JavaScript for impatient programmers

Dr. Axel Rauschmayer

2019

"An exhaustive resource, yet cuts out the fluff that clutters many programming books – with explanations that are understandable and to the point, as promised by the title! The quizzes and exercises are a very useful feature to check and lock in your knowledge. And you can definitely tear through the book fairly quickly, to get up and running in JavaScript."
— **Pam Selle**, thewebivore.com

"The best introductory book for modern JavaScript."
— **Tejinder Singh**, Senior Software Engineer, IBM

"This is JavaScript. No filler. No frameworks. No third-party libraries. If you want to learn JavaScript, you need this book."
— **Shelley Powers**, Software Engineer/Writer

Copyright © 2019 by Dr. Axel Rauschmayer
Cover by Fran Caye

All rights reserved. This book or any portion thereof may not be reproduced or used in any manner whatsoever without the express written permission of the publisher except for the use of brief quotations in a book review or scholarly journal.

ISBN 978-1-09-121009-7

exploringjs.com

Contents

I Background — 13

1 About this book (ES2019 edition) — 15
- 1.1 About the content — 15
- 1.2 Previewing and buying this book — 16
- 1.3 About the author — 16
- 1.4 Acknowledgements — 17

2 FAQ: Book and supplementary material — 19
- 2.1 How to read this book — 19
- 2.2 I own a digital edition — 20
- 2.3 I own the print edition — 21
- 2.4 Notations and conventions — 21

3 Why JavaScript? (bonus) — 23
- 3.1 The cons of JavaScript — 23
- 3.2 The pros of JavaScript — 24
- 3.3 Pro and con of JavaScript: innovation — 25

4 The nature of JavaScript (bonus) — 27
- 4.1 JavaScript's influences — 27
- 4.2 The nature of JavaScript — 27
- 4.3 Tips for getting started with JavaScript — 28

5 History and evolution of JavaScript — 31
- 5.1 How JavaScript was created — 31
- 5.2 Standardizing JavaScript — 32
- 5.3 Timeline of ECMAScript versions — 32
- 5.4 Ecma Technical Committee 39 (TC39) — 33
- 5.5 The TC39 process — 33
- 5.6 FAQ: TC39 process — 35
- 5.7 Evolving JavaScript: Don't break the web — 35

6 FAQ: JavaScript — 37
- 6.1 What are good references for JavaScript? — 37
- 6.2 How do I find out what JavaScript features are supported where? — 37
- 6.3 Where can I look up what features are planned for JavaScript? — 38
- 6.4 Why does JavaScript fail silently so often? — 38

		6.5	Why can't we clean up JavaScript, by removing quirks and outdated features?	38
		6.6	How can I quickly try out a piece of JavaScript code?	38

II First steps   39

7 The big picture   41
  7.1 What are you learning in this book?   41
  7.2 The structure of browsers and Node.js   41
  7.3 JavaScript references   42
  7.4 Further reading   42

8 Syntax   43
  8.1 An overview of JavaScript's syntax   44
  8.2 (Advanced)   49
  8.3 Identifiers   49
  8.4 Statement vs. expression   50
  8.5 Ambiguous syntax   51
  8.6 Semicolons   52
  8.7 Automatic semicolon insertion (ASI)   53
  8.8 Semicolons: best practices   55
  8.9 Strict mode vs. sloppy mode   55

9 Consoles: interactive JavaScript command lines   59
  9.1 Trying out JavaScript code   59
  9.2 The `console.*` API: printing data and more   61

10 Assertion API   65
  10.1 Assertions in software development   65
  10.2 How assertions are used in this book   65
  10.3 Normal comparison vs. deep comparison   66
  10.4 Quick reference: module `assert`   67

11 Getting started with quizzes and exercises   71
  11.1 Quizzes   71
  11.2 Exercises   71
  11.3 Unit tests in JavaScript   72

III Variables and values   75

12 Variables and assignment   77
  12.1 `let`   78
  12.2 `const`   78
  12.3 Deciding between `const` and `let`   79
  12.4 The scope of a variable   79
  12.5 (Advanced)   81
  12.6 Terminology: static vs. dynamic   81
  12.7 Global variables and the global object   82

        12.8 Declarations: scope and activation 84
        12.9 Closures 88
        12.10 Further reading 90

13 **Values**   **91**
        13.1 What's a type? 91
        13.2 JavaScript's type hierarchy 92
        13.3 The types of the language specification 92
        13.4 Primitive values vs. objects 93
        13.5 The operators typeof and instanceof: what's the type of a value? 95
        13.6 Classes and constructor functions 97
        13.7 Converting between types 98

14 **Operators**   **101**
        14.1 Making sense of operators 101
        14.2 The plus operator (+) 102
        14.3 Assignment operators 103
        14.4 Equality: == vs. === 104
        14.5 Ordering operators 107
        14.6 Various other operators 107

IV Primitive values   **109**

15 **The non-values undefined and null**   **111**
        15.1 undefined vs. null 111
        15.2 Occurrences of undefined and null 112
        15.3 Checking for undefined or null 113
        15.4 undefined and null don't have properties 113
        15.5 The history of undefined and null 114

16 **Booleans**   **115**
        16.1 Converting to boolean 115
        16.2 Falsy and truthy values 116
        16.3 Truthiness-based existence checks 117
        16.4 Conditional operator (? :) 119
        16.5 Binary logical operators: And (x && y), Or (x || y) 119
        16.6 Logical Not (!) 121

17 **Numbers**   **123**
        17.1 JavaScript only has floating point numbers 124
        17.2 Number literals 124
        17.3 Arithmetic operators 125
        17.4 Converting to number 127
        17.5 Error values 128
        17.6 Error value: NaN 128
        17.7 Error value: Infinity 130
        17.8 The precision of numbers: careful with decimal fractions 131
        17.9 (Advanced) 131

17.10 Background: floating point precision 131
17.11 Integers in JavaScript 133
17.12 Bitwise operators 136
17.13 Quick reference: numbers 138

18 Math 145
18.1 Data properties 145
18.2 Exponents, roots, logarithms 146
18.3 Rounding 147
18.4 Trigonometric Functions 148
18.5 Various other functions 150
18.6 Sources 151

19 Unicode – a brief introduction (advanced) 153
19.1 Code points vs. code units 153
19.2 Encodings used in web development: UTF-16 and UTF-8 156
19.3 Grapheme clusters – the real characters 156

20 Strings 159
20.1 Plain string literals 160
20.2 Accessing characters and code points 160
20.3 String concatenation via + ... 161
20.4 Converting to string 161
20.5 Comparing strings 163
20.6 Atoms of text: Unicode characters, JavaScript characters, grapheme clusters 164
20.7 Quick reference: Strings 166

21 Using template literals and tagged templates 175
21.1 Disambiguation: "template" 175
21.2 Template literals 176
21.3 Tagged templates 177
21.4 Raw string literals 179
21.5 (Advanced) 180
21.6 Multiline template literals and indentation 180
21.7 Simple templating via template literals 182

22 Symbols 185
22.1 Use cases for symbols 186
22.2 Publicly known symbols 188
22.3 Converting symbols 188

V Control flow and data flow 191

23 Control flow statements 193
23.1 Conditions of control flow statements 194
23.2 Controlling loops: `break` and `continue` 194
23.3 `if` statements 196
23.4 `switch` statements 197
23.5 `while` loops 199

CONTENTS 7

    23.6 `do-while` loops 200
    23.7 `for` loops 200
    23.8 `for-of` loops 202
    23.9 `for-await-of` loops 203
    23.10 `for-in` loops (avoid) 203

24 Exception handling   205
    24.1 Motivation: throwing and catching exceptions 205
    24.2 `throw` 206
    24.3 The `try` statement 207
    24.4 Error classes 209

25 Callable values   211
    25.1 Kinds of functions 211
    25.2 Ordinary functions 212
    25.3 Specialized functions 214
    25.4 More kinds of functions and methods 217
    25.5 Returning values from functions and methods 218
    25.6 Parameter handling 219
    25.7 Dynamically evaluating code: `eval()`, `new Function()` (advanced) . . . 224

26 Environments: under the hood of variables (bonus)   227
    26.1 Environment: data structure for managing variables 227
    26.2 Recursion via environments 227
    26.3 Nested scopes via environments 228
    26.4 Closures and environments 232

VI   Modularity   235

27 Modules   237
    27.1 Overview: syntax of ECMAScript modules 238
    27.2 JavaScript source code formats 239
    27.3 Before we had modules, we had scripts 239
    27.4 Module systems created prior to ES6 240
    27.5 ECMAScript modules 243
    27.6 Named exports and imports 243
    27.7 Default exports and imports 246
    27.8 More details on exporting and importing 248
    27.9 npm packages 249
    27.10 Naming modules 251
    27.11 Module specifiers 252
    27.12 Loading modules dynamically via `import()` 254
    27.13 Preview: `import.meta.url` 256
    27.14 Polyfills: emulating native web platform features (advanced) 258

28 Single objects   261
    28.1 What is an object? 262
    28.2 Objects as records 263

	28.3 Spreading into object literals (...)	266
	28.4 Methods	268
	28.5 Objects as dictionaries (advanced)	275
	28.6 Standard methods (advanced)	283
	28.7 Advanced topics	283
29	**Prototype chains and classes**	**287**
	29.1 Prototype chains	288
	29.2 Classes	293
	29.3 Private data for classes	297
	29.4 Subclassing	299
	29.5 FAQ: objects	307

VII Collections   309

30	**Synchronous iteration**	**311**
	30.1 What is synchronous iteration about?	311
	30.2 Core iteration constructs: iterables and iterators	312
	30.3 Iterating manually	313
	30.4 Iteration in practice	314
	30.5 Quick reference: synchronous iteration	315
31	**Arrays (`Array`)**	**317**
	31.1 The two roles of Arrays in JavaScript	318
	31.2 Basic Array operations	318
	31.3 `for-of` and Arrays	321
	31.4 Array-like objects	322
	31.5 Converting iterable and Array-like values to Arrays	323
	31.6 Creating and filling Arrays with arbitrary lengths	324
	31.7 Multidimensional Arrays	325
	31.8 More Array features (advanced)	326
	31.9 Adding and removing elements (destructively and non-destructively)	329
	31.10 Methods: iteration and transformation (`.find()`, `.map()`, `.filter()`, etc.)	331
	31.11 `.sort()`: sorting Arrays	338
	31.12 Quick reference: `Array<T>`	340
32	**Typed Arrays: handling binary data (Advanced)**	**349**
	32.1 The basics of the API	350
	32.2 Element types	352
	32.3 More information on Typed Arrays	355
	32.4 Quick references: indices vs. offsets	358
	32.5 Quick reference: ArrayBuffers	359
	32.6 Quick reference: Typed Arrays	360
	32.7 Quick reference: DataViews	363
33	**Maps (`Map`)**	**365**
	33.1 Using Maps	366
	33.2 Example: Counting characters	369

CONTENTS

33.3 A few more details about the keys of Maps (advanced) 369
33.4 Missing Map operations 370
33.5 Quick reference: `Map<K,V>` 372
33.6 FAQ: Maps 374

34 WeakMaps (`WeakMap`)   377
34.1 WeakMaps are black boxes 377
34.2 The keys of a WeakMap are *weakly held* 378
34.3 Examples 379
34.4 WeakMap API 380

35 Sets (`Set`)   381
35.1 Using Sets 382
35.2 Examples of using Sets 383
35.3 What Set elements are considered equal? 383
35.4 Missing Set operations 384
35.5 Quick reference: `Set<T>` 385
35.6 FAQ: Sets 387

36 WeakSets (`WeakSet`)   389
36.1 Example: Marking objects as safe to use with a method 389
36.2 WeakSet API 390

37 Destructuring   391
37.1 A first taste of destructuring 392
37.2 Constructing vs. extracting 392
37.3 Where can we destructure? 393
37.4 Object-destructuring 394
37.5 Array-destructuring 395
37.6 Examples of destructuring 396
37.7 What happens if a pattern part does not match anything? 398
37.8 What values can't be destructured? 398
37.9 (Advanced) 399
37.10 Default values 399
37.11 Parameter definitions are similar to destructuring 400
37.12 Nested destructuring 401

38 Synchronous generators (advanced)   403
38.1 What are synchronous generators? 403
38.2 Calling generators from generators (advanced) 407
38.3 Background: external iteration vs. internal iteration 409
38.4 Use case for generators: reusing traversals 410
38.5 Advanced features of generators 411

VIII   Asynchronicity   413

39 Asynchronous programming in JavaScript   415
39.1 A roadmap for asynchronous programming in JavaScript 416
39.2 The call stack 418

39.3	The event loop	419
39.4	How to avoid blocking the JavaScript process	420
39.5	Patterns for delivering asynchronous results	422
39.6	Asynchronous code: the downsides	425
39.7	Resources	426

40 Promises for asynchronous programming — 427

40.1	The basics of using Promises	428
40.2	Examples	433
40.3	Error handling: don't mix rejections and exceptions	437
40.4	Promise-based functions start synchronously, settle asynchronously	439
40.5	`Promise.all()`: concurrency and Arrays of Promises	440
40.6	Tips for chaining Promises	443
40.7	Advanced topics	445

41 Async functions — 447

41.1	Async functions: the basics	447
41.2	Returning from async functions	449
41.3	`await`: working with Promises	451
41.4	(Advanced)	453
41.5	Immediately invoked async arrow functions	453
41.6	Concurrency and `await`	454
41.7	Tips for using async functions	455

42 Asynchronous iteration — 457

42.1	Basic asynchronous iteration	457
42.2	Asynchronous generators	460
42.3	Async iteration over Node.js streams	464

IX More standard library — 467

43 Regular expressions (`RegExp`) — 469

43.1	Creating regular expressions	470
43.2	Syntax	471
43.3	Flags	475
43.4	Properties of regular expression objects	479
43.5	Methods for working with regular expressions	480
43.6	Flag `/g` and its pitfalls	484
43.7	Techniques for working with regular expressions	487

44 Dates (`Date`) — 489

44.1	Best practice: avoid the built-in `Date`	489
44.2	Time standards	490
44.3	Background: date time formats (ISO)	492
44.4	Time values	493
44.5	Creating Dates	494
44.6	Getters and setters	495
44.7	Converting Dates to strings	495

45 Creating and parsing JSON (`JSON`) — 497
- 45.1 The discovery and standardization of JSON 498
- 45.2 JSON syntax 498
- 45.3 Using the `JSON` API 499
- 45.4 Customizing stringification and parsing (advanced) 501
- 45.5 FAQ 505

X Miscellaneous topics — 507

46 Next steps: overview of web development (bonus) — 509
- 46.1 Tips against feeling overwhelmed 509
- 46.2 Things worth learning for web development 510
- 46.3 Example: tool-based JavaScript workflow 512
- 46.4 An overview of JavaScript tools 514
- 46.5 Tools not related to JavaScript 517

XI Appendices — 519

47 Index — 521

Part I

Background

Chapter 1

About this book (ES2019 edition)

Contents

1.1	About the content	15
	1.1.1 What's in this book?	15
	1.1.2 What is not covered by this book?	15
	1.1.3 Isn't this book too long for impatient people?	16
1.2	Previewing and buying this book	16
	1.2.1 How can I preview the book, the exercises, and the quizzes?	16
	1.2.2 How can I buy a digital edition of this book?	16
	1.2.3 How can I buy the print edition of this book?	16
1.3	About the author	16
1.4	Acknowledgements	17

1.1 About the content

1.1.1 What's in this book?

This book makes JavaScript less challenging to learn for newcomers by offering a modern view that is as consistent as possible.

Highlights:

- Get started quickly by initially focusing on modern features.
- Test-driven exercises and quizzes available for most chapters.
- Covers all essential features of JavaScript, up to and including ES2019.
- Optional advanced sections let you dig deeper.

No prior knowledge of JavaScript is required, but you should know how to program.

1.1.2 What is not covered by this book?

- Some advanced language features are not explained, but references to appropriate material are provided – for example, to my other JavaScript books at Explor-

ingJS.com[1], which are free to read online.
- This book deliberately focuses on the language. Browser-only features, etc. are not described.

1.1.3 Isn't this book too long for impatient people?

There are several ways in which you can read this book. One of them involves skipping much of the content in order to get started quickly. For details, see §2.1.1 "In which order should I read the content in this book?" (p. 19).

1.2 Previewing and buying this book

1.2.1 How can I preview the book, the exercises, and the quizzes?

Go to the homepage of this book[2]:

- All essential chapters of this book can be read online.
- The first half of the test-driven exercises can be downloaded.
- The first half of the quizzes can be tried online.

1.2.2 How can I buy a digital edition of this book?

There are two digital editions of *JavaScript for impatient programmers*:

- Ebooks: PDF, EPUB, MOBI, HTML (all without DRM)
- Ebooks plus exercises and quizzes

The home page of this book[3] describes how you can buy them.

1.2.3 How can I buy the print edition of this book?

The print edition of *JavaScript for impatient programmers* is available on Amazon.

1.3 About the author

Dr. Axel Rauschmayer specializes in JavaScript and web development. He has been developing web applications since 1995. In 1999, he was technical manager at a German internet startup that later expanded internationally. In 2006, he held his first talk on Ajax. In 2010, he received a PhD in Informatics from the University of Munich.

Since 2011, he has been blogging about web development at 2ality.com and has written several books on JavaScript. He has held trainings and talks for companies such as eBay, Bank of America, and O'Reilly Media.

He lives in Munich, Germany.

---

[1] https://exploringjs.com/
[2] https://exploringjs.com/impatient-js/
[3] https://exploringjs.com/impatient-js/#buy

1.4 Acknowledgements

- Cover by Fran Caye[4]
- Parts of this book were edited by Adaobi Obi Tulton[5].
- Thanks for answering questions, discussing language topics, etc.:
    - Allen Wirfs-Brock (`@awbjs`[6])
    - Benedikt Meurer (`@bmeurer`[7])
    - Brian Terlson (`@bterlson`[8])
    - Daniel Ehrenberg (`@littledan`[9])
    - Jordan Harband (`@ljharb`[10])
    - Mathias Bynens (`@mathias`[11])
    - Myles Borins (`@MylesBorins`[12])
    - Rob Palmer (`@robpalmer2`[13])
    - Šime Vidas (`@simevidas`[14])
    - And many others
- Thanks for reviewing:
    - Johannes Weber (`@jowe`[15])

---

[4] http://francaye.net
[5] http://www.serendipity23editorial.com
[6] https://twitter.com/awbjs
[7] https://twitter.com/bmeurer
[8] https://twitter.com/bterlson
[9] https://twitter.com/littledan
[10] https://twitter.com/ljharb
[11] https://twitter.com/mathias
[12] https://twitter.com/MylesBorins
[13] https://twitter.com/robpalmer2
[14] https://twitter.com/simevidas
[15] https://twitter.com/jowe

Chapter 2

FAQ: Book and supplementary material

Contents

2.1	How to read this book		19
	2.1.1	In which order should I read the content in this book?	19
	2.1.2	Why are some chapters and sections marked with "(advanced)"?	20
	2.1.3	Why are some chapters marked with "(bonus)"?	20
2.2	I own a digital edition		20
	2.2.1	How do I submit feedback and corrections?	20
	2.2.2	How do I get updates for the downloads I bought at Payhip?	20
	2.2.3	Can I upgrade from package "Ebooks" to package "Ebooks + exercises + quizzes"?	20
2.3	I own the print edition		21
	2.3.1	Can I get a discount for a digital edition?	21
	2.3.2	Can I submit an error or see submitted errors?	21
	2.3.3	Is there an online list with the URLs in this book?	21
2.4	Notations and conventions		21
	2.4.1	What is a type signature? Why am I seeing static types in this book?	21
	2.4.2	What do the notes with icons mean?	21

This chapter answers questions you may have and gives tips for reading this book.

2.1 How to read this book

2.1.1 In which order should I read the content in this book?

This book is three books in one:

- You can use it to get started with JavaScript as quickly as possible. This "mode" is for impatient people:

- Start reading with §7 "The big picture" (p. 41).
- Skip all chapters and sections marked as "advanced", and all quick references.
* It gives you a comprehensive look at current JavaScript. In this "mode", you read everything and don't skip advanced content and quick references.
* It serves as a reference. If there is a topic that you are interested in, you can find information on it via the table of contents or via the index. Due to basic and advanced content being mixed, everything you need is usually in a single location.

The quizzes and exercises (p. 71) play an important part in helping you practice and retain what you have learned.

2.1.2 Why are some chapters and sections marked with "(advanced)"?

Several chapters and sections are marked with "(advanced)". The idea is that you can initially skip them. That is, you can get a quick working knowledge of JavaScript by only reading the basic (non-advanced) content.

As your knowledge evolves, you can later come back to some or all of the advanced content.

2.1.3 Why are some chapters marked with "(bonus)"?

The bonus chapters are only available in the paid versions of this book (print and ebook). They are listed in the full table of contents[1].

2.2 I own a digital edition

2.2.1 How do I submit feedback and corrections?

The HTML version of this book (online, or ad-free archive in the paid version) has a link at the end of each chapter that enables you to give feedback.

2.2.2 How do I get updates for the downloads I bought at Payhip?

* The receipt email for the purchase includes a link. You'll always be able to download the latest version of the files at that location.

* If you opted into emails while buying, you'll get an email whenever there is new content. To opt in later, you must contact Payhip (see bottom of `payhip.com`).

2.2.3 Can I upgrade from package "Ebooks" to package "Ebooks + exercises + quizzes"?

Yes. The instructions for doing so are on the homepage of this book[2].

---

[1]https://exploringjs.com/impatient-js/downloads/complete-toc.html
[2]https://exploringjs.com/impatient-js/#upgrades

2.3 I own the print edition

2.3.1 Can I get a discount for a digital edition?

If you bought the print edition, you can get a discount for a digital edition. The homepage of the print edition[3] explains how.

Alas, the reverse is not possible: you cannot get a discount for the print edition if you bought a digital edition.

2.3.2 Can I submit an error or see submitted errors?

On the homepage of the print edition[4], you can submit errors and see submitted errors.

2.3.3 Is there an online list with the URLs in this book?

The homepage of the print edition[5] has a list with all the URLs that you see in the footnotes of the print edition.

2.4 Notations and conventions

2.4.1 What is a type signature? Why am I seeing static types in this book?

For example, you may see:

```
Number.isFinite(num: number): boolean
```

That is called the *type signature* of `Number.isFinite()`. This notation, especially the static types `number` of `num` and `boolean` of the result, are not real JavaScript. The notation is borrowed from the compile-to-JavaScript language TypeScript (which is mostly just JavaScript plus static typing).

Why is this notation being used? It helps give you a quick idea of how a function works. The notation is explained in detail in a 2ality blog post[6], but is usually relatively intuitive.

2.4.2 What do the notes with icons mean?

👁 **Reading instructions**

Explains how to best read the content.

↗ **External content**

---

[3] https://exploringjs.com/impatient-js/es2019/
[4] https://exploringjs.com/impatient-js/es2019/
[5] https://exploringjs.com/impatient-js/es2019/
[6] https://2ality.com/2018/04/type-notation-typescript.html

> Points to additional, external, content.

> 💡 **Tip**
>
> Gives a tip related to the current content.

> ❓ **Question**
>
> Asks and answers a question pertinent to the current content (think FAQ).

> ⚠ **Warning**
>
> Warns about pitfalls, etc.

> ⚙ **Details**
>
> Provides additional details, complementing the current content. It is similar to a footnote.

> 🧩 **Exercise**
>
> Mentions the path of a test-driven exercise that you can do at that point.

> ≡ **Quiz**
>
> Indicates that there is a quiz for the current (part of a) chapter.

Chapter 3

Why JavaScript? (bonus)

Contents

3.1	The cons of JavaScript	23
3.2	The pros of JavaScript	24
	3.2.1 Community	24
	3.2.2 Practically useful	24
	3.2.3 Language	25
3.3	Pro and con of JavaScript: innovation	25

In this chapter, we examine the pros and cons of JavaScript.

> 👁 **"ECMAScript 6" and "ES6" refer to versions of JavaScript**
>
> ECMAScript is the name of the language standard; the number refers to the version of that standard. For more information, consult §5.2 "Standardizing JavaScript" (p. 32).

3.1 The cons of JavaScript

Among programmers, JavaScript isn't always well liked. One reason is that it has a fair amount of quirks. Some of them are just unusual ways of doing something. Others are considered bugs. Either way, learning *why* JavaScript does something the way it does, helps with dealing with the quirks and with accepting JavaScript (maybe even liking it). Hopefully, this book can be of assistance here.

Additionally, many traditional quirks have been eliminated now. For example:

- Traditionally, JavaScript variables weren't block-scoped. ES6 introduced `let` and `const`, which let you declare block-scoped variables.

- Prior to ES6, implementing object factories and inheritance via `function` and `.prototype` was clumsy. ES6 introduced classes, which provide more convenient syntax for these mechanisms.
- Traditionally, JavaScript did not have built-in modules. ES6 added them to the language.

Lastly, JavaScript's standard library is limited, but:

- There are plans[1] for adding more functionality.
- Many libraries are easily available via the npm software registry[2].

3.2 The pros of JavaScript

On the plus side, JavaScript offers many benefits.

3.2.1 Community

JavaScript's popularity means that it's well supported and well documented. Whenever you create something in JavaScript, you can rely on many people being (potentially) interested. And there is a large pool of JavaScript programmers from which you can hire, if you need to.

No single party controls JavaScript – it is evolved by TC39 (p. 33), a committee comprising many organizations. The language is evolved via an open process that encourages feedback from the public.

3.2.2 Practically useful

With JavaScript, you can write apps for many client platforms. These are a few example technologies:

- *Progressive Web Apps*[3] can be installed natively on Android and many desktop operating systems.
- *Electron*[4] lets you build cross-platform desktop apps.
- *React Native*[5] lets you write apps for iOS and Android that have native user interfaces.
- *Node.js*[6] provides extensive support for writing shell scripts (in addition to being a platform for web servers).

JavaScript is supported by many server platforms and services – for example:

- Node.js (many of the following services are based on Node.js or support its APIs)
- ZEIT Now
- Microsoft Azure Functions
- AWS Lambda

---

[1] https://github.com/tc39/proposal-javascript-standard-library
[2] https://www.npmjs.com
[3] https://developers.google.com/web/progressive-web-apps/
[4] https://electronjs.org
[5] https://facebook.github.io/react-native/
[6] https://nodejs.org/

- Google Cloud Functions

There are many data technologies available for JavaScript: many databases support it and intermediate layers (such as GraphQL) exist. Additionally, the standard data format *JSON* (*JavaScript Object Notation*, p. 497) is based on JavaScript and supported by its standard library.

Lastly, many, if not most, tools for JavaScript are written in JavaScript. That includes IDEs, build tools, and more. As a consequence, you install them the same way you install your libraries and you can customize them in JavaScript.

3.2.3 Language

- Many libraries are available, via the de-facto standard in the JavaScript universe, the npm software registry[7].
- If you are unhappy with "plain" JavaScript, it is relatively easy to add more features:
  - You can compile future and modern language features to current and past versions of JavaScript, via Babel[8].
  - You can add static typing, via TypeScript[9] and Flow[10].
  - You can work with ReasonML, which is, roughly, OCaml with JavaScript syntax. It can be compiled to JavaScript or native code.
- The language is flexible: it is dynamic and supports both object-oriented programming and functional programming.
- JavaScript has become suprisingly fast for such a dynamic language.
  - Whenever it isn't fast enough, you can switch to WebAssembly (p. 511), a universal virtual machine built into most JavaScript engines. It can run static code at nearly native speeds.

3.3 Pro and con of JavaScript: innovation

There is much innovation in the JavaScript ecosystem: new approaches to implementing user interfaces, new ways of optimizing the delivery of software, and more. The upside is that you will constantly learn new things. The downside is that the constant change can be exhausting at times. Thankfully, things have somewhat slowed down, recently: all of ES6 (which was a considerable modernization of the language) is becoming established, as are certain tools and workflows.

Quiz

See quiz app (p. 71).

---

[7]https://www.npmjs.com
[8]https://babeljs.io
[9]https://www.typescriptlang.org
[10]https://flow.org

Chapter 4

The nature of JavaScript (bonus)

Contents

4.1	JavaScript's influences	27
4.2	The nature of JavaScript	27
	4.2.1 JavaScript often fails silently	28
4.3	Tips for getting started with JavaScript	28

4.1 JavaScript's influences

When JavaScript was created in 1995, it was influenced by several programming languages:

- JavaScript's syntax is largely based on Java.
- Self inspired JavaScript's prototypal inheritance.
- Closures and environments were borrowed from Scheme.
- AWK influenced JavaScript's functions (including the keyword `function`).
- JavaScript's strings, Arrays, and regular expressions take cues from Perl.
- HyperTalk inspired event handling via `onclick` in web browsers.

With ECMAScript 6, new influences came to JavaScript:

- Generators were borrowed from Python.
- The syntax of arrow functions came from CoffeeScript.
- C++ contributed the keyword `const`.
- Destructuring was inspired by Lisp's *destructuring bind*.
- Template literals came from the E language (where they are called *quasi literals*).

4.2 The nature of JavaScript

These are a few traits of the language:

- Its syntax is part of the C family of languages (curly braces, etc.).

- It is a dynamic language: most objects can be changed in various ways at runtime, objects can be created directly, etc.
- It is a dynamically typed language: variables don't have fixed static types and you can assign any value to a given (mutable) variable.
- It has functional programming features: first-class functions, closures, partial application via `bind()`, etc.
- It has object-oriented features: mutable state, objects, inheritance, classes, etc.
- It often fails silently: see the next subsection for details.
- It is deployed as source code. But that source code is often *minified* (rewritten to require less storage). And there are plans for a binary source code format[1].
- JavaScript is part of the web platform – it is the language built into web browsers. But it is also used elsewhere – for example, in Node.js, for server things, and shell scripting.
- JavaScript engines often optimize less-efficient language mechanisms under the hood. For example, in principle, JavaScript Arrays are dictionaries. But under the hood, engines store Arrays contiguously if they have contiguous indices.

4.2.1 JavaScript often fails silently

JavaScript often fails silently. Let's look at two examples.

First example: If the operands of an operator don't have the appropriate types, they are converted as necessary.

```
> '3' * '5'
15
```

Second example: If an arithmetic computation fails, you get an error value, not an exception.

```
> 1 / 0
Infinity
```

The reason for the silent failures is historical: JavaScript did not have exceptions until ECMAScript 3. Since then, its designers have tried to avoid silent failures.

4.3 Tips for getting started with JavaScript

These are a few tips to help you get started with JavaScript:

- Take your time to really get to know this language. The conventional C-style syntax hides that this is a very unconventional language. Learn especially the quirks and the rationales behind them. Then you will understand and appreciate the language better.

---
[1] https://github.com/tc39/proposal-binary-ast

4.3 Tips for getting started with JavaScript

   - In addition to details, this book also teaches simple rules of thumb to be safe – for example, "Always use === to determine if two values are equal, never ==."
- Language tools make it easier to work with JavaScript. For example:
   - You can statically type JavaScript via TypeScript[2] or Flow[3].
   - You can check for problems and anti-patterns via linters such as ESLint[4].
   - You can format your code automatically via code formatters such as Prettier[5].
- Get in contact with the community:
   - Twitter is popular among JavaScript programmers. As a mode of communication that sits between the spoken and the written word, it is well suited for exchanging knowledge.
   - Many cities have regular free meetups where people come together to learn topics related to JavaScript.
   - JavaScript conferences are another convenient way of meeting other JavaScript programmers.
- Read books and blogs. Much material is free online!

---

[2] https://www.typescriptlang.org
[3] https://flow.org
[4] https://eslint.org
[5] https://prettier.io

Chapter 5

History and evolution of JavaScript

Contents

5.1	How JavaScript was created	31
5.2	Standardizing JavaScript	32
5.3	Timeline of ECMAScript versions	32
5.4	Ecma Technical Committee 39 (TC39)	33
5.5	The TC39 process	33
	5.5.1 Tip: Think in individual features and stages, not ECMAScript versions	33
5.6	FAQ: TC39 process	35
	5.6.1 How is [my favorite proposed feature] doing?	35
	5.6.2 Is there an official list of ECMAScript features?	35
5.7	Evolving JavaScript: Don't break the web	35

5.1 How JavaScript was created

JavaScript was created in May 1995 in 10 days, by Brendan Eich. Eich worked at Netscape and implemented JavaScript for their web browser, *Netscape Navigator*.

The idea was that major interactive parts of the client-side web were to be implemented in Java. JavaScript was supposed to be a glue language for those parts and to also make HTML slightly more interactive. Given its role of assisting Java, JavaScript had to look like Java. That ruled out existing solutions such as Perl, Python, TCL, and others.

Initially, JavaScript's name changed several times:

- Its code name was *Mocha*.
- In the Netscape Navigator 2.0 betas (September 1995), it was called *LiveScript*.
- In Netscape Navigator 2.0 beta 3 (December 1995), it got its final name, *JavaScript*.

5.2 Standardizing JavaScript

There are two standards for JavaScript:

- ECMA-262 is hosted by Ecma International. It is the primary standard.
- ISO/IEC 16262 is hosted by the International Organization for Standardization (ISO) and the International Electrotechnical Commission (IEC). This is a secondary standard.

The language described by these standards is called *ECMAScript*, not *JavaScript*. A different name was chosen because Sun (now Oracle) had a trademark for the latter name. The "ECMA" in "ECMAScript" comes from the organization that hosts the primary standard.

The original name of that organization was *ECMA*, an acronym for *European Computer Manufacturers Association*. It was later changed to *Ecma International* (with "Ecma" being a proper name, not an acronym) because the organization's activities had expanded beyond Europe. The initial all-caps acronym explains the spelling of ECMAScript.

In principle, JavaScript and ECMAScript mean the same thing. Sometimes the following distinction is made:

- The term *JavaScript* refers to the language and its implementations.
- The term *ECMAScript* refers to the language standard and language versions.

Therefore, *ECMAScript 6* is a version of the language (its 6th edition).

5.3 Timeline of ECMAScript versions

This is a brief timeline of ECMAScript versions:

- ECMAScript 1 (June 1997): First version of the standard.
- ECMAScript 2 (June 1998): Small update to keep ECMA-262 in sync with the ISO standard.
- ECMAScript 3 (December 1999): Adds many core features – "[…] regular expressions, better string handling, new control statements [do-while, switch], try/catch exception handling, […]"
- ECMAScript 4 (abandoned in July 2008): Would have been a massive upgrade (with static typing, modules, namespaces, and more), but ended up being too ambitious and dividing the language's stewards.
- ECMAScript 5 (December 2009): Brought minor improvements – a few standard library features and *strict mode* (p. 55).
- ECMAScript 5.1 (June 2011): Another small update to keep Ecma and ISO standards in sync.
- ECMAScript 6 (June 2015): A large update that fulfilled many of the promises of ECMAScript 4. This version is the first one whose official name – *ECMAScript 2015* – is based on the year of publication.
- ECMAScript 2016 (June 2016): First yearly release. The shorter release life cycle resulted in fewer new features compared to the large ES6.
- ECMAScript 2017 (June 2017). Second yearly release.
- Subsequent ECMAScript versions (ES2018, etc.) are always ratified in June.

5.4 Ecma Technical Committee 39 (TC39)

TC39 is the committee that evolves JavaScript. Its member are, strictly speaking, companies: Adobe, Apple, Facebook, Google, Microsoft, Mozilla, Opera, Twitter, and others. That is, companies that are usually fierce competitors are working together for the good of the language.

Every two months, TC39 has meetings that member-appointed delegates and invited experts attend. The minutes of those meetings are public in a GitHub repository[1].

5.5 The TC39 process

With ECMAScript 6, two issues with the release process used at that time became obvious:

- If too much time passes between releases then features that are ready early, have to wait a long time until they can be released. And features that are ready late, risk being rushed to make the deadline.

- Features were often designed long before they were implemented and used. Design deficiencies related to implementation and use were therefore discovered too late.

In response to these issues, TC39 instituted the new *TC39 process*:

- ECMAScript features are designed independently and go through stages, starting at 0 ("strawman"), ending at 4 ("finished").
- Especially the later stages require prototype implementations and real-world testing, leading to feedback loops between designs and implementations.
- ECMAScript versions are released once per year and include all features that have reached stage 4 prior to a release deadline.

The result: smaller, incremental releases, whose features have already been field-tested. Fig. 5.1 illustrates the TC39 process.

ES2016 was the first ECMAScript version that was designed according to the TC39 process.

5.5.1 Tip: Think in individual features and stages, not ECMAScript versions

Up to and including ES6, it was most common to think about JavaScript in terms of ECMAScript versions – for example, "Does this browser support ES6 yet?"

Starting with ES2016, it's better to think in individual features: once a feature reaches stage 4, you can safely use it (if it's supported by the JavaScript engines you are targeting). You don't have to wait until the next ECMAScript release.

---

[1] https://github.com/tc39/tc39-notes/

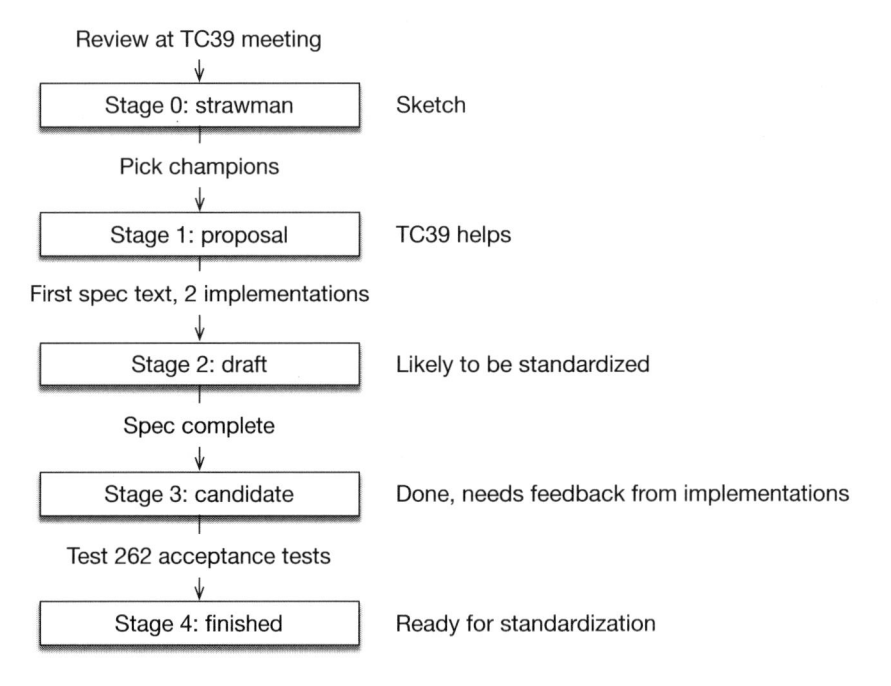

```
Review at TC39 meeting
          ↓
┌─────────────────────┐
│ Stage 0: strawman   │   Sketch
└─────────────────────┘
     Pick champions
          ↓
┌─────────────────────┐
│ Stage 1: proposal   │   TC39 helps
└─────────────────────┘
First spec text, 2 implementations
          ↓
┌─────────────────────┐
│ Stage 2: draft      │   Likely to be standardized
└─────────────────────┘
      Spec complete
          ↓
┌─────────────────────┐
│ Stage 3: candidate  │   Done, needs feedback from implementations
└─────────────────────┘
  Test 262 acceptance tests
          ↓
┌─────────────────────┐
│ Stage 4: finished   │   Ready for standardization
└─────────────────────┘
```

Figure 5.1: Each ECMAScript feature proposal goes through stages that are numbered from 0 to 4. *Champions* are TC39 members that support the authors of a feature. Test 262 is a suite of tests that checks JavaScript engines for compliance with the language specification.

5.6 FAQ: TC39 process

5.6.1 How is [my favorite proposed feature] doing?

If you are wondering what stages various proposed features are in, consult the GitHub repository proposals[2].

5.6.2 Is there an official list of ECMAScript features?

Yes, the TC39 repo lists finished proposals[3] and mentions in which ECMAScript versions they were introduced.

5.7 Evolving JavaScript: Don't break the web

One idea that occasionally comes up is to clean up JavaScript by removing old features and quirks. While the appeal of that idea is obvious, it has significant downsides.

Let's assume we create a new version of JavaScript that is not backward compatible and fix all of its flaws. As a result, we'd encounter the following problems:

- JavaScript engines become bloated: they need to support both the old and the new version. The same is true for tools such as IDEs and build tools.
- Programmers need to know, and be continually conscious of, the differences between the versions.
- You can either migrate all of an existing code base to the new version (which can be a lot of work). Or you can mix versions and refactoring becomes harder because you can't move code between versions without changing it.
- You somehow have to specify per piece of code – be it a file or code embedded in a web page – what version it is written in. Every conceivable solution has pros and cons. For example, *strict mode* (p. 55) is a slightly cleaner version of ES5. One of the reasons why it wasn't as popular as it should have been: it was a hassle to opt in via a directive at the beginning of a file or a function.

So what is the solution? Can we have our cake and eat it? The approach that was chosen for ES6 is called "One JavaScript":

- New versions are always completely backward compatible (but there may occasionally be minor, hardly noticeable clean-ups).
- Old features aren't removed or fixed. Instead, better versions of them are introduced. One example is declaring variables via let – which is an improved version of var.
- If aspects of the language are changed, it is done inside new syntactic constructs. That is, you opt in implicitly. For example, yield is only a keyword inside generators (which were introduced in ES6). And all code inside modules and classes (both introduced in ES6) is implicitly in strict mode.

---

[2]https://github.com/tc39/proposals
[3]https://github.com/tc39/proposals/blob/master/finished-proposals.md

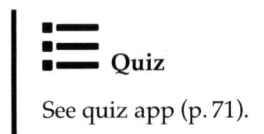

Quiz

See quiz app (p. 71).

Chapter 6

FAQ: JavaScript

Contents

6.1	What are good references for JavaScript?	37
6.2	How do I find out what JavaScript features are supported where?	37
6.3	Where can I look up what features are planned for JavaScript?	38
6.4	Why does JavaScript fail silently so often?	38
6.5	Why can't we clean up JavaScript, by removing quirks and outdated features?	38
6.6	How can I quickly try out a piece of JavaScript code?	38

6.1 What are good references for JavaScript?

Please consult §7.3 "JavaScript references" (p. 42).

6.2 How do I find out what JavaScript features are supported where?

This book usually mentions if a feature is part of ECMAScript 5 (as required by older browsers) or a newer version. For more detailed information (including pre-ES5 versions), there are several good compatibility tables available online:

- ECMAScript compatibility tables for various engines[1] (by kangax[2], webbedspace[3], zloirock[4])
- Node.js compatibility tables[5] (by William Kapke[6])

---

[1] http://kangax.github.io/compat-table/es5/
[2] https://twitter.com/kangax
[3] https://twitter.com/webbedspace
[4] https://twitter.com/zloirock
[5] https://node.green
[6] https://twitter.com/williamkapke

- Mozilla's MDN web docs[7] have tables for each feature that describe relevant ECMAScript versions and browser support.
- "Can I use…"[8] documents what features (including JavaScript language features) are supported by web browsers.

6.3 Where can I look up what features are planned for JavaScript?

Please consult the following sources:

- §5.5 "The TC39 process" (p. 33) describes how upcoming features are planned.
- §5.6 "FAQ: TC39 process" (p. 35) answers various questions regarding upcoming features.

6.4 Why does JavaScript fail silently so often?

JavaScript often fails silently. Let's look at two examples.

First example: If the operands of an operator don't have the appropriate types, they are converted as necessary.

```
> '3' * '5'
15
```

Second example: If an arithmetic computation fails, you get an error value, not an exception.

```
> 1 / 0
Infinity
```

The reason for the silent failures is historical: JavaScript did not have exceptions until ECMAScript 3. Since then, its designers have tried to avoid silent failures.

6.5 Why can't we clean up JavaScript, by removing quirks and outdated features?

This question is answered in §5.7 "Evolving JavaScript: Don't break the web" (p. 35).

6.6 How can I quickly try out a piece of JavaScript code?

§9.1 "Trying out JavaScript code" (p. 59) explains how to do that.

---

[7]https://developer.mozilla.org/en-US/docs/Web/JavaScript
[8]https://caniuse.com/

Part II

First steps

Chapter 7

The big picture

Contents

7.1	What are you learning in this book?	41
7.2	The structure of browsers and Node.js	41
7.3	JavaScript references	42
7.4	Further reading	42

In this chapter, I'd like to paint the big picture: what are you learning in this book, and how does it fit into the overall landscape of web development?

7.1 What are you learning in this book?

This book teaches the JavaScript language. It focuses on just the language, but offers occasional glimpses at two platforms where JavaScript can be used:

- Web browser
- Node.js

Node.js is important for web development in three ways:

- You can use it to write server-side software in JavaScript.
- You can also use it to write software for the command line (think Unix shell, Windows PowerShell, etc.). Many JavaScript-related tools are based on (and executed via) Node.js.
- Node's software registry, npm, has become the dominant way of installing tools (such as compilers and build tools) and libraries – even for client-side development.

7.2 The structure of browsers and Node.js

The structures of the two JavaScript platforms *web browser* and *Node.js* are similar (fig. 7.1):

- The foundational layer consists of the JavaScript engine and platform-specific "core" functionality.

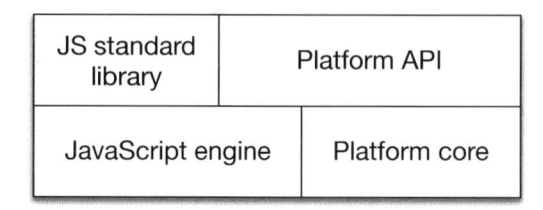

JS standard library	Platform API
JavaScript engine	Platform core

Figure 7.1: The structure of the two JavaScript platforms *web browser* and *Node.js*. The APIs "standard library" and "platform API" are hosted on top of a foundational layer with a JavaScript engine and a platform-specific "core".

- Two APIs are hosted on top of this foundation:
  - The JavaScript standard library is part of JavaScript proper and runs on top of the engine.
  - The platform API are also available from JavaScript – it provides access to platform-specific functionality. For example:
    * In browsers, you need to use the platform-specific API if you want to do anything related to the user interface: react to mouse clicks, play sounds, etc.
    * In Node.js, the platform-specific API lets you read and write files, download data via HTTP, etc.

7.3 JavaScript references

When you have a question about a JavaScript, a web search usually helps. I can recommend the following online sources:

- MDN web docs[1]: cover various web technologies such as CSS, HTML, JavaScript, and more. An excellent reference.
- Node.js Docs[2]: document the Node.js API.
- ExploringJS.com[3]: My other books on JavaScript go into greater detail than this book and are free to read online. You can look up features by ECMAScript version:
  - ES1–ES5: *Speaking JavaScript*[4]
  - ES6: *Exploring ES6*[5]
  - ES2016–ES2017: *Exploring ES2016 and ES2017*[6]
  - Etc.

7.4 Further reading

- §46 "Next steps: overview of web development" (p. 509) provides a more comprehensive look at web development.

---

[1] https://developer.mozilla.org/en-US/
[2] https://nodejs.org/en/docs/
[3] https://exploringjs.com
[4] http://speakingjs.com/
[5] https://exploringjs.com/es6.html
[6] https://exploringjs.com/es2016-es2017.html

Chapter 8

Syntax

Contents

- 8.1 An overview of JavaScript's syntax 44
  - 8.1.1 Basic syntax 44
  - 8.1.2 Modules 46
  - 8.1.3 Legal variable and property names 47
  - 8.1.4 Casing styles 47
  - 8.1.5 Capitalization of names 47
  - 8.1.6 More naming conventions 48
  - 8.1.7 Where to put semicolons? 48
- 8.2 (Advanced) 49
- 8.3 Identifiers 49
  - 8.3.1 Valid identifiers (variable names, etc.) 49
  - 8.3.2 Reserved words 49
- 8.4 Statement vs. expression 50
  - 8.4.1 Statements 50
  - 8.4.2 Expressions 50
  - 8.4.3 What is allowed where? 51
- 8.5 Ambiguous syntax 51
  - 8.5.1 Same syntax: function declaration and function expression .. 51
  - 8.5.2 Same syntax: object literal and block 52
  - 8.5.3 Disambiguation 52
- 8.6 Semicolons 52
  - 8.6.1 Rule of thumb for semicolons 52
  - 8.6.2 Semicolons: control statements 53
- 8.7 Automatic semicolon insertion (ASI) 53
  - 8.7.1 ASI triggered unexpectedly 54
  - 8.7.2 ASI unexpectedly not triggered 54
- 8.8 Semicolons: best practices 55
- 8.9 Strict mode vs. sloppy mode 55

| 8.9.1 | Switching on strict mode | . . . . | 56 |
| 8.9.2 | Improvements in strict mode | . . . . | 56 |

8.1 An overview of JavaScript's syntax

8.1.1 Basic syntax

Comments:

```
// single-line comment

/*
Comment with
multiple lines
*/
```

Primitive (atomic) values:

```
// Booleans
true
false

// Numbers (JavaScript only has a single type for numbers)
-123
1.141

// Strings (JavaScript has no type for characters)
'abc'
"abc"
```

An *assertion* describes what the result of a computation is expected to look like and throws an exception if those expectations aren't correct. For example, the following assertion states that the result of the computation 7 plus 1 must be 8:

```
assert.equal(7 + 1, 8);
```

assert.equal() is a method call (the object is assert, the method is .equal()) with two arguments: the actual result and the expected result. It is part of a Node.js assertion API that is explained later in this book (p. 65).

Logging to the console (p. 59) of a browser or Node.js:

```
// Printing a value to standard out (another method call)
console.log('Hello!');

// Printing error information to standard error
console.error('Something went wrong!');
```

Operators:

```
// Operators for booleans
assert.equal(true && false, false); // And
```

8.1 An overview of JavaScript's syntax

```js
assert.equal(true || false, true); // Or

// Operators for numbers
assert.equal(3 + 4, 7);
assert.equal(5 - 1, 4);
assert.equal(3 * 4, 12);
assert.equal(9 / 3, 3);

// Operators for strings
assert.equal('a' + 'b', 'ab');
assert.equal('I see ' + 3 + ' monkeys', 'I see 3 monkeys');

// Comparison operators
assert.equal(3 < 4, true);
assert.equal(3 <= 4, true);
assert.equal('abc' === 'abc', true);
assert.equal('abc' !== 'def', true);
```

Declaring variables:

```js
let x; // declaring x (mutable)
x = 3 * 5; // assign a value to x

let y = 3 * 5; // declaring and assigning

const z = 8; // declaring z (immutable)
```

Control flow statements:

```js
// Conditional statement
if (x < 0) { // is x less than zero?
  x = -x;
}
```

Ordinary function declarations:

```js
// add1() has the parameters a and b
function add1(a, b) {
  return a + b;
}
// Calling function add1()
assert.equal(add1(5, 2), 7);
```

Arrow function expressions (used especially as arguments of function calls and method calls):

```js
const add2 = (a, b) => { return a + b };
// Calling function add2()
assert.equal(add2(5, 2), 7);

// Equivalent to add2:
const add3 = (a, b) => a + b;
```

The previous code contains the following two arrow functions (the terms *expression* and *statement* are explained later in this chapter (p. 50)):

```
// An arrow function whose body is a code block
(a, b) => { return a + b }

// An arrow function whose body is an expression
(a, b) => a + b
```

Objects:

```
// Creating a plain object via an object literal
const obj = {
  first: 'Jane', // property
  last: 'Doe', // property
  getFullName() { // property (method)
    return this.first + ' ' + this.last;
  },
};

// Getting a property value
assert.equal(obj.first, 'Jane');
// Setting a property value
obj.first = 'Janey';

// Calling the method
assert.equal(obj.getFullName(), 'Janey Doe');
```

Arrays (Arrays are also objects):

```
// Creating an Array via an Array literal
const arr = ['a', 'b', 'c'];

// Getting an Array element
assert.equal(arr[1], 'b');
// Setting an Array element
arr[1] = 'β';
```

8.1.2 Modules

Each module is a single file. Consider, for example, the following two files with modules in them:

```
file-tools.mjs
main.mjs
```

The module in `file-tools.mjs` exports its function `isTextFilePath()`:

```
export function isTextFilePath(filePath) {
  return filePath.endsWith('.txt');
}
```

8.1 An overview of JavaScript's syntax 47

The module in `main.mjs` imports the whole module `path` and the function `isTextFilePath()`:

```
// Import whole module as namespace object `path`
import * as path from 'path';
// Import a single export of module file-tools.mjs
import {isTextFilePath} from './file-tools.mjs';
```

8.1.3 Legal variable and property names

The grammatical category of variable names and property names is called *identifier*.

Identifiers are allowed to have the following characters:

- Unicode letters: A–Z, a–z (etc.)
- $, _
- Unicode digits: 0–9 (etc.)
    - Variable names can't start with a digit

Some words have special meaning in JavaScript and are called *reserved*. Examples include: `if`, `true`, `const`.

Reserved words can't be used as variable names:

```
const if = 123;
  // SyntaxError: Unexpected token if
```

But they are allowed as names of properties:

```
> const obj = { if: 123 };
> obj.if
123
```

8.1.4 Casing styles

Common casing styles for concatenating words are:

- Camel case: `threeConcatenatedWords`
- Underscore case (also called *snake case*): `three_concatenated_words`
- Dash case (also called *kebab case*): `three-concatenated-words`

8.1.5 Capitalization of names

In general, JavaScript uses camel case, except for constants.

Lowercase:

- Functions, variables: `myFunction`
- Methods: `obj.myMethod`
- CSS:
    - CSS entity: `special-class`
    - Corresponding JavaScript variable: `specialClass`

Uppercase:

- Classes: `MyClass`
- Constants: `MY_CONSTANT`
    - Constants are also often written in camel case: `myConstant`

8.1.6 More naming conventions

The following naming conventions are popular in JavaScript.

If the name of a parameter starts with an underscore (or is an underscore) it means that this parameter is not used – for example:

```
arr.map((_x, i) => i)
```

If the name of a property of an object starts with an underscore then that property is considered private:

```
class ValueWrapper {
  constructor(value) {
    this._value = value;
  }
}
```

8.1.7 Where to put semicolons?

At the end of a statement:

```
const x = 123;
func();
```

But not if that statement ends with a curly brace:

```
while (false) {
  // ···
} // no semicolon

function func() {
  // ···
} // no semicolon
```

However, adding a semicolon after such a statement is not a syntax error – it is interpreted as an empty statement:

```
// Function declaration followed by empty statement:
function func() {
  // ···
};
```

Quiz: basic

See quiz app (p. 71).

8.2 (Advanced)

All remaining sections of this chapter are advanced.

8.3 Identifiers

8.3.1 Valid identifiers (variable names, etc.)

First character:

- Unicode letter (including accented characters such as é and ü and characters from non-latin alphabets, such as α)
- $
- _

Subsequent characters:

- Legal first characters
- Unicode digits (including Eastern Arabic numerals)
- Some other Unicode marks and punctuations

Examples:

```
const ε = 0.0001;
const строка = '';
let _tmp = 0;
const $foo2 = true;
```

8.3.2 Reserved words

Reserved words can't be variable names, but they can be property names.

All JavaScript *keywords* are reserved words:

```
await break case catch class const continue debugger default delete
do else export extends finally for function if import in instanceof
let new return static super switch this throw try typeof var void while
with yield
```

The following tokens are also keywords, but currently not used in the language:

```
enum implements package protected interface private public
```

The following literals are reserved words:

```
true false null
```

Technically, these words are not reserved, but you should avoid them, too, because they effectively are keywords:

```
Infinity NaN undefined async
```

You shouldn't use the names of global variables (String, Math, etc.) for your own variables and parameters, either.

8.4 Statement vs. expression

In this section, we explore how JavaScript distinguishes two kinds of syntactic constructs: *statements* and *expressions*. Afterward, we'll see that that can cause problems because the same syntax can mean different things, depending on where it is used.

> ⚙ **We pretend there are only statements and expressions**
>
> For the sake of simplicity, we pretend that there are only statements and expressions in JavaScript.

8.4.1 Statements

A *statement* is a piece of code that can be executed and performs some kind of action. For example, if is a statement:

```
let myStr;
if (myBool) {
  myStr = 'Yes';
} else {
  myStr = 'No';
}
```

One more example of a statement: a function declaration.

```
function twice(x) {
  return x + x;
}
```

8.4.2 Expressions

An *expression* is a piece of code that can be *evaluated* to produce a value. For example, the code between the parentheses is an expression:

```
let myStr = (myBool ? 'Yes' : 'No');
```

The operator _?_:_ used between the parentheses is called the *ternary operator*. It is the expression version of the if statement.

Let's look at more examples of expressions. We enter expressions and the REPL evaluates them for us:

```
> 'ab' + 'cd'
'abcd'
> Number('123')
123
> true || false
true
```

8.4.3 What is allowed where?

The current location within JavaScript source code determines which kind of syntactic constructs you are allowed to use:

- The body of a function must be a sequence of statements:

    ```
    function max(x, y) {
      if (x > y) {
        return x;
      } else {
        return y;
      }
    }
    ```

- The arguments of a function call or a method call must be expressions:

    ```
    console.log('ab' + 'cd', Number('123'));
    ```

However, expressions can be used as statements. Then they are called *expression statements*. The opposite is not true: when the context requires an expression, you can't use a statement.

The following code demonstrates that any expression bar() can be either expression or statement – it depends on the context:

```
function f() {
  console.log(bar()); // bar() is expression
  bar(); // bar(); is (expression) statement
}
```

8.5 Ambiguous syntax

JavaScript has several programming constructs that are syntactically ambiguous: the same syntax is interpreted differently, depending on whether it is used in statement context or in expression context. This section explores the phenomenon and the pitfalls it causes.

8.5.1 Same syntax: function declaration and function expression

A *function declaration* is a statement:

```
function id(x) {
  return x;
}
```

A *function expression* is an expression (right-hand side of =):

```
const id = function me(x) {
  return x;
};
```

8.5.2 Same syntax: object literal and block

In the following code, {} is an *object literal*: an expression that creates an empty object.

```
const obj = {};
```

This is an empty code block (a statement):

```
{
}
```

8.5.3 Disambiguation

The ambiguities are only a problem in statement context: If the JavaScript parser encounters ambiguous syntax, it doesn't know if it's a plain statement or an expression statement. For example:

- If a statement starts with `function`: Is it a function declaration or a function expression?
- If a statement starts with `{`: Is it an object literal or a code block?

To resolve the ambiguity, statements starting with `function` or `{` are never interpreted as expressions. If you want an expression statement to start with either one of these tokens, you must wrap it in parentheses:

```
(function (x) { console.log(x) })('abc');

// Output:
// 'abc'
```

In this code:

1. We first create a function via a function expression:

    ```
    function (x) { console.log(x) }
    ```

2. Then we invoke that function: `('abc')`

The code fragment shown in (1) is only interpreted as an expression because we wrap it in parentheses. If we didn't, we would get a syntax error because then JavaScript expects a function declaration and complains about the missing function name. Additionally, you can't put a function call immediately after a function declaration.

Later in this book, we'll see more examples of pitfalls caused by syntactic ambiguity:

- Assigning via object destructuring (p. 395)
- Returning an object literal from an arrow function (p. 217)

8.6 Semicolons

8.6.1 Rule of thumb for semicolons

Each statement is terminated by a semicolon:

8.7 Automatic semicolon insertion (ASI)

```
const x = 3;
someFunction('abc');
i++;
```

except statements ending with blocks:

```
function foo() {
  // ···
}
if (y > 0) {
  // ···
}
```

The following case is slightly tricky:

```
const func = () => {}; // semicolon!
```

The whole `const` declaration (a statement) ends with a semicolon, but inside it, there is an arrow function expression. That is, it's not the statement per se that ends with a curly brace; it's the embedded arrow function expression. That's why there is a semicolon at the end.

8.6.2 Semicolons: control statements

The body of a control statement is itself a statement. For example, this is the syntax of the `while` loop:

```
while (condition)
  statement
```

The body can be a single statement:

```
while (a > 0) a--;
```

But blocks are also statements and therefore legal bodies of control statements:

```
while (a > 0) {
  a--;
}
```

If you want a loop to have an empty body, your first option is an empty statement (which is just a semicolon):

```
while (processNextItem() > 0);
```

Your second option is an empty block:

```
while (processNextItem() > 0) {}
```

8.7 Automatic semicolon insertion (ASI)

While I recommend to always write semicolons, most of them are optional in JavaScript. The mechanism that makes this possible is called *automatic semicolon insertion* (ASI). In a way, it corrects syntax errors.

ASI works as follows. Parsing of a statement continues until there is either:

- A semicolon
- A line terminator followed by an illegal token

In other words, ASI can be seen as inserting semicolons at line breaks. The next subsections cover the pitfalls of ASI.

8.7.1 ASI triggered unexpectedly

The good news about ASI is that – if you don't rely on it and always write semicolons – there is only one pitfall that you need to be aware of. It is that JavaScript forbids line breaks after some tokens. If you do insert a line break, a semicolon will be inserted, too.

The token where this is most practically relevant is `return`. Consider, for example, the following code:

```
return
{
  first: 'jane'
};
```

This code is parsed as:

```
return;
{
  first: 'jane';
}
;
```

That is:

- Return statement without operand: `return;`
- Start of code block: `{`
- Expression statement `'jane';` with label (p. 195) `first:`
- End of code block: `}`
- Empty statement: `;`

Why does JavaScript do this? It protects against accidentally returning a value in a line after a `return`.

8.7.2 ASI unexpectedly not triggered

In some cases, ASI is *not* triggered when you think it should be. That makes life more complicated for people who don't like semicolons because they need to be aware of those cases. The following are three examples. There are more.

Example 1: Unintended function call.

```
a = b + c
(d + e).print()
```

Parsed as:

```
a = b + c(d + e).print();
```

Example 2: Unintended division.

```
a = b
/hi/g.exec(c).map(d)
```

Parsed as:

```
a = b / hi / g.exec(c).map(d);
```

Example 3: Unintended property access.

```
someFunction()
['ul', 'ol'].map(x => x + x)
```

Executed as:

```
const propKey = ('ul','ol'); // comma operator
assert.equal(propKey, 'ol');

someFunction()[propKey].map(x => x + x);
```

8.8 Semicolons: best practices

I recommend that you always write semicolons:

- I like the visual structure it gives code – you clearly see when a statement ends.
- There are less rules to keep in mind.
- The majority of JavaScript programmers use semicolons.

However, there are also many people who don't like the added visual clutter of semicolons. If you are one of them: Code without them *is* legal. I recommend that you use tools to help you avoid mistakes. The following are two examples:

- The automatic code formatter Prettier[1] can be configured to not use semicolons. It then automatically fixes problems. For example, if it encounters a line that starts with a square bracket, it prefixes that line with a semicolon.
- The static checker ESLint[2] has a rule[3] that you tell your preferred style (always semicolons or as few semicolons as possible) and that warns you about critical issues.

8.9 Strict mode vs. sloppy mode

Starting with ECMAScript 5, JavaScript has two *modes* in which JavaScript can be executed:

- Normal "sloppy" mode is the default in scripts (code fragments that are a precursor to modules and supported by browsers).

---

[1] https://prettier.io
[2] https://eslint.org
[3] https://eslint.org/docs/rules/semi

- Strict mode is the default in modules and classes, and can be switched on in scripts (how, is explained later). In this mode, several pitfalls of normal mode are removed and more exceptions are thrown.

You'll rarely encounter sloppy mode in modern JavaScript code, which is almost always located in modules. In this book, I assume that strict mode is always switched on.

8.9.1 Switching on strict mode

In script files and CommonJS modules, you switch on strict mode for a complete file, by putting the following code in the first line:

```
'use strict';
```

The neat thing about this "directive" is that ECMAScript versions before 5 simply ignore it: it's an expression statement that does nothing.

You can also switch on strict mode for just a single function:

```
function functionInStrictMode() {
  'use strict';
}
```

8.9.2 Improvements in strict mode

Let's look at three things that strict mode does better than sloppy mode. Just in this one section, all code fragments are executed in sloppy mode.

8.9.2.1 Sloppy mode pitfall: changing an undeclared variable creates a global variable

In non-strict mode, changing an undeclared variable creates a global variable.

```
function sloppyFunc() {
  undeclaredVar1 = 123;
}
sloppyFunc();
// Created global variable `undeclaredVar1`:
assert.equal(undeclaredVar1, 123);
```

Strict mode does it better and throws a `ReferenceError`. That makes it easier to detect typos.

```
function strictFunc() {
  'use strict';
  undeclaredVar2 = 123;
}
assert.throws(
  () => strictFunc(),
  {
    name: 'ReferenceError',
    message: 'undeclaredVar2 is not defined',
  });
```

8.9 Strict mode vs. sloppy mode

The `assert.throws()` states that its first argument, a function, throws a `ReferenceError` when it is called.

8.9.2.2 Function declarations are block-scoped in strict mode, function-scoped in sloppy mode

In strict mode, a variable created via a function declaration only exists within the innermost enclosing block:

```
function strictFunc() {
  'use strict';
  {
    function foo() { return 123 }
  }
  return foo(); // ReferenceError
}
assert.throws(
  () => strictFunc(),
  {
    name: 'ReferenceError',
    message: 'foo is not defined',
  });
```

In sloppy mode, function declarations are function-scoped:

```
function sloppyFunc() {
  {
    function foo() { return 123 }
  }
  return foo(); // works
}
assert.equal(sloppyFunc(), 123);
```

8.9.2.3 Sloppy mode doesn't throw exceptions when changing immutable data

In strict mode, you get an exception if you try to change immutable data:

```
function strictFunc() {
  'use strict';
  true.prop = 1; // TypeError
}
assert.throws(
  () => strictFunc(),
  {
    name: 'TypeError',
    message: "Cannot create property 'prop' on boolean 'true'",
  });
```

In sloppy mode, the assignment fails silently:

```
function sloppyFunc() {
  true.prop = 1; // fails silently
```

```
    return true.prop;
}
assert.equal(sloppyFunc(), undefined);
```

⬈ Further reading: sloppy mode

For more information on how sloppy mode differs from strict mode, see MDN[a].

[a]https://developer.mozilla.org/en-US/docs/Web/JavaScript/Reference/Strict_mode

≔ Quiz: advanced

See quiz app (p. 71).

Chapter 9

Consoles: interactive JavaScript command lines

Contents

9.1	Trying out JavaScript code	59
	9.1.1 Browser consoles	59
	9.1.2 The Node.js REPL	60
	9.1.3 Other options	60
9.2	The console.* API: printing data and more	61
	9.2.1 Printing values: `console.log()` (stdout)	61
	9.2.2 Printing error information: `console.error()` (stderr)	62
	9.2.3 Printing nested objects via `JSON.stringify()`	62

9.1 Trying out JavaScript code

You have many options for quickly running pieces of JavaScript code. The following subsections describe a few of them.

9.1.1 Browser consoles

Web browsers have so-called *consoles*: interactive command lines to which you can print text via `console.log()` and where you can run pieces of code. How to open the console differs from browser to browser. Fig. 9.1 shows the console of Google Chrome.

To find out how to open the console in your web browser, you can do a web search for "console «name-of-your-browser»". These are pages for a few commonly used web browsers:

- Apple Safari[1]
- Google Chrome[2]

---
[1]https://developer.apple.com/safari/tools/
[2]https://developers.google.com/web/tools/chrome-devtools/console/

- Microsoft Edge[3]
- Mozilla Firefox[4]

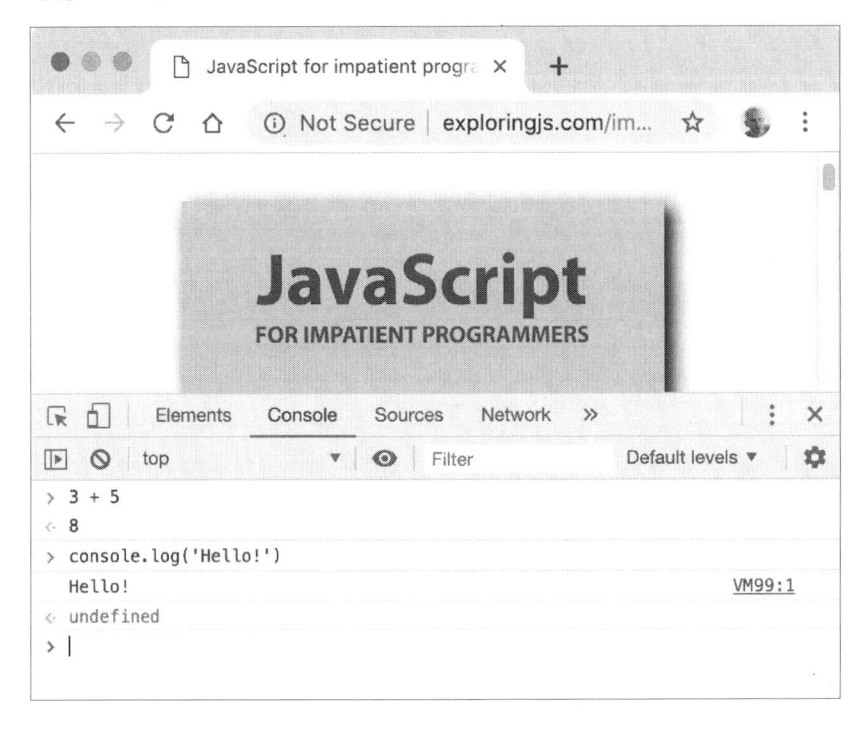

Figure 9.1: The console of the web browser "Google Chrome" is open (in the bottom half of window) while visiting a web page.

9.1.2 The Node.js REPL

REPL stands for *read-eval-print loop* and basically means *command line*. To use it, you must first start Node.js from an operating system command line, via the command node. Then an interaction with it looks as depicted in fig. 9.2: The text after > is input from the user; everything else is output from Node.js.

> **Reading: REPL interactions**
>
> I occasionally demonstrate JavaScript via REPL interactions. Then I also use greater-than symbols (>) to mark input – for example:
>
> ```
> > 3 + 5
> 8
> ```

9.1.3 Other options

Other options include:

---

[3]https://docs.microsoft.com/en-us/microsoft-edge/devtools-guide/console
[4]https://developer.mozilla.org/en-US/docs/Tools/Web_Console/Opening_the_Web_Console

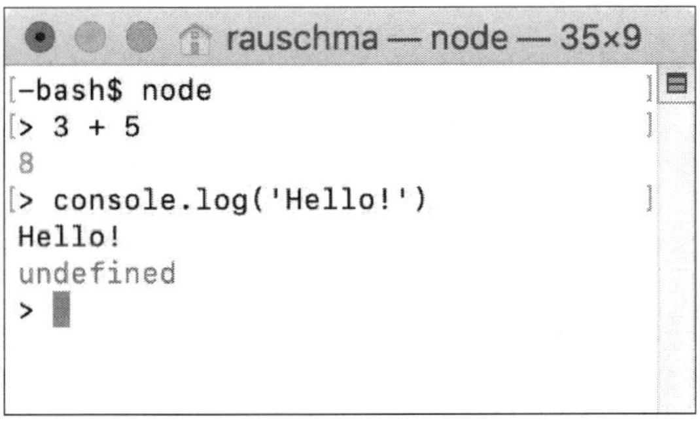

9.2 The `console.*` API: printing data and more

Figure 9.2: Starting and using the Node.js REPL (interactive command line).

- There are many web apps that let you experiment with JavaScript in web browsers – for example, Babel's REPL[5].
- There are also native apps and IDE plugins for running JavaScript.

> ⚠️ **Consoles often run in non-strict mode**
>
> In modern JavaScript, most code (e.g., modules) is executed in strict mode (p. 55). However, consoles often run in non-strict mode. Therefore, you may occasionally get slightly different results when using a console to execute code from this book.

9.2 The `console.*` API: printing data and more

In browsers, the console is something you can bring up that is normally hidden. For Node.js, the console is the terminal that Node.js is currently running in.

The full `console.*` API is documented on MDN web docs[6] and on the Node.js website[7]. It is not part of the JavaScript language standard, but much functionality is supported by both browsers and Node.js.

In this chapter, we only look at the following two methods for printing data ("printing" means displaying in the console):

- `console.log()`
- `console.error()`

9.2.1 Printing values: `console.log()` (stdout)

There are two variants of this operation:

```
console.log(...values: any[]): void
console.log(pattern: string, ...values: any[]): void
```

---
[5]https://babeljs.io/repl
[6]https://developer.mozilla.org/en-US/docs/Web/API/console
[7]https://nodejs.org/api/console.html

9.2.1.1 Printing multiple values

The first variant prints (text representations of) values on the console:

```
console.log('abc', 123, true);
// Output:
// abc 123 true
```

At the end, `console.log()` always prints a newline. Therefore, if you call it with zero arguments, it just prints a newline.

9.2.1.2 Printing a string with substitutions

The second variant performs string substitution:

```
console.log('Test: %s %j', 123, 'abc');
// Output:
// Test: 123 "abc"
```

These are some of the directives you can use for substitutions:

- `%s` converts the corresponding value to a string and inserts it.

    ```
    console.log('%s %s', 'abc', 123);
    // Output:
    // abc 123
    ```

- `%o` inserts a string representation of an object.

    ```
    console.log('%o', {foo: 123, bar: 'abc'});
    // Output:
    // { foo: 123, bar: 'abc' }
    ```

- `%j` converts a value to a JSON string and inserts it.

    ```
    console.log('%j', {foo: 123, bar: 'abc'});
    // Output:
    // {"foo":123,"bar":"abc"}
    ```

- `%%` inserts a single %.

    ```
    console.log('%s%%', 99);
    // Output:
    // 99%
    ```

9.2.2 Printing error information: `console.error()` (stderr)

`console.error()` works the same as `console.log()`, but what it logs is considered error information. For Node.js, that means that the output goes to stderr instead of stdout on Unix.

9.2.3 Printing nested objects via `JSON.stringify()`

`JSON.stringify()` (p. 499) is occasionally useful for printing nested objects:

9.2 The `console.*` API: printing data and more

```
console.log(JSON.stringify({first: 'Jane', last: 'Doe'}, null, 2));
```

Output:

```
{
  "first": "Jane",
  "last": "Doe"
}
```

Chapter 10

Assertion API

Contents

10.1 Assertions in software development	65
10.2 How assertions are used in this book	65
10.2.1 Documenting results in code examples via assertions	66
10.2.2 Implementing test-driven exercises via assertions	66
10.3 Normal comparison vs. deep comparison	66
10.4 Quick reference: module `assert`	67
10.4.1 Normal equality	67
10.4.2 Deep equality	67
10.4.3 Expecting exceptions	68
10.4.4 Another tool function	68

10.1 Assertions in software development

In software development, *assertions* state facts about values or pieces of code that must be true. If they aren't, an exception is thrown. Node.js supports assertions via its built-in module `assert` – for example:

```
import {strict as assert} from 'assert';
assert.equal(3 + 5, 8);
```

This assertion states that the expected result of 3 plus 5 is 8. The import statement uses the recommended `strict` version[1] of `assert`.

10.2 How assertions are used in this book

In this book, assertions are used in two ways: to document results in code examples and to implement test-driven exercises.

---

[1] https://nodejs.org/api/assert.html#assert_strict_mode

10.2.1 Documenting results in code examples via assertions

In code examples, assertions express expected results. Take, for example, the following function:

```
function id(x) {
  return x;
}
```

`id()` returns its parameter. We can show it in action via an assertion:

```
assert.equal(id('abc'), 'abc');
```

In the examples, I usually omit the statement for importing `assert`.

The motivation behind using assertions is:

- You can specify precisely what is expected.
- Code examples can be tested automatically, which ensures that they really work.

10.2.2 Implementing test-driven exercises via assertions

The exercises for this book are test-driven, via the test framework AVA. Checks inside the tests are made via methods of `assert`.

The following is an example of such a test:

```
// For the exercise, you must implement the function hello().
// The test checks if you have done it properly.
test('First exercise', t => {
  assert.equal(hello('world'), 'Hello world!');
  assert.equal(hello('Jane'), 'Hello Jane!');
  assert.equal(hello('John'), 'Hello John!');
  assert.equal(hello(''), 'Hello !');
});
```

For more information, consult §11 "Getting started with quizzes and exercises" (p. 71).

10.3 Normal comparison vs. deep comparison

The strict `equal()` uses `===` to compare values. Therefore, an object is only equal to itself – even if another object has the same content (because `===` does not compare the contents of objects, only their identities):

```
assert.notEqual({foo: 1}, {foo: 1});
```

`deepEqual()` is a better choice for comparing objects:

```
assert.deepEqual({foo: 1}, {foo: 1});
```

This method works for Arrays, too:

```
assert.notEqual(['a', 'b', 'c'], ['a', 'b', 'c']);
assert.deepEqual(['a', 'b', 'c'], ['a', 'b', 'c']);
```

10.4 Quick reference: module `assert`

For the full documentation, see the Node.js docs[2].

10.4.1 Normal equality

- `function equal(actual: any, expected: any, message?: string): void`

  `actual === expected` must be true. If not, an `AssertionError` is thrown.

  ```
  assert.equal(3+3, 6);
  ```

- `function notEqual(actual: any, expected: any, message?: string): void`

  `actual !== expected` must be true. If not, an `AssertionError` is thrown.

  ```
  assert.notEqual(3+3, 22);
  ```

The optional last parameter `message` can be used to explain what is asserted. If the assertion fails, the message is used to set up the `AssertionError` that is thrown.

```
let e;
try {
  const x = 3;
  assert.equal(x, 8, 'x must be equal to 8')
} catch (err) {
  assert.equal(
    String(err),
    'AssertionError [ERR_ASSERTION]: x must be equal to 8');
}
```

10.4.2 Deep equality

- `function deepEqual(actual: any, expected: any, message?: string): void`

  `actual` must be deeply equal to `expected`. If not, an `AssertionError` is thrown.

  ```
  assert.deepEqual([1,2,3], [1,2,3]);
  assert.deepEqual([], []);

  // To .equal(), an object is only equal to itself:
  assert.notEqual([], []);
  ```

- `function notDeepEqual(actual: any, expected: any, message?: string): void`

  `actual` must not be deeply equal to `expected`. If it is, an `AssertionError` is thrown.

  ```
  assert.notDeepEqual([1,2,3], [1,2]);
  ```

---

[2]https://nodejs.org/api/assert.html

10.4.3 Expecting exceptions

If you want to (or expect to) receive an exception, you need `throws()`: This function calls its first parameter, the function `block`, and only succeeds if it throws an exception. Additional parameters can be used to specify what that exception must look like.

- function throws(block: Function, message?: string): void

  ```
  assert.throws(
    () => {
      null.prop;
    }
  );
  ```

- function throws(block: Function, error: Function, message?: string): void

  ```
  assert.throws(
    () => {
      null.prop;
    },
    TypeError
  );
  ```

- function throws(block: Function, error: RegExp, message?: string): void

  ```
  assert.throws(
    () => {
      null.prop;
    },
    /^TypeError: Cannot read property 'prop' of null$/
  );
  ```

- function throws(block: Function, error: Object, message?: string): void

  ```
  assert.throws(
    () => {
      null.prop;
    },
    {
      name: 'TypeError',
      message: `Cannot read property 'prop' of null`,
    }
  );
  ```

10.4.4 Another tool function

- function fail(message: string | Error): never

  Always throws an `AssertionError` when it is called. That is occasionally useful for unit testing.

  ```
  try {
    functionThatShouldThrow();
  ```

10.4 Quick reference: module `assert`

```
    assert.fail();
} catch (_) {
    // Success
}
```

Quiz

See quiz app (p. 71).

Chapter 11

Getting started with quizzes and exercises

Contents

11.1 Quizzes	71
11.2 Exercises	71
11.2.1 Installing the exercises	71
11.2.2 Running exercises	72
11.3 Unit tests in JavaScript	72
11.3.1 A typical test	72
11.3.2 Asynchronous tests in AVA	73

Throughout most chapters, there are quizzes and exercises. These are a paid feature, but a comprehensive preview is available. This chapter explains how to get started with them.

11.1 Quizzes

Installation:

- Download and unzip `impatient-js-quiz.zip`

Running the quiz app:

- Open `impatient-js-quiz/index.html` in a web browser
- You'll see a TOC of all the quizzes.

11.2 Exercises

11.2.1 Installing the exercises

To install the exercises:

- Download and unzip `impatient-js-code.zip`
- Follow the instructions in `README.txt`

11.2.2 Running exercises

- Exercises are referred to by path in this book.
  - For example: `exercises/quizzes-exercises/first_module_test.mjs`
- Within each file:
  - The first line contains the command for running the exercise.
  - The following lines describe what you have to do.

11.3 Unit tests in JavaScript

All exercises in this book are tests that are run via the test framework AVA[1]. This section gives a brief introduction.

11.3.1 A typical test

Typical test code is split into two parts:

- Part 1: the code to be tested.
- Part 2: the tests for the code.

Take, for example, the following two files:

- `id.mjs` (code to be tested)
- `id_test.mjs` (tests)

11.3.1.1 Part 1: the code

The code itself resides in `id.mjs`:

```
export function id(x) {
  return x;
}
```

The key thing here is: everything you want to test must be exported. Otherwise, the test code can't access it.

11.3.1.2 Part 2: the tests

> 👁 **Don't worry about the exact details of tests**
>
> You don't need to worry about the exact details of tests: They are always implemented for you. Therefore, you only need to read them, but not write them.

The tests for the code reside in `id_test.mjs`:

---
[1] https://github.com/avajs/ava

11.3 Unit tests in JavaScript

```
// npm t demos/quizzes-exercises/id_test.mjs

import test from 'ava'; // (A)
import {strict as assert} from 'assert'; // (B)
import {id} from './id.mjs'; // (C)

test('My test', t => { // (D)
  assert.equal(id('abc'), 'abc'); // (E)
});
```

The core of this test file is line E – an assertion (p. 65): `assert.equal()` specifies that the expected result of `id('abc')` is `'abc'`.

As for the other lines:

- The comment at the very beginning shows the shell command for running the test.
- Line A: We import the test framework.
- Line B: We import the assertion library. AVA has built-in assertions, but module `assert` lets us remain compatible with plain Node.js.
- Line C: We import the function to test.
- Line D: We define a test. This is done by calling the function `test()`:
  - First parameter: the name of the test.
  - Second parameter: the test code, which is provided via an arrow function. The parameter `t` gives us access to AVA's testing API (assertions, etc.).

To run the test, we execute the following in a command line:

```
npm t demos/quizzes-exercises/id_test.mjs
```

The `t` is an abbreviation for `test`. That is, the long version of this command is:

```
npm test demos/quizzes-exercises/id_test.mjs
```

Exercise: Your first exercise

The following exercise gives you a first taste of what exercises are like:

- `exercises/quizzes-exercises/first_module_test.mjs`

11.3.2 Asynchronous tests in AVA

Reading

You can postpone reading this section until you get to the chapters on asynchronous programming.

Writing tests for asynchronous code requires extra work: The test receives its results later and has to signal to AVA that it isn't finished yet when it returns. The following subsections examine three ways of doing so.

11.3.2.1 Asynchronicity via callbacks

If we call `test.cb()` instead of `test()`, AVA switches to callback-based asynchronicity. When we are done with our asynchronous work, we have to call `t.end()`:

```
test.cb('divideCallback', t => {
  divideCallback(8, 4, (error, result) => {
    if (error) {
      t.end(error);
    } else {
      assert.strictEqual(result, 2);
      t.end();
    }
  });
});
```

11.3.2.2 Asynchronicity via Promises

If a test returns a Promise, AVA switches to Promise-based asynchronicity. A test is considered successful if the Promise is fulfilled and failed if the Promise is rejected.

```
test('dividePromise 1', t => {
  return dividePromise(8, 4)
  .then(result => {
    assert.strictEqual(result, 2);
  });
});
```

11.3.2.3 Async functions as test "bodies"

Async functions always return Promises. Therefore, an async function is a convenient way of implementing an asynchronous test. The following code is equivalent to the previous example.

```
test('dividePromise 2', async t => {
  const result = await dividePromise(8, 4);
  assert.strictEqual(result, 2);
  // No explicit return necessary!
});
```

You don't need to explicitly return anything: The implicitly returned `undefined` is used to fulfill the Promise returned by this async function. And if the test code throws an exception, then the async function takes care of rejecting the returned Promise.

Part III

Variables and values

Chapter 12

Variables and assignment

Contents

12.1 `let` 78
12.2 `const` 78
    12.2.1 `const` and immutability 78
    12.2.2 `const` and loops 79
12.3 Deciding between `const` and `let` 79
12.4 The scope of a variable 79
    12.4.1 Shadowing variables 80
12.5 (Advanced) 81
12.6 Terminology: static vs. dynamic 81
    12.6.1 Static phenomenon: scopes of variables 81
    12.6.2 Dynamic phenomenon: function calls 81
12.7 Global variables and the global object 82
    12.7.1 `globalThis` 82
12.8 Declarations: scope and activation 84
    12.8.1 `const` and `let`: temporal dead zone 84
    12.8.2 Function declarations and early activation 86
    12.8.3 Class declarations are not activated early 87
    12.8.4 `var`: hoisting (partial early activation) 88
12.9 Closures 88
    12.9.1 Bound variables vs. free variables 88
    12.9.2 What is a closure? 89
    12.9.3 Example: A factory for incrementors 89
    12.9.4 Use cases for closures 90
12.10 Further reading 90

These are JavaScript's main ways of declaring variables:

- `let` declares mutable variables.
- `const` declares *constants* (immutable variables).

Before ES6, there was also var. But it has several quirks, so it's best to avoid it in modern JavaScript. You can read more about it in *Speaking JavaScript*[1].

12.1 let

Variables declared via let are mutable:

```
let i;
i = 0;
i = i + 1;
assert.equal(i, 1);
```

You can also declare and assign at the same time:

```
let i = 0;
```

12.2 const

Variables declared via const are immutable. You must always initialize immediately:

```
const i = 0; // must initialize

assert.throws(
  () => { i = i + 1 },
  {
    name: 'TypeError',
    message: 'Assignment to constant variable.',
  }
);
```

12.2.1 const and immutability

In JavaScript, const only means that the *binding* (the association between variable name and variable value) is immutable. The value itself may be mutable, like obj in the following example.

```
const obj = { prop: 0 };

// Allowed: changing properties of `obj`
obj.prop = obj.prop + 1;
assert.equal(obj.prop, 1);

// Not allowed: assigning to `obj`
assert.throws(
  () => { obj = {} },
  {
    name: 'TypeError',
    message: 'Assignment to constant variable.',
```

---
[1] http://speakingjs.com/es5/ch16.html

```
    }
);
```

12.2.2 const and loops

You can use const with for-of loops, where a fresh binding is created for each iteration:

```
const arr = ['hello', 'world'];
for (const elem of arr) {
  console.log(elem);
}
// Output:
// 'hello'
// 'world'
```

In plain for loops, you must use let, however:

```
const arr = ['hello', 'world'];
for (let i=0; i<arr.length; i++) {
  const elem = arr[i];
  console.log(elem);
}
```

12.3 Deciding between const and let

I recommend the following rules to decide between const and let:

- const indicates an immutable binding and that a variable never changes its value. Prefer it.
- let indicates that the value of a variable changes. Use it only when you can't use const.

Exercise: const

exercises/variables-assignment/const_exrc.mjs

12.4 The scope of a variable

The *scope* of a variable is the region of a program where it can be accessed. Consider the following code.

```
{ // // Scope A. Accessible: x
  const x = 0;
  assert.equal(x, 0);
  { // Scope B. Accessible: x, y
    const y = 1;
    assert.equal(x, 0);
    assert.equal(y, 1);
    { // Scope C. Accessible: x, y, z
```

```
      const z = 2;
      assert.equal(x, 0);
      assert.equal(y, 1);
      assert.equal(z, 2);
    }
  }
}
// Outside. Not accessible: x, y, z
assert.throws(
  () => console.log(x),
  {
    name: 'ReferenceError',
    message: 'x is not defined',
  }
);
```

- Scope A is the *(direct) scope* of x.
- Scopes B and C are *inner scopes* of scope A.
- Scope A is an *outer scope* of scope B and scope C.

Each variable is accessible in its direct scope and all scopes nested within that scope.

The variables declared via const and let are called *block-scoped* because their scopes are always the innermost surrounding blocks.

12.4.1 Shadowing variables

You can't declare the same variable twice at the same level:

```
assert.throws(
  () => {
    eval('let x = 1; let x = 2;');
  },
  {
    name: 'SyntaxError',
    message: "Identifier 'x' has already been declared",
  });
```

> ⚙️ **Why eval()?**
>
> eval() (p. 224) delays parsing (and therefore the SyntaxError), until the callback of assert.throws() is executed. If we didn't use it, we'd already get an error when this code is parsed and assert.throws() wouldn't even be executed.

You can, however, nest a block and use the same variable name x that you used outside the block:

```
const x = 1;
assert.equal(x, 1);
{
```

```
  const x = 2;
  assert.equal(x, 2);
}
assert.equal(x, 1);
```

Inside the block, the inner x is the only accessible variable with that name. The inner x is said to *shadow* the outer x. Once you leave the block, you can access the old value again.

> **Quiz: basic**
>
> See quiz app (p. 71).

12.5 (Advanced)

All remaining sections are advanced.

12.6 Terminology: static vs. dynamic

These two adjectives describe phenomena in programming languages:

- *Static* means that something is related to source code and can be determined without executing code.
- *Dynamic* means at runtime.

Let's look at examples for these two terms.

12.6.1 Static phenomenon: scopes of variables

Variable scopes are a static phenomenon. Consider the following code:

```
function f() {
  const x = 3;
  // ···
}
```

x is *statically* (or *lexically*) *scoped*. That is, its scope is fixed and doesn't change at runtime.

Variable scopes form a static tree (via static nesting).

12.6.2 Dynamic phenomenon: function calls

Function calls are a dynamic phenomenon. Consider the following code:

```
function g(x) {}
function h(y) {
  if (Math.random()) g(y); // (A)
}
```

Whether or not the function call in line A happens, can only be decided at runtime.

Function calls form a dynamic tree (via dynamic calls).

12.7 Global variables and the global object

JavaScript's variable scopes are nested. They form a tree:

- The outermost scope is the root of the tree.
- The scopes directly contained in that scope are the children of the root.
- And so on.

The root is also called the *global scope*. In web browsers, the only location where one is directly in that scope is at the top level of a script. The variables of the global scope are called *global variables* and accessible everywhere. There are two kinds of global variables:

- *Global declarative variables* are normal variables.
    - They can only be created while at the top level of a script, via const, 'let, and class declarations.
- *Global object variables* are stored in properties of the so-called *global object*.
    - They are created in the top level of a script, via var and function declarations.
    - The global object can be accessed via the global variable globalThis. It can be used to create, read, and delete global object variables.
    - Other than that, global object variables work like normal variables.

The following HTML fragment demonstrates globalThis and the two kinds of global variables.

```
<script>
  const declarativeVariable = 'd';
  var objectVariable = 'o';
</script>
<script>
  // All scripts share the same top-level scope:
  console.log(declarativeVariable); // 'd'
  console.log(objectVariable); // 'o'

  // Not all declarations create properties of the global object:
  console.log(globalThis.declarativeVariable); // undefined
  console.log(globalThis.objectVariable); // 'o'
</script>
```

Each ECMAScript module has its own scope. Therefore, variables that exist at the top level of a module are not global. Fig. 12.1 illustrates how the various scopes are related.

12.7.1 globalThis

> ⚠ **globalThis is new**
>
> globalThis is a new feature. Be sure that the JavaScript engines you are targeting support it. If they don't, switch to one of the alternatives mentioned below.

The global variable globalThis is the new standard way of accessing the global object. It got its name from the fact that it has the same value as this in global scope.

12.7 Global variables and the global object

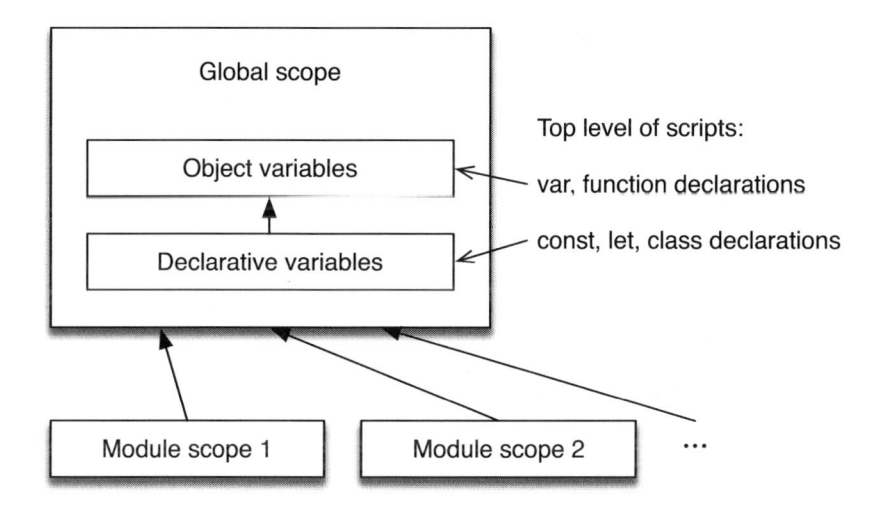

Figure 12.1: The global scope is JavaScript's outermost scope. It has two kinds of variables: *object variables* (managed via the *global object*) and normal *declarative variables*. Each ECMAScript module has its own scope which is contained in the global scope.

> ⚙ **globalThis does not always directly point to the global object**
>
> For example, in browsers, there is an indirection[a]. That indirection is normally not noticeable, but it is there and can be observed.
>
> ---
> [a]https://2ality.com/2019/08/global-this.html#window-proxy

12.7.1.1 Alternatives to `globalThis`

Older ways of accessing the global object depend on the platform:

- Global variable `window`: is the classic way of referring to the global object. But it doesn't work in Node.js and in Web Workers.
- Global variable `self`: is available in Web Workers and browsers in general. But it isn't supported by Node.js.
- Global variable `global`: is only available in Node.js.

12.7.1.2 Use cases for `globalThis`

The global object is now considered a mistake that JavaScript can't get rid of, due to backward compatibility. It affects performance negatively and is generally confusing.

ECMAScript 6 introduced several features that make it easier to avoid the global object – for example:

- `const`, `let`, and `class` declarations don't create global object properties when used in global scope.
- Each ECMAScript module has its own local scope.

It is usually better to access global object variables via variables and not via properties of `globalThis`. The former has always worked the same on all JavaScript platforms.

Tutorials on the web occasionally access global variables `globVar` via `window.globVar`. But the prefix "`window.`" is not necessary and I recommend to omit it:

```
window.encodeURIComponent(str); // no
encodeURIComponent(str); // yes
```

Therefore, there are relatively few use cases for `globalThis` – for example:

- *Polyfills* (p. 258) that add new features to old JavaScript engines.
- Feature detection, to find out what features a JavaScript engine supports.

12.8 Declarations: scope and activation

These are two key aspects of declarations:

- Scope: Where can a declared entity be seen? This is a static trait.
- Activation: When can I access an entity? This is a dynamic trait. Some entities can be accessed as soon as we enter their scopes. For others, we have to wait until execution reaches their declarations.

Tbl. 12.1 summarizes how various declarations handle these aspects.

> Table 12.1: Aspects of declarations. "Duplicates" describes if a declaration can be used twice with the same name (per scope). "Global prop." describes if a declaration adds a property to the global object, when it is executed in the global scope of a script. *TDZ* means *temporal dead zone* (which is explained later). (*) Function declarations are normally block-scoped, but function-scoped in sloppy mode (p. 55).

	Scope	Activation	Duplicates	Global prop.
const	Block	decl. (TDZ)	✗	✗
let	Block	decl. (TDZ)	✗	✗
function	Block (*)	start	✓	✓
class	Block	decl. (TDZ)	✗	✗
import	Module	same as export	✗	✗
var	Function	start, partially	✓	✓

`import` is described in §27.5 "ECMAScript modules" (p. 243). The following sections describe the other constructs in more detail.

12.8.1 const and let: temporal dead zone

For JavaScript, TC39 needed to decide what happens if you access a constant in its direct scope, before its declaration:

```
{
  console.log(x); // What happens here?
```

12.8 Declarations: scope and activation

```
    const x;
}
```

Some possible approaches are:

1. The name is resolved in the scope surrounding the current scope.
2. You get undefined.
3. There is an error.

Approach 1 was rejected because there is no precedent in the language for this approach. It would therefore not be intuitive to JavaScript programmers.

Approach 2 was rejected because then x wouldn't be a constant – it would have different values before and after its declaration.

let uses the same approach 3 as const, so that both work similarly and it's easy to switch between them.

The time between entering the scope of a variable and executing its declaration is called the *temporal dead zone* (TDZ) of that variable:

- During this time, the variable is considered to be uninitialized (as if that were a special value it has).
- If you access an uninitialized variable, you get a ReferenceError.
- Once you reach a variable declaration, the variable is set to either the value of the initializer (specified via the assignment symbol) or undefined – if there is no initializer.

The following code illustrates the temporal dead zone:

```
if (true) { // entering scope of `tmp`, TDZ starts
  // `tmp` is uninitialized:
  assert.throws(() => (tmp = 'abc'), ReferenceError);
  assert.throws(() => console.log(tmp), ReferenceError);

  let tmp; // TDZ ends
  assert.equal(tmp, undefined);
}
```

The next example shows that the temporal dead zone is truly *temporal* (related to time):

```
if (true) { // entering scope of `myVar`, TDZ starts
  const func = () => {
    console.log(myVar); // executed later
  };

  // We are within the TDZ:
  // Accessing `myVar` causes `ReferenceError`

  let myVar = 3; // TDZ ends
  func(); // OK, called outside TDZ
}
```

Even though `func()` is located before the declaration of `myVar` and uses that variable, we can call `func()`. But we have to wait until the temporal dead zone of `myVar` is over.

12.8.2 Function declarations and early activation

> 👁 **More information on functions**
>
> In this section, we are using functions – before we had a chance to learn them properly. Hopefully, everything still makes sense. Whenever it doesn't, please see §25 "Callable values" (p. 211).

A function declaration is always executed when entering its scope, regardless of where it is located within that scope. That enables you to call a function `foo()` before it is declared:

```
assert.equal(foo(), 123); // OK
function foo() { return 123; }
```

The early activation of `foo()` means that the previous code is equivalent to:

```
function foo() { return 123; }
assert.equal(foo(), 123);
```

If you declare a function via `const` or `let`, then it is not activated early. In the following example, you can only use `bar()` after its declaration.

```
assert.throws(
  () => bar(), // before declaration
  ReferenceError);

const bar = () => { return 123; };

assert.equal(bar(), 123); // after declaration
```

12.8.2.1 Calling ahead without early activation

Even if a function `g()` is not activated early, it can be called by a preceding function `f()` (in the same scope) if we adhere to the following rule: `f()` must be invoked after the declaration of `g()`.

```
const f = () => g();
const g = () => 123;

// We call f() after g() was declared:
assert.equal(f(), 123);
```

The functions of a module are usually invoked after its complete body is executed. Therefore, in modules, you rarely need to worry about the order of functions.

Lastly, note how early activation automatically keeps the aforementioned rule: when entering a scope, all function declarations are executed first, before any calls are made.

12.8.2.2 A pitfall of early activation

If you rely on early activation to call a function before its declaration, then you need to be careful that it doesn't access data that isn't activated early.

```
funcDecl();

const MY_STR = 'abc';
function funcDecl() {
  assert.throws(
    () => MY_STR,
    ReferenceError);
}
```

The problem goes away if you make the call to `funcDecl()` after the declaration of `MY_STR`.

12.8.2.3 The pros and cons of early activation

We have seen that early activation has a pitfall and that you can get most of its benefits without using it. Therefore, it is better to avoid early activation. But I don't feel strongly about this and, as mentioned before, often use function declarations because I like their syntax.

12.8.3 Class declarations are not activated early

Even though they are similar to function declarations in some ways, class declarations (p. 293) are not activated early:

```
assert.throws(
  () => new MyClass(),
  ReferenceError);

class MyClass {}

assert.equal(new MyClass() instanceof MyClass, true);
```

Why is that? Consider the following class declaration:

```
class MyClass extends Object {}
```

The operand of `extends` is an expression. Therefore, you can do things like this:

```
const identity = x => x;
class MyClass extends identity(Object) {}
```

Evaluating such an expression must be done at the location where it is mentioned. Anything else would be confusing. That explains why class declarations are not activated early.

12.8.4 var: hoisting (partial early activation)

var is an older way of declaring variables that predates const and let (which are preferred now). Consider the following var declaration.

```
var x = 123;
```

This declaration has two parts:

- Declaration var x: The scope of a var-declared variable is the innermost surrounding function and not the innermost surrounding block, as for most other declarations. Such a variable is already active at the beginning of its scope and initialized with undefined.
- Assignment x = 123: The assignment is always executed in place.

The following code demonstrates the effects of var:

```
function f() {
  // Partial early activation:
  assert.equal(x, undefined);
  if (true) {
    var x = 123;
    // The assignment is executed in place:
    assert.equal(x, 123);
  }
  // Scope is function, not block:
  assert.equal(x, 123);
}
```

12.9 Closures

Before we can explore closures, we need to learn about bound variables and free variables.

12.9.1 Bound variables vs. free variables

Per scope, there is a set of variables that are mentioned. Among these variables we distinguish:

- *Bound variables* are declared within the scope. They are parameters and local variables.
- *Free variables* are declared externally. They are also called *non-local variables*.

Consider the following code:

```
function func(x) {
  const y = 123;
  console.log(z);
}
```

In the body of func(), x and y are bound variables. z is a free variable.

12.9.2 What is a closure?

What is a closure then?

> A *closure* is a function plus a connection to the variables that exist at its "birth place".

What is the point of keeping this connection? It provides the values for the free variables of the function – for example:

```
function funcFactory(value) {
  return () => {
    return value;
  };
}

const func = funcFactory('abc');
assert.equal(func(), 'abc'); // (A)
```

`funcFactory` returns a closure that is assigned to `func`. Because `func` has the connection to the variables at its birth place, it can still access the free variable `value` when it is called in line A (even though it "escaped" its scope).

> **All functions in JavaScript are closures**
>
> Static scoping is supported via closures in JavaScript. Therefore, every function is a closure.

12.9.3 Example: A factory for incrementors

The following function returns *incrementors* (a name that I just made up). An incrementor is a function that internally stores a number. When it is called, it updates that number by adding the argument to it and returns the new value.

```
function createInc(startValue) {
  return (step) => { // (A)
    startValue += step;
    return startValue;
  };
}
const inc = createInc(5);
assert.equal(inc(2), 7);
```

We can see that the function created in line A keeps its internal number in the free variable `startValue`. This time, we don't just read from the birth scope, we use it to store data that we change and that persists across function calls.

We can create more storage slots in the birth scope, via local variables:

```
function createInc(startValue) {
  let index = -1;
  return (step) => {
```

```
    startValue += step;
    index++;
    return [index, startValue];
  };
}
const inc = createInc(5);
assert.deepEqual(inc(2), [0, 7]);
assert.deepEqual(inc(2), [1, 9]);
assert.deepEqual(inc(2), [2, 11]);
```

12.9.4 Use cases for closures

What are closures good for?

- For starters, they are simply an implementation of static scoping. As such, they provide context data for callbacks.
- They can also be used by functions to store state that persists across function calls. `createInc()` is an example of that.
- And they can provide private data for objects (produced via literals or classes). The details of how that works are explained in *Exploring ES6*[2].

Quiz: advanced

See quiz app (p. 71).

12.10 Further reading

For more information on how variables are handled under the hood (as described in the ECMAScript specification), consult §26.4 "Closures and environments" (p. 232).

---

[2]https://exploringjs.com/es6/ch_classes.html#_private-data-via-constructor-environments

Chapter 13

Values

Contents

13.1 What's a type?	91
13.2 JavaScript's type hierarchy	92
13.3 The types of the language specification	92
13.4 Primitive values vs. objects	93
13.4.1 Primitive values (short: primitives)	93
13.4.2 Objects	94
13.5 The operators `typeof` and `instanceof`: what's the type of a value?	95
13.5.1 `typeof`	96
13.5.2 `instanceof`	96
13.6 Classes and constructor functions	97
13.6.1 Constructor functions associated with primitive types	97
13.7 Converting between types	98
13.7.1 Explicit conversion between types	98
13.7.2 Coercion (automatic conversion between types)	99

In this chapter, we'll examine what kinds of values JavaScript has.

> 👁 **Supporting tool: `===`**
>
> In this chapter, we'll occasionally use the strict equality operator. `a === b` evaluates to `true` if a and b are equal. What exactly that means is explained in §14.4.2 "Strict equality (=== and !==)" (p. 105).

13.1 What's a type?

For this chapter, I consider types to be sets of values – for example, the type `boolean` is the set { `false`, `true` }.

13.2 JavaScript's type hierarchy

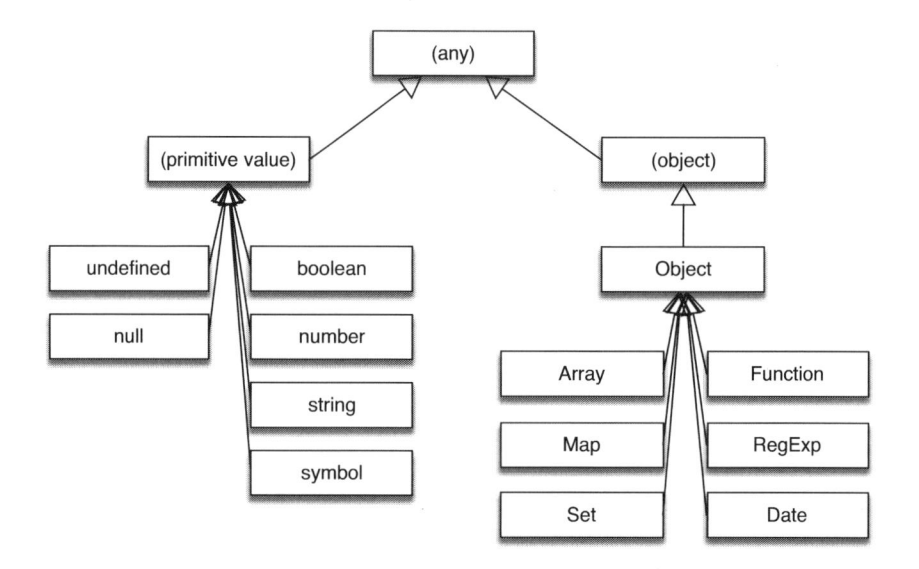

Figure 13.1: A partial hierarchy of JavaScript's types. Missing are the classes for errors, the classes associated with primitive types, and more. The diagram hints at the fact that not all objects are instances of Object.

Fig. 13.1 shows JavaScript's type hierarchy. What do we learn from that diagram?

- JavaScript distinguishes two kinds of values: primitive values and objects. We'll see soon what the difference is.
- The diagram differentiates objects and instances of class Object. Each instance of Object is also an object, but not vice versa. However, virtually all objects that you'll encounter in practice are instances of Object – for example, objects created via object literals. More details on this topic are explained in §29.4.3.4 "Objects that aren't instances of Object" (p. 303).

13.3 The types of the language specification

The ECMAScript specification only knows a total of seven types. The names of those types are (I'm using TypeScript's names, not the spec's names):

- undefined with the only element undefined
- null with the only element null
- boolean with the elements false and true
- number the type of all numbers (e.g., -123, 3.141)
- string the type of all strings (e.g., 'abc')
- symbol the type of all symbols (e.g., Symbol('My Symbol'))
- object the type of all objects (different from Object, the type of all instances of class Object and its subclasses)

13.4 Primitive values vs. objects

The specification makes an important distinction between values:

- *Primitive values* are the elements of the types `undefined`, `null`, `boolean`, `number`, `string`, `symbol`.
- All other values are *objects*.

In contrast to Java (that inspired JavaScript here), primitive values are not second-class citizens. The difference between them and objects is more subtle. In a nutshell:

- Primitive values: are atomic building blocks of data in JavaScript.
    - They are *passed by value*: when primitive values are assigned to variables or passed to functions, their contents are copied.
    - They are *compared by value*: when comparing two primitive values, their contents are compared.
- Objects: are compound pieces of data.
    - They are *passed by identity* (my term): when objects are assigned to variables or passed to functions, their *identities* (think pointers) are copied.
    - They are *compared by identity* (my term): when comparing two objects, their identities are compared.

Other than that, primitive values and objects are quite similar: they both have *properties* (key-value entries) and can be used in the same locations.

Next, we'll look at primitive values and objects in more depth.

13.4.1 Primitive values (short: primitives)

13.4.1.1 Primitives are immutable

You can't change, add, or remove properties of primitives:

```
let str = 'abc';
assert.equal(str.length, 3);
assert.throws(
  () => { str.length = 1 },
  /^TypeError: Cannot assign to read only property 'length'/
);
```

13.4.1.2 Primitives are *passed by value*

Primitives are *passed by value*: variables (including parameters) store the contents of the primitives. When assigning a primitive value to a variable or passing it as an argument to a function, its content is copied.

```
let x = 123;
let y = x;
assert.equal(y, 123);
```

13.4.1.3 Primitives are *compared by value*

Primitives are *compared by value*: when comparing two primitive values, we compare their contents.

```
assert.equal(123 === 123, true);
assert.equal('abc' === 'abc', true);
```

To see what's so special about this way of comparing, read on and find out how objects are compared.

13.4.2 Objects

Objects are covered in detail in §28 "Single objects" (p. 261) and the following chapter. Here, we mainly focus on how they differ from primitive values.

Let's first explore two common ways of creating objects:

- Object literal:

    ```
    const obj = {
      first: 'Jane',
      last: 'Doe',
    };
    ```

    The object literal starts and ends with curly braces {}. It creates an object with two properties. The first property has the key `'first'` (a string) and the value `'Jane'`. The second property has the key `'last'` and the value `'Doe'`. For more information on object literals, consult §28.2.1 "Object literals: properties" (p. 263).

- Array literal:

    ```
    const arr = ['foo', 'bar'];
    ```

    The Array literal starts and ends with square brackets []. It creates an Array with two *elements*: `'foo'` and `'bar'`. For more information on Array literals, consult §31.2.1 "Creating, reading, writing Arrays" (p. 318).

13.4.2.1 Objects are mutable by default

By default, you can freely change, add, and remove the properties of objects:

```
const obj = {};

obj.foo = 'abc'; // add a property
assert.equal(obj.foo, 'abc');

obj.foo = 'def'; // change a property
assert.equal(obj.foo, 'def');
```

13.4.2.2 Objects are *passed by identity*

Objects are *passed by identity* (my term): variables (including parameters) store the *identities* of objects.

13.5 The operators `typeof` and `instanceof`: what's the type of a value? 95

The identity of an object is like a pointer (or a transparent reference) to the object's actual data on the *heap* (think shared main memory of a JavaScript engine).

When assigning an object to a variable or passing it as an argument to a function, its identity is copied. Each object literal creates a fresh object on the heap and returns its identity.

```
const a = {}; // fresh empty object
// Pass the identity in `a` to `b`:
const b = a;

// Now `a` and `b` point to the same object
// (they "share" that object):
assert.equal(a === b, true);

// Changing `a` also changes `b`:
a.foo = 123;
assert.equal(b.foo, 123);
```

JavaScript uses *garbage collection* to automatically manage memory:

```
let obj = { prop: 'value' };
obj = {};
```

Now the old value `{ prop: 'value' }` of `obj` is *garbage* (not used anymore). JavaScript will automatically *garbage-collect* it (remove it from memory), at some point in time (possibly never if there is enough free memory).

> ⚙ **Details: passing by identity**
>
> "Passing by identity" means that the identity of an object (a transparent reference) is passed by value. This approach is also called "passing by sharing"[a].
>
> ---
> [a] https://en.wikipedia.org/wiki/Evaluation_strategy#Call_by_sharing

13.4.2.3 Objects are *compared by identity*

Objects are *compared by identity* (my term): two variables are only equal if they contain the same object identity. They are not equal if they refer to different objects with the same content.

```
const obj = {}; // fresh empty object
assert.equal(obj === obj, true); // same identity
assert.equal({} === {}, false); // different identities, same content
```

13.5 The operators `typeof` and `instanceof`: what's the type of a value?

The two operators `typeof` and `instanceof` let you determine what type a given value x has:

```
if (typeof x === 'string') ···
if (x instanceof Array) ···
```

How do they differ?

- `typeof` distinguishes the 7 types of the specification (minus one omission, plus one addition).
- `instanceof` tests which class created a given value.

> Rule of thumb: `typeof` is for primitive values; `instanceof` is for objects

13.5.1 `typeof`

Table 13.1: The results of the `typeof` operator.

x	typeof x
undefined	`'undefined'`
null	`'object'`
Boolean	`'boolean'`
Number	`'number'`
String	`'string'`
Symbol	`'symbol'`
Function	`'function'`
All other objects	`'object'`

Tbl. 13.1 lists all results of `typeof`. They roughly correspond to the 7 types of the language specification. Alas, there are two differences, and they are language quirks:

- `typeof null` returns `'object'` and not `'null'`. That's a bug. Unfortunately, it can't be fixed. TC39 tried to do that, but it broke too much code on the web.
- `typeof` of a function should be `'object'` (functions are objects). Introducing a separate category for functions is confusing.

> Exercises: Two exercises on `typeof`
>
> - `exercises/values/typeof_exrc.mjs`
> - Bonus: `exercises/values/is_object_test.mjs`

13.5.2 `instanceof`

This operator answers the question: has a value x been created by a class C?

```
x instanceof C
```

For example:

```
> (function() {}) instanceof Function
true
> ({}) instanceof Object
true
> [] instanceof Array
true
```

Primitive values are not instances of anything:

```
> 123 instanceof Number
false
> '' instanceof String
false
> '' instanceof Object
false
```

> **Exercise: `instanceof`**
> `exercises/values/instanceof_exrc.mjs`

13.6 Classes and constructor functions

JavaScript's original factories for objects are *constructor functions*: ordinary functions that return "instances" of themselves if you invoke them via the `new` operator.

ES6 introduced *classes*, which are mainly better syntax for constructor functions.

In this book, I'm using the terms *constructor function* and *class* interchangeably.

Classes can be seen as partitioning the single type `object` of the specification into subtypes – they give us more types than the limited 7 ones of the specification. Each class is the type of the objects that were created by it.

13.6.1 Constructor functions associated with primitive types

Each primitive type (except for the spec-internal types for `undefined` and `null`) has an associated *constructor function* (think class):

- The constructor function `Boolean` is associated with booleans.
- The constructor function `Number` is associated with numbers.
- The constructor function `String` is associated with strings.
- The constructor function `Symbol` is associated with symbols.

Each of these functions plays several roles – for example, `Number`:

- You can use it as a function and convert values to numbers:

    ```
    assert.equal(Number('123'), 123);
    ```

- `Number.prototype` provides the properties for numbers – for example, method `.toString()`:

```
assert.equal((123).toString, Number.prototype.toString);
```

- `Number` is a namespace/container object for tool functions for numbers – for example:
  ```
  assert.equal(Number.isInteger(123), true);
  ```
- Lastly, you can also use `Number` as a class and create number objects. These objects are different from real numbers and should be avoided.
  ```
  assert.notEqual(new Number(123), 123);
  assert.equal(new Number(123).valueOf(), 123);
  ```

13.6.1.1 Wrapping primitive values

The constructor functions related to primitive types are also called *wrapper types* because they provide the canonical way of converting primitive values to objects. In the process, primitive values are "wrapped" in objects.

```
const prim = true;
assert.equal(typeof prim, 'boolean');
assert.equal(prim instanceof Boolean, false);

const wrapped = Object(prim);
assert.equal(typeof wrapped, 'object');
assert.equal(wrapped instanceof Boolean, true);

assert.equal(wrapped.valueOf(), prim); // unwrap
```

Wrapping rarely matters in practice, but it is used internally in the language specification, to give primitives properties.

13.7 Converting between types

There are two ways in which values are converted to other types in JavaScript:

- Explicit conversion: via functions such as `String()`.
- *Coercion* (automatic conversion): happens when an operation receives operands/parameters that it can't work with.

13.7.1 Explicit conversion between types

The function associated with a primitive type explicitly converts values to that type:

```
> Boolean(0)
false
> Number('123')
123
> String(123)
'123'
```

You can also use `Object()` to convert values to objects:

13.7 Converting between types

```
> typeof Object(123)
'object'
```

13.7.2 Coercion (automatic conversion between types)

For many operations, JavaScript automatically converts the operands/parameters if their types don't fit. This kind of automatic conversion is called *coercion*.

For example, the multiplication operator coerces its operands to numbers:

```
> '7' * '3'
21
```

Many built-in functions coerce, too. For example, `parseInt()` coerces its parameter to string (parsing stops at the first character that is not a digit):

```
> parseInt(123.45)
123
```

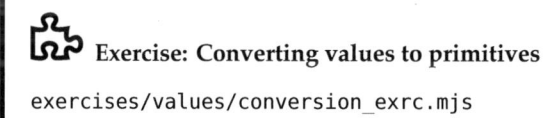

> **Exercise: Converting values to primitives**
>
> exercises/values/conversion_exrc.mjs

> **Quiz**
>
> See quiz app (p. 71).

Chapter 14

Operators

Contents

- 14.1 Making sense of operators 101
  - 14.1.1 Operators coerce their operands to appropriate types 102
  - 14.1.2 Most operators only work with primitive values 102
- 14.2 The plus operator (+) 102
- 14.3 Assignment operators 103
  - 14.3.1 The plain assignment operator 103
  - 14.3.2 Compound assignment operators 103
  - 14.3.3 A list of all compound assignment operators 103
- 14.4 Equality: == vs. === 104
  - 14.4.1 Loose equality (== and !=) 104
  - 14.4.2 Strict equality (=== and !==) 105
  - 14.4.3 Recommendation: always use strict equality 105
  - 14.4.4 Even stricter than ===: `Object.is()` 106
- 14.5 Ordering operators 107
- 14.6 Various other operators 107
  - 14.6.1 Comma operator 107
  - 14.6.2 `void` operator 107

14.1 Making sense of operators

JavaScript's operators may seem quirky. With the following two rules, they are easier to understand:

- Operators coerce their operands to appropriate types
- Most operators only work with primitive values

14.1.1 Operators coerce their operands to appropriate types

If an operator gets operands that don't have the proper types, it rarely throws an exception. Instead, it *coerces* (automatically converts) the operands so that it can work with them. Let's look at two examples.

First, the multiplication operator can only work with numbers. Therefore, it converts strings to numbers before computing its result.

```
> '7' * '3'
21
```

Second, the square brackets operator ([ ]) for accessing the properties of an object can only handle strings and symbols. All other values are coerced to string:

```
const obj = {};
obj['true'] = 123;

// Coerce true to the string 'true'
assert.equal(obj[true], 123);
```

14.1.2 Most operators only work with primitive values

As mentioned before, most operators only work with primitive values. If an operand is an object, it is usually coerced to a primitive value – for example:

```
> [1,2,3] + [4,5,6]
'1,2,34,5,6'
```

Why? The plus operator first coerces its operands to primitive values:

```
> String([1,2,3])
'1,2,3'
> String([4,5,6])
'4,5,6'
```

Next, it concatenates the two strings:

```
> '1,2,3' + '4,5,6'
'1,2,34,5,6'
```

14.2 The plus operator (+)

The plus operator works as follows in JavaScript:

- First, it converts both operands to primitive values. Then it switches to one of two modes:
    - String mode: If one of the two primitive values is a string, then it converts the other one to a string, concatenates both strings, and returns the result.
    - Number mode: Otherwise, It converts both operands to numbers, adds them, and returns the result.

String mode lets us use + to assemble strings:

14.3 Assignment operators

```
> 'There are ' + 3 + ' items'
'There are 3 items'
```

Number mode means that if neither operand is a string (or an object that becomes a string) then everything is coerced to numbers:

```
> 4 + true
5
```

`Number(true)` is 1.

14.3 Assignment operators

14.3.1 The plain assignment operator

The plain assignment operator is used to change storage locations:

```
x = value; // assign to a previously declared variable
obj.propKey = value; // assign to a property
arr[index] = value; // assign to an Array element
```

Initializers in variable declarations can also be viewed as a form of assignment:

```
const x = value;
let y = value;
```

14.3.2 Compound assignment operators

Given an operator op, the following two ways of assigning are equivalent:

```
myvar op= value
myvar = myvar op value
```

If, for example, op is +, then we get the operator += that works as follows.

```
let str = '';
str += '<b>';
str += 'Hello!';
str += '</b>';

assert.equal(str, '<b>Hello!</b>');
```

14.3.3 A list of all compound assignment operators

- Arithmetic operators:

    += -= *= /= %= **=

    += also works for string concatenation

- Bitwise operators:

    <<= >>= >>>= &= ^= |=

14.4 Equality: == vs. ===

JavaScript has two kinds of equality operators: loose equality (==) and strict equality (===). The recommendation is to always use the latter.

> **Other names for == and ===**
>
> - == is also called *double equals*. Its official name in the language specification is *abstract equality comparison*[a].
> - === is also called *triple equals*.
>
> ---
> [a]https://tc39.github.io/ecma262/#sec-abstract-equality-comparison

14.4.1 Loose equality (== and !=)

Loose equality is one of JavaScript's quirks. It often coerces operands. Some of those coercions make sense:

```
> '123' == 123
true
> false == 0
true
```

Others less so:

```
> '' == 0
true
```

Objects are coerced to primitives if (and only if!) the other operand is primitive:

```
> [1, 2, 3] == '1,2,3'
true
> ['1', '2', '3'] == '1,2,3'
true
```

If both operands are objects, they are only equal if they are the same object:

```
> [1, 2, 3] == ['1', '2', '3']
false
> [1, 2, 3] == [1, 2, 3]
false

> const arr = [1, 2, 3];
> arr == arr
true
```

Lastly, == considers undefined and null to be equal:

```
> undefined == null
true
```

14.4.2 Strict equality (=== and !==)

Strict equality never coerces. Two values are only equal if they have the same type. Let's revisit our previous interaction with the == operator and see what the === operator does:

```
> false === 0
false
> '123' === 123
false
```

An object is only equal to another value if that value is the same object:

```
> [1, 2, 3] === '1,2,3'
false
> ['1', '2', '3'] === '1,2,3'
false

> [1, 2, 3] === ['1', '2', '3']
false
> [1, 2, 3] === [1, 2, 3]
false

> const arr = [1, 2, 3];
> arr === arr
true
```

The === operator does not consider undefined and null to be equal:

```
> undefined === null
false
```

14.4.3 Recommendation: always use strict equality

I recommend to always use ===. It makes your code easier to understand and spares you from having to think about the quirks of ==.

Let's look at two use cases for == and what I recommend to do instead.

14.4.3.1 Use case for ==: comparing with a number or a string

== lets you check if a value x is a number or that number as a string – with a single comparison:

```
if (x == 123) {
  // x is either 123 or '123'
}
```

I prefer either of the following two alternatives:

```
if (x === 123 || x === '123') ···
if (Number(x) === 123) ···
```

You can also convert x to a number when you first encounter it.

14.4.3.2 Use case for ==: comparing with undefined or null

Another use case for == is to check if a value x is either undefined or null:

```
if (x == null) {
  // x is either null or undefined
}
```

The problem with this code is that you can't be sure if someone meant to write it that way or if they made a typo and meant === null.

I prefer either of the following two alternatives:

```
if (x === undefined || x === null) ···
if (!x) ···
```

A downside of the second alternative is that it accepts values other than undefined and null, but it is a well-established pattern in JavaScript (to be explained in detail in §16.3 "Truthiness-based existence checks" (p. 117)).

The following three conditions are also roughly equivalent:

```
if (x != null) ···
if (x !== undefined && x !== null) ···
if (x) ···
```

14.4.4 Even stricter than ===: Object.is()

Method Object.is() compares two values:

```
> Object.is(123, 123)
true
> Object.is(123, '123')
false
```

It is even stricter than ===. For example, it considers NaN, the error value for computations involving numbers (p. 128), to be equal to itself:

```
> Object.is(NaN, NaN)
true
> NaN === NaN
false
```

That is occasionally useful. For example, you can use it to implement an improved version of the Array method .indexOf():

```
const myIndexOf = (arr, elem) => {
  return arr.findIndex(x => Object.is(x, elem));
};
```

myIndexOf() finds NaN in an Array, while .indexOf() doesn't:

```
> myIndexOf([0,NaN,2], NaN)
1
> [0,NaN,2].indexOf(NaN)
-1
```

The result -1 means that `.indexOf()` couldn't find its argument in the Array.

14.5 Ordering operators

Table 14.1: JavaScript's ordering operators.

Operator	name
<	less than
<=	Less than or equal
>	Greater than
>=	Greater than or equal

JavaScript's ordering operators (tbl. 14.1) work for both numbers and strings:

```
> 5 >= 2
true
> 'bar' < 'foo'
true
```

<= and >= are based on strict equality.

> ⚠ **The ordering operators don't work well for human languages**
>
> The ordering operators don't work well for comparing text in a human language, e.g., when capitalization or accents are involved. The details are explained in §20.5 "Comparing strings" (p. 163).

14.6 Various other operators

Operators for booleans, strings, numbers, objects: are covered elsewhere in this book.

The next two subsections discuss two operators that are rarely used.

14.6.1 Comma operator

The comma operator has two operands, evaluates both of them and returns the second one:

```
> 'a', 'b'
'b'
```

For more information on this operator, see *Speaking JavaScript*[1].

14.6.2 `void` operator

The `void` operator evaluates its operand and returns `undefined`:

---
[1] http://speakingjs.com/es5/ch09.html#comma_operator

```
> void (3 + 2)
undefined
```

For more information on this operator, see *Speaking JavaScript*[2].

Quiz

See quiz app (p. 71).

---
[2]http://speakingjs.com/es5/ch09.html#void_operator

Part IV

Primitive values

Chapter 15

The non-values `undefined` and `null`

Contents

15.1 undefined vs. null	111
15.2 Occurrences of undefined and null	112
15.2.1 Occurrences of undefined	112
15.2.2 Occurrences of null	112
15.3 Checking for undefined or null	113
15.4 undefined and null don't have properties	113
15.5 The history of undefined and null	114

Many programming languages have one "non-value" called `null`. It indicates that a variable does not currently point to an object – for example, when it hasn't been initialized yet.

In contrast, JavaScript has two of them: `undefined` and `null`.

15.1 `undefined` vs. `null`

Both values are very similar and often used interchangeably. How they differ is therefore subtle. The language itself makes the following distinction:

- `undefined` means "not initialized" (e.g., a variable) or "not existing" (e.g., a property of an object).
- `null` means "the intentional absence of any object value" (a quote from the language specification[1]).

Programmers may make the following distinction:

---
[1] https://tc39.github.io/ecma262/#sec-null-value

- `undefined` is the non-value used by the language (when something is uninitialized, etc.).
- `null` means "explicitly switched off". That is, it helps implement a type that comprises both meaningful values and a meta-value that stands for "no meaningful value". Such a type is called *option type* or *maybe type*[2] in functional programming.

15.2 Occurrences of `undefined` and `null`

The following subsections describe where `undefined` and `null` appear in the language. We'll encounter several mechanisms that are explained in more detail later in this book.

15.2.1 Occurrences of `undefined`

Uninitialized variable `myVar`:

```
let myVar;
assert.equal(myVar, undefined);
```

Parameter x is not provided:

```
function func(x) {
  return x;
}
assert.equal(func(), undefined);
```

Property `.unknownProp` is missing:

```
const obj = {};
assert.equal(obj.unknownProp, undefined);
```

If you don't explicitly specify the result of a function via a `return` statement, JavaScript returns `undefined` for you:

```
function func() {}
assert.equal(func(), undefined);
```

15.2.2 Occurrences of `null`

The prototype of an object is either an object or, at the end of a chain of prototypes, `null`. `Object.prototype` does not have a prototype:

```
> Object.getPrototypeOf(Object.prototype)
null
```

If you match a regular expression (such as `/a/`) against a string (such as `'x'`), you either get an object with matching data (if matching was successful) or `null` (if matching failed):

```
> /a/.exec('x')
null
```

The JSON data format (p. 497) does not support `undefined`, only `null`:

---

[2]https://en.wikipedia.org/wiki/Option_type

15.3 Checking for `undefined` or `null`

```
> JSON.stringify({a: undefined, b: null})
'{"b":null}'
```

15.3 Checking for `undefined` or `null`

Checking for either:

```
if (x === null) ···
if (x === undefined) ···
```

Does x have a value?

```
if (x !== undefined && x !== null) {
  // ···
}
if (x) { // truthy?
  // x is neither: undefined, null, false, 0, NaN, ''
}
```

Is x either undefined or null?

```
if (x === undefined || x === null) {
  // ···
}
if (!x) { // falsy?
  // x is: undefined, null, false, 0, NaN, ''
}
```

Truthy means "is `true` if coerced to boolean". *Falsy* means "is `false` if coerced to boolean". Both concepts are explained properly in §16.2 "Falsy and truthy values" (p. 116).

15.4 `undefined` and `null` don't have properties

`undefined` and `null` are the two only JavaScript values where you get an exception if you try to read a property. To explore this phenomenon, let's use the following function, which reads ("gets") property `.foo` and returns the result.

```
function getFoo(x) {
  return x.foo;
}
```

If we apply `getFoo()` to various values, we can see that it only fails for undefined and null:

```
> getFoo(undefined)
TypeError: Cannot read property 'foo' of undefined
> getFoo(null)
TypeError: Cannot read property 'foo' of null

> getFoo(true)
undefined
```

```
> getFoo({})
undefined
```

15.5 The history of `undefined` and `null`

In Java (which inspired many aspects of JavaScript), initialization values depend on the static type of a variable:

- Variables with object types are initialized with `null`.
- Each primitive type has its own initialization value. For example, `int` variables are initialized with `0`.

In JavaScript, each variable can hold both object values and primitive values. Therefore, if `null` means "not an object", JavaScript also needs an initialization value that means "neither an object nor a primitive value". That initialization value is `undefined`.

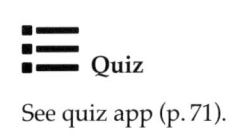

> **Quiz**
>
> See quiz app (p. 71).

Chapter 16

Booleans

Contents

16.1	Converting to boolean	115
16.2	Falsy and truthy values	116
	16.2.1 Checking for truthiness or falsiness	117
16.3	Truthiness-based existence checks	117
	16.3.1 Pitfall: truthiness-based existence checks are imprecise	118
	16.3.2 Use case: was a parameter provided?	118
	16.3.3 Use case: does a property exist?	118
16.4	Conditional operator (? :)	119
16.5	Binary logical operators: And (x && y), Or (x || y)	119
	16.5.1 Logical And (x && y)	120
	16.5.2 Logical Or (||)	120
	16.5.3 Default values via logical Or (||)	121
16.6	Logical Not (!)	121

The primitive type *boolean* comprises two values – `false` and `true`:

```
> typeof false
'boolean'
> typeof true
'boolean'
```

16.1 Converting to boolean

> ⚙ **The meaning of "converting to [type]"**
>
> "Converting to [type]" is short for "Converting arbitrary values to values of type [type]".

These are three ways in which you can convert an arbitrary value x to a boolean.

- `Boolean(x)`
  Most descriptive; recommended.

- `x ? true : false`
  Uses the conditional operator (explained later in this chapter (p. 119)).

- `!!x`
  Uses the logical Not operator (`!`, p. 121). This operator coerces its operand to boolean. It is applied a second time to get a non-negated result.

Tbl. 16.1 describes how various values are converted to boolean.

Table 16.1: Converting values to booleans.

x	Boolean(x)
`undefined`	`false`
`null`	`false`
boolean value	x (no change)
number value	`0` → `false`, `NaN` → `false`
	other numbers → `true`
string value	`''` → `false`
	other strings → `true`
object value	always `true`

16.2 Falsy and truthy values

When checking the condition of an `if` statement, a `while` loop, or a `do-while` loop, JavaScript works differently than you may expect. Take, for example, the following condition:

```
if (value) {}
```

In many programming languages, this condition is equivalent to:

```
if (value === true) {}
```

However, in JavaScript, it is equivalent to:

```
if (Boolean(value) === true) {}
```

That is, JavaScript checks if `value` is `true` when converted to boolean. This kind of check is so common that the following names were introduced:

- A value is called *truthy* if it is `true` when converted to boolean.
- A value is called *falsy* if it is `false` when converted to boolean.

Each value is either truthy or falsy. Consulting tbl. 16.1, we can make an exhaustive list of falsy values:

- `undefined`, `null`
- `false`
- `0`, `NaN`

16.3 Truthiness-based existence checks

- `''`

All other values (including all objects) are truthy:

```
> Boolean('abc')
true
> Boolean([])
true
> Boolean({})
true
```

16.2.1 Checking for truthiness or falsiness

```
if (x) {
  // x is truthy
}

if (!x) {
  // x is falsy
}

if (x) {
  // x is truthy
} else {
  // x is falsy
}

const result = x ? 'truthy' : 'falsy';
```

The conditional operator that is used in the last line, is explained later in this chapter (p. 119).

Exercise: Truthiness

`exercises/booleans/truthiness_exrc.mjs`

16.3 Truthiness-based existence checks

In JavaScript, if you read something that doesn't exist (e.g., a missing parameter or a missing property), you usually get `undefined` as a result. In these cases, an existence check amounts to comparing a value with `undefined`. For example, the following code checks if object `obj` has the property `.prop`:

```
if (obj.prop !== undefined) {
  // obj has property .prop
}
```

Due to undefined being falsy, we can shorten this check to:

```
if (obj.prop) {
  // obj has property .prop
}
```

16.3.1 Pitfall: truthiness-based existence checks are imprecise

Truthiness-based existence checks have one pitfall: they are not very precise. Consider this previous example:

```
if (obj.prop) {
  // obj has property .prop
}
```

The body of the `if` statement is skipped if:

- `obj.prop` is missing (in which case, JavaScript returns `undefined`).

However, it is also skipped if:

- `obj.prop` is `undefined`.
- `obj.prop` is any other falsy value (`null`, `0`, `' '`, etc.).

In practice, this rarely causes problems, but you have to be aware of this pitfall.

16.3.2 Use case: was a parameter provided?

A truthiness check is often used to determine if the caller of a function provided a parameter:

```
function func(x) {
  if (!x) {
    throw new Error('Missing parameter x');
  }
  // ···
}
```

On the plus side, this pattern is established and short. It correctly throws errors for undefined and null.

On the minus side, there is the previously mentioned pitfall: the code also throws errors for all other falsy values.

An alternative is to check for `undefined`:

```
if (x === undefined) {
  throw new Error('Missing parameter x');
}
```

16.3.3 Use case: does a property exist?

Truthiness checks are also often used to determine if a property exists:

```
function readFile(fileDesc) {
  if (!fileDesc.path) {
```

```
    throw new Error('Missing property: .path');
  }
  // ...
}
readFile({ path: 'foo.txt' }); // no error
```

This pattern is also established and has the usual caveat: it not only throws if the property is missing, but also if it exists and has any of the falsy values.

If you truly want to check if the property exists, you have to use the `in` operator (p. 277):

```
if (! ('path' in fileDesc)) {
  throw new Error('Missing property: .path');
}
```

16.4 Conditional operator (? :)

The conditional operator is the expression version of the `if` statement. Its syntax is:

«condition» ? «thenExpression» : «elseExpression»

It is evaluated as follows:

- If condition is truthy, evaluate and return thenExpression.
- Otherwise, evaluate and return elseExpression.

The conditional operator is also called *ternary operator* because it has three operands.

Examples:

```
> true ? 'yes' : 'no'
'yes'
> false ? 'yes' : 'no'
'no'
> '' ? 'yes' : 'no'
'no'
```

The following code demonstrates that whichever of the two branches "then" and "else" is chosen via the condition, only that branch is evaluated. The other branch isn't.

```
const x = (true ? console.log('then') : console.log('else'));

// Output:
// 'then'
```

16.5 Binary logical operators: And (x && y), Or (x || y)

The operators && and || are *value-preserving* and *short-circuiting*. What does that mean?

Value-preservation means that operands are interpreted as booleans but returned unchanged:

```
> 12 || 'hello'
12
> 0 || 'hello'
'hello'
```

Short-circuiting means if the first operand already determines the result, then the second operand is not evaluated. The only other operator that delays evaluating its operands is the conditional operator. Usually, all operands are evaluated before performing an operation.

For example, logical And (&&) does not evaluate its second operand if the first one is falsy:

```
const x = false && console.log('hello');
// No output
```

If the first operand is truthy, `console.log()` is executed:

```
const x = true && console.log('hello');

// Output:
// 'hello'
```

16.5.1 Logical And (x && y)

The expression a && b ("a And b") is evaluated as follows:

1. Evaluate a.
2. Is the result falsy? Return it.
3. Otherwise, evaluate b and return the result.

In other words, the following two expressions are roughly equivalent:

```
a && b
!a ? a : b
```

Examples:

```
> false && true
false
> false && 'abc'
false

> true && false
false
> true && 'abc'
'abc'

> '' && 'abc'
''
```

16.5.2 Logical Or (||)

The expression a || b ("a Or b") is evaluated as follows:

16.6 Logical Not (!)   121

1. Evaluate a.
2. Is the result truthy? Return it.
3. Otherwise, evaluate b and return the result.

In other words, the following two expressions are roughly equivalent:

```
a || b
a ? a : b
```

Examples:

```
> true || false
true
> true || 'abc'
true

> false || true
true
> false || 'abc'
'abc'

> 'abc' || 'def'
'abc'
```

16.5.3   Default values via logical Or (||)

Sometimes you receive a value and only want to use it if it isn't either null or undefined. Otherwise, you'd like to use a default value, as a fallback. You can do that via the || operator:

```
const valueToUse = valueReceived || defaultValue;
```

The following code shows a real-world example:

```
function countMatches(regex, str) {
  const matchResult = str.match(regex); // null or Array
  return (matchResult || []).length;
}
```

If there are one or more matches for regex inside str then .match() returns an Array. If there are no matches, it unfortunately returns null (and not the empty Array). We fix that via the || operator.

Exercise: Default values via the Or operator (||)

exercises/booleans/default_via_or_exrc.mjs

16.6   Logical Not (!)

The expression !x ("Not x") is evaluated as follows:

1. Evaluate x.
2. Is it truthy? Return `false`.
3. Otherwise, return `true`.

Examples:

```
> !false
true
> !true
false

> !0
true
> !123
false

> !''
true
> !'abc'
false
```

Quiz

See quiz app (p. 71).

Chapter 17

Numbers

Contents

17.1 JavaScript only has floating point numbers 124
17.2 Number literals 124
    17.2.1 Integer literals 124
    17.2.2 Floating point literals 125
    17.2.3 Syntactic pitfall: properties of integer literals 125
17.3 Arithmetic operators 125
    17.3.1 Binary arithmetic operators 125
    17.3.2 Unary plus (+) and negation (-) 126
    17.3.3 Incrementing (++) and decrementing (--) 126
17.4 Converting to number 127
17.5 Error values 128
17.6 Error value: `NaN` 128
    17.6.1 Checking for `NaN` 129
    17.6.2 Finding `NaN` in Arrays 129
17.7 Error value: `Infinity` 130
    17.7.1 `Infinity` as a default value 130
    17.7.2 Checking for `Infinity` 130
17.8 The precision of numbers: careful with decimal fractions 131
17.9 (Advanced) 131
17.10 Background: floating point precision 131
    17.10.1 A simplified representation of floating point numbers 132
17.11 Integers in JavaScript 133
    17.11.1 Converting to integer 133
    17.11.2 Ranges of integers in JavaScript 134
    17.11.3 Safe integers 134
17.12 Bitwise operators 136
    17.12.1 Internally, bitwise operators work with 32-bit integers 136
    17.12.2 Binary bitwise operators 136

17.12.3 Bitwise Not 137
17.12.4 Bitwise shift operators 137
17.12.5 b32(): displaying unsigned 32-bit integers in binary notation . 138
17.13 Quick reference: numbers **138**
17.13.1 Global functions for numbers 138
17.13.2 Static properties of Number 138
17.13.3 Static methods of Number 139
17.13.4 Methods of Number.prototype 141
17.13.5 Sources 142

This chapter covers JavaScript's single type for numbers, number.

17.1 JavaScript only has floating point numbers

You can express both integers and floating point numbers in JavaScript:

```
98
123.45
```

However, there is only a single type for all numbers: they are all *doubles*, 64-bit floating point numbers implemented according to the IEEE Standard for Floating-Point Arithmetic (IEEE 754).

Integers are simply floating point numbers without a decimal fraction:

```
> 98 === 98.0
true
```

Note that, under the hood, most JavaScript engines are often able to use real integers, with all associated performance and storage size benefits.

17.2 Number literals

Let's examine literals for numbers.

17.2.1 Integer literals

Several *integer literals* let you express integers with various bases:

```
// Binary (base 2)
assert.equal(0b11, 3);

// Octal (base 8)
assert.equal(0o10, 8);

// Decimal (base 10):
assert.equal(35, 35);

// Hexadecimal (base 16)
assert.equal(0xE7, 231);
```

17.2.2 Floating point literals

Floating point numbers can only be expressed in base 10.

Fractions:

```
> 35.0
35
```

Exponent: eN means $\times 10^N$

```
> 3e2
300
> 3e-2
0.03
> 0.3e2
30
```

17.2.3 Syntactic pitfall: properties of integer literals

Accessing a property of an integer literal entails a pitfall: If the integer literal is immediately followed by a dot, then that dot is interpreted as a decimal dot:

```
7.toString(); // syntax error
```

There are four ways to work around this pitfall:

```
7.0.toString()
(7).toString()
7..toString()
7 .toString()   // space before dot
```

17.3 Arithmetic operators

17.3.1 Binary arithmetic operators

Tbl. 17.1 lists JavaScript's binary arithmetic operators.

Table 17.1: Binary arithmetic operators.

Operator	Name		Example
n + m	Addition	ES1	3 + 4 → 7
n - m	Subtraction	ES1	9 - 1 → 8
n * m	Multiplication	ES1	3 * 2.25 → 6.75
n / m	Division	ES1	5.625 / 5 → 1.125
n % m	Remainder	ES1	8 % 5 → 3
			-8 % 5 → -3
n ** m	Exponentiation	ES2016	4 ** 2 → 16

17.3.1.1 % is a remainder operator

% is a remainder operator, not a modulo operator. Its result has the sign of the first operand:

```
> 5 % 3
2
> -5 % 3
-2
```

For more information on the difference between remainder and modulo, see the blog post "Remainder operator vs. modulo operator (with JavaScript code)"[1] on 2ality.

17.3.2 Unary plus (+) and negation (-)

Tbl. 17.2 summarizes the two operators *unary plus* (+) and *negation* (-).

Table 17.2: The operators unary plus (+) and negation (-).

Operator	Name		Example
+n	Unary plus	ES1	+(-7) → -7
-n	Unary negation	ES1	-(-7) → 7

Both operators coerce their operands to numbers:

```
> +'5'
5
> +'-12'
-12
> -'9'
-9
```

Thus, unary plus lets us convert arbitrary values to numbers.

17.3.3 Incrementing (++) and decrementing (--)

The incrementation operator ++ exists in a prefix version and a suffix version. In both versions, it destructively adds one to its operand. Therefore, its operand must be a storage location that can be changed.

The decrementation operator -- works the same, but subtracts one from its operand. The next two examples explain the difference between the prefix and the suffix version.

Tbl. 17.3 summarizes the incrementation and decrementation operators.

Table 17.3: Incrementation operators and decrementation operators.

Operator	Name		Example
v++	Increment	ES1	let v=0; [v++, v] → [0, 1]

[1] https://2ality.com/2019/08/remainder-vs-modulo.html

17.4 Converting to number

Operator	Name		Example
++v	Increment	ES1	`let v=0; [++v, v] → [1, 1]`
v--	Decrement	ES1	`let v=1; [v--, v] → [1, 0]`
--v	Decrement	ES1	`let v=1; [--v, v] → [0, 0]`

Next, we'll look at examples of these operators in use.

Prefix ++ and prefix -- change their operands and then return them.

```
let foo = 3;
assert.equal(++foo, 4);
assert.equal(foo, 4);

let bar = 3;
assert.equal(--bar, 2);
assert.equal(bar, 2);
```

Suffix ++ and suffix -- return their operands and then change them.

```
let foo = 3;
assert.equal(foo++, 3);
assert.equal(foo, 4);

let bar = 3;
assert.equal(bar--, 3);
assert.equal(bar, 2);
```

17.3.3.1 Operands: not just variables

You can also apply these operators to property values:

```
const obj = { a: 1 };
++obj.a;
assert.equal(obj.a, 2);
```

And to Array elements:

```
const arr = [ 4 ];
arr[0]++;
assert.deepEqual(arr, [5]);
```

Exercise: Number operators

`exercises/numbers-math/is_odd_test.mjs`

17.4 Converting to number

These are three ways of converting values to numbers:

- `Number(value)`

- `+value`
- `parseFloat(value)` (avoid; different than the other two!)

Recommendation: use the descriptive `Number()`. Tbl. 17.4 summarizes how it works.

Table 17.4: Converting values to numbers.

x	Number(x)
undefined	NaN
null	0
boolean	false → 0, true → 1
number	x (no change)
string	'' → 0
	other → parsed number, ignoring leading/trailing whitespace
object	configurable (e.g. via .valueOf())

Examples:

```
assert.equal(Number(123.45), 123.45);

assert.equal(Number(''), 0);
assert.equal(Number('\n 123.45 \t'), 123.45);
assert.equal(Number('xyz'), NaN);
```

How objects are converted to numbers can be configured – for example, by overriding `.valueOf()`:

```
> Number({ valueOf() { return 123 } })
123
```

Exercise: Converting to number

`exercises/numbers-math/parse_number_test.mjs`

17.5 Error values

Two number values are returned when errors happen:

- NaN
- Infinity

17.6 Error value: NaN

NaN is an abbreviation of "not a number". Ironically, JavaScript considers it to be a number:

```
> typeof NaN
'number'
```

17.6 Error value: NaN

When is `NaN` returned?

`NaN` is returned if a number can't be parsed:

```
> Number('$$$')
NaN
> Number(undefined)
NaN
```

`NaN` is returned if an operation can't be performed:

```
> Math.log(-1)
NaN
> Math.sqrt(-1)
NaN
```

`NaN` is returned if an operand or argument is `NaN` (to propagate errors):

```
> NaN - 3
NaN
> 7 ** NaN
NaN
```

17.6.1 Checking for NaN

`NaN` is the only JavaScript value that is not strictly equal to itself:

```
const n = NaN;
assert.equal(n === n, false);
```

These are several ways of checking if a value x is `NaN`:

```
const x = NaN;

assert.equal(Number.isNaN(x), true); // preferred
assert.equal(Object.is(x, NaN), true);
assert.equal(x !== x, true);
```

In the last line, we use the comparison quirk to detect `NaN`.

17.6.2 Finding NaN in Arrays

Some Array methods can't find `NaN`:

```
> [NaN].indexOf(NaN)
-1
```

Others can:

```
> [NaN].includes(NaN)
true
> [NaN].findIndex(x => Number.isNaN(x))
0
> [NaN].find(x => Number.isNaN(x))
NaN
```

Alas, there is no simple rule of thumb. You have to check for each method how it handles NaN.

17.7 Error value: `Infinity`

When is the error value `Infinity` returned?

`Infinity` is returned if a number is too large:

```
> Math.pow(2, 1023)
8.98846567431158e+307
> Math.pow(2, 1024)
Infinity
```

`Infinity` is returned if there is a division by zero:

```
> 5 / 0
Infinity
> -5 / 0
-Infinity
```

17.7.1 `Infinity` as a default value

`Infinity` is larger than all other numbers (except `NaN`), making it a good default value:

```
function findMinimum(numbers) {
  let min = Infinity;
  for (const n of numbers) {
    if (n < min) min = n;
  }
  return min;
}

assert.equal(findMinimum([5, -1, 2]), -1);
assert.equal(findMinimum([]), Infinity);
```

17.7.2 Checking for `Infinity`

These are two common ways of checking if a value x is `Infinity`:

```
const x = Infinity;

assert.equal(x === Infinity, true);
assert.equal(Number.isFinite(x), false);
```

> **Exercise: Comparing numbers**
> `exercises/numbers-math/find_max_test.mjs`

17.8 The precision of numbers: careful with decimal fractions

Internally, JavaScript floating point numbers are represented with base 2 (according to the IEEE 754 standard). That means that decimal fractions (base 10) can't always be represented precisely:

```
> 0.1 + 0.2
0.30000000000000004
> 1.3 * 3
3.9000000000000004
> 1.4 * 100000000000000
139999999999999.98
```

You therefore need to take rounding errors into consideration when performing arithmetic in JavaScript.

Read on for an explanation of this phenomenon.

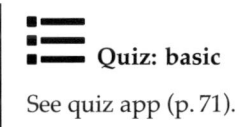

Quiz: basic

See quiz app (p. 71).

17.9 (Advanced)

All remaining sections of this chapter are advanced.

17.10 Background: floating point precision

In JavaScript, computations with numbers don't always produce correct results – for example:

```
> 0.1 + 0.2
0.30000000000000004
```

To understand why, we need to explore how JavaScript represents floating point numbers internally. It uses three integers to do so, which take up a total of 64 bits of storage (double precision):

Component	Size	Integer range
Sign	1 bit	[0, 1]
Fraction	52 bits	[0, $2^{52}-1$]
Exponent	11 bits	[−1023, 1024]

The floating point number represented by these integers is computed as follows:

$$(-1)^{\text{sign}} \times 0b1.\text{fraction} \times 2^{\text{exponent}}$$

This representation can't encode a zero because its second component (involving the fraction) always has a leading 1. Therefore, a zero is encoded via the special exponent −1023 and a fraction 0.

17.10.1 A simplified representation of floating point numbers

To make further discussions easier, we simplify the previous representation:

- Instead of base 2 (binary), we use base 10 (decimal) because that's what most people are more familiar with.
- The *fraction* is a natural number that is interpreted as a fraction (digits after a point). We switch to a *mantissa*, an integer that is interpreted as itself. As a consequence, the exponent is used differently, but its fundamental role doesn't change.
- As the mantissa is an integer (with its own sign), we don't need a separate sign, anymore.

The new representation works like this:

$$\text{mantissa} \times 10^{\text{exponent}}$$

Let's try out this representation for a few floating point numbers.

- For the integer −123, we mainly need the mantissa:

  ```
  > -123 * (10 ** 0)
  -123
  ```

- For the number 1.5, we imagine there being a point after the mantissa. We use a negative exponent to move that point one digit to the left:

  ```
  > 15 * (10 ** -1)
  1.5
  ```

- For the number 0.25, we move the point two digits to the left:

  ```
  > 25 * (10 ** -2)
  0.25
  ```

Representations with negative exponents can also be written as fractions with positive exponents in the denominators:

```
> 15 * (10 ** -1) === 15 / (10 ** 1)
true
> 25 * (10 ** -2) === 25 / (10 ** 2)
true
```

These fractions help with understanding why there are numbers that our encoding cannot represent:

- 1/10 can be represented. It already has the required format: a power of 10 in the denominator.
- 1/2 can be represented as 5/10. We turned the 2 in the denominator into a power of 10 by multiplying the numerator and denominator by 5.

- 1/4 can be represented as 25/100. We turned the 4 in the denominator into a power of 10 by multiplying the numerator and denominator by 25.

- 1/3 cannot be represented. There is no way to turn the denominator into a power of 10. (The prime factors of 10 are 2 and 5. Therefore, any denominator that only has these prime factors can be converted to a power of 10, by multiplying both the numerator and denominator by enough twos and fives. If a denominator has a different prime factor, then there's nothing we can do.)

To conclude our excursion, we switch back to base 2:

- `0.5 = 1/2` can be represented with base 2 because the denominator is already a power of 2.
- `0.25 = 1/4` can be represented with base 2 because the denominator is already a power of 2.
- `0.1 = 1/10` cannot be represented because the denominator cannot be converted to a power of 2.
- `0.2 = 2/10` cannot be represented because the denominator cannot be converted to a power of 2.

Now we can see why `0.1 + 0.2` doesn't produce a correct result: internally, neither of the two operands can be represented precisely.

The only way to compute precisely with decimal fractions is by internally switching to base 10. For many programming languages, base 2 is the default and base 10 an option. For example, Java has the class `BigDecimal`[2] and Python has the module `decimal`[3]. There are tentative plans to add something similar to JavaScript: the ECMAScript proposal "Decimal"[4] is currently at stage 0.

17.11 Integers in JavaScript

JavaScript doesn't have a special type for integers. Instead, they are simply normal (floating point) numbers without a decimal fraction:

```
> 1 === 1.0
true
> Number.isInteger(1.0)
true
```

In this section, we'll look at a few tools for working with these pseudo-integers.

17.11.1 Converting to integer

The recommended way of converting numbers to integers is to use one of the rounding methods of the `Math` object:

- `Math.floor(n)`: returns the largest integer $i \leq n$

---
[2]https://docs.oracle.com/javase/8/docs/api/java/math/BigDecimal.html
[3]https://docs.python.org/3/library/decimal.html
[4]https://github.com/tc39/proposals/blob/master/stage-0-proposals.md

```
> Math.floor(2.1)
2
> Math.floor(2.9)
2
```

- `Math.ceil(n)`: returns the smallest integer $i \geq n$

    ```
    > Math.ceil(2.1)
    3
    > Math.ceil(2.9)
    3
    ```

- `Math.round(n)`: returns the integer that is "closest" to n with __.5 being rounded up – for example:

    ```
    > Math.round(2.4)
    2
    > Math.round(2.5)
    3
    ```

- `Math.trunc(n)`: removes any decimal fraction (after the point) that n has, therefore turning it into an integer.

    ```
    > Math.trunc(2.1)
    2
    > Math.trunc(2.9)
    2
    ```

For more information on rounding, consult §18.3 "Rounding" (p. 147).

17.11.2 Ranges of integers in JavaScript

These are important ranges of integers in JavaScript:

- **Safe integers:** can be represented "safely" by JavaScript (more on what that means in the next subsection)
    - Precision: 53 bits plus sign
    - Range: $(-2^{53}, 2^{53})$
- **Array indices**
    - Precision: 32 bits, unsigned
    - Range: $[0, 2^{32}-1)$ (excluding the maximum length)
    - Typed Arrays have a larger range of 53 bits (safe and unsigned)
- **Bitwise operators** (bitwise Or, etc.)
    - Precision: 32 bits
    - Range of unsigned right shift (>>>): unsigned, $[0, 2^{32})$
    - Range of all other bitwise operators: signed, $[-2^{31}, 2^{31})$

17.11.3 Safe integers

This is the range of integers that are *safe* in JavaScript (53 bits plus a sign):

$$[-2^{53}-1, 2^{53}-1]$$

17.11 Integers in JavaScript

An integer is *safe* if it is represented by exactly one JavaScript number. Given that JavaScript numbers are encoded as a fraction multiplied by 2 to the power of an exponent, higher integers can also be represented, but then there are gaps between them.

For example (18014398509481984 is 2^{54}):

```
> 18014398509481984
18014398509481984
> 18014398509481985
18014398509481984
> 18014398509481986
18014398509481984
> 18014398509481987
18014398509481988
```

The following properties of Number help determine if an integer is safe:

```
assert.equal(Number.MAX_SAFE_INTEGER, (2 ** 53) - 1);
assert.equal(Number.MIN_SAFE_INTEGER, -Number.MAX_SAFE_INTEGER);

assert.equal(Number.isSafeInteger(5), true);
assert.equal(Number.isSafeInteger('5'), false);
assert.equal(Number.isSafeInteger(5.1), false);
assert.equal(Number.isSafeInteger(Number.MAX_SAFE_INTEGER), true);
assert.equal(Number.isSafeInteger(Number.MAX_SAFE_INTEGER+1), false);
```

> **Exercise: Detecting safe integers**
> exercises/numbers-math/is_safe_integer_test.mjs

17.11.3.1 Safe computations

Let's look at computations involving unsafe integers.

The following result is incorrect and unsafe, even though both of its operands are safe:

```
> 9007199254740990 + 3
9007199254740992
```

The following result is safe, but incorrect. The first operand is unsafe; the second operand is safe:

```
> 9007199254740995 - 10
9007199254740986
```

Therefore, the result of an expression a op b is correct if and only if:

```
isSafeInteger(a) && isSafeInteger(b) && isSafeInteger(a op b)
```

That is, both operands and the result must be safe.

17.12 Bitwise operators

17.12.1 Internally, bitwise operators work with 32-bit integers

Internally, JavaScript's bitwise operators work with 32-bit integers. They produce their results in the following steps:

- Input (JavaScript numbers): The 1–2 operands are first converted to JavaScript numbers (64-bit floating point numbers) and then to 32-bit integers.
- Computation (32-bit integers): The actual operation processes 32-bit integers and produces a 32-bit integer.
- Output (JavaScript number): Before returning the result, it is converted back to a JavaScript number.

17.12.1.1 The types of operands and results

For each bitwise operator, this book mentions the types of its operands and its result. Each type is always one of the following two:

Type	Description	Size	Range
Int32	signed 32-bit integer	32 bits incl. sign	$[-2^{31}, 2^{31})$
Uint32	unsigned 32-bit integer	32 bits	$[0, 2^{32})$

Considering the previously mentioned steps, I recommend to pretend that bitwise operators internally work with unsigned 32-bit integers (step "computation") and that Int32 and Uint32 only affect how JavaScript numbers are converted to and from integers (steps "input" and "output").

17.12.1.2 Displaying JavaScript numbers as unsigned 32-bit integers

While exploring the bitwise operators, it occasionally helps to display JavaScript numbers as unsigned 32-bit integers in binary notation. That's what b32() does (whose implementation is shown later):

```
assert.equal(
  b32(-1),
  '11111111111111111111111111111111');
assert.equal(
  b32(1),
  '00000000000000000000000000000001');
assert.equal(
  b32(2 ** 31),
  '10000000000000000000000000000000');
```

17.12.2 Binary bitwise operators

17.12 Bitwise operators

Table 17.7: Binary bitwise operators.

Operation	Name	Type signature	
num1 & num2	Bitwise And	Int32 × Int32 → Int32	ES1
num1 | num2	Bitwise Or	Int32 × Int32 → Int32	ES1
num1 ^ num2	Bitwise Xor	Int32 × Int32 → Int32	ES1

The binary bitwise operators (tbl. 17.7) combine the bits of their operands to produce their results:

```
> (0b1010 & 0b0011).toString(2).padStart(4, '0')
'0010'
> (0b1010 | 0b0011).toString(2).padStart(4, '0')
'1011'
> (0b1010 ^ 0b0011).toString(2).padStart(4, '0')
'1001'
```

17.12.3 Bitwise Not

Table 17.8: The bitwise Not operator.

Operation	Name	Type signature	
~num	Bitwise Not, ones' complement	Int32 → Int32	ES1

The bitwise Not operator (tbl. 17.8) inverts each binary digit of its operand:

```
> b32(~0b100)
'11111111111111111111111111111011'
```

17.12.4 Bitwise shift operators

Table 17.9: Bitwise shift operators.

Operation	Name	Type signature	
num << count	Left shift	Int32 × Uint32 → Int32	ES1
num >> count	Signed right shift	Int32 × Uint32 → Int32	ES1
num >>> count	Unsigned right shift	Uint32 × Uint32 → Uint32	ES1

The shift operators (tbl. 17.9) move binary digits to the left or to the right:

```
> (0b10 << 1).toString(2)
'100'
```

\>> preserves highest bit, >>> doesn't:

```
> b32(0b10000000000000000000000000000010 >> 1)
```

```
'11000000000000000000000000000001'
> b32(0b10000000000000000000000000000010 >>> 1)
'01000000000000000000000000000001'
```

17.12.5 b32(): displaying unsigned 32-bit integers in binary notation

We have now used b32() a few times. The following code is an implementation of it:

```
/**
 * Return a string representing n as a 32-bit unsigned integer,
 * in binary notation.
 */
function b32(n) {
  // >>> ensures highest bit isn't interpreted as a sign
  return (n >>> 0).toString(2).padStart(32, '0');
}
assert.equal(
  b32(6),
  '00000000000000000000000000000110');
```

n >>> 0 means that we are shifting n zero bits to the right. Therefore, in principle, the >>> operator does nothing, but it still coerces n to an unsigned 32-bit integer:

```
> 12 >>> 0
12
> -12 >>> 0
4294967284
> (2**32 + 1) >>> 0
1
```

17.13 Quick reference: numbers

17.13.1 Global functions for numbers

JavaScript has the following four global functions for numbers:

- isFinite()
- isNaN()
- parseFloat()
- parseInt()

However, it is better to use the corresponding methods of Number (Number.isFinite(), etc.), which have fewer pitfalls. They were introduced with ES6 and are discussed below.

17.13.2 Static properties of Number

- .EPSILON: number [ES6]

  The difference between 1 and the next representable floating point number. In general, a machine epsilon[5] provides an upper bound for rounding errors in floating

---
[5]https://en.wikipedia.org/wiki/Machine_epsilon

17.13 Quick reference: numbers

point arithmetic.

- Approximately: $2.2204460492503130808472633361816 \times 10^{-16}$

- `.MAX_SAFE_INTEGER: number` [ES6]

    The largest integer that JavaScript can represent unambiguously ($2^{53}-1$).

- `.MAX_VALUE: number` [ES1]

    The largest positive finite JavaScript number.

    - Approximately: $1.7976931348623157 \times 10^{308}$

- `.MIN_SAFE_INTEGER: number` [ES6]

    The smallest integer that JavaScript can represent unambiguously ($-2^{53}+1$).

- `.MIN_VALUE: number` [ES1]

    The smallest positive JavaScript number. Approximately 5×10^{-324}.

- `.NaN: number` [ES1]

    The same as the global variable `NaN`.

- `.NEGATIVE_INFINITY: number` [ES1]

    The same as `-Number.POSITIVE_INFINITY`.

- `.POSITIVE_INFINITY: number` [ES1]

    The same as the global variable `Infinity`.

17.13.3 Static methods of Number

- `.isFinite(num: number): boolean` [ES6]

    Returns `true` if `num` is an actual number (neither `Infinity` nor `-Infinity` nor `NaN`).

    ```
    > Number.isFinite(Infinity)
    false
    > Number.isFinite(-Infinity)
    false
    > Number.isFinite(NaN)
    false
    > Number.isFinite(123)
    true
    ```

- `.isInteger(num: number): boolean` [ES6]

    Returns `true` if `num` is a number and does not have a decimal fraction.

    ```
    > Number.isInteger(-17)
    true
    > Number.isInteger(33)
    true
    > Number.isInteger(33.1)
    ```

```
false
> Number.isInteger('33')
false
> Number.isInteger(NaN)
false
> Number.isInteger(Infinity)
false
```

- .isNaN(num: number): boolean [ES6]

    Returns true if num is the value NaN:

    ```
    > Number.isNaN(NaN)
    true
    > Number.isNaN(123)
    false
    > Number.isNaN('abc')
    false
    ```

- .isSafeInteger(num: number): boolean [ES6]

    Returns true if num is a number and unambiguously represents an integer.

- .parseFloat(str: string): number [ES6]

    Coerces its parameter to string and parses it as a floating point number. For converting strings to numbers, Number() (which ignores leading and trailing whitespace) is usually a better choice than Number.parseFloat() (which ignores leading whitespace and illegal trailing characters and can hide problems).

    ```
    > Number.parseFloat(' 123.4#')
    123.4
    > Number(' 123.4#')
    NaN
    ```

- .parseInt(str: string, radix=10): number [ES6]

    Coerces its parameter to string and parses it as an integer, ignoring leading whitespace and illegal trailing characters:

    ```
    > Number.parseInt('   123#')
    123
    ```

    The parameter radix specifies the base of the number to be parsed:

    ```
    > Number.parseInt('101', 2)
    5
    > Number.parseInt('FF', 16)
    255
    ```

    Do not use this method to convert numbers to integers: coercing to string is inefficient. And stopping before the first non-digit is not a good algorithm for removing the fraction of a number. Here is an example where it goes wrong:

17.13 Quick reference: numbers

```
> Number.parseInt(1e21, 10) // wrong
1
```

It is better to use one of the rounding functions of Math to convert a number to an integer:

```
> Math.trunc(1e21) // correct
1e+21
```

17.13.4 Methods of `Number.prototype`

(Number.prototype is where the methods of numbers are stored.)

- `.toExponential(fractionDigits?: number): string` [ES3]

    Returns a string that represents the number via exponential notation. With fractionDigits, you can specify, how many digits should be shown of the number that is multiplied with the exponent (the default is to show as many digits as necessary).

    Example: number too small to get a positive exponent via `.toString()`.

    ```
    > 1234..toString()
    '1234'
    
    > 1234..toExponential() // 3 fraction digits
    '1.234e+3'
    > 1234..toExponential(5)
    '1.23400e+3'
    > 1234..toExponential(1)
    '1.2e+3'
    ```

    Example: fraction not small enough to get a negative exponent via `.toString()`.

    ```
    > 0.003.toString()
    '0.003'
    > 0.003.toExponential()
    '3e-3'
    ```

- `.toFixed(fractionDigits=0): string` [ES3]

    Returns an exponent-free representation of the number, rounded to fractionDigits digits.

    ```
    > 0.00000012.toString() // with exponent
    '1.2e-7'
    
    > 0.00000012.toFixed(10) // no exponent
    '0.0000001200'
    > 0.00000012.toFixed()
    '0'
    ```

    If the number is 10^{21} or greater, even `.toFixed()` uses an exponent:

    ```
    > (10 ** 21).toFixed()
    '1e+21'
    ```

- .toPrecision(precision?: number): string [ES3]

    Works like .toString(), but precision specifies how many digits should be shown. If precision is missing, .toString() is used.

    ```
    > 1234..toPrecision(3)  // requires exponential notation
    '1.23e+3'

    > 1234..toPrecision(4)
    '1234'

    > 1234..toPrecision(5)
    '1234.0'

    > 1.234.toPrecision(3)
    '1.23'
    ```

- .toString(radix=10): string [ES1]

    Returns a string representation of the number.

    By default, you get a base 10 numeral as a result:

    ```
    > 123.456.toString()
    '123.456'
    ```

    If you want the numeral to have a different base, you can specify it via radix:

    ```
    > 4..toString(2) // binary (base 2)
    '100'
    > 4.5.toString(2)
    '100.1'

    > 255..toString(16) // hexadecimal (base 16)
    'ff'
    > 255.66796875.toString(16)
    'ff.ab'

    > 1234567890..toString(36)
    'kf12oi'
    ```

    parseInt() provides the inverse operation: it converts a string that contains an integer (no fraction!) numeral with a given base, to a number.

    ```
    > parseInt('kf12oi', 36)
    1234567890
    ```

17.13.5 Sources

- Wikipedia
- TypeScript's built-in typings[6]

---

[6]https://github.com/Microsoft/TypeScript/blob/master/lib/

- MDN web docs for JavaScript[7]
- ECMAScript language specification[8]

☰ Quiz: advanced

See quiz app (p. 71).

---

[7]https://developer.mozilla.org/en-US/docs/Web/JavaScript
[8]https://tc39.github.io/ecma262/

Chapter 18

Math

Contents

18.1 Data properties	145
18.2 Exponents, roots, logarithms	146
18.3 Rounding	147
18.4 Trigonometric Functions	148
18.5 Various other functions	150
18.6 Sources	151

`Math` is an object with data properties and methods for processing numbers. You can see it as a poor man's module: It was created long before JavaScript had modules.

18.1 Data properties

- `Math.E: number` [ES1]

    Euler's number, base of the natural logarithms, approximately 2.7182818284590452354.

- `Math.LN10: number` [ES1]

    The natural logarithm of 10, approximately 2.302585092994046.

- `Math.LN2: number` [ES1]

    The natural logarithm of 2, approximately 0.6931471805599453.

- `Math.LOG10E: number` [ES1]

    The logarithm of e to base 10, approximately 0.4342944819032518.

- `Math.LOG2E: number` [ES1]

    The logarithm of e to base 2, approximately 1.4426950408889634.

- `Math.PI: number` [ES1]

The mathematical constant π, ratio of a circle's circumference to its diameter, approximately 3.1415926535897932.

- `Math.SQRT1_2: number` [ES1]

  The square root of 1/2, approximately 0.7071067811865476.

- `Math.SQRT2: number` [ES1]

  The square root of 2, approximately 1.4142135623730951.

18.2 Exponents, roots, logarithms

- `Math.cbrt(x: number): number` [ES6]

  Returns the cube root of x.

  ```
  > Math.cbrt(8)
  2
  ```

- `Math.exp(x: number): number` [ES1]

  Returns e^x (*e* being Euler's number). The inverse of `Math.log()`.

  ```
  > Math.exp(0)
  1
  > Math.exp(1) === Math.E
  true
  ```

- `Math.expm1(x: number): number` [ES6]

  Returns `Math.exp(x)-1`. The inverse of `Math.log1p()`. Very small numbers (fractions close to 0) are represented with a higher precision. Therefore, this function returns more precise values whenever `.exp()` returns values close to 1.

- `Math.log(x: number): number` [ES1]

  Returns the natural logarithm of x (to base *e*, Euler's number). The inverse of `Math.exp()`.

  ```
  > Math.log(1)
  0
  > Math.log(Math.E)
  1
  > Math.log(Math.E ** 2)
  2
  ```

- `Math.log1p(x: number): number` [ES6]

  Returns `Math.log(1 + x)`. The inverse of `Math.expm1()`. Very small numbers (fractions close to 0) are represented with a higher precision. Therefore, you can provide this function with a more precise argument whenever the argument for `.log()` is close to 1.

- `Math.log10(x: number): number` [ES6]

Returns the logarithm of x to base 10. The inverse of `10 ** x`.

```
> Math.log10(1)
0
> Math.log10(10)
1
> Math.log10(100)
2
```

- `Math.log2(x: number): number` [ES6]

    Returns the logarithm of x to base 2. The inverse of `2 ** x`.

    ```
    > Math.log2(1)
    0
    > Math.log2(2)
    1
    > Math.log2(4)
    2
    ```

- `Math.pow(x: number, y: number): number` [ES1]

    Returns x^y, x to the power of y. The same as `x ** y`.

    ```
    > Math.pow(2, 3)
    8
    > Math.pow(25, 0.5)
    5
    ```

- `Math.sqrt(x: number): number` [ES1]

    Returns the square root of x. The inverse of `x ** 2`.

    ```
    > Math.sqrt(9)
    3
    ```

18.3 Rounding

Rounding means converting an arbitrary number to an integer (a number without a decimal fraction). The following functions implement different approaches to rounding.

- `Math.ceil(x: number): number` [ES1]

    Returns the smallest (closest to $-\infty$) integer i with x ≤ i.

    ```
    > Math.ceil(2.1)
    3
    > Math.ceil(2.9)
    3
    ```

- `Math.floor(x: number): number` [ES1]

    Returns the largest (closest to $+\infty$) integer i with i ≤ x.

```
> Math.floor(2.1)
2
> Math.floor(2.9)
2
```

- Math.round(x: number): number [ES1]

    Returns the integer that is closest to x. If the decimal fraction of x is .5 then .round() rounds up (to the integer closer to positive infinity):

    ```
    > Math.round(2.4)
    2
    > Math.round(2.5)
    3
    ```

- Math.trunc(x: number): number [ES6]

    Removes the decimal fraction of x and returns the resulting integer.

    ```
    > Math.trunc(2.1)
    2
    > Math.trunc(2.9)
    2
    ```

Tbl. 18.1 shows the results of the rounding functions for a few representative inputs.

Table 18.1: Rounding functions of Math. Note how things change with negative numbers because "larger" always means "closer to positive infinity".

	-2.9	-2.5	-2.1	2.1	2.5	2.9
Math.floor	-3	-3	-3	2	2	2
Math.ceil	-2	-2	-2	3	3	3
Math.round	-3	-2	-2	2	3	3
Math.trunc	-2	-2	-2	2	2	2

18.4 Trigonometric Functions

All angles are specified in radians. Use the following two functions to convert between degrees and radians.

```
function degreesToRadians(degrees) {
  return degrees / 180 * Math.PI;
}
assert.equal(degreesToRadians(90), Math.PI/2);

function radiansToDegrees(radians) {
  return radians / Math.PI * 180;
}
assert.equal(radiansToDegrees(Math.PI), 180);
```

18.4 Trigonometric Functions

- `Math.acos(x: number): number` [ES1]

  Returns the arc cosine (inverse cosine) of x.

  ```
  > Math.acos(0)
  1.5707963267948966
  > Math.acos(1)
  0
  ```

- `Math.acosh(x: number): number` [ES6]

  Returns the inverse hyperbolic cosine of x.

- `Math.asin(x: number): number` [ES1]

  Returns the arc sine (inverse sine) of x.

  ```
  > Math.asin(0)
  0
  > Math.asin(1)
  1.5707963267948966
  ```

- `Math.asinh(x: number): number` [ES6]

  Returns the inverse hyperbolic sine of x.

- `Math.atan(x: number): number` [ES1]

  Returns the arc tangent (inverse tangent) of x.

- `Math.atanh(x: number): number` [ES6]

  Returns the inverse hyperbolic tangent of x.

- `Math.atan2(y: number, x: number): number` [ES1]

  Returns the arc tangent of the quotient y/x.

- `Math.cos(x: number): number` [ES1]

  Returns the cosine of x.

  ```
  > Math.cos(0)
  1
  > Math.cos(Math.PI)
  -1
  ```

- `Math.cosh(x: number): number` [ES6]

  Returns the hyperbolic cosine of x.

- `Math.hypot(...values: number[]): number` [ES6]

  Returns the square root of the sum of the squares of `values` (Pythagoras' theorem):

  ```
  > Math.hypot(3, 4)
  5
  ```

- `Math.sin(x: number): number` [ES1]

    Returns the sine of x.

    ```
    > Math.sin(0)
    0
    > Math.sin(Math.PI / 2)
    1
    ```

- `Math.sinh(x: number): number` [ES6]

    Returns the hyperbolic sine of x.

- `Math.tan(x: number): number` [ES1]

    Returns the tangent of x.

    ```
    > Math.tan(0)
    0
    > Math.tan(1)
    1.5574077246549023
    ```

- `Math.tanh(x: number): number;` [ES6]

    Returns the hyperbolic tangent of x.

18.5 Various other functions

- `Math.abs(x: number): number` [ES1]

    Returns the absolute value of x.

    ```
    > Math.abs(3)
    3
    > Math.abs(-3)
    3
    > Math.abs(0)
    0
    ```

- `Math.clz32(x: number): number` [ES6]

    Counts the leading zero bits in the 32-bit integer x. Used in DSP algorithms.

    ```
    > Math.clz32(0b01000000000000000000000000000000)
    1
    > Math.clz32(0b00100000000000000000000000000000)
    2
    > Math.clz32(2)
    30
    > Math.clz32(1)
    31
    ```

- `Math.max(...values: number[]): number` [ES1]

    Converts values to numbers and returns the largest one.

```
> Math.max(3, -5, 24)
24
```

- `Math.min(...values: number[]): number` [ES1]

    Converts values to numbers and returns the smallest one.

    ```
    > Math.min(3, -5, 24)
    -5
    ```

- `Math.random(): number` [ES1]

    Returns a pseudo-random number n where $0 \leq n < 1$.

    Computing a random integer i where $0 \leq i < max$:

    ```
    function getRandomInteger(max) {
      return Math.floor(Math.random() * max);
    }
    ```

- `Math.sign(x: number): number` [ES6]

    Returns the sign of a number:

    ```
    > Math.sign(-8)
    -1
    > Math.sign(0)
    0
    > Math.sign(3)
    1
    ```

18.6 Sources

- Wikipedia
- TypeScript's built-in typings[1]
- MDN web docs for JavaScript[2]
- ECMAScript language specification[3]

---

[1] https://github.com/Microsoft/TypeScript/blob/master/lib/
[2] https://developer.mozilla.org/en-US/docs/Web/JavaScript
[3] https://tc39.github.io/ecma262/

Chapter 19

Unicode – a brief introduction (advanced)

Contents

19.1 Code points vs. code units	**153**
19.1.1 Code points	154
19.1.2 Encoding Unicode code points: UTF-32, UTF-16, UTF-8	154
19.2 Encodings used in web development: UTF-16 and UTF-8	**156**
19.2.1 Source code internally: UTF-16	156
19.2.2 Strings: UTF-16	156
19.2.3 Source code in files: UTF-8	156
19.3 Grapheme clusters – the real characters	**156**

Unicode is a standard for representing and managing text in most of the world's writing systems. Virtually all modern software that works with text, supports Unicode. The standard is maintained by the Unicode Consortium. A new version of the standard is published every year (with new emojis, etc.). Unicode version 1.0.0 was published in October 1991.

19.1 Code points vs. code units

Two concepts are crucial for understanding Unicode:

- *Code points* are numbers that represent Unicode characters.
- *Code units* are numbers that encode code points, to store or transmit Unicode text. One or more code units encode a single code point. Each code unit has the same size, which depends on the *encoding format* that is used. The most popular format, UTF-8, has 8-bit code units.

19.1.1 Code points

The first version of Unicode had 16-bit code points. Since then, the number of characters has grown considerably and the size of code points was extended to 21 bits. These 21 bits are partitioned in 17 planes, with 16 bits each:

- Plane 0: **Basic Multilingual Plane (BMP)**, 0x0000–0xFFFF
  - Contains characters for almost all modern languages (Latin characters, Asian characters, etc.) and many symbols.
- Plane 1: Supplementary Multilingual Plane (SMP), 0x10000–0x1FFFF
  - Supports historic writing systems (e.g., Egyptian hieroglyphs and cuneiform) and additional modern writing systems.
  - Supports emojis and many other symbols.
- Plane 2: Supplementary Ideographic Plane (SIP), 0x20000–0x2FFFF
  - Contains additional CJK (Chinese, Japanese, Korean) ideographs.
- Plane 3–13: Unassigned
- Plane 14: Supplementary Special-Purpose Plane (SSP), 0xE0000–0xEFFFF
  - Contains non-graphical characters such as tag characters and glyph variation selectors.
- Plane 15–16: Supplementary Private Use Area (S PUA A/B), 0x0F0000–0x10FFFF
  - Available for character assignment by parties outside the ISO and the Unicode Consortium. Not standardized.

Planes 1-16 are called supplementary planes or **astral planes**.

Let's check the code points of a few characters:

```
> 'A'.codePointAt(0).toString(16)
'41'
> 'ü'.codePointAt(0).toString(16)
'fc'
> 'π'.codePointAt(0).toString(16)
'3c0'
> '🙂'.codePointAt(0).toString(16)
'1f642'
```

The hexadecimal numbers of the code points tell us that the first three characters reside in plane 0 (within 16 bits), while the emoji resides in plane 1.

19.1.2 Encoding Unicode code points: UTF-32, UTF-16, UTF-8

The main ways of encoding code points are three *Unicode Transformation Formats* (UTFs): UTF-32, UTF-16, UTF-8. The number at the end of each format indicates the size (in bits) of its code units.

19.1.2.1 UTF-32 (Unicode Transformation Format 32)

UTF-32 uses 32 bits to store code units, resulting in one code unit per code point. This format is the only one with *fixed-length encoding*; all others use a varying number of code units to encode a single code point.

19.1 Code points vs. code units

19.1.2.2 UTF-16 (Unicode Transformation Format 16)

UTF-16 uses 16-bit code units. It encodes code points as follows:

- The BMP (first 16 bits of Unicode) is stored in single code units.
- Astral planes: The BMP comprises 0x10_000 code points. Given that Unicode has a total of 0x110_000 code points, we still need to encode the remaining 0x100_000 code points (20 bits). The BMP has two ranges of unassigned code points that provide the necessary storage:
    - Most significant 10 bits (*leading surrogate*): 0xD800-0xDBFF
    - Least significant 10 bits (*trailing surrogate*): 0xDC00-0xDFFF

In other words, the two hexadecimal digits at the end contribute 8 bits. But we can only use those 8 bits if a BMP starts with one of the following 2-digit pairs:

- D8, D9, DA, DB
- DC, DD, DE, DF

Per surrogate, we have a choice between 4 pairs, which is where the remaining 2 bits come from.

As a consequence, each UTF-16 code unit is always either a leading surrogate, a trailing surrogate, or encodes a BMP code point.

These are two examples of UTF-16-encoded code points:

- Code point 0x03C0 (π) is in the BMP and can therefore be represented by a single UTF-16 code unit: 0x03C0.
- Code point 0x1F642 (☺) is in an astral plane and represented by two code units: 0xD83D and 0xDE42.

19.1.2.3 UTF-8 (Unicode Transformation Format 8)

UTF-8 has 8-bit code units. It uses 1–4 code units to encode a code point:

Code points	Code units
0000–007F	0bbbbbbb (7 bits)
0080–07FF	110bbbbb, 10bbbbbb (5+6 bits)
0800–FFFF	1110bbbb, 10bbbbbb, 10bbbbbb (4+6+6 bits)
10000–1FFFFF	11110bbb, 10bbbbbb, 10bbbbbb, 10bbbbbb (3+6+6+6 bits)

Notes:

- The bit prefix of each code unit tells us:
    - Is it first in a series of code units? If yes, how many code units will follow?
    - Is it second or later in a series of code units?
- The character mappings in the 0000–007F range are the same as ASCII, which leads to a degree of backward compatibility with older software.

Three examples:

Character	Code point	Code units
A	0x0041	01000001
π	0x03C0	11001111, 10000000
☺	0x1F642	11110000, 10011111, 10011001, 10000010

19.2 Encodings used in web development: UTF-16 and UTF-8

The Unicode encoding formats that are used in web development are: UTF-16 and UTF-8.

19.2.1 Source code internally: UTF-16

The ECMAScript specification internally represents source code as UTF-16.

19.2.2 Strings: UTF-16

The characters in JavaScript strings are based on UTF-16 code units:

```
> const smiley = '☺';
> smiley.length
2
> smiley === '\uD83D\uDE42' // code units
true
```

For more information on Unicode and strings, consult §20.6 "Atoms of text: Unicode characters, JavaScript characters, grapheme clusters" (p. 164).

19.2.3 Source code in files: UTF-8

HTML and JavaScript are almost always encoded as UTF-8 these days.

For example, this is how HTML files usually start now:

```
<!doctype html>
<html>
<head>
  <meta charset="UTF-8">
...
```

For HTML modules loaded in web browsers, the standard encoding[1] is also UTF-8.

19.3 Grapheme clusters – the real characters

The concept of a character becomes remarkably complex once you consider many of the world's writing systems.

On one hand, there are Unicode characters, as represented by code points.

---

[1] https://html.spec.whatwg.org/multipage/webappapis.html#fetch-a-single-module-script

19.3 Grapheme clusters – the real characters

On the other hand, there are *grapheme clusters*. A grapheme cluster corresponds most closely to a symbol displayed on screen or paper. It is defined as "a horizontally segmentable unit of text". Therefore, official Unicode documents[2] also call it a *user-perceived character*. One or more code point characters are needed to encode a grapheme cluster.

For example, the Devanagari *kshi* is encoded by 4 code points. We use spreading (...) to split a string into an Array with code point characters (for details, consult §20.6.1 "Working with code points" (p. 164)):

```
> [...'क्षि']
[ 'क', 'ो', 'ष', 'fि' ]
```

Flag emojis are also grapheme clusters and composed of two code point characters – for example, the flag of Japan:

```
> [...'🇯🇵']
[ '🇯', '🇵' ]
```

⬈ More information on grapheme clusters

For more information, consult "Let's Stop Ascribing Meaning to Code Points"[a] by Manish Goregaokar.

[a]https://manishearth.github.io/blog/2017/01/14/stop-ascribing-meaning-to-unicode-code-points/

≡ Quiz

See quiz app (p. 71).

---

[2]https://unicode.org/reports/tr29/#Grapheme_Cluster_Boundaries

Chapter 20

Strings

Contents

- 20.1 Plain string literals 160
  - 20.1.1 Escaping 160
- 20.2 Accessing characters and code points 160
  - 20.2.1 Accessing JavaScript characters 160
  - 20.2.2 Accessing Unicode code point characters via `for-of` and spreading 160
- 20.3 String concatenation via + ... 161
- 20.4 Converting to string 161
  - 20.4.1 Stringifying objects 162
  - 20.4.2 Customizing the stringification of objects 163
  - 20.4.3 An alternate way of stringifying values 163
- 20.5 Comparing strings 163
- 20.6 Atoms of text: Unicode characters, JavaScript characters, grapheme clusters 164
  - 20.6.1 Working with code points 164
  - 20.6.2 Working with code units (char codes) 165
  - 20.6.3 Caveat: grapheme clusters 166
- 20.7 Quick reference: Strings 166
  - 20.7.1 Converting to string 166
  - 20.7.2 Numeric values of characters 166
  - 20.7.3 String operators 167
  - 20.7.4 `String.prototype`: finding and matching 167
  - 20.7.5 `String.prototype`: extracting 169
  - 20.7.6 `String.prototype`: combining 170
  - 20.7.7 `String.prototype`: transforming 170
  - 20.7.8 Sources 173

Strings are primitive values in JavaScript and immutable. That is, string-related operations always produce new strings and never change existing strings.

20.1 Plain string literals

Plain string literals are delimited by either single quotes or double quotes:

```
const str1 = 'abc';
const str2 = "abc";
assert.equal(str1, str2);
```

Single quotes are used more often because it makes it easier to mention HTML, where double quotes are preferred.

The next chapter (p. 175) covers *template literals*, which give you:

- String interpolation
- Multiple lines
- Raw string literals (backslash has no special meaning)

20.1.1 Escaping

The backslash lets you create special characters:

- Unix line break: `'\n'`
- Windows line break: `'\r\n'`
- Tab: `'\t'`
- Backslash: `'\\'`

The backslash also lets you use the delimiter of a string literal inside that literal:

```
assert.equal(
  'She said: "Let\'s go!"',
  "She said: \"Let's go!\"");
```

20.2 Accessing characters and code points

20.2.1 Accessing JavaScript characters

JavaScript has no extra data type for characters – characters are always represented as strings.

```
const str = 'abc';

// Reading a character at a given index
assert.equal(str[1], 'b');

// Counting the characters in a string:
assert.equal(str.length, 3);
```

20.2.2 Accessing Unicode code point characters via `for-of` and spreading

Iterating over strings via `for-of` or spreading (...) visits Unicode code point characters. Each code point character is encoded by 1–2 JavaScript characters. For more information,

20.3 String concatenation via +

see §20.6 "Atoms of text: Unicode characters, JavaScript characters, grapheme clusters" (p. 164).

This is how you iterate over the code point characters of a string via `for-of`:

```
for (const ch of 'x☺y') {
  console.log(ch);
}
// Output:
// 'x'
// '☺'
// 'y'
```

And this is how you convert a string into an Array of code point characters via spreading:

```
assert.deepEqual([...'x☺y'], ['x', '☺', 'y']);
```

20.3 String concatenation via +

If at least one operand is a string, the plus operator (+) converts any non-strings to strings and concatenates the result:

```
assert.equal(3 + ' times ' + 4, '3 times 4');
```

The assignment operator += is useful if you want to assemble a string, piece by piece:

```
let str = ''; // must be `let`!
str += 'Say it';
str += ' one more';
str += ' time';

assert.equal(str, 'Say it one more time');
```

> **Concatenating via + is efficient**
>
> Using + to assemble strings is quite efficient because most JavaScript engines internally optimize it.

> **Exercise: Concatenating strings**
>
> `exercises/strings/concat_string_array_test.mjs`

20.4 Converting to string

These are three ways of converting a value x to a string:

- `String(x)`
- `''+x`

- `x.toString()` (does not work for `undefined` and `null`)

Recommendation: use the descriptive and safe `String()`.

Examples:

```
assert.equal(String(undefined), 'undefined');
assert.equal(String(null), 'null');

assert.equal(String(false), 'false');
assert.equal(String(true), 'true');

assert.equal(String(123.45), '123.45');
```

Pitfall for booleans: If you convert a boolean to a string via `String()`, you generally can't convert it back via `Boolean()`:

```
> String(false)
'false'
> Boolean('false')
true
```

The only string for which `Boolean()` returns `false`, is the empty string.

20.4.1 Stringifying objects

Plain objects have a default string representation that is not very useful:

```
> String({a: 1})
'[object Object]'
```

Arrays have a better string representation, but it still hides much information:

```
> String(['a', 'b'])
'a,b'
> String(['a', ['b']])
'a,b'

> String([1, 2])
'1,2'
> String(['1', '2'])
'1,2'

> String([true])
'true'
> String(['true'])
'true'
> String(true)
'true'
```

Stringifying functions, returns their source code:

```
> String(function f() {return 4})
'function f() {return 4}'
```

20.4.2 Customizing the stringification of objects

You can override the built-in way of stringifying objects by implementing the method toString():

```
const obj = {
  toString() {
    return 'hello';
  }
};

assert.equal(String(obj), 'hello');
```

20.4.3 An alternate way of stringifying values

The JSON data format is a text representation of JavaScript values. Therefore, JSON.stringify() (p. 499) can also be used to convert values to strings:

```
> JSON.stringify({a: 1})
'{"a":1}'
> JSON.stringify(['a', ['b']])
'["a",["b"]]'
```

The caveat is that JSON only supports null, booleans, numbers, strings, Arrays, and objects (which it always treats as if they were created by object literals).

Tip: The third parameter lets you switch on multiline output and specify how much to indent – for example:

```
console.log(JSON.stringify({first: 'Jane', last: 'Doe'}, null, 2));
```

This statement produces the following output:

```
{
  "first": "Jane",
  "last": "Doe"
}
```

20.5 Comparing strings

Strings can be compared via the following operators:

```
< <= > >=
```

There is one important caveat to consider: These operators compare based on the numeric values of JavaScript characters. That means that the order that JavaScript uses for strings is different from the one used in dictionaries and phone books:

```
> 'A' < 'B' // ok
true
> 'a' < 'B' // not ok
false
```

```
> 'ä' < 'b' // not ok
false
```

Properly comparing text is beyond the scope of this book. It is supported via the ECMAScript Internationalization API (Intl)[1].

20.6 Atoms of text: Unicode characters, JavaScript characters, grapheme clusters

Quick recap of §19 "Unicode – a brief introduction" (p. 153):

- Unicode characters are represented by *code points* – numbers which have a range of 21 bits.
- In JavaScript strings, Unicode is implemented via *code units* based on the encoding format UTF-16. Each code unit is a 16-bit number. One to two of code units are needed to encode a single code point.
    - Therefore, each JavaScript character is represented by a code unit. In the JavaScript standard library, code units are also called *char codes*. Which is what they are: numbers for JavaScript characters.
- *Grapheme clusters* (*user-perceived characters*) are written symbols, as displayed on screen or paper. One or more Unicode characters are needed to encode a single grapheme cluster.

The following code demonstrates that a single Unicode character comprises one or two JavaScript characters. We count the latter via .length:

```
// 3 Unicode characters, 3 JavaScript characters:
assert.equal('abc'.length, 3);

// 1 Unicode character, 2 JavaScript characters:
assert.equal('☺'.length, 2);
```

The following table summarizes the concepts we have just explored:

Entity	Numeric representation	Size	Encoded via
Grapheme cluster			1+ code points
Unicode character	Code point	21 bits	1–2 code units
JavaScript character	UTF-16 code unit	16 bits	–

20.6.1 Working with code points

Let's explore JavaScript's tools for working with code points.

A *code point escape* lets you specify a code point hexadecimally. It produces one or two JavaScript characters.

---

[1]https://developer.mozilla.org/en/docs/Web/JavaScript/Reference/Global_Objects/Intl

20.6 Atoms of text: Unicode characters, JavaScript characters, grapheme clusters

```
> '\u{1F642}'
'🙂'
```

`String.fromCodePoint()` converts a single code point to 1–2 JavaScript characters:

```
> String.fromCodePoint(0x1F642)
'🙂'
```

`.codePointAt()` converts 1–2 JavaScript characters to a single code point:

```
> '🙂'.codePointAt(0).toString(16)
'1f642'
```

You can *iterate* over a string, which visits Unicode characters (not JavaScript characters). Iteration is described later in this book (p. 311). One way of iterating is via a `for-of` loop:

```
const str = '🙂a';
assert.equal(str.length, 3);

for (const codePointChar of str) {
  console.log(codePointChar);
}

// Output:
// '🙂'
// 'a'
```

Spreading (...) into Array literals (p. 320) is also based on iteration and visits Unicode characters:

```
> [...'🙂a']
[ '🙂', 'a' ]
```

That makes it a good tool for counting Unicode characters:

```
> [...'🙂a'].length
2
> '🙂a'.length
3
```

20.6.2 Working with code units (char codes)

Indices and lengths of strings are based on JavaScript characters (as represented by UTF-16 code units).

To specify a code unit hexadecimally, you can use a *code unit escape*:

```
> '\uD83D\uDE42'
'🙂'
```

And you can use `String.fromCharCode()`. *Char code* is the standard library's name for *code unit*:

```
> String.fromCharCode(0xD83D) + String.fromCharCode(0xDE42)
'🙂'
```

To get the char code of a character, use `.charCodeAt()`:

```
> '☺'.charCodeAt(0).toString(16)
'd83d'
```

20.6.3 Caveat: grapheme clusters

When working with text that may be written in any human language, it's best to split at the boundaries of grapheme clusters, not at the boundaries of Unicode characters.

TC39 is working on `Intl.Segmenter`[2], a proposal for the ECMAScript Internationalization API to support Unicode segmentation (along grapheme cluster boundaries, word boundaries, sentence boundaries, etc.).

Until that proposal becomes a standard, you can use one of several libraries that are available (do a web search for "JavaScript grapheme").

20.7 Quick reference: Strings

Strings are immutable; none of the string methods ever modify their strings.

20.7.1 Converting to string

Tbl. 20.2 describes how various values are converted to strings.

Table 20.2: Converting values to strings.

x	String(x)
undefined	'undefined'
null	'null'
Boolean value	false → 'false', true → 'true'
Number value	Example: 123 → '123'
String value	x (input, unchanged)
An object	Configurable via, e.g., `toString()`

20.7.2 Numeric values of characters

- **Char code:** represents a JavaScript character numerically. JavaScript's name for *Unicode code unit*.
    - Size: 16 bits, unsigned
    - Convert number to character: `String.fromCharCode()` [ES1]
    - Convert character to number: string method `.charCodeAt()` [ES1]
- **Code point:** represents a Unicode character numerically.
    - Size: 21 bits, unsigned (17 planes, 16 bits each)
    - Convert number to character: `String.fromCodePoint()` [ES6]
    - Convert character to number: string method `.codePointAt()` [ES6]

---

[2]https://github.com/tc39/proposal-intl-segmenter

20.7.3 String operators

```
// Access characters via []
const str = 'abc';
assert.equal(str[1], 'b');

// Concatenate strings via +
assert.equal('a' + 'b' + 'c', 'abc');
assert.equal('take ' + 3 + ' oranges', 'take 3 oranges');
```

20.7.4 String.prototype: finding and matching

(String.prototype is where the methods of strings are stored.)

- .endsWith(searchString: string, endPos=this.length): boolean [ES6]

    Returns true if the string would end with searchString if its length were endPos. Returns false otherwise.

    ```
    > 'foo.txt'.endsWith('.txt')
    true
    > 'abcde'.endsWith('cd', 4)
    true
    ```

- .includes(searchString: string, startPos=0): boolean [ES6]

    Returns true if the string contains the searchString and false otherwise. The search starts at startPos.

    ```
    > 'abc'.includes('b')
    true
    > 'abc'.includes('b', 2)
    false
    ```

- .indexOf(searchString: string, minIndex=0): number [ES1]

    Returns the lowest index at which searchString appears within the string or -1, otherwise. Any returned index will be minIndex' or higher.

    ```
    > 'abab'.indexOf('a')
    0
    > 'abab'.indexOf('a', 1)
    2
    > 'abab'.indexOf('c')
    -1
    ```

- .lastIndexOf(searchString: string, maxIndex=Infinity): number [ES1]

    Returns the highest index at which searchString appears within the string or -1, otherwise. Any returned index will be maxIndex' or lower.

    ```
    > 'abab'.lastIndexOf('ab', 2)
    2
    > 'abab'.lastIndexOf('ab', 1)
    ```

```
0
> 'abab'.lastIndexOf('ab')
2
```

- [1 of 2] `.match(regExp: string | RegExp): RegExpMatchArray | null` [ES3]

  If `regExp` is a regular expression with flag `/g` not set, then `.match()` returns the first match for `regExp` within the string. Or `null` if there is no match. If `regExp` is a string, it is used to create a regular expression (think parameter of `new RegExp()`) before performing the previously mentioned steps.

  The result has the following type:

  ```
  interface RegExpMatchArray extends Array<string> {
    index: number;
    input: string;
    groups: undefined | {
      [key: string]: string
    };
  }
  ```

  Numbered capture groups become Array indices (which is why this type extends `Array`). Named capture groups (p. 481) (ES2018) become properties of `.groups`. In this mode, `.match()` works like `RegExp.prototype.exec()`.

  Examples:

  ```
  > 'ababb'.match(/a(b+)/)
  { 0: 'ab', 1: 'b', index: 0, input: 'ababb', groups: undefined }
  > 'ababb'.match(/a(?<foo>b+)/)
  { 0: 'ab', 1: 'b', index: 0, input: 'ababb', groups: { foo: 'b' } }
  > 'abab'.match(/x/)
  null
  ```

- [2 of 2] `.match(regExp: RegExp): string[] | null` [ES3]

  If flag `/g` of `regExp` is set, `.match()` returns either an Array with all matches or `null` if there was no match.

  ```
  > 'ababb'.match(/a(b+)/g)
  [ 'ab', 'abb' ]
  > 'ababb'.match(/a(?<foo>b+)/g)
  [ 'ab', 'abb' ]
  > 'abab'.match(/x/g)
  null
  ```

- `.search(regExp: string | RegExp): number` [ES3]

  Returns the index at which `regExp` occurs within the string. If `regExp` is a string, it is used to create a regular expression (think parameter of `new RegExp()`).

  ```
  > 'a2b'.search(/[0-9]/)
  1
  ```

20.7 Quick reference: Strings

```
> 'a2b'.search('[0-9]')
1
```

- `.startsWith(searchString: string, startPos=0): boolean` [ES6]

    Returns `true` if `searchString` occurs in the string at index `startPos`. Returns `false` otherwise.

    ```
    > '.gitignore'.startsWith('.')
    true
    > 'abcde'.startsWith('bc', 1)
    true
    ```

20.7.5 String.prototype: extracting

- `.slice(start=0, end=this.length): string` [ES3]

    Returns the substring of the string that starts at (including) index `start` and ends at (excluding) index end. If an index is negative, it is added to `.length` before it is used (-1 becomes `this.length-1`, etc.).

    ```
    > 'abc'.slice(1, 3)
    'bc'
    > 'abc'.slice(1)
    'bc'
    > 'abc'.slice(-2)
    'bc'
    ```

- `.split(separator: string | RegExp, limit?: number): string[]` [ES3]

    Splits the string into an Array of substrings – the strings that occur between the separators. The separator can be a string:

    ```
    > 'a | b | c'.split('|')
    [ 'a ', ' b ', ' c' ]
    ```

    It can also be a regular expression:

    ```
    > 'a : b : c'.split(/ *: */)
    [ 'a', 'b', 'c' ]
    > 'a : b : c'.split(/( *):( *)/)
    [ 'a', ' ', ' ', 'b', ' ', ' ', 'c' ]
    ```

    The last invocation demonstrates that captures made by groups in the regular expression become elements of the returned Array.

    Warning: `.split('')` splits a string into JavaScript characters. That doesn't work well when dealing with astral Unicode characters (which are encoded as two JavaScript characters). For example, emojis are astral:

    ```
    > '😂X😂'.split('')
    [ '\uD83D', '\uDE42', 'X', '\uD83D', '\uDE42' ]
    ```

    Instead, it is better to use spreading:

```
> [...'☺X☺']
[ '☺', 'X', '☺' ]
```

- `.substring(start: number, end=this.length): string` [ES1]

    Use `.slice()` instead of this method. `.substring()` wasn't implemented consistently in older engines and doesn't support negative indices.

20.7.6 `String.prototype`: combining

- `.concat(...strings: string[]): string` [ES3]

    Returns the concatenation of the string and `strings`. `'a'.concat('b')` is equivalent to `'a'+'b'`. The latter is much more popular.

    ```
    > 'ab'.concat('cd', 'ef', 'gh')
    'abcdefgh'
    ```

- `.padEnd(len: number, fillString=' '): string` [ES2017]

    Appends (fragments of) `fillString` to the string until it has the desired length `len`. If it already has or exceeds `len`, then it is returned without any changes.

    ```
    > '#'.padEnd(2)
    '# '
    > 'abc'.padEnd(2)
    'abc'
    > '#'.padEnd(5, 'abc')
    '#abca'
    ```

- `.padStart(len: number, fillString=' '): string` [ES2017]

    Prepends (fragments of) `fillString` to the string until it has the desired length `len`. If it already has or exceeds `len`, then it is returned without any changes.

    ```
    > '#'.padStart(2)
    ' #'
    > 'abc'.padStart(2)
    'abc'
    > '#'.padStart(5, 'abc')
    'abca#'
    ```

- `.repeat(count=0): string` [ES6]

    Returns the string, concatenated `count` times.

    ```
    > '*'.repeat()
    ''
    > '*'.repeat(3)
    '***'
    ```

20.7.7 `String.prototype`: transforming

- `.normalize(form: 'NFC'|'NFD'|'NFKC'|'NFKD' = 'NFC'): string` [ES6]

20.7 Quick reference: Strings

Normalizes the string according to the Unicode Normalization Forms[3].

- [1 of 2] `.replace(searchValue: string | RegExp, replaceValue: string): string` [ES3]

  Replace matches of `searchValue` with `replaceValue`. If `searchValue` is a string, only the first verbatim occurrence is replaced. If `searchValue` is a regular expression without flag `/g`, only the first match is replaced. If `searchValue` is a regular expression with `/g` then all matches are replaced.

  ```
  > 'x.x.'.replace('.', '#')
  'x#x.'
  > 'x.x.'.replace(/./, '#')
  '#.x.'
  > 'x.x.'.replace(/./g, '#')
  '####'
  ```

  Special characters in `replaceValue` are:

  - `$$`: becomes `$`
  - `$n`: becomes the capture of numbered group n (alas, `$0` stands for the string `'$0'`, it does not refer to the complete match)
  - `$&`: becomes the complete match
  - `` $` ``: becomes everything before the match
  - `$'`: becomes everything after the match

  Examples:

  ```
  > 'a 2020-04 b'.replace(/([0-9]{4})-([0-9]{2})/, '|$2|')
  'a |04| b'
  > 'a 2020-04 b'.replace(/([0-9]{4})-([0-9]{2})/, '|$&|')
  'a |2020-04| b'
  > 'a 2020-04 b'.replace(/([0-9]{4})-([0-9]{2})/, '|$`|')
  'a |a | b'
  ```

  Named capture groups (p. 481) (ES2018) are supported, too:

  - `$<name>` becomes the capture of named group name

  Example:

  ```
  assert.equal(
    'a 2020-04 b'.replace(
      /(?<year>[0-9]{4})-(?<month>[0-9]{2})/, '|$<month>|'),
    'a |04| b');
  ```

- [2 of 2] `.replace(searchValue: string | RegExp, replacer: (...args: any[]) => string): string` [ES3]

  If the second parameter is a function, occurrences are replaced with the strings it returns. Its parameters `args` are:

  - `matched: string`. The complete match

---
[3] https://unicode.org/reports/tr15/

- g1: string|undefined. The capture of numbered group 1
- g2: string|undefined. The capture of numbered group 2
- (Etc.)
- offset: number. Where was the match found in the input string?
- input: string. The whole input string

```
const regexp = /([0-9]{4})-([0-9]{2})/;
const replacer = (all, year, month) => '|' + all + '|';
assert.equal(
  'a 2020-04 b'.replace(regexp, replacer),
  'a |2020-04| b');
```

Named capture groups (p. 481) (ES2018) are supported, too. If there are any, an argument is added at the end with an object whose properties contain the captures:

```
const regexp = /(?<year>[0-9]{4})-(?<month>[0-9]{2})/;
const replacer = (...args) => {
  const groups=args.pop();
  return '|' + groups.month + '|';
};
assert.equal(
  'a 2020-04 b'.replace(regexp, replacer),
  'a |04| b');
```

- .toUpperCase(): string [ES1]

    Returns a copy of the string in which all lowercase alphabetic characters are converted to uppercase. How well that works for various alphabets, depends on the JavaScript engine.

    ```
    > '-a2b-'.toUpperCase()
    '-A2B-'
    > 'αβγ'.toUpperCase()
    'ΑΒΓ'
    ```

- .toLowerCase(): string [ES1]

    Returns a copy of the string in which all uppercase alphabetic characters are converted to lowercase. How well that works for various alphabets, depends on the JavaScript engine.

    ```
    > '-A2B-'.toLowerCase()
    '-a2b-'
    > 'ΑΒΓ'.toLowerCase()
    'αβγ'
    ```

- .trim(): string [ES5]

    Returns a copy of the string in which all leading and trailing whitespace (spaces, tabs, line terminators, etc.) is gone.

    ```
    > '\r\n#\t  '.trim()
    '#'
    ```

```
>   '  abc  '.trim()
'abc'
```

- `.trimEnd(): string` [ES2019]

    Similar to `.trim()` but only the end of the string is trimmed:

    ```
    >   '  abc  '.trimEnd()
    '  abc'
    ```

- `.trimStart(): string` [ES2019]

    Similar to `.trim()` but only the beginning of the string is trimmed:

    ```
    >   '  abc  '.trimStart()
    'abc  '
    ```

20.7.8 Sources

- TypeScript's built-in typings[4]
- MDN web docs for JavaScript[5]
- ECMAScript language specification[6]

Exercise: Using string methods

`exercises/strings/remove_extension_test.mjs`

Quiz

See quiz app (p. 71).

---

[4]https://github.com/Microsoft/TypeScript/blob/master/lib/
[5]https://developer.mozilla.org/en-US/docs/Web/JavaScript
[6]https://tc39.github.io/ecma262/

Chapter 21

Using template literals and tagged templates

Contents

21.1 Disambiguation: "template"	175
21.2 Template literals	176
21.3 Tagged templates	177
21.3.1 Cooked vs. raw template strings (advanced)	177
21.3.2 Tag function library: lit-html	178
21.3.3 Tag function library: re-template-tag	179
21.3.4 Tag function library: graphql-tag	179
21.4 Raw string literals	179
21.5 (Advanced)	180
21.6 Multiline template literals and indentation	180
21.6.1 Fix: template tag for dedenting	180
21.6.2 Fix: `.trim()`	181
21.7 Simple templating via template literals	182
21.7.1 A more complex example	182
21.7.2 Simple HTML-escaping	183

Before we dig into the two features *template literal* and *tagged template*, let's first examine the multiple meanings of the term *template*.

21.1 Disambiguation: "template"

The following three things are significantly different despite all having *template* in their names and despite all of them looking similar:

- A *text template* is a function from data to text. It is frequently used in web development and often defined via text files. For example, the following text defines a template for the library Handlebars[1]:

  ```
  <div class="entry">
    <h1>{{title}}</h1>
    <div class="body">
      {{body}}
    </div>
  </div>
  ```

  This template has two blanks to be filled in: `title` and `body`. It is used like this:

  ```
  // First step: retrieve the template text, e.g. from a text file.
  const tmplFunc = Handlebars.compile(TMPL_TEXT); // compile string
  const data = {title: 'My page', body: 'Welcome to my page!'};
  const html = tmplFunc(data);
  ```

- A *template literal* is similar to a string literal, but has additional features – for example, interpolation. It is delimited by backticks:

  ```
  const num = 5;
  assert.equal(`Count: ${num}!`, 'Count: 5!');
  ```

- Syntactically, a *tagged template* is a template literal that follows a function (or rather, an expression that evaluates to a function). That leads to the function being called. Its arguments are derived from the contents of the template literal.

  ```
  const getArgs = (...args) => args;
  assert.deepEqual(
    getArgs`Count: ${5}!`,
    [['Count: ', '!'], 5] );
  ```

  Note that `getArgs()` receives both the text of the literal and the data interpolated via `${}`.

21.2 Template literals

A template literal has two new features compared to a normal string literal.

First, it supports *string interpolation*: if you put a dynamically computed value inside a `${}`, it is converted to a string and inserted into the string returned by the literal.

```
const MAX = 100;
function doSomeWork(x) {
  if (x > MAX) {
    throw new Error(`At most ${MAX} allowed: ${x}!`);
  }
  // ···
}
assert.throws(
```

---
[1] https://handlebarsjs.com

21.3 Tagged templates

```
      () => doSomeWork(101),
      {message: 'At most 100 allowed: 101!'});
```

Second, template literals can span multiple lines:

```
const str = `this is
a text with
multiple lines`;
```

Template literals always produce strings.

21.3 Tagged templates

The expression in line A is a *tagged template*. It is equivalent to invoking `tagFunc()` with the arguments listed in the Array in line B.

```
function tagFunc(...args) {
  return args;
}

const setting = 'dark mode';
const value = true;

assert.deepEqual(
  tagFunc`Setting ${setting} is ${value}!`, // (A)
  [['Setting ', ' is ', '!'], 'dark mode', true] // (B)
);
```

The function `tagFunc` before the first backtick is called a *tag function*. Its arguments are:

- *Template strings* (first argument): an Array with the text fragments surrounding the interpolations ${}.
    - In the example: `['Setting ', ' is ', '!']`
- *Substitutions* (remaining arguments): the interpolated values.
    - In the example: `'dark mode'` and `true`

The static (fixed) parts of the literal (the template strings) are kept separate from the dynamic parts (the substitutions).

A tag function can return arbitrary values.

21.3.1 Cooked vs. raw template strings (advanced)

So far, we have only seen the *cooked interpretation* of template strings. But tag functions actually get two interpretations:

- A *cooked interpretation* where backslashes have special meaning. For example, \t produces a tab character. This interpretation of the template strings is stored as an Array in the first argument.

- A *raw interpretation* where backslashes do not have special meaning. For example, \t produces two characters – a backslash and a t. This interpretation of the template strings is stored in property .raw of the first argument (an Array).

The following tag function cookedRaw uses both interpretations:

```
function cookedRaw(templateStrings, ...substitutions) {
  return {
    cooked: [...templateStrings], // copy just the Array elements
    raw: templateStrings.raw,
    substitutions,
  };
}
assert.deepEqual(
  cookedRaw`\tab${'subst'}\newline\\`,
  {
    cooked: ['\tab', '\newline\\'],
    raw:    ['\\tab', '\\newline\\\\'],
    substitutions: ['subst'],
  });
```

The raw interpretation enables raw string literals via String.raw (described later, p. 179) and similar applications.

Tagged templates are great for supporting small embedded languages (so-called *domain-specific languages*). We'll continue with a few examples.

21.3.2   Tag function library: lit-html

lit-html[2] is a templating library that is based on tagged templates and used by the front-end framework Polymer[3]:

```
import {html, render} from 'lit-html';

const template = (items) => html`
  <ul>
    ${
      repeat(items,
        (item) => item.id,
        (item, index) => html`<li>${index}. ${item.name}</li>`
      )
    }
  </ul>
`;
```

repeat() is a custom function for looping. Its 2nd parameter produces unique keys for the values returned by the 3rd parameter. Note the nested tagged template used by that parameter.

---

[2]https://github.com/Polymer/lit-html
[3]https://www.polymer-project.org/

21.3.3 Tag function library: re-template-tag

re-template-tag[4] is a simple library for composing regular expressions. Templates tagged with re produce regular expressions. The main benefit is that you can interpolate regular expressions and plain text via ${} (line A):

```
const RE_YEAR = re`(?<year>[0-9]{4})`;
const RE_MONTH = re`(?<month>[0-9]{2})`;
const RE_DAY = re`(?<day>[0-9]{2})`;
const RE_DATE = re`/${RE_YEAR}-${RE_MONTH}-${RE_DAY}/u`; // (A)

const match = RE_DATE.exec('2017-01-27');
assert.equal(match.groups.year, '2017');
```

21.3.4 Tag function library: graphql-tag

The library graphql-tag[5] lets you create GraphQL queries via tagged templates:

```
import gql from 'graphql-tag';

const query = gql`
  {
    user(id: 5) {
      firstName
      lastName
    }
  }
`;
```

Additionally, there are plugins for pre-compiling such queries in Babel, TypeScript, etc.

21.4 Raw string literals

Raw string literals are implemented via the tag function String.raw. They are string literals where backslashes don't do anything special (such as escaping characters, etc.):

```
assert.equal(String.raw`\back`, '\\back');
```

This helps whenever data contains backslashes – for example, strings with regular expressions:

```
const regex1 = /^\./;
const regex2 = new RegExp('^\\.');
const regex3 = new RegExp(String.raw`^\.`);
```

All three regular expressions are equivalent. With a normal string literal, you have to write the backslash twice, to escape it for that literal. With a raw string literal, you don't have to do that.

Raw string literals are also useful for specifying Windows filename paths:

---
[4]https://github.com/rauschma/re-template-tag
[5]https://github.com/apollographql/graphql-tag

```
const WIN_PATH = String.raw`C:\foo\bar`;
assert.equal(WIN_PATH, 'C:\\foo\\bar');
```

21.5 (Advanced)

All remaining sections are advanced

21.6 Multiline template literals and indentation

If you put multiline text in template literals, two goals are in conflict: On one hand, the template literal should be indented to fit inside the source code. On the other hand, the lines of its content should start in the leftmost column.

For example:

```
function div(text) {
  return `
    <div>
      ${text}
    </div>
  `;
}
console.log('Output:');
console.log(
  div('Hello!')
  // Replace spaces with mid-dots:
  .replace(/ /g, '·')
  // Replace \n with #\n:
  .replace(/\n/g, '#\n')
);
```

Due to the indentation, the template literal fits well into the source code. Alas, the output is also indented. And we don't want the return at the beginning and the return plus two spaces at the end.

```
Output:
#
····<div>#
······Hello!#
····</div>#
··
```

There are two ways to fix this: via a tagged template or by trimming the result of the template literal.

21.6.1 Fix: template tag for dedenting

The first fix is to use a custom template tag that removes the unwanted whitespace. It uses the first line after the initial line break to determine in which column the text starts

21.6 Multiline template literals and indentation 181

and shortens the indentation everywhere. It also removes the line break at the very beginning and the indentation at the very end. One such template tag is dedent by Desmond Brand[6]:

```
import dedent from 'dedent';
function divDedented(text) {
  return dedent`
    <div>
      ${text}
    </div>
  `.replace(/\n/g, '#\n');
}
console.log('Output:');
console.log(divDedented('Hello!'));
```

This time, the output is not indented:

```
Output:
<div>#
  Hello!#
</div>
```

21.6.2 Fix: .trim()

The second fix is quicker, but also dirtier:

```
function divDedented(text) {
  return `
<div>
  ${text}
</div>
  `.trim().replace(/\n/g, '#\n');
}
console.log('Output:');
console.log(divDedented('Hello!'));
```

The string method .trim() removes the superfluous whitespace at the beginning and at the end, but the content itself must start in the leftmost column. The advantage of this solution is that you don't need a custom tag function. The downside is that it looks ugly.

The output is the same as with dedent:

```
Output:
<div>#
  Hello!#
</div>
```

---
[6]https://github.com/dmnd/dedent

21.7 Simple templating via template literals

While template literals look like text templates, it is not immediately obvious how to use them for (text) templating: A text template gets its data from an object, while a template literal gets its data from variables. The solution is to use a template literal in the body of a function whose parameter receives the templating data – for example:

```
const tmpl = (data) => `Hello ${data.name}!`;
assert.equal(tmpl({name: 'Jane'}), 'Hello Jane!');
```

21.7.1 A more complex example

As a more complex example, we'd like to take an Array of addresses and produce an HTML table. This is the Array:

```
const addresses = [
  { first: '<Jane>', last: 'Bond' },
  { first: 'Lars', last: '<Croft>' },
];
```

The function `tmpl()` that produces the HTML table looks as follows:

```
1  const tmpl = (addrs) => `
2  <table>
3    ${addrs.map(
4      (addr) => `
5        <tr>
6          <td>${escapeHtml(addr.first)}</td>
7          <td>${escapeHtml(addr.last)}</td>
8        </tr>
9      `.trim()
10     ).join('')}
11 </table>
12 `.trim();
```

This code contains two templating functions:

- The first one (line 1) takes `addrs`, an Array with addresses, and returns a string with a table.
- The second one (line 4) takes `addr`, an object containing an address, and returns a string with a table row. Note the `.trim()` at the end, which removes unnecessary whitespace.

The first templating function produces its result by wrapping a table element around an Array that it joins into a string (line 10). That Array is produced by mapping the second templating function to each element of `addrs` (line 3). It therefore contains strings with table rows.

The helper function `escapeHtml()` is used to escape special HTML characters (line 6 and line 7). Its implementation is shown in the next subsection.

Let us call `tmpl()` with the addresses and log the result:

21.7 Simple templating via template literals

```
console.log(tmpl(addresses));
```

The output is:

```
<table>
  <tr>
        <td>&lt;Jane&gt;</td>
        <td>Bond</td>
      </tr><tr>
        <td>Lars</td>
        <td>&lt;Croft&gt;</td>
      </tr>
</table>
```

21.7.2 Simple HTML-escaping

The following function escapes plain text so that it is displayed verbatim in HTML:

```
function escapeHtml(str) {
  return str
    .replace(/&/g, '&amp;') // first!
    .replace(/>/g, '&gt;')
    .replace(/</g, '&lt;')
    .replace(/"/g, '&quot;')
    .replace(/'/g, '&#39;')
    .replace(/`/g, '&#96;')
    ;
}
assert.equal(
  escapeHtml('Rock & Roll'), 'Rock &amp; Roll');
assert.equal(
  escapeHtml('<blank>'), '&lt;blank&gt;');
```

Exercise: HTML templating

Exercise with bonus challenge: `exercises/template-literals/templating_test.mjs`

Quiz

See quiz app (p. 71).

Chapter 22

Symbols

Contents

22.1 Use cases for symbols	186
22.1.1 Symbols: values for constants	186
22.1.2 Symbols: unique property keys	187
22.2 Publicly known symbols	188
22.3 Converting symbols	188

Symbols are primitive values that are created via the factory function `Symbol()`:

```
const mySymbol = Symbol('mySymbol');
```

The parameter is optional and provides a description, which is mainly useful for debugging.

On one hand, symbols are like objects in that each value created by `Symbol()` is unique and not compared by value:

```
> Symbol() === Symbol()
false
```

On the other hand, they also behave like primitive values. They have to be categorized via `typeof`:

```
const sym = Symbol();
assert.equal(typeof sym, 'symbol');
```

And they can be property keys in objects:

```
const obj = {
  [sym]: 123,
};
```

22.1 Use cases for symbols

The main use cases for symbols, are:

- Values for constants
- Unique property keys

22.1.1 Symbols: values for constants

Let's assume you want to create constants representing the colors red, orange, yellow, green, blue, and violet. One simple way of doing so would be to use strings:

```
const COLOR_BLUE = 'Blue';
```

On the plus side, logging that constant produces helpful output. On the minus side, there is a risk of mistaking an unrelated value for a color because two strings with the same content are considered equal:

```
const MOOD_BLUE = 'Blue';
assert.equal(COLOR_BLUE, MOOD_BLUE);
```

We can fix that problem via symbols:

```
const COLOR_BLUE = Symbol('Blue');
const MOOD_BLUE = Symbol('Blue');

assert.notEqual(COLOR_BLUE, MOOD_BLUE);
```

Let's use symbol-valued constants to implement a function:

```
const COLOR_RED    = Symbol('Red');
const COLOR_ORANGE = Symbol('Orange');
const COLOR_YELLOW = Symbol('Yellow');
const COLOR_GREEN  = Symbol('Green');
const COLOR_BLUE   = Symbol('Blue');
const COLOR_VIOLET = Symbol('Violet');

function getComplement(color) {
  switch (color) {
    case COLOR_RED:
      return COLOR_GREEN;
    case COLOR_ORANGE:
      return COLOR_BLUE;
    case COLOR_YELLOW:
      return COLOR_VIOLET;
    case COLOR_GREEN:
      return COLOR_RED;
    case COLOR_BLUE:
      return COLOR_ORANGE;
    case COLOR_VIOLET:
      return COLOR_YELLOW;
    default:
```

```
      throw new Exception('Unknown color: '+color);
  }
}
assert.equal(getComplement(COLOR_YELLOW), COLOR_VIOLET);
```

22.1.2 Symbols: unique property keys

The keys of properties (fields) in objects are used at two levels:

- The program operates at a *base level*. The keys at that level reflect the problem that the program solves.

- Libraries and ECMAScript operate at a *meta-level*. The keys at that level are used by services operating on base-level data and code. One such key is 'toString'.

The following code demonstrates the difference:

```
const pt = {
  x: 7,
  y: 4,
  toString() {
    return `(${this.x}, ${this.y})`;
  },
};
assert.equal(String(pt), '(7, 4)');
```

Properties .x and .y exist at the base level. They hold the coordinates of the point represented by pt and are used to solve a problem – computing with points. Method .toString() exists at a meta-level. It is used by JavaScript to convert this object to a string.

Meta-level properties must never interfere with base-level properties. That is, their keys must never overlap. That is difficult when both language and libraries contribute to the meta-level. For example, it is now impossible to give new meta-level methods simple names, such as toString because they might clash with existing base-level names. Python's solution to this problem is to prefix and suffix special names with two underscores: __init__, __iter__, __hash__, etc. However, even with this solution, libraries can't have their own meta-level properties because those might be in conflict with future language properties.

Symbols, used as property keys, help us here: Each symbol is unique and a symbol key never clashes with any other string or symbol key.

22.1.2.1 Example: a library with a meta-level method

As an example, let's assume we are writing a library that treats objects differently if they implement a special method. This is what defining a property key for such a method and implementing it for an object would look like:

```
const specialMethod = Symbol('specialMethod');
const obj = {
  _id: 'kf12oi',
```

```
  [specialMethod]() { // (A)
    return this._id;
  }
};
assert.equal(obj[specialMethod](), 'kf12oi');
```

The square brackets in line A enable us to specify that the method must have the key specialMethod. More details are explained in §28.5.2 "Computed property keys" (p. 276).

22.2 Publicly known symbols

Symbols that play special roles within ECMAScript are called *publicly known symbols*. Examples include:

- Symbol.iterator: makes an object *iterable*. It's the key of a method that returns an iterator. For more information on this topic, see §30 "Synchronous iteration" (p. 311).

- Symbol.hasInstance: customizes how instanceof works. If an object implements a method with that key, it can be used at the right-hand side of that operator. For example:

  ```
  const PrimitiveNull = {
    [Symbol.hasInstance](x) {
      return x === null;
    }
  };
  assert.equal(null instanceof PrimitiveNull, true);
  ```

- Symbol.toStringTag: influences the default .toString() method.

  ```
  > String({})
  '[object Object]'
  > String({ [Symbol.toStringTag]: 'is no money' })
  '[object is no money]'
  ```

  Note: It's usually better to override .toString().

> **Exercises: Publicly known symbols**
> - Symbol.toStringTag: exercises/symbols/to_string_tag_test.mjs
> - Symbol.hasInstance: exercises/symbols/has_instance_test.mjs

22.3 Converting symbols

What happens if we convert a symbol sym to another primitive type? Tbl. 22.1 has the answers.

22.3 Converting symbols

Table 22.1: The results of converting symbols to other primitive types.

Convert to	Explicit conversion	Coercion (implicit conv.)
boolean	Boolean(sym) → OK	!sym → OK
number	Number(sym) → TypeError	sym*2 → TypeError
string	String(sym) → OK	''+sym → TypeError
	sym.toString() → OK	`${sym}` → TypeError

One key pitfall with symbols is how often exceptions are thrown when converting them to something else. What is the thinking behind that? First, conversion to number never makes sense and should be warned about. Second, converting a symbol to a string is indeed useful for diagnostic output. But it also makes sense to warn about accidentally turning a symbol into a string (which is a different kind of property key):

```
const obj = {};
const sym = Symbol();
assert.throws(
  () => { obj['__'+sym+'__'] = true },
  { message: 'Cannot convert a Symbol value to a string' });
```

The downside is that the exceptions make working with symbols more complicated. You have to explicitly convert symbols when assembling strings via the plus operator:

```
> const mySymbol = Symbol('mySymbol');
> 'Symbol I used: ' + mySymbol
TypeError: Cannot convert a Symbol value to a string
> 'Symbol I used: ' + String(mySymbol)
'Symbol I used: Symbol(mySymbol)'
```

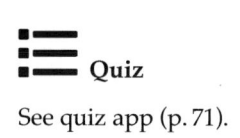

Quiz

See quiz app (p. 71).

Part V

Control flow and data flow

Chapter 23

Control flow statements

Contents

23.1 Conditions of control flow statements 194
23.2 Controlling loops: `break` and `continue` 194
    23.2.1 `break` 194
    23.2.2 `break` plus label: leaving any labeled statement 195
    23.2.3 `continue` 195
23.3 `if` statements 196
    23.3.1 The syntax of `if` statements 196
23.4 `switch` statements 197
    23.4.1 A first example of a `switch` statement 197
    23.4.2 Don't forget to `return` or `break`! 198
    23.4.3 Empty case clauses 198
    23.4.4 Checking for illegal values via a `default` clause 199
23.5 `while` loops 199
    23.5.1 Examples of `while` loops 200
23.6 `do-while` loops 200
23.7 `for` loops 200
    23.7.1 Examples of `for` loops 201
23.8 `for-of` loops 202
    23.8.1 `const`: `for-of` vs. `for` 202
    23.8.2 Iterating over iterables 202
    23.8.3 Iterating over [index, element] pairs of Arrays 202
23.9 `for-await-of` loops 203
23.10 `for-in` loops (avoid) 203

This chapter covers the following control flow statements:

- `if` statement (ES1)
- `switch` statement (ES3)
- `while` loop (ES1)

- `do-while` loop (ES3)
- `for` loop (ES1)
- `for-of` loop (ES6)
- `for-await-of` loop (ES2018)
- `for-in` loop (ES1)

Before we get to the actual control flow statements, let's take a look at two operators for controlling loops.

23.1 Conditions of control flow statements

`if`, `while`, and `do-while` have conditions that are, in principle, boolean. However, a condition only has to be *truthy* (true if coerced to boolean) in order to be accepted. In other words, the following two control flow statements are equivalent:

```
if (value) {}
if (Boolean(value) === true) {}
```

This is a list of all *falsy* values:

- `undefined`, `null`
- `false`
- `0`, `NaN`
- `''`

All other values are truthy. For more information, see §16.2 "Falsy and truthy values" (p. 116).

23.2 Controlling loops: `break` and `continue`

The two operators `break` and `continue` can be used to control loops and other statements while you are inside them.

23.2.1 `break`

There are two versions of `break`: one with an operand and one without an operand. The latter version works inside the following statements: `while`, `do-while`, `for`, `for-of`, `for-await-of`, `for-in` and `switch`. It immediately leaves the current statement:

```
for (const x of ['a', 'b', 'c']) {
  console.log(x);
  if (x === 'b') break;
  console.log('---')
}

// Output:
// 'a'
// '---'
// 'b'
```

23.2.2 break plus label: leaving any labeled statement

break with an operand works everywhere. Its operand is a *label*. Labels can be put in front of any statement, including blocks. break foo leaves the statement whose label is foo:

```
foo: { // label
  if (condition) break foo; // labeled break
  // ···
}
```

In the following example, we use break with a label to leave a loop differently when we succeeded (line A). Then we skip what comes directly after the loop, which is where we end up if we failed.

```
function findSuffix(stringArray, suffix) {
  let result;
  search_block: {
    for (const str of stringArray) {
      if (str.endsWith(suffix)) {
        // Success:
        result = str;
        break search_block; // (A)
      }
    } // for
    // Failure:
    result = '(Untitled)';
  } // search_block

  return { suffix, result };
    // Same as: {suffix: suffix, result: result}
}
assert.deepEqual(
  findSuffix(['foo.txt', 'bar.html'], '.html'),
  { suffix: '.html', result: 'bar.html' }
);
assert.deepEqual(
  findSuffix(['foo.txt', 'bar.html'], '.mjs'),
  { suffix: '.mjs', result: '(Untitled)' }
);
```

23.2.3 continue

continue only works inside while, do-while, for, for-of, for-await-of, and for-in. It immediately leaves the current loop iteration and continues with the next one – for example:

```
const lines = [
  'Normal line',
  '# Comment',
```

```
  'Another normal line',
];
for (const line of lines) {
  if (line.startsWith('#')) continue;
  console.log(line);
}
// Output:
// 'Normal line'
// 'Another normal line'
```

23.3 `if` statements

These are two simple `if` statements: one with just a "then" branch and one with both a "then" branch and an "else" branch:

```
if (cond) {
  // then branch
}

if (cond) {
  // then branch
} else {
  // else branch
}
```

Instead of the block, `else` can also be followed by another `if` statement:

```
if (cond1) {
  // ···
} else if (cond2) {
  // ···
}

if (cond1) {
  // ···
} else if (cond2) {
  // ···
} else {
  // ···
}
```

You can continue this chain with more `else if`s.

23.3.1 The syntax of `if` statements

The general syntax of `if` statements is:

```
if (cond) «then_statement»
else «else_statement»
```

23.4 switch statements

So far, the then_statement has always been a block, but we can use any statement. That statement must be terminated with a semicolon:

```
if (true) console.log('Yes'); else console.log('No');
```

That means that else if is not its own construct; it's simply an if statement whose else_statement is another if statement.

23.4 switch statements

A switch statement looks as follows:

```
switch («switch_expression») {
  «switch_body»
}
```

The body of switch consists of zero or more case clauses:

```
case «case_expression»:
  «statements»
```

And, optionally, a default clause:

```
default:
  «statements»
```

A switch is executed as follows:

- It evaluates the switch expression.
- It jumps to the first case clause whose expression has the same result as the switch expression.
- Otherwise, if there is no such clause, it jumps to the default clause.
- Otherwise, if there is no default clause, it does nothing.

23.4.1 A first example of a switch statement

Let's look at an example: The following function converts a number from 1–7 to the name of a weekday.

```
function dayOfTheWeek(num) {
  switch (num) {
    case 1:
      return 'Monday';
    case 2:
      return 'Tuesday';
    case 3:
      return 'Wednesday';
    case 4:
      return 'Thursday';
    case 5:
      return 'Friday';
    case 6:
```

```
      return 'Saturday';
    case 7:
      return 'Sunday';
  }
}
assert.equal(dayOfTheWeek(5), 'Friday');
```

23.4.2 Don't forget to return or break!

At the end of a case clause, execution continues with the next case clause, unless you return or break – for example:

```
function englishToFrench(english) {
  let french;
  switch (english) {
    case 'hello':
      french = 'bonjour';
    case 'goodbye':
      french = 'au revoir';
  }
  return french;
}
// The result should be 'bonjour'!
assert.equal(englishToFrench('hello'), 'au revoir');
```

That is, our implementation of dayOfTheWeek() only worked because we used return. We can fix englishToFrench() by using break:

```
function englishToFrench(english) {
  let french;
  switch (english) {
    case 'hello':
      french = 'bonjour';
      break;
    case 'goodbye':
      french = 'au revoir';
      break;
  }
  return french;
}
assert.equal(englishToFrench('hello'), 'bonjour'); // ok
```

23.4.3 Empty case clauses

The statements of a case clause can be omitted, which effectively gives us multiple case expressions per case clause:

```
function isWeekDay(name) {
  switch (name) {
    case 'Monday':
```

23.5 while loops

```
      case 'Tuesday':
      case 'Wednesday':
      case 'Thursday':
      case 'Friday':
        return true;
      case 'Saturday':
      case 'Sunday':
        return false;
    }
}
assert.equal(isWeekDay('Wednesday'), true);
assert.equal(isWeekDay('Sunday'), false);
```

23.4.4 Checking for illegal values via a `default` clause

A `default` clause is jumped to if the `switch` expression has no other match. That makes it useful for error checking:

```
function isWeekDay(name) {
  switch (name) {
    case 'Monday':
    case 'Tuesday':
    case 'Wednesday':
    case 'Thursday':
    case 'Friday':
      return true;
    case 'Saturday':
    case 'Sunday':
      return false;
    default:
      throw new Error('Illegal value: '+name);
  }
}
assert.throws(
  () => isWeekDay('January'),
  {message: 'Illegal value: January'});
```

> **Exercises: `switch`**
>
> - exercises/control-flow/number_to_month_test.mjs
> - Bonus: exercises/control-flow/is_object_via_switch_test.mjs

23.5 while loops

A while loop has the following syntax:

```
while («condition») {
  «statements»
}
```

Before each loop iteration, `while` evaluates `condition`:

- If the result is falsy, the loop is finished.
- If the result is truthy, the `while` body is executed one more time.

23.5.1 Examples of `while` loops

The following code uses a `while` loop. In each loop iteration, it removes the first element of arr via `.shift()` and logs it.

```
const arr = ['a', 'b', 'c'];
while (arr.length > 0) {
  const elem = arr.shift(); // remove first element
  console.log(elem);
}
// Output:
// 'a'
// 'b'
// 'c'
```

If the condition always evaluates to `true`, then `while` is an infinite loop:

```
while (true) {
  if (Math.random() === 0) break;
}
```

23.6 `do-while` loops

The `do-while` loop works much like `while`, but it checks its condition *after* each loop iteration, not before.

```
let input;
do {
  input = prompt('Enter text:');
  console.log(input);
} while (input !== ':q');
```

`prompt()`[1] is a global function that is available in web browsers. It prompts the user to input text and returns it.

23.7 `for` loops

A `for` loop has the following syntax:

---
[1] https://developer.mozilla.org/en-US/docs/Web/API/Window/prompt

23.7 for loops

```
for («initialization»; «condition»; «post_iteration») {
  «statements»
}
```

The first line is the *head* of the loop and controls how often the *body* (the remainder of the loop) is executed. It has three parts and each of them is optional:

- initialization: sets up variables, etc. for the loop. Variables declared here via let or const only exist inside the loop.
- condition: This condition is checked before each loop iteration. If it is falsy, the loop stops.
- post_iteration: This code is executed after each loop iteration.

A for loop is therefore roughly equivalent to the following while loop:

```
«initialization»
while («condition») {
  «statements»
  «post_iteration»
}
```

23.7.1 Examples of for loops

As an example, this is how to count from zero to two via a for loop:

```
for (let i=0; i<3; i++) {
  console.log(i);
}

// Output:
// 0
// 1
// 2
```

This is how to log the contents of an Array via a for loop:

```
const arr = ['a', 'b', 'c'];
for (let i=0; i<arr.length; i++) {
  console.log(arr[i]);
}

// Output:
// 'a'
// 'b'
// 'c'
```

If you omit all three parts of the head, you get an infinite loop:

```
for (;;) {
  if (Math.random() === 0) break;
}
```

23.8 for-of loops

A `for-of` loop iterates over an *iterable* – a data container that supports the *iteration protocol* (p. 311). Each iterated value is stored in a variable, as specified in the head:

```
for («iteration_variable» of «iterable») {
  «statements»
}
```

The iteration variable is usually created via a variable declaration:

```
const iterable = ['hello', 'world'];
for (const elem of iterable) {
  console.log(elem);
}
// Output:
// 'hello'
// 'world'
```

But you can also use a (mutable) variable that already exists:

```
const iterable = ['hello', 'world'];
let elem;
for (elem of iterable) {
  console.log(elem);
}
```

23.8.1 const: for-of vs. for

Note that in `for-of` loops you can use `const`. The iteration variable can still be different for each iteration (it just can't change during the iteration). Think of it as a new `const` declaration being executed each time in a fresh scope.

In contrast, in `for` loops you must declare variables via `let` or `var` if their values change.

23.8.2 Iterating over iterables

As mentioned before, `for-of` works with any iterable object, not just with Arrays – for example, with Sets:

```
const set = new Set(['hello', 'world']);
for (const elem of set) {
  console.log(elem);
}
```

23.8.3 Iterating over [index, element] pairs of Arrays

Lastly, you can also use `for-of` to iterate over the [index, element] entries of Arrays:

```
const arr = ['a', 'b', 'c'];
for (const [index, elem] of arr.entries()) {
  console.log(`${index} -> ${elem}`);
```

```
}
// Output:
// '0 -> a'
// '1 -> b'
// '2 -> c'
```

With `[index, element]`, we are using *destructuring* (p. 391) to access Array elements.

Exercise: `for-of`

`exercises/control-flow/array_to_string_test.mjs`

23.9 for-await-of loops

`for-await-of` is like `for-of`, but it works with asynchronous iterables instead of synchronous ones. And it can only be used inside async functions and async generators.

```
for await (const item of asyncIterable) {
  // ···
}
```

`for-await-of` is described in detail in the chapter on asynchronous iteration (p. 460).

23.10 for-in loops (avoid)

Recommendation: don't use `for-in` loops

`for-in` has several pitfalls. Therefore, it is usually best to avoid it.

This is an example of using `for-in` properly, which involves boilerplate code (line A):

```
function getOwnPropertyNames(obj) {
  const result = [];
  for (const key in obj) {
    if ({}.hasOwnProperty.call(obj, key)) { // (A)
      result.push(key);
    }
  }
  return result;
}
assert.deepEqual(
  getOwnPropertyNames({ a: 1, b:2 }),
  ['a', 'b']);
assert.deepEqual(
  getOwnPropertyNames(['a', 'b']),
  ['0', '1']); // strings!
```

We can implement the same functionality without `for-in`, which is almost always better:

```
function getOwnPropertyNames(obj) {
  const result = [];
  for (const key of Object.keys(obj)) {
    result.push(key);
  }
  return result;
}
```

Quiz

See quiz app (p. 71).

Chapter 24

Exception handling

Contents

24.1 Motivation: throwing and catching exceptions	205
24.2 throw	206
24.2.1 Options for creating error objects	207
24.3 The try statement	207
24.3.1 The try block	207
24.3.2 The catch clause	207
24.3.3 The finally clause	208
24.4 Error classes	209
24.4.1 Properties of error objects	209

This chapter covers how JavaScript handles exceptions.

> **Why doesn't JavaScript throw exceptions more often?**
>
> JavaScript didn't support exceptions until ES3. That explains why they are used sparingly by the language and its standard library.

24.1 Motivation: throwing and catching exceptions

Consider the following code. It reads profiles stored in files into an Array with instances of class `Profile`:

```
function readProfiles(filePaths) {
  const profiles = [];
  for (const filePath of filePaths) {
    try {
      const profile = readOneProfile(filePath);
      profiles.push(profile);
```

```
    } catch (err) { // (A)
      console.log('Error in: '+filePath, err);
    }
  }
}
function readOneProfile(filePath) {
  const profile = new Profile();
  const file = openFile(filePath);
  // ··· (Read the data in `file` into `profile`)
  return profile;
}
function openFile(filePath) {
  if (!fs.existsSync(filePath)) {
    throw new Error('Could not find file '+filePath); // (B)
  }
  // ··· (Open the file whose path is `filePath`)
}
```

Let's examine what happens in line B: An error occurred, but the best place to handle the problem is not the current location, it's line A. There, we can skip the current file and move on to the next one.

Therefore:

- In line B, we use a `throw` statement to indicate that there was a problem.
- In line A, we use a `try-catch` statement to handle the problem.

When we throw, the following constructs are active:

```
readProfiles(···)
  for (const filePath of filePaths)
    try
      readOneProfile(···)
        openFile(···)
          if (!fs.existsSync(filePath))
            throw
```

One by one, `throw` exits the nested constructs, until it encounters a `try` statement. Execution continues in the `catch` clause of that `try` statement.

24.2 `throw`

This is the syntax of the `throw` statement:

```
throw «value»;
```

Any value can be thrown, but it's best to throw an instance of `Error` or its subclasses.

```
throw new Error('Problem!');
```

24.2.1 Options for creating error objects

- Use class `Error`. That is less limiting in JavaScript than in a more static language because you can add your own properties to instances:

  ```
  const err = new Error('Could not find the file');
  err.filePath = filePath;
  throw err;
  ```

- Use one of JavaScript's subclasses of `Error` (which are listed later (p. 209)).
- Subclass `Error` yourself.

  ```
  class MyError extends Error {
  }
  function func() {
    throw new MyError('Problem!');
  }
  assert.throws(
    () => func(),
    MyError);
  ```

24.3 The try statement

The maximal version of the `try` statement looks as follows:

```
try {
  «try_statements»
} catch (error) {
  «catch_statements»
} finally {
  «finally_statements»
}
```

You can combine these clauses as follows:

- try-catch
- try-finally
- try-catch-finally

Since ECMAScript 2019, you can omit the `catch` parameter (`error`), if you are not interested in the value that was thrown.

24.3.1 The try block

The `try` block can be considered the body of the statement. This is where we execute the regular code.

24.3.2 The catch clause

If an exception reaches the `try` block, then it is assigned to the parameter of the `catch` clause and the code in that clause is executed. Next, execution normally continues after the `try` statement. That may change if:

- There is a `return`, `break`, or `throw` inside the `catch` block.
- There is a `finally` clause (which is always executed before the `try` statement ends).

The following code demonstrates that the value that is thrown in line A is indeed caught in line B.

```
const errorObject = new Error();
function func() {
  throw errorObject; // (A)
}

try {
  func();
} catch (err) { // (B)
  assert.equal(err, errorObject);
}
```

24.3.3 The finally clause

The code inside the `finally` clause is always executed at the end of a `try` statement – no matter what happens in the `try` block or the `catch` clause.

Let's look at a common use case for `finally`: You have created a resource and want to always destroy it when you are done with it, no matter what happens while working with it. You'd implement that as follows:

```
const resource = createResource();
try {
  // Work with `resource`. Errors may be thrown.
} finally {
  resource.destroy();
}
```

24.3.3.1 finally is always executed

The `finally` clause is always executed, even if an error is thrown (line A):

```
let finallyWasExecuted = false;
assert.throws(
  () => {
    try {
      throw new Error(); // (A)
    } finally {
      finallyWasExecuted = true;
    }
  },
  Error
);
assert.equal(finallyWasExecuted, true);
```

24.4 Error classes

And even if there is a `return` statement (line A):

```
let finallyWasExecuted = false;
function func() {
  try {
    return; // (A)
  } finally {
    finallyWasExecuted = true;
  }
}
func();
assert.equal(finallyWasExecuted, true);
```

24.4 Error classes

`Error` is the common superclass of all built-in error classes. It has the following subclasses (I'm quoting the ECMAScript specification[1]):

- `RangeError`: Indicates a value that is not in the set or range of allowable values.
- `ReferenceError`: Indicate that an invalid reference value has been detected.
- `SyntaxError`: Indicates that a parsing error has occurred.
- `TypeError`: is used to indicate an unsuccessful operation when none of the other *NativeError* objects are an appropriate indication of the failure cause.
- `URIError`: Indicates that one of the global URI handling functions was used in a way that is incompatible with its definition.

24.4.1 Properties of error objects

Consider `err`, an instance of `Error`:

```
const err = new Error('Hello!');
assert.equal(String(err), 'Error: Hello!');
```

Two properties of `err` are especially useful:

- `.message`: contains just the error message.

    ```
    assert.equal(err.message, 'Hello!');
    ```

- `.stack`: contains a stack trace. It is supported by all mainstream browsers.

    ```
    assert.equal(
    err.stack,
    `
    Error: Hello!
        at ch_exception-handling.mjs:1:13
    `.trim());
    ```

---

[1]https://tc39.github.io/ecma262/#sec-native-error-types-used-in-this-standard

🧩 Exercise: Exception handling

`exercises/exception-handling/call_function_test.mjs`

≣ Quiz

See quiz app (p. 71).

Chapter 25

Callable values

Contents

25.1 Kinds of functions	211
25.2 Ordinary functions	212
25.2.1 Parts of a function declaration	212
25.2.2 Roles played by ordinary functions	213
25.2.3 Names of ordinary functions	213
25.3 Specialized functions	214
25.3.1 Specialized functions are still functions	214
25.3.2 Recommendation: prefer specialized functions	215
25.3.3 Arrow functions	215
25.4 More kinds of functions and methods	217
25.5 Returning values from functions and methods	218
25.6 Parameter handling	219
25.6.1 Terminology: parameters vs. arguments	219
25.6.2 Terminology: callback	219
25.6.3 Too many or not enough arguments	220
25.6.4 Parameter default values	220
25.6.5 Rest parameters	220
25.6.6 Named parameters	221
25.6.7 Simulating named parameters	222
25.6.8 Spreading (...) into function calls	222
25.7 Dynamically evaluating code: `eval()`, `new Function()` (advanced)	224
25.7.1 `eval()`	224
25.7.2 `new Function()`	224
25.7.3 Recommendations	225

25.1 Kinds of functions

JavaScript has two categories of functions:

- An *ordinary function* can play several roles:
  - Real function
  - Method
  - Constructor function
- A *specialized function* can only play one of those roles – for example:
  - An *arrow function* can only be a real function.
  - A *method* can only be a method.
  - A *class* can only be a constructor function.

The next two sections explain what all of those things mean.

25.2 Ordinary functions

The following code shows three ways of doing (roughly) the same thing: creating an ordinary function.

```
// Function declaration (a statement)
function ordinary1(a, b, c) {
  // ···
}

// const plus anonymous function expression
const ordinary2 = function (a, b, c) {
  // ···
};

// const plus named function expression
const ordinary3 = function myName(a, b, c) {
  // `myName` is only accessible in here
};
```

As we have seen in §12.8 "Declarations: scope and activation" (p. 84), function declarations are activated early, while variable declarations (e.g., via `const`) are not.

The syntax of function declarations and function expressions is very similar. The context determines which is which. For more information on this kind of syntactic ambiguity, consult §8.5 "Ambiguous syntax" (p. 51).

25.2.1 Parts of a function declaration

Let's examine the parts of a function declaration via an example:

```
function add(x, y) {
  return x + y;
}
```

- add is the *name* of the function declaration.
- add(x, y) is the *head* of the function declaration.
- x and y are the *parameters*.
- The curly braces ({ and }) and everything between them are the *body* of the function declaration.

25.2 Ordinary functions

- The `return` statement explicitly returns a value from the function.

25.2.2 Roles played by ordinary functions

Consider the following function declaration from the previous section:

```
function add(x, y) {
  return x + y;
}
```

This function declaration creates an ordinary function whose name is add. As an ordinary function, `add()` can play three roles:

- Real function: invoked via a function call.

    ```
    assert.equal(add(2, 1), 3);
    ```

- Method: stored in property, invoked via a method call.

    ```
    const obj = { addAsMethod: add };
    assert.equal(obj.addAsMethod(2, 4), 6); // (A)
    ```

    In line A, `obj` is called the *receiver* of the method call. It can be accessed via `this` inside the method.

- Constructor function/class: invoked via `new`.

    ```
    const inst = new add();
    assert.equal(inst instanceof add, true);
    ```

    (As an aside, the names of classes normally start with capital letters.)

> ⚙ **Ordinary function vs. real function**
>
> In JavaScript, we distinguish:
>
> - The entity *ordinary function*
> - The role *real function*, as played by an ordinary function
>
> In many other programming languages, the entity *function* only plays one role – *function*. Therefore, the same name *function* can be used for both.

25.2.3 Names of ordinary functions

The name of a function expression is only accessible inside the function, where the function can use it to refer to itself (e.g., for self-recursion):

```
const func = function funcExpr() { return funcExpr };
assert.equal(func(), func);

// The name `funcExpr` only exists inside the function:
assert.throws(() => funcExpr(), ReferenceError);
```

In contrast, the name of a function declaration is accessible inside the current scope:

```
function funcDecl() { return funcDecl }

// The name `funcDecl` exists in the current scope
assert.equal(funcDecl(), funcDecl);
```

25.3 Specialized functions

Specialized functions are single-purpose versions of ordinary functions. Each one of them specializes in a single role:

- The purpose of an *arrow function* is to be a real function:
  ```
  const arrow = () => { return 123 };
  assert.equal(arrow(), 123);
  ```

- The purpose of a *method* is to be a method:
  ```
  const obj = { method() { return 'abc' } };
  assert.equal(obj.method(), 'abc');
  ```

- The purpose of a *class* is to be a constructor function:
  ```
  class MyClass { /* ··· */ }
  const inst = new MyClass();
  ```

Apart from nicer syntax, each kind of specialized function also supports new features, making them better at their jobs than ordinary functions.

- Arrow functions are explained later in this chapter.
- Methods are explained in the chapter on single objects (p. 268).
- Classes are explained in the chapter on classes (p. 293).

Tbl. 25.1 lists the capabilities of ordinary and specialized functions.

> Table 25.1: Capabilities of four kinds of functions. "Lexical this" (p. 216) means that this is defined by the surroundings of an arrow function, not by method calls.

	Function call	Method call	Constructor call
Ordinary function	(this === undefined)	✓	✓
Arrow function	✓	(lexical this)	✗
Method	(this === undefined)	✓	✗
Class	✗	✗	✓

25.3.1 Specialized functions are still functions

It's important to note that arrow functions, methods, and classes are still categorized as functions:

```
> (() => {}) instanceof Function
true
```

```
> ({ method() {} }.method) instanceof Function
true
> (class SomeClass {}) instanceof Function
true
```

25.3.2 Recommendation: prefer specialized functions

Normally, you should prefer specialized functions over ordinary functions, especially classes and methods. The choice between an arrow function and an ordinary function is less clear-cut, though:

- On one hand, an ordinary function has this as an implicit parameter. That parameter is set to undefined during function calls – which is not what you want. An arrow function treats this like any other variable. For details, see §28.4.6 "Avoiding the pitfalls of this" (p. 274).

- On the other hand, I like the syntax of a function declaration (which produces an ordinary function). If you don't use this inside it, it is mostly equivalent to const plus arrow function:

  ```
  function funcDecl(x, y) {
    return x * y;
  }
  const arrowFunc = (x, y) => {
    return x * y;
  };
  ```

25.3.3 Arrow functions

Arrow functions were added to JavaScript for two reasons:

1. To provide a more concise way for creating functions.
2. To make working with real functions easier: You can't refer to the this of the surrounding scope inside an ordinary function.

Next, we'll first look at the syntax of arrow functions and then how they help with this.

25.3.3.1 The syntax of arrow functions

Let's review the syntax of an anonymous function expression:

```
const f = function (x, y, z) { return 123 };
```

The (roughly) equivalent arrow function looks as follows. Arrow functions are expressions.

```
const f = (x, y, z) => { return 123 };
```

Here, the body of the arrow function is a block. But it can also be an expression. The following arrow function works exactly like the previous one.

```
const f = (x, y, z) => 123;
```

If an arrow function has only a single parameter and that parameter is an identifier (not a destructuring pattern (p. 391)) then you can omit the parentheses around the parameter:

```
const id = x => x;
```

That is convenient when passing arrow functions as parameters to other functions or methods:

```
> [1,2,3].map(x => x+1)
[ 2, 3, 4 ]
```

This previous example demonstrates one benefit of arrow functions – conciseness. If we perform the same task with a function expression, our code is more verbose:

```
[1,2,3].map(function (x) { return x+1 });
```

25.3.3.2 Arrow functions: lexical `this`

Ordinary functions can be both methods and real functions. Alas, the two roles are in conflict:

- As each ordinary function can be a method, it has its own `this`.
- The own `this` makes it impossible to access the `this` of the surrounding scope from inside an ordinary function. And that is inconvenient for real functions.

The following code demonstrates the issue:

```
const person = {
  name: 'Jill',
  someMethod() {
    const ordinaryFunc = function () {
      assert.throws(
        () => this.name, // (A)
        /^TypeError: Cannot read property 'name' of undefined$/);
    };
    const arrowFunc = () => {
      assert.equal(this.name, 'Jill'); // (B)
    };

    ordinaryFunc();
    arrowFunc();
  },
}
```

In this code, we can observe two ways of handling `this`:

- Dynamic `this`: In line A, we try to access the `this` of .someMethod() from an ordinary function. There, it is *shadowed* by the function's own `this`, which is undefined (as filled in by the function call). Given that ordinary functions receive their `this` via (dynamic) function or method calls, their `this` is called *dynamic*.

- Lexical `this`: In line B, we again try to access the `this` of .someMethod(). This time, we succeed because the arrow function does not have its own `this`. this is resolved *lexically*, just like any other variable. That's why the `this` of arrow functions is called *lexical*.

25.3.3.3 Syntax pitfall: returning an object literal from an arrow function

If you want the expression body of an arrow function to be an object literal, you must put the literal in parentheses:

```
const func1 = () => ({a: 1});
assert.deepEqual(func1(), { a: 1 });
```

If you don't, JavaScript thinks, the arrow function has a block body (that doesn't return anything):

```
const func2 = () => {a: 1};
assert.deepEqual(func2(), undefined);
```

`{a: 1}` is interpreted as a block with the label `a:` (p. 195) and the expression statement `1`. Without an explicit `return` statement, the block body returns `undefined`.

This pitfall is caused by syntactic ambiguity (p. 51): object literals and code blocks have the same syntax. We use the parentheses to tell JavaScript that the body is an expression (an object literal) and not a statement (a block).

For more information on shadowing `this`, consult §28.4.5 "`this` pitfall: accidentally shadowing `this`" (p. 272).

25.4 More kinds of functions and methods

> 👁 **This section is a summary of upcoming content**
>
> This section mainly serves as a reference for the current and upcoming chapters. Don't worry if you don't understand everything.

So far, all (real) functions and methods, that we have seen, were:

- Single-result
- Synchronous

Later chapters will cover other modes of programming:

- *Iteration* treats objects as containers of data (so-called *iterables*) and provides a standardized way for retrieving what is inside them. If a function or a method returns an iterable, it returns multiple values.
- *Asynchronous programming* deals with handling a long-running computation. You are notified when the computation is finished and can do something else in between. The standard pattern for asynchronously delivering single results is called *Promise*.

These modes can be combined – for example, there are synchronous iterables and asynchronous iterables.

Several new kinds of functions and methods help with some of the mode combinations:

- *Async functions* help implement functions that return Promises. There are also *async methods*.
- *Synchronous generator functions* help implement functions that return synchronous iterables. There are also *synchronous generator methods*.
- *Asynchronous generator functions* help implement functions that return asynchronous iterables. There are also *asynchronous generator methods*.

That leaves us with 4 kinds (2 × 2) of functions and methods:

- Synchronous vs. asynchronous
- Generator vs. single-result

Tbl. 25.2 gives an overview of the syntax for creating these 4 kinds of functions and methods.

Table 25.2: Syntax for creating functions and methods. The last column specifies how many values are produced by an entity.

		Result	Values
Sync function `function f() {}` `f = function () {}` `f = () => {}`	**Sync method** `{ m() {} }`	value	1
Sync generator function `function* f() {}` `f = function* () {}`	**Sync gen. method** `{ * m() {} }`	iterable	0+
Async function `async function f() {}` `f = async function () {}` `f = async () => {}`	**Async method** `{ async m() {} }`	Promise	1
Async generator function `async function* f() {}` `f = async function* () {}`	**Async gen. method** `{ async * m() {} }`	async iterable	0+

25.5 Returning values from functions and methods

(Everything mentioned in this section applies to both functions and methods.)

The `return` statement explicitly returns a value from a function:

```
function func() {
  return 123;
}
assert.equal(func(), 123);
```

Another example:

```
function boolToYesNo(bool) {
  if (bool) {
```

25.6 Parameter handling

```
    return 'Yes';
  } else {
    return 'No';
  }
}
assert.equal(boolToYesNo(true), 'Yes');
assert.equal(boolToYesNo(false), 'No');
```

If, at the end of a function, you haven't returned anything explicitly, JavaScript returns undefined for you:

```
function noReturn() {
  // No explicit return
}
assert.equal(noReturn(), undefined);
```

25.6 Parameter handling

Once again, I am only mentioning functions in this section, but everything also applies to methods.

25.6.1 Terminology: parameters vs. arguments

The term *parameter* and the term *argument* basically mean the same thing. If you want to, you can make the following distinction:

- *Parameters* are part of a function definition. They are also called *formal parameters* and *formal arguments*.
- *Arguments* are part of a function call. They are also called *actual parameters* and *actual arguments*.

25.6.2 Terminology: callback

A *callback* or *callback function* is a function that is an argument of a function or method call.

The following is an example of a callback:

```
const myArray = ['a', 'b'];
const callback = (x) => console.log(x);
myArray.forEach(callback);

// Output:
// 'a'
// 'b'
```

> ⚙️ **JavaScript uses the term *callback* broadly**
>
> In other programming languages, the term *callback* often has a narrower meaning:

it refers to a pattern for delivering results asynchronously, via a function-valued parameter. In this meaning, the *callback* (or *continuation*) is invoked after a function has completely finished its computation.

Callbacks as an asynchronous pattern, are described in the chapter on asynchronous programming (p. 425).

25.6.3 Too many or not enough arguments

JavaScript does not complain if a function call provides a different number of arguments than expected by the function definition:

- Extra arguments are ignored.
- Missing parameters are set to undefined.

For example:

```
function foo(x, y) {
  return [x, y];
}

// Too many arguments:
assert.deepEqual(foo('a', 'b', 'c'), ['a', 'b']);

// The expected number of arguments:
assert.deepEqual(foo('a', 'b'), ['a', 'b']);

// Not enough arguments:
assert.deepEqual(foo('a'), ['a', undefined]);
```

25.6.4 Parameter default values

Parameter default values specify the value to use if a parameter has not been provided – for example:

```
function f(x, y=0) {
  return [x, y];
}

assert.deepEqual(f(1), [1, 0]);
assert.deepEqual(f(), [undefined, 0]);
```

undefined also triggers the default value:

```
assert.deepEqual(
  f(undefined, undefined),
  [undefined, 0]);
```

25.6.5 Rest parameters

A rest parameter is declared by prefixing an identifier with three dots (...). During a function or method call, it receives an Array with all remaining arguments. If there are

25.6 Parameter handling

no extra arguments at the end, it is an empty Array – for example:

```
function f(x, ...y) {
  return [x, y];
}
assert.deepEqual(
  f('a', 'b', 'c'),
  ['a', ['b', 'c']]);
assert.deepEqual(
  f(),
  [undefined, []]);
```

25.6.5.1 Enforcing a certain number of arguments via a rest parameter

You can use a rest parameter to enforce a certain number of arguments. Take, for example, the following function:

```
function createPoint(x, y) {
  return {x, y};
    // same as {x: x, y: y}
}
```

This is how we force callers to always provide two arguments:

```
function createPoint(...args) {
  if (args.length !== 2) {
    throw new Error('Please provide exactly 2 arguments!');
  }
  const [x, y] = args; // (A)
  return {x, y};
}
```

In line A, we access the elements of `args` via *destructuring* (p. 391).

25.6.6 Named parameters

When someone calls a function, the arguments provided by the caller are assigned to the parameters received by the callee. Two common ways of performing the mapping are:

1. Positional parameters: An argument is assigned to a parameter if they have the same position. A function call with only positional arguments looks as follows.

    ```
    selectEntries(3, 20, 2)
    ```

2. Named parameters: An argument is assigned to a parameter if they have the same name. JavaScript doesn't have named parameters, but you can simulate them. For example, this is a function call with only (simulated) named arguments:

    ```
    selectEntries({start: 3, end: 20, step: 2})
    ```

Named parameters have several benefits:

- They lead to more self-explanatory code because each argument has a descriptive label. Just compare the two versions of `selectEntries()`: with the second one, it is much easier to see what happens.

- The order of the arguments doesn't matter (as long as the names are correct).

- Handling more than one optional parameter is more convenient: callers can easily provide any subset of all optional parameters and don't have to be aware of the ones they omit (with positional parameters, you have to fill in preceding optional parameters, with `undefined`).

25.6.7 Simulating named parameters

JavaScript doesn't have real named parameters. The official way of simulating them is via object literals:

```
function selectEntries({start=0, end=-1, step=1}) {
  return {start, end, step};
}
```

This function uses *destructuring* (p. 391) to access the properties of its single parameter. The pattern it uses is an abbreviation for the following pattern:

```
{start: start=0, end: end=-1, step: step=1}
```

This destructuring pattern works for empty object literals:

```
> selectEntries({})
{ start: 0, end: -1, step: 1 }
```

But it does not work if you call the function without any parameters:

```
> selectEntries()
TypeError: Cannot destructure property `start` of 'undefined' or 'null'.
```

You can fix this by providing a default value for the whole pattern. This default value works the same as default values for simpler parameter definitions: if the parameter is missing, the default is used.

```
function selectEntries({start=0, end=-1, step=1} = {}) {
  return {start, end, step};
}
assert.deepEqual(
  selectEntries(),
  { start: 0, end: -1, step: 1 });
```

25.6.8 Spreading (...) into function calls

If you put three dots (...) in front of the argument of a function call, then you *spread* it. That means that the argument must be an *iterable* object (p. 311) and the iterated values all become arguments. In other words, a single argument is expanded into multiple arguments – for example:

25.6 Parameter handling

```
function func(x, y) {
  console.log(x);
  console.log(y);
}
const someIterable = ['a', 'b'];
func(...someIterable);
  // same as func('a', 'b')

// Output:
// 'a'
// 'b'
```

Spreading and rest parameters use the same syntax (...), but they serve opposite purposes:

- Rest parameters are used when defining functions or methods. They collect arguments into Arrays.
- Spread arguments are used when calling functions or methods. They turn iterable objects into arguments.

25.6.8.1 Example: spreading into `Math.max()`

`Math.max()` returns the largest one of its zero or more arguments. Alas, it can't be used for Arrays, but spreading gives us a way out:

```
> Math.max(-1, 5, 11, 3)
11
> Math.max(...[-1, 5, 11, 3])
11
> Math.max(-1, ...[-5, 11], 3)
11
```

25.6.8.2 Example: spreading into `Array.prototype.push()`

Similarly, the Array method `.push()` destructively adds its zero or more parameters to the end of its Array. JavaScript has no method for destructively appending an Array to another one. Once again, we are saved by spreading:

```
const arr1 = ['a', 'b'];
const arr2 = ['c', 'd'];

arr1.push(...arr2);
assert.deepEqual(arr1, ['a', 'b', 'c', 'd']);
```

Exercises: Parameter handling

- Positional parameters: `exercises/callables/positional_parameters_test.mjs`
- Named parameters: `exercises/callables/named_parameters_test.mjs`

25.7 Dynamically evaluating code: `eval()`, `new Function()` (advanced)

Next, we'll look at two ways of evaluating code dynamically: `eval()` and `new Function()`.

25.7.1 `eval()`

Given a string `str` with JavaScript code, `eval(str)` evaluates that code and returns the result:

```
> eval('2 ** 4')
16
```

There are two ways of invoking `eval()`:

- *Directly*, via a function call. Then the code in its argument is evaluated inside the current scope.
- *Indirectly*, not via a function call. Then it evaluates its code in global scope.

"Not via a function call" means "anything that looks different than `eval(···)`":

- `eval.call(undefined, '···')`
- `(0, eval)('···')` (uses the comma operator)
- `globalThis.eval('···')`
- `const e = eval; e('···')`
- Etc.

The following code illustrates the difference:

```
globalThis.myVariable = 'global';
function func() {
  const myVariable = 'local';

  // Direct eval
  assert.equal(eval('myVariable'), 'local');

  // Indirect eval
  assert.equal(eval.call(undefined, 'myVariable'), 'global');
}
```

Evaluating code in global context is safer because the code has access to fewer internals.

25.7.2 `new Function()`

`new Function()` creates a function object and is invoked as follows:

```
const func = new Function('«param_1»', ···, '«param_n»', '«func_body»');
```

The previous statement is equivalent to the next statement. Note that «param_1», etc., are not inside string literals, anymore.

25.7 Dynamically evaluating code: `eval()`, `new Function()` (advanced)

```
const func = function («param_1», ···, «param_n») {
  «func_body»
};
```

In the next example, we create the same function twice, first via `new Function()`, then via a function expression:

```
const times1 = new Function('a', 'b', 'return a * b');
const times2 = function (a, b) { return a * b };
```

> ⚠️ **`new Function()` creates non-strict mode functions**
>
> Functions created via `new Function()` are sloppy (p. 55).

25.7.3 Recommendations

Avoid dynamic evaluation of code as much as you can:

- It's a security risk because it may enable an attacker to execute arbitrary code with the privileges of your code.
- It may be switched off – for example, in browsers, via a Content Security Policy[1].

Very often, JavaScript is dynamic enough so that you don't need `eval()` or similar. In the following example, what we are doing with `eval()` (line A) can be achieved just as well without it (line B).

```
const obj = {a: 1, b: 2};
const propKey = 'b';

assert.equal(eval('obj.' + propKey), 2); // (A)
assert.equal(obj[propKey], 2); // (B)
```

If you have to dynamically evaluate code:

- Prefer `new Function()` over `eval()`: it always executes its code in global context and a function provides a clean interface to the evaluated code.
- Prefer indirect `eval` over direct `eval`: evaluating code in global context is safer.

> ≣ **Quiz**
>
> See quiz app (p. 71).

---

[1] https://developer.mozilla.org/en-US/docs/Web/HTTP/CSP

Chapter 26

Environments: under the hood of variables (bonus)

Contents

26.1 Environment: data structure for managing variables 227
26.2 Recursion via environments 227
    26.2.1 Executing the code 228
26.3 Nested scopes via environments 228
    26.3.1 Executing the code 230
26.4 Closures and environments 232

In this chapter, we take a closer look at how the ECMAScript language specification handles variables.

26.1 Environment: data structure for managing variables

An environment is the data structure that the ECMAScript specification uses to manage variables. It is a dictionary whose keys are variable names and whose values are the values of those variables. Each scope has its associated environment. Environments must be able to support the following phenomena related to variables:

- Recursion
- Nested scopes
- Closures

We'll use examples to illustrate how that is done for each phenomenon.

26.2 Recursion via environments

We'll tackle recursion first. Consider the following code:

```
function f(x) {
  return x * 2;
}
function g(y) {
  const tmp = y + 1;
  return f(tmp);
}
assert.equal(g(3), 8);
```

For each function call, you need fresh storage space for the variables (parameters and local variables) of the called function. This is managed via a stack of so-called *execution contexts*, which are references to environments (for the purpose of this chapter). Environments themselves are stored on the heap. That is necessary because they occasionally live on after execution has left their scopes (we'll see that when exploring *closures*). Therefore, they themselves can't be managed via a stack.

26.2.1 Executing the code

While executing the code, we make the following pauses:

```
function f(x) {
  // Pause 3
  return x * 2;
}
function g(y) {
  const tmp = y + 1;
  // Pause 2
  return f(tmp);
}
// Pause 1
assert.equal(g(3), 8);
```

This is what happens:

- Pause 1 – before calling `g()` (fig. 26.1).
- Pause 2 – while executing `g()` (fig. 26.2).
- Pause 3 – while executing `f()` (fig. 26.3).
- Remaining steps: Every time there is a `return`, one execution context is removed from the stack.

26.3 Nested scopes via environments

We use the following code to explore how nested scopes are implemented via environments.

```
function f(x) {
  function square() {
    const result = x * x;
```

26.3 Nested scopes via environments

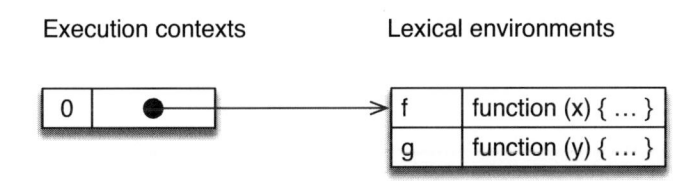

Figure 26.1: Recursion, pause 1 – before calling `g()`: The execution context stack has one entry, which points to the top-level environment. In that environment, there are two entries; one for `f()` and one for `g()`.

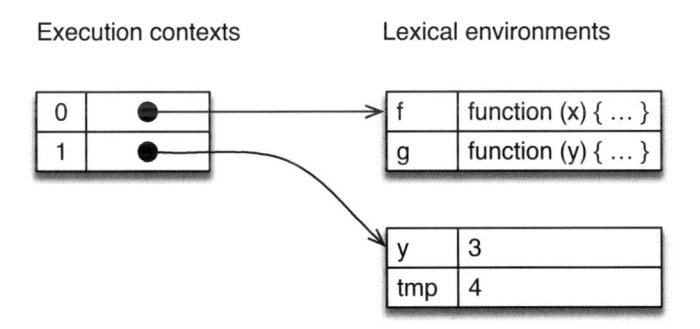

Figure 26.2: Recursion, pause 2 – while executing `g()`: The top of the execution context stack points to the environment that was created for `g()`. That environment contains entries for the argument y and for the local variable tmp.

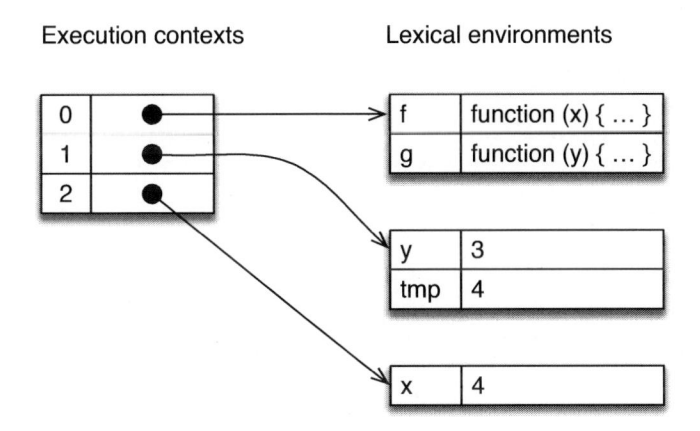

Figure 26.3: Recursion, pause 3 – while executing `f()`: The top execution context now points to the environment for `f()`.

```
    return result;
  }
  return square();
}
assert.equal(f(6), 36);
```

Here, we have three nested scopes: The top-level scope, the scope of `f()`, and the scope of `square()`. Observations:

- The scopes are connected. An inner scope "inherits" all the variables of an outer scope (minus the ones it shadows).
- Nesting scopes as a mechanism is independent of recursion. The latter is best managed by a stack of independent environments. The former is a relationship that each environment has with the environment "in which" it is created.

Therefore, the environment of each scope points to the environment of the surrounding scope via a field called `outer`. When we are looking up the value of a variable, we first search for its name in the current environment, then in the outer environment, then in the outer environment's outer environment, etc. The whole chain of outer environments contains all variables that can currently be accessed (minus shadowed variables).

When you make a function call, you create a new environment. The outer environment of that environment is the environment in which the function was created. To help set up the field `outer` of environments created via function calls, each function has an internal property named `[[Scope]]` that points to its "birth environment".

26.3.1 Executing the code

These are the pauses we are making while executing the code:

```
function f(x) {
  function square() {
    const result = x * x;
    // Pause 3
    return result;
  }
  // Pause 2
  return square();
}
// Pause 1
assert.equal(f(6), 36);
```

This is what happens:

- Pause 1 – before calling `f()` (fig. 26.4).
- Pause 2 – while executing `f()` (fig. 26.5).
- Pause 3 – while executing `square()` (fig. 26.6).
- After that, `return` statements pop execution entries off the stack.

26.3 Nested scopes via environments

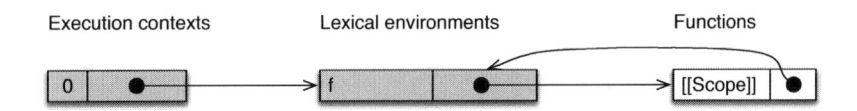

Figure 26.4: Nested scopes, pause 1 – before calling f(): The top-level environment has a single entry, for f(). The birth environment of f() is the top-level environment. Therefore, f's [[Scope]] points to it.

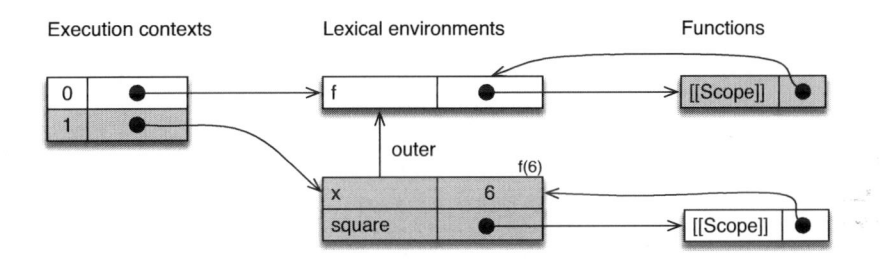

Figure 26.5: Nested scopes, pause 2 – while executing f(): There is now an environment for the function call f(6). The outer environment of that environment is the birth environment of f() (the top-level environment at index 0). We can see that the field outer was set to the value of f's [[Scope]]. Furthermore, the [[Scope]] of the new function square() is the environment that was just created.

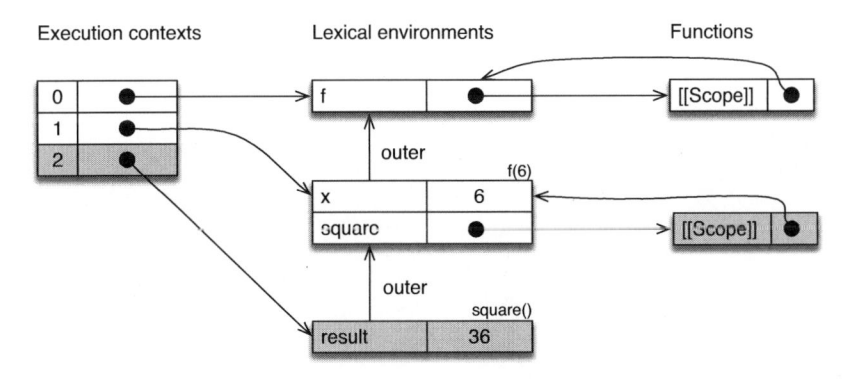

Figure 26.6: Nested scopes, pause 3 – while executing square(): The previous pattern was repeated: the outer of the most recent environment was set up via the [[Scope]] of the function that we just called. The chain of scopes created via outer, contains all variables that are active right now. For example, we can access result, square, and f if we want to. Environments reflect two aspects of variables. First, the chain of outer environments reflects the nested static scopes. Second, the stack of execution contexts reflects what function calls were made, dynamically.

26.4 Closures and environments

To see how environments are used to implement closures (p. 88), we are using the following example:

```
function add(x) {
  return (y) => { // (A)
    return x + y;
  };
}
assert.equal(add(3)(1), 4); // (B)
```

What is going on here? `add()` is a function that returns a function. When we make the nested function call `add(3)(1)` in line B, the first parameter is for `add()`, the second parameter is for the function it returns. This works because the function created in line A does not lose the connection to its birth scope when it leaves that scope. The associated environment is kept alive by that connection and the function still has access to variable x in that environment (x is free inside the function).

This nested way of calling `add()` has an advantage: if you only make the first function call, you get a version of `add()` whose parameter x is already filled in:

```
const plus2 = add(2);
assert.equal(plus2(5), 7);
```

Converting a function with two parameters into two nested functions with one parameter each, is called *currying*. `add()` is a curried function.

Only filling in some of the parameters of a function is called *partial application* (the function has not been fully applied yet). Method `.bind()` of functions (p. 270) performs partial application. In the previous example, we can see that partial application is simple if a function is curried.

26.4.0.1 Executing the code

As we are executing the following code, we are making three pauses:

```
function add(x) {
  return (y) => {
    // Pause 3: plus2(5)
    return x + y;
  }; // Pause 1: add(2)
}
const plus2 = add(2);
// Pause 2
assert.equal(plus2(5), 7);
```

This is what happens:

- Pause 1 – during the execution of `add(2)` (fig. 26.7).
- Pause 2 – after the execution of `add(2)` (fig. 26.8).
- Pause 3 – while executing `plus2(5)` (fig. 26.9).

26.4 Closures and environments

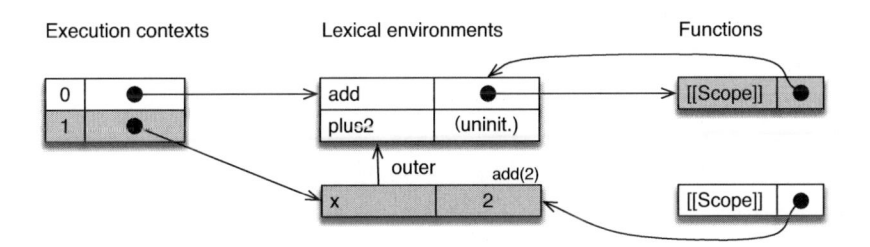

Figure 26.7: Closures, pause 1 – during the execution of add(2): We can see that the function returned by add() already exists (see bottom right corner) and that it points to its birth environment via its internal property [[Scope]]. Note that plus2 is still in its temporal dead zone and uninitialized.

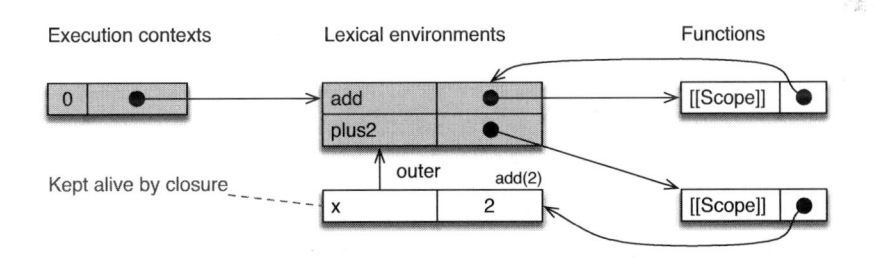

Figure 26.8: Closures, pause 2 – after the execution of add(2): plus2 now points to the function returned by add(2). That function keeps its birth environment (the environment of add(2)) alive via its [[Scope]].

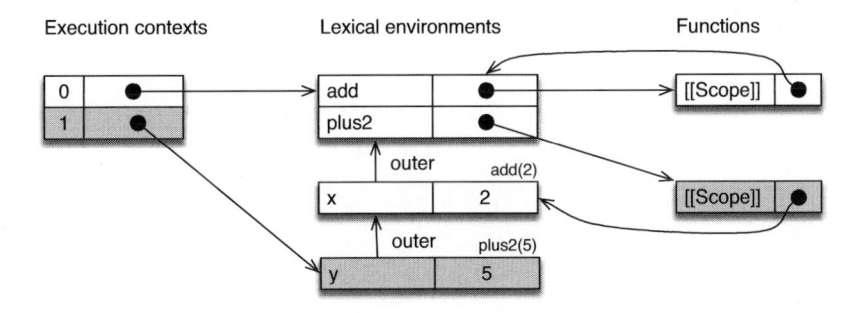

Figure 26.9: Closures, pause 3 – while executing plus2(5): The [[Scope]] of plus2 is used to set up the outer of the new environment. That's how the current function gets access to x.

Part VI

Modularity

Chapter 27

Modules

Contents

27.1 Overview: syntax of ECMAScript modules 238
    27.1.1 Exporting 238
    27.1.2 Importing 238
27.2 JavaScript source code formats 239
    27.2.1 Code before built-in modules was written in ECMAScript 5 . . 239
27.3 Before we had modules, we had scripts 239
27.4 Module systems created prior to ES6 240
    27.4.1 Server side: CommonJS modules 241
    27.4.2 Client side: AMD (Asynchronous Module Definition) modules 241
    27.4.3 Characteristics of JavaScript modules 242
27.5 ECMAScript modules 243
    27.5.1 ES modules: syntax, semantics, loader API 243
27.6 Named exports and imports 243
    27.6.1 Named exports 243
    27.6.2 Named imports 244
    27.6.3 Namespace imports 245
    27.6.4 Named exporting styles: inline versus clause (advanced) . . . 245
27.7 Default exports and imports 246
    27.7.1 The two styles of default-exporting 246
    27.7.2 The default export as a named export (advanced) 247
27.8 More details on exporting and importing 248
    27.8.1 Imports are read-only views on exports 248
    27.8.2 ESM's transparent support for cyclic imports (advanced) . . . 249
27.9 npm packages 249
    27.9.1 Packages are installed inside a directory `node_modules/` 250
    27.9.2 Why can npm be used to install frontend libraries? 251
27.10 Naming modules 251
27.11 Module specifiers 252

27.11.1 Categories of module specifiers 252
27.11.2 ES module specifiers in browsers 252
27.11.3 ES module specifiers on Node.js 253
27.12 Loading modules dynamically via `import()` 254
27.12.1 Example: loading a module dynamically 254
27.12.2 Use cases for `import()` 256
27.13 Preview: `import.meta.url` 256
27.13.1 `import.meta.url` and class `URL` 256
27.13.2 `import.meta.url` on Node.js 257
27.14 Polyfills: emulating native web platform features (advanced) 258
27.14.1 Sources of this section 259

27.1 Overview: syntax of ECMAScript modules

27.1.1 Exporting

```
// Named exports
export function f() {}
export const one = 1;
export {foo, b as bar};

// Default exports
export default function f() {} // declaration with optional name
// Replacement for `const` (there must be exactly one value)
export default 123;

// Re-exporting from another module
export * from './some-module.mjs';
export {foo, b as bar} from './some-module.mjs';
```

27.1.2 Importing

```
// Named imports
import {foo, bar as b} from './some-module.mjs';
// Namespace import
import * as someModule from './some-module.mjs';
// Default import
import someModule from './some-module.mjs';

// Combinations:
import someModule, * as someModule from './some-module.mjs';
import someModule, {foo, bar as b} from './some-module.mjs';

// Empty import (for modules with side effects)
import './some-module.mjs';
```

27.2 JavaScript source code formats

The current landscape of JavaScript modules is quite diverse: ES6 brought built-in modules, but the source code formats that came before them, are still around, too. Understanding the latter helps understand the former, so let's investigate. The next sections describe the following ways of delivering JavaScript source code:

- *Scripts* are code fragments that browsers run in global scope. They are precursors of modules.
- *CommonJS modules* are a module format that is mainly used on servers (e.g., via Node.js).
- *AMD modules* are a module format that is mainly used in browsers.
- *ECMAScript modules* are JavaScript's built-in module format. It supersedes all previous formats.

Tbl. 27.1 gives an overview of these code formats. Note that for CommonJS modules and ECMAScript modules, two filename extensions are commonly used. Which one is appropriate depends on how you want to use a file. Details are given later in this chapter.

Table 27.1: Ways of delivering JavaScript source code.

	Runs on	Loaded	Filename ext.
Script	browsers	async	`.js`
CommonJS module	servers	sync	`.js` `.cjs`
AMD module	browsers	async	`.js`
ECMAScript module	browsers and servers	async	`.js` `.mjs`

27.2.1 Code before built-in modules was written in ECMAScript 5

Before we get to built-in modules (which were introduced with ES6), all code that you'll see, will be written in ES5. Among other things:

- ES5 did not have `const` and `let`, only `var`.
- ES5 did not have arrow functions, only function expressions.

27.3 Before we had modules, we had scripts

Initially, browsers only had *scripts* – pieces of code that were executed in global scope. As an example, consider an HTML file that loads script files via the following HTML:

```
<script src="other-module1.js"></script>
<script src="other-module2.js"></script>
<script src="my-module.js"></script>
```

The main file is `my-module.js`, where we simulate a module:

```
var myModule = (function () { // Open IIFE
  // Imports (via global variables)
  var importedFunc1 = otherModule1.importedFunc1;
```

```
    var importedFunc2 = otherModule2.importedFunc2;

    // Body
    function internalFunc() {
      // ···
    }
    function exportedFunc() {
      importedFunc1();
      importedFunc2();
      internalFunc();
    }

    // Exports (assigned to global variable `myModule`)
    return {
      exportedFunc: exportedFunc,
    };
})(); // Close IIFE
```

myModule is a global variable that is assigned the result of immediately invoking a function expression. The function expression starts in the first line. It is invoked in the last line.

This way of wrapping a code fragment is called *immediately invoked function expression* (IIFE, coined by Ben Alman). What do we gain from an IIFE? var is not block-scoped (like const and let), it is function-scoped: the only way to create new scopes for var-declared variables is via functions or methods (with const and let, you can use either functions, methods, or blocks {}). Therefore, the IIFE in the example hides all of the following variables from global scope and minimizes name clashes: importedFunc1, importedFunc2, internalFunc, exportedFunc.

Note that we are using an IIFE in a particular manner: at the end, we pick what we want to export and return it via an object literal. That is called the *revealing module pattern* (coined by Christian Heilmann).

This way of simulating modules, has several issues:

- Libraries in script files export and import functionality via global variables, which risks name clashes.
- Dependencies are not stated explicitly, and there is no built-in way for a script to load the scripts it depends on. Therefore, the web page has to load not just the scripts that are needed by the page but also the dependencies of those scripts, the dependencies' dependencies, etc. And it has to do so in the right order!

27.4 Module systems created prior to ES6

Prior to ECMAScript 6, JavaScript did not have built-in modules. Therefore, the flexible syntax of the language was used to implement custom module systems *within* the language. Two popular ones are:

- CommonJS (targeting the server side)

27.4 Module systems created prior to ES6

- AMD (Asynchronous Module Definition, targeting the client side)

27.4.1 Server side: CommonJS modules

The original CommonJS standard for modules was created for server and desktop platforms. It was the foundation of the original Node.js module system, where it achieved enormous popularity. Contributing to that popularity were the npm package manager for Node and tools that enabled using Node modules on the client side (browserify, webpack, and others).

From now on, *CommonJS module* means the Node.js version of this standard (which has a few additional features). This is an example of a CommonJS module:

```
// Imports
var importedFunc1 = require('./other-module1.js').importedFunc1;
var importedFunc2 = require('./other-module2.js').importedFunc2;

// Body
function internalFunc() {
  // ···
}
function exportedFunc() {
  importedFunc1();
  importedFunc2();
  internalFunc();
}

// Exports
module.exports = {
  exportedFunc: exportedFunc,
};
```

CommonJS can be characterized as follows:

- Designed for servers.
- Modules are meant to be loaded *synchronously* (the importer waits while the imported module is loaded and executed).
- Compact syntax.

27.4.2 Client side: AMD (Asynchronous Module Definition) modules

The AMD module format was created to be easier to use in browsers than the CommonJS format. Its most popular implementation is RequireJS[1]. The following is an example of an AMD module.

```
define(['./other-module1.js', './other-module2.js'],
  function (otherModule1, otherModule2) {
    var importedFunc1 = otherModule1.importedFunc1;
    var importedFunc2 = otherModule2.importedFunc2;
```

---
[1] https://requirejs.org

```
    function internalFunc() {
      // ···
    }
    function exportedFunc() {
      importedFunc1();
      importedFunc2();
      internalFunc();
    }

    return {
      exportedFunc: exportedFunc,
    };
  });
```

AMD can be characterized as follows:

- Designed for browsers.
- Modules are meant to be loaded *asynchronously*. That's a crucial requirement for browsers, where code can't wait until a module has finished downloading. It has to be notified once the module is available.
- The syntax is slightly more complicated.

On the plus side, AMD modules can be executed directly. In contrast, CommonJS modules must either be compiled before deployment or custom source code must be generated and evaluated dynamically (think `eval()`, p. 224). That isn't always permitted on the web.

27.4.3 Characteristics of JavaScript modules

Looking at CommonJS and AMD, similarities between JavaScript module systems emerge:

- There is one module per file.
- Such a file is basically a piece of code that is executed:
  - Local scope: The code is executed in a local "module scope". Therefore, by default, all of the variables, functions, and classes declared in it are internal and not global.
  - Exports: If you want any declared entity to be exported, you must explicitly mark it as an export.
  - Imports: Each module can import exported entities from other modules. Those other modules are identified via *module specifiers* (usually paths, occasionally full URLs).
- Modules are *singletons*: Even if a module is imported multiple times, only a single "instance" of it exists.
- No global variables are used. Instead, module specifiers serve as global IDs.

27.5 ECMAScript modules

ECMAScript modules (*ES modules* or *ESM*) were introduced with ES6. They continue the tradition of JavaScript modules and have all of their aforementioned characteristics. Additionally:

- With CommonJS, ES modules share the compact syntax and support for cyclic dependencies.
- With AMD, ES modules share being designed for asynchronous loading.

ES modules also have new benefits:

- The syntax is even more compact than CommonJS's.
- Modules have *static* structures (which can't be changed at runtime). That helps with static checking, optimized access of imports, dead code elimination, and more.
- Support for cyclic imports is completely transparent.

This is an example of ES module syntax:

```
import {importedFunc1} from './other-module1.mjs';
import {importedFunc2} from './other-module2.mjs';

function internalFunc() {
  ...
}

export function exportedFunc() {
  importedFunc1();
  importedFunc2();
  internalFunc();
}
```

From now on, "module" means "ECMAScript module".

27.5.1 ES modules: syntax, semantics, loader API

The full standard of ES modules comprises the following parts:

1. Syntax (how code is written): What is a module? How are imports and exports declared? Etc.
2. Semantics (how code is executed): How are variable bindings exported? How are imports connected with exports? Etc.
3. A programmatic loader API for configuring module loading.

Parts 1 and 2 were introduced with ES6. Work on part 3 is ongoing.

27.6 Named exports and imports

27.6.1 Named exports

Each module can have zero or more *named exports*.

As an example, consider the following two files:

```
lib/my-math.mjs
main.mjs
```

Module `my-math.mjs` has two named exports: `square` and `LIGHTSPEED`.

```
// Not exported, private to module
function times(a, b) {
  return a * b;
}
export function square(x) {
  return times(x, x);
}
export const LIGHTSPEED = 299792458;
```

To export something, we put the keyword `export` in front of a declaration. Entities that are not exported are private to a module and can't be accessed from outside.

27.6.2 Named imports

Module `main.mjs` has a single named import, `square`:

```
import {square} from './lib/my-math.mjs';
assert.equal(square(3), 9);
```

It can also rename its import:

```
import {square as sq} from './lib/my-math.mjs';
assert.equal(sq(3), 9);
```

27.6.2.1 Syntactic pitfall: named importing is not destructuring

Both named importing and destructuring look similar:

```
import {foo} from './bar.mjs'; // import
const {foo} = require('./bar.mjs'); // destructuring
```

But they are quite different:

- Imports remain connected with their exports.

- You can destructure again inside a destructuring pattern, but the {} in an import statement can't be nested.

- The syntax for renaming is different:

    ```
    import {foo as f} from './bar.mjs'; // importing
    const {foo: f} = require('./bar.mjs'); // destructuring
    ```

    Rationale: Destructuring is reminiscent of an object literal (including nesting), while importing evokes the idea of renaming.

> ![puzzle] **Exercise: Named exports**
> `exercises/modules/export_named_test.mjs`

27.6.3 Namespace imports

Namespace imports are an alternative to named imports. If we namespace-import a module, it becomes an object whose properties are the named exports. This is what `main.mjs` looks like if we use a namespace import:

```
import * as myMath from './lib/my-math.mjs';
assert.equal(myMath.square(3), 9);

assert.deepEqual(
  Object.keys(myMath), ['LIGHTSPEED', 'square']);
```

27.6.4 Named exporting styles: inline versus clause (advanced)

The named export style we have seen so far was *inline*: We exported entities by prefixing them with the keyword `export`.

But we can also use separate *export clauses*. For example, this is what `lib/my-math.mjs` looks like with an export clause:

```
function times(a, b) {
  return a * b;
}
function square(x) {
  return times(x, x);
}
const LIGHTSPEED = 299792458;

export { square, LIGHTSPEED }; // semicolon!
```

With an export clause, we can rename before exporting and use different names internally:

```
function times(a, b) {
  return a * b;
}
function sq(x) {
  return times(x, x);
}
const LS = 299792458;

export {
  sq as square,
  LS as LIGHTSPEED, // trailing comma is optional
};
```

27.7 Default exports and imports

Each module can have at most one *default export*. The idea is that the module *is* the default-exported value.

> 💡 **Avoid mixing named exports and default exports**
>
> A module can have both named exports and a default export, but it's usually better to stick to one export style per module.

As an example for default exports, consider the following two files:

```
my-func.mjs
main.mjs
```

Module `my-func.mjs` has a default export:

```
const GREETING = 'Hello!';
export default function () {
  return GREETING;
}
```

Module `main.mjs` default-imports the exported function:

```
import myFunc from './my-func.mjs';
assert.equal(myFunc(), 'Hello!');
```

Note the syntactic difference: the curly braces around named imports indicate that we are reaching *into* the module, while a default import *is* the module.

> ❓ **What are use cases for default exports?**
>
> The most common use case for a default export is a module that contains a single function or a single class.

27.7.1 The two styles of default-exporting

There are two styles of doing default exports.

First, you can label existing declarations with `export default`:

```
export default function foo() {} // no semicolon!
export default class Bar {} // no semicolon!
```

Second, you can directly default-export values. In that style, `export default` is itself much like a declaration.

```
export default 'abc';
export default foo();
export default /^xyz$/;
```

27.7 Default exports and imports

```
export default 5 * 7;
export default { no: false, yes: true };
```

27.7.1.1 Why are there two default export styles?

The reason is that `export default` can't be used to label `const`: `const` may define multiple values, but `export default` needs exactly one value. Consider the following hypothetical code:

```
// Not legal JavaScript!
export default const foo = 1, bar = 2, baz = 3;
```

With this code, you don't know which one of the three values is the default export.

> Exercise: Default exports
> `exercises/modules/export_default_test.mjs`

27.7.2 The default export as a named export (advanced)

Internally, a default export is simply a named export whose name is `default`. As an example, consider the previous module `my-func.mjs` with a default export:

```
const GREETING = 'Hello!';
export default function () {
  return GREETING;
}
```

The following module `my-func2.mjs` is equivalent to that module:

```
const GREETING = 'Hello!';
function greet() {
  return GREETING;
}

export {
  greet as default,
};
```

For importing, we can use a normal default import:

```
import myFunc from './my-func2.mjs';
assert.equal(myFunc(), 'Hello!');
```

Or we can use a named import:

```
import {default as myFunc} from './my-func2.mjs';
assert.equal(myFunc(), 'Hello!');
```

The default export is also available via property `.default` of namespace imports:

```
import * as mf from './my-func2.mjs';
assert.equal(mf.default(), 'Hello!');
```

> **? Isn't default illegal as a variable name?**
>
> `default` can't be a variable name, but it can be an export name and it can be a property name:
>
> ```
> const obj = {
>   default: 123,
> };
> assert.equal(obj.default, 123);
> ```

27.8 More details on exporting and importing

27.8.1 Imports are read-only views on exports

So far, we have used imports and exports intuitively, and everything seems to have worked as expected. But now it is time to take a closer look at how imports and exports are really related.

Consider the following two modules:

```
counter.mjs
main.mjs
```

`counter.mjs` exports a (mutable!) variable and a function:

```
export let counter = 3;
export function incCounter() {
  counter++;
}
```

`main.mjs` name-imports both exports. When we use `incCounter()`, we discover that the connection to `counter` is live – we can always access the live state of that variable:

```
import { counter, incCounter } from './counter.mjs';

// The imported value `counter` is live
assert.equal(counter, 3);
incCounter();
assert.equal(counter, 4);
```

Note that while the connection is live and we can read `counter`, we cannot change this variable (e.g., via `counter++`).

There are two benefits to handling imports this way:

- It is easier to split modules because previously shared variables can become exports.
- This behavior is crucial for supporting transparent cyclic imports. Read on for more information.

27.8.2 ESM's transparent support for cyclic imports (advanced)

ESM supports cyclic imports transparently. To understand how that is achieved, consider the following example: fig. 27.1 shows a directed graph of modules importing other modules. P importing M is the cycle in this case.

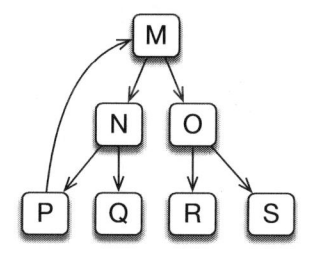

Figure 27.1: A directed graph of modules importing modules: M imports N and O, N imports P and Q, etc.

After parsing, these modules are set up in two phases:

- Instantiation: Every module is visited and its imports are connected to its exports. Before a parent can be instantiated, all of its children must be instantiated.
- Evaluation: The bodies of the modules are executed. Once again, children are evaluated before parents.

This approach handles cyclic imports correctly, due to two features of ES modules:

- Due to the static structure of ES modules, the exports are already known after parsing. That makes it possible to instantiate P before its child M: P can already look up M's exports.

- When P is evaluated, M hasn't been evaluated, yet. However, entities in P can already mention imports from M. They just can't use them, yet, because the imported values are filled in later. For example, a function in P can access an import from M. The only limitation is that we must wait until after the evaluation of M, before calling that function.

  Imports being filled in later is enabled by them being "live immutable views" on exports.

27.9 npm packages

The *npm software registry* is the dominant way of distributing JavaScript libraries and apps for Node.js and web browsers. It is managed via the *npm package manager* (short: *npm*). Software is distributed as so-called *packages*. A package is a directory containing arbitrary files and a file `package.json` at the top level that describes the package. For example, when npm creates an empty package inside a directory `foo/`, you get this `package.json`:

```
{
  "name": "foo",
  "version": "1.0.0",
```

```
  "description": "",
  "main": "index.js",
  "scripts": {
    "test": "echo \"Error: no test specified\" && exit 1"
  },
  "keywords": [],
  "author": "",
  "license": "ISC"
}
```

Some of these properties contain simple metadata:

- `name` specifies the name of this package. Once it is uploaded to the npm registry, it can be installed via `npm install foo`.
- `version` is used for version management and follows semantic versioning[2], with three numbers:
  - Major version: is incremented when incompatible API changes are made.
  - Minor version: is incremented when functionality is added in a backward compatible manner.
  - Patch version: is incremented when backward compatible changes are made.
- `description`, `keywords`, `author` make it easier to find packages.
- `license` clarifies how you can use this package.

Other properties enable advanced configuration:

- `main`: specifies the module that "is" the package (explained later in this chapter).
- `scripts`: are commands that you can execute via `npm run`. For example, the script `test` can be executed via `npm run test`.

For more information on `package.json`, consult the npm documentation[3].

27.9.1 Packages are installed inside a directory `node_modules/`

npm always installs packages inside a directory `node_modules`. There are usually many of these directories. Which one npm uses, depends on the directory where one currently is. For example, if we are inside a directory `/tmp/a/b/`, npm tries to find a `node_modules` in the current directory, its parent directory, the parent directory of the parent, etc. In other words, it searches the following *chain* of locations:

- `/tmp/a/b/node_modules`
- `/tmp/a/node_modules`
- `/tmp/node_modules`

When installing a package `foo`, npm uses the closest `node_modules`. If, for example, we are inside `/tmp/a/b/` and there is a `node_modules` in that directory, then npm puts the package inside the directory:

`/tmp/a/b/node_modules/foo/`

---

[2] https://semver.org
[3] https://docs.npmjs.com/files/package.json

When importing a module, we can use a special module specifier to tell Node.js that we want to import it from an installed package. How exactly that works, is explained later. For now, consider the following example:

```
// /home/jane/proj/main.mjs
import * as theModule from 'the-package/the-module.mjs';
```

To find `the-module.mjs` (Node.js prefers the filename extension `.mjs` for ES modules), Node.js walks up the `node_module` chain and searches the following locations:

- `/home/jane/proj/node_modules/the-package/the-module.mjs`
- `/home/jane/node_modules/the-package/the-module.mjs`
- `/home/node_modules/the-package/the-module.mjs`

27.9.2 Why can npm be used to install frontend libraries?

Finding installed modules in `node_modules` directories is only supported on Node.js. So why can we also use npm to install libraries for browsers?

That is enabled via bundling tools (p. 515), such as webpack, that compile and optimize code before it is deployed online. During this compilation process, the code in npm packages is adapted so that it works in browsers.

27.10 Naming modules

There are no established best practices for naming module files and the variables they are imported into.

In this chapter, I'm using the following naming style:

- The names of module files are dash-cased and start with lowercase letters:

    ```
    ./my-module.mjs
    ./some-func.mjs
    ```

- The names of namespace imports are lowercased and camel-cased:

    ```
    import * as myModule from './my-module.mjs';
    ```

- The names of default imports are lowercased and camel-cased:

    ```
    import someFunc from './some-func.mjs';
    ```

What are the rationales behind this style?

- npm doesn't allow uppercase letters in package names (source[4]). Thus, we avoid camel case, so that "local" files have names that are consistent with those of npm packages. Using only lowercase letters also minimizes conflicts between file systems that are case-sensitive and file systems that aren't: the former distinguish files whose names have the same letters, but with different cases; the latter don't.

---

[4]https://docs.npmjs.com/files/package.json#name

- There are clear rules for translating dash-cased file names to camel-cased JavaScript variable names. Due to how we name namespace imports, these rules work for both namespace imports and default imports.

I also like underscore-cased module file names because you can directly use these names for namespace imports (without any translation):

```
import * as my_module from './my_module.mjs';
```

But that style does not work for default imports: I like underscore-casing for namespace objects, but it is not a good choice for functions, etc.

27.11 Module specifiers

Module specifiers are the strings that identify modules. They work slightly differently in browsers and Node.js. Before we can look at the differences, we need to learn about the different categories of module specifiers.

27.11.1 Categories of module specifiers

In ES modules, we distinguish the following categories of specifiers. These categories originated with CommonJS modules.

- Relative path: starts with a dot. Examples:

    ```
    './some/other/module.mjs'
    '../../lib/counter.mjs'
    ```

- Absolute path: starts with a slash. Example:

    ```
    '/home/jane/file-tools.mjs'
    ```

- URL: includes a protocol (technically, paths are URLs, too). Examples:

    ```
    'https://example.com/some-module.mjs'
    'file:///home/john/tmp/main.mjs'
    ```

- Bare path: does not start with a dot, a slash or a protocol, and consists of a single filename without an extension. Examples:

    ```
    'lodash'
    'the-package'
    ```

- Deep import path: starts with a bare path and has at least one slash. Example:

    ```
    'the-package/dist/the-module.mjs'
    ```

27.11.2 ES module specifiers in browsers

Browsers handle module specifiers as follows:

- Relative paths, absolute paths, and URLs work as expected. They all must point to real files (in contrast to CommonJS, which lets you omit filename extensions and more).

27.11 Module specifiers

- The file name extensions of modules don't matter, as long as they are served with the content type text/javascript.
- How bare paths will end up being handled is not yet clear. You will probably eventually be able to map them to other specifiers via lookup tables.

Note that bundling tools (p. 515) such as webpack, which combine modules into fewer files, are often less strict with specifiers than browsers. That's because they operate at build/compile time (not at runtime) and can search for files by traversing the file system.

27.11.3 ES module specifiers on Node.js

> ⚠ **Support for ES modules on Node.js is still new**
>
> You may have to switch it on via a command line flag. See the Node.js documentation[a] for details.
>
> [a]https://nodejs.org/api/esm.html

Node.js handles module specifiers as follows:

- Relative paths are resolved as they are in web browsers – relative to the path of the current module.
- Absolute paths are currently not supported. As a workaround, you can use URLs that start with file:///. You can create such URLs via url.pathToFileURL() (p. 257).
- Only file: is supported as a protocol for URL specifiers.
- A bare path is interpreted as a package name and resolved relative to the closest node_modules directory. What module should be loaded, is determined by looking at property "main" of the package's package.json (similarly to CommonJS).
- Deep import paths are also resolved relatively to the closest node_modules directory. They contain file names, so it is always clear which module is meant.

All specifiers, except bare paths, must refer to actual files. That is, ESM does not support the following CommonJS features:

- CommonJS automatically adds missing filename extensions.
- CommonJS can import a directory foo if there is a foo/package.json with a "main" property.
- CommonJS can import a directory foo if there is a module foo/index.js.

All built-in Node.js modules are available via bare paths and have named ESM exports – for example:

```
import * as path from 'path';
import {strict as assert} from 'assert';
```

```
assert.equal(
  path.join('a/b/c', '../d'), 'a/b/d');
```

27.11.3.1 Filename extensions on Node.js

Node.js supports the following default filename extensions:

- `.mjs` for ES modules
- `.cjs` for CommonJS modules

The filename extension `.js` stands for either ESM or CommonJS. Which one it is is configured via the "closest" `package.json` (in the current directory, the parent directory, etc.). Using `package.json` in this manner is independent of packages.

In that `package.json`, there is a property `"type"`, which has two settings:

- `"commonjs"` (the default): files with the extension `.js` or without an extension are interpreted as CommonJS modules.
- `"module"`: files with the extension `.js` or without an extension are interpreted as ESM modules.

27.11.3.2 Interpreting non-file source code as either CommonJS or ESM

Not all source code executed by Node.js comes from files. You can also send it code via stdin, `--eval`, and `--print`. The command line option `--input-type` lets you specify how such code is interpreted:

- As CommonJS (the default): `--input-type=commonjs`
- As ESM: `--input-type=module`

27.12 Loading modules dynamically via `import()`

So far, the only way to import a module has been via an `import` statement. That statement has several limitations:

- You must use it at the top level of a module. That is, you can't, for example, import something when you are inside a block.
- The module specifier is always fixed. That is, you can't change what you import depending on a condition. And you can't assemble a specifier dynamically.

The `import()` operator changes that. Let's look at an example of it being used.

27.12.1 Example: loading a module dynamically

Consider the following files:

```
lib/my-math.mjs
main1.mjs
main2.mjs
```

We have already seen module `my-math.mjs`:

27.12 Loading modules dynamically via `import()`

```
// Not exported, private to module
function times(a, b) {
  return a * b;
}
export function square(x) {
  return times(x, x);
}
export const LIGHTSPEED = 299792458;
```

This is what using `import()` looks like in `main1.mjs`:

```
const dir = './lib/';
const moduleSpecifier = dir + 'my-math.mjs';

function loadConstant() {
  return import(moduleSpecifier)
  .then(myMath => {
    const result = myMath.LIGHTSPEED;
    assert.equal(result, 299792458);
    return result;
  });
}
```

Method `.then()` is part of *Promises*, a mechanism for handling asynchronous results, which is covered later in this book (p. 427).

Two things in this code weren't possible before:

- We are importing inside a function (not at the top level).
- The module specifier comes from a variable.

Next, we'll implement the exact same functionality in `main2.mjs` but via a so-called *async function*, which provides nicer syntax for Promises.

```
const dir = './lib/';
const moduleSpecifier = dir + 'my-math.mjs';

async function loadConstant() {
  const myMath = await import(moduleSpecifier);
  const result = myMath.LIGHTSPEED;
  assert.equal(result, 299792458);
  return result;
}
```

> **❓ Why is `import()` an operator and not a function?**
>
> Even though it works much like a function, `import()` is an operator: in order to resolve module specifiers relatively to the current module, it needs to know from which module it is invoked. A normal function cannot receive this information as implicitly as an operator can. It would need, for example, a parameter.

27.12.2 Use cases for `import()`

27.12.2.1 Loading code on demand

Some functionality of web apps doesn't have to be present when they start, it can be loaded on demand. Then `import()` helps because you can put such functionality into modules – for example:

```
button.addEventListener('click', event => {
  import('./dialogBox.mjs')
    .then(dialogBox => {
      dialogBox.open();
    })
    .catch(error => {
      /* Error handling */
    })
});
```

27.12.2.2 Conditional loading of modules

We may want to load a module depending on whether a condition is true. For example, a module with a polyfill (p. 258) that makes a new feature available on legacy platforms:

```
if (isLegacyPlatform()) {
  import('./my-polyfill.mjs')
    .then(···);
}
```

27.12.2.3 Computed module specifiers

For applications such as internationalization, it helps if you can dynamically compute module specifiers:

```
import(`messages_${getLocale()}.mjs`)
  .then(···);
```

27.13 Preview: `import.meta.url`

"import.meta"[5] is an ECMAScript feature proposed by Domenic Denicola. The object `import.meta` holds metadata for the current module.

Its most important property is `import.meta.url`, which contains a string with the URL of the current module file. For example:

```
'https://example.com/code/main.mjs'
```

27.13.1 `import.meta.url` and class `URL`

Class URL is available via a global variable in browsers and on Node.js. You can look up its full functionality in the Node.js documentation[6]. When working with `import.meta.url`,

---

[5] https://github.com/tc39/proposal-import-meta
[6] https://nodejs.org/api/url.html#url_class_url

27.13 Preview: `import.meta.url`

its constructor is especially useful:

```
new URL(input: string, base?: string|URL)
```

Parameter `input` contains the URL to be parsed. It can be relative if the second parameter, `base`, is provided.

In other words, this constructor lets us resolve a relative path against a base URL:

```
> new URL('other.mjs', 'https://example.com/code/main.mjs').href
'https://example.com/code/other.mjs'
> new URL('../other.mjs', 'https://example.com/code/main.mjs').href
'https://example.com/other.mjs'
```

This is how we get a URL instance that points to a file `data.txt` that sits next to the current module:

```
const urlOfData = new URL('data.txt', import.meta.url);
```

27.13.2 `import.meta.url` on Node.js

On Node.js, `import.meta.url` is always a string with a `file:` URL – for example:

```
'file:///Users/rauschma/my-module.mjs'
```

27.13.2.1 Example: reading a sibling file of a module

Many Node.js file system operations accept either strings with paths or instances of URL. That enables us to read a sibling file `data.txt` of the current module:

```
import {promises as fs} from 'fs';

async function main() {
  const urlOfData = new URL('data.txt', import.meta.url);
  const str = await fs.readFile(urlOfData, {encoding: 'UTF-8'});
  assert.equal(str, 'This is textual data.\n');
}
main();
```

`main()` is an async function, as explained in §41 "Async functions" (p. 447).

`fs.promises`[7] contains a Promise-based version of the `fs` API, which can be used with async functions.

27.13.2.2 Converting between `file:` URLs and paths

The Node.js module `url`[8] has two functions for converting between `file:` URLs and paths:

- `fileURLToPath(url: URL|string): string`
  Converts a `file:` URL to a path.

---
[7] https://nodejs.org/api/fs.html#fs_fs_promises_api
[8] https://nodejs.org/api/url.html

- pathToFileURL(path: string): URL
  Converts a path to a `file:` URL.

If you need a path that can be used in the local file system, then property `.pathname` of URL instances does not always work:

```
assert.equal(
  new URL('file:///tmp/with%20space.txt').pathname,
  '/tmp/with%20space.txt');
```

Therefore, it is better to use `fileURLToPath()`:

```
import * as url from 'url';
assert.equal(
  url.fileURLToPath('file:///tmp/with%20space.txt'),
  '/tmp/with space.txt'); // result on Unix
```

Similarly, `pathToFileURL()` does more than just prepend `'file://'` to an absolute path.

27.14 Polyfills: emulating native web platform features (advanced)

> **Backends have polyfills, too**
>
> This section is about frontend development and web browsers, but similar ideas apply to backend development.

Polyfills help with a conflict that we are facing when developing a web application in JavaScript:

- On one hand, we want to use modern web platform features that make the app better and/or development easier.
- On the other hand, the app should run on as many browsers as possible.

Given a web platform feature X:

- A *polyfill* for X is a piece of code. If it is executed on a platform that already has built-in support for X, it does nothing. Otherwise, it makes the feature available on the platform. In the latter case, the polyfilled feature is (mostly) indistinguishable from a native implementation. In order to achieve that, the polyfill usually makes global changes. For example, it may modify global data or configure a global module loader. Polyfills are often packaged as modules.
    - The term *polyfill*[9] was coined by Remy Sharp.
- A *speculative polyfill* is a polyfill for a proposed web platform feature (that is not standardized, yet).
    - Alternative term: *prollyfill*
- A *replica* of X is a library that reproduces the API and functionality of X locally. Such a library exists independently of a native (and global) implementation of X.
    - *Replica* is a new term introduced in this section. Alternative term: *ponyfill*

---
[9] https://remysharp.com/2010/10/08/what-is-a-polyfill

27.14 Polyfills: emulating native web platform features (advanced)

- There is also the term *shim*, but it doesn't have a universally agreed upon definition. It often means roughly the same as *polyfill*.

Every time our web applications starts, it must first execute all polyfills for features that may not be available everywhere. Afterwards, we can be sure that those features are available natively.

27.14.1 Sources of this section

- "What is a Polyfill?"[10] by Remy Sharp
- Inspiration for the term *replica*: The Eiffel Tower in Las Vegas[11]
- Useful clarification of "polyfill" and related terms: "Polyfills and the evolution of the Web"[12]. Edited by Andrew Betts.

Quiz

See quiz app (p. 71).

---

[10]https://remysharp.com/2010/10/08/what-is-a-polyfill
[11]https://en.wikipedia.org/wiki/Paris_Las_Vegas
[12]https://www.w3.org/2001/tag/doc/polyfills/

Chapter 28

Single objects

Contents

- **28.1 What is an object?** 262
  - 28.1.1 Roles of objects: record vs. dictionary 263
- **28.2 Objects as records** 263
  - 28.2.1 Object literals: properties 263
  - 28.2.2 Object literals: property value shorthands 264
  - 28.2.3 Getting properties 264
  - 28.2.4 Setting properties 264
  - 28.2.5 Object literals: methods 265
  - 28.2.6 Object literals: accessors 265
- **28.3 Spreading into object literals (...)** 266
  - 28.3.1 Use case for spreading: copying objects 267
  - 28.3.2 Use case for spreading: default values for missing properties 267
  - 28.3.3 Use case for spreading: non-destructively changing properties 268
- **28.4 Methods** 268
  - 28.4.1 Methods are properties whose values are functions 268
  - 28.4.2 `.call()`: specifying `this` via a parameter 269
  - 28.4.3 `.bind()`: pre-filling `this` and parameters of functions 270
  - 28.4.4 `this` pitfall: extracting methods 271
  - 28.4.5 `this` pitfall: accidentally shadowing `this` 272
  - 28.4.6 Avoiding the pitfalls of `this` 274
  - 28.4.7 The value of `this` in various contexts 274
- **28.5 Objects as dictionaries (advanced)** 275
  - 28.5.1 Arbitrary fixed strings as property keys 275
  - 28.5.2 Computed property keys 276
  - 28.5.3 The `in` operator: is there a property with a given key? 277
  - 28.5.4 Deleting properties 277
  - 28.5.5 Listing property keys 277
  - 28.5.6 Listing property values via `Object.values()` 279

28.5.7 Listing property entries via `Object.entries()` 279
28.5.8 Properties are listed deterministically 279
28.5.9 Assembling objects via `Object.fromEntries()` 280
28.5.10 The pitfalls of using an object as a dictionary 282
28.6 Standard methods (advanced) **283**
28.6.1 `.toString()` 283
28.6.2 `.valueOf()` 283
28.7 Advanced topics **283**
28.7.1 `Object.assign()` 283
28.7.2 Freezing objects 284
28.7.3 Property attributes and property descriptors 284

In this book, JavaScript's style of object-oriented programming (OOP) is introduced in four steps. This chapter covers step 1; the next chapter (p. 287) covers steps 2–4. The steps are (fig. 28.1):

1. **Single objects (this chapter):** How do *objects*, JavaScript's basic OOP building blocks, work in isolation?
2. **Prototype chains (next chapter):** Each object has a chain of zero or more *prototype objects*. Prototypes are JavaScript's core inheritance mechanism.
3. **Classes (next chapter):** JavaScript's *classes* are factories for objects. The relationship between a class and its instances is based on prototypal inheritance.
4. **Subclassing (next chapter):** The relationship between a *subclass* and its *superclass* is also based on prototypal inheritance.

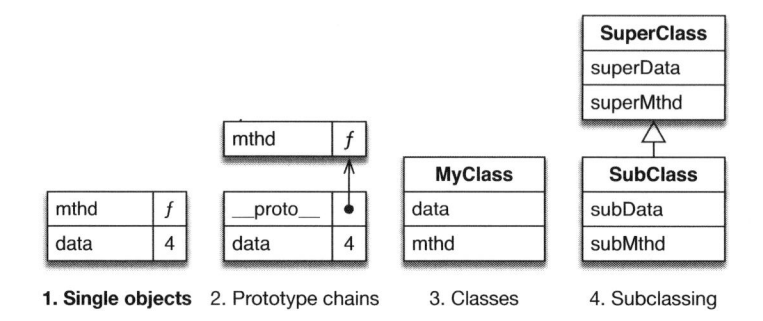

Figure 28.1: This book introduces object-oriented programming in JavaScript in four steps.

28.1 What is an object?

In JavaScript:

- An object is a set of *properties* (key-value entries).
- A property key can only be a string or a symbol.

28.1.1 Roles of objects: record vs. dictionary

Objects play two roles in JavaScript:

- Records: Objects-as-records have a fixed number of properties, whose keys are known at development time. Their values can have different types.

- Dictionaries: Objects-as-dictionaries have a variable number of properties, whose keys are not known at development time. All of their values have the same type.

These roles influence how objects are explained in this chapter:

- First, we'll explore objects-as-records. Even though property keys are strings or symbols under the hood, they will appear as fixed identifiers to us, in this part of the chapter.
- Later, we'll explore objects-as-dictionaries. Note that Maps (p. 365) are usually better dictionaries than objects. However, some of the operations that we'll encounter, can also be useful for objects-as-records.

28.2 Objects as records

Let's first explore the role *record* of objects.

28.2.1 Object literals: properties

Object literals are one way of creating objects-as-records. They are a stand-out feature of JavaScript: you can directly create objects – no need for classes! This is an example:

```
const jane = {
  first: 'Jane',
  last: 'Doe', // optional trailing comma
};
```

In the example, we created an object via an object literal, which starts and ends with curly braces {}. Inside it, we defined two *properties* (key-value entries):

- The first property has the key first and the value 'Jane'.
- The second property has the key last and the value 'Doe'.

We will later see other ways of specifying property keys, but with this way of specifying them, they must follow the rules of JavaScript variable names. For example, you can use first_name as a property key, but not first-name). However, reserved words are allowed:

```
const obj = {
  if: true,
  const: true,
};
```

In order to check the effects of various operations on objects, we'll occasionally use Object.keys() in this part of the chapter. It lists property keys:

```
> Object.keys({a:1, b:2})
[ 'a', 'b' ]
```

28.2.2 Object literals: property value shorthands

Whenever the value of a property is defined via a variable name and that name is the same as the key, you can omit the key.

```
function createPoint(x, y) {
  return {x, y};
}
assert.deepEqual(
  createPoint(9, 2),
  { x: 9, y: 2 }
);
```

28.2.3 Getting properties

This is how you *get* (read) a property (line A):

```
const jane = {
  first: 'Jane',
  last: 'Doe',
};

// Get property .first
assert.equal(jane.first, 'Jane'); // (A)
```

Getting an unknown property produces `undefined`:

```
assert.equal(jane.unknownProperty, undefined);
```

28.2.4 Setting properties

This is how you *set* (write to) a property:

```
const obj = {
  prop: 1,
};
assert.equal(obj.prop, 1);
obj.prop = 2; // (A)
assert.equal(obj.prop, 2);
```

We just changed an existing property via setting. If we set an unknown property, we create a new entry:

```
const obj = {}; // empty object
assert.deepEqual(
  Object.keys(obj), []);

obj.unknownProperty = 'abc';
```

28.2 Objects as records

```
assert.deepEqual(
  Object.keys(obj), ['unknownProperty']);
```

28.2.5 Object literals: methods

The following code shows how to create the method .says() via an object literal:

```
const jane = {
  first: 'Jane', // data property
  says(text) {   // method
    return `${this.first} says "${text}"`; // (A)
  }, // comma as separator (optional at end)
};
assert.equal(jane.says('hello'), 'Jane says "hello"');
```

During the method call jane.says('hello'), jane is called the *receiver* of the method call and assigned to the special variable this. That enables method .says() to access the sibling property .first in line A.

28.2.6 Object literals: accessors

There are two kinds of accessors in JavaScript:

- A *getter* is a method-like entity that is invoked by getting a property.
- A *setter* is a method-like entity that is invoked by setting a property.

28.2.6.1 Getters

A getter is created by prefixing a method definition with the modifier get:

```
const jane = {
  first: 'Jane',
  last: 'Doe',
  get full() {
    return `${this.first} ${this.last}`;
  },
};

assert.equal(jane.full, 'Jane Doe');
jane.first = 'John';
assert.equal(jane.full, 'John Doe');
```

28.2.6.2 Setters

A setter is created by prefixing a method definition with the modifier set:

```
const jane = {
  first: 'Jane',
  last: 'Doe',
  set full(fullName) {
    const parts = fullName.split(' ');
```

```
    this.first = parts[0];
    this.last = parts[1];
  },
};

jane.full = 'Richard Roe';
assert.equal(jane.first, 'Richard');
assert.equal(jane.last, 'Roe');
```

> **Exercise: Creating an object via an object literal**
> `exercises/single-objects/color_point_object_test.mjs`

28.3 Spreading into object literals (...)

Inside a function call (p. 222), spreading (...) turns the iterated values of an *iterable* object (p. 311) into arguments.

Inside an object literal, a *spread property* adds the properties of another object to the current one:

```
> const obj = {foo: 1, bar: 2};
> {...obj, baz: 3}
{ foo: 1, bar: 2, baz: 3 }
```

If property keys clash, the property that is mentioned last "wins":

```
> const obj = {foo: 1, bar: 2, baz: 3};
> {...obj, foo: true}
{ foo: true, bar: 2, baz: 3 }
> {foo: true, ...obj}
{ foo: 1, bar: 2, baz: 3 }
```

All values are spreadable, even `undefined` and `null`:

```
> {...undefined}
{}
> {...null}
{}
> {...123}
{}
> {...'abc'}
{ '0': 'a', '1': 'b', '2': 'c' }
> {...['a', 'b']}
{ '0': 'a', '1': 'b' }
```

Property `.length` of strings and of Arrays is hidden from this kind of operation (it is not *enumerable*; see §28.7.3 "Property attributes and property descriptors" (p. 284) for more information).

28.3.1 Use case for spreading: copying objects

You can use spreading to create a copy of an object `original`:

```
const copy = {...original};
```

Caveat – copying is *shallow*: `copy` is a fresh object with duplicates of all properties (key-value entries) of `original`. But if property values are objects, then those are not copied themselves; they are shared between `original` and `copy`. Let's look at an example:

```
const original = { a: 1, b: {foo: true} };
const copy = {...original};
```

The first level of `copy` is really a copy: If you change any properties at that level, it does not affect the original:

```
copy.a = 2;
assert.deepEqual(
  original, { a: 1, b: {foo: true} }); // no change
```

However, deeper levels are not copied. For example, the value of `.b` is shared between `original` and `copy`. Changing `.b` in the copy also changes it in the original.

```
copy.b.foo = false;
assert.deepEqual(
  original, { a: 1, b: {foo: false} });
```

> ⚠️ **JavaScript doesn't have built-in support for deep copying**
>
> *Deep copies* of objects (where all levels are copied) are notoriously difficult to do generically. Therefore, JavaScript does not have a built-in operation for them (for now). If you need such an operation, you have to implement it yourself.

28.3.2 Use case for spreading: default values for missing properties

If one of the inputs of your code is an object with data, you can make properties optional by specifying default values that are used if those properties are missing. One technique for doing so is via an object whose properties contain the default values. In the following example, that object is `DEFAULTS`:

```
const DEFAULTS = {foo: 'a', bar: 'b'};
const providedData = {foo: 1};

const allData = {...DEFAULTS, ...providedData};
assert.deepEqual(allData, {foo: 1, bar: 'b'});
```

The result, the object `allData`, is created by copying `DEFAULTS` and overriding its properties with those of `providedData`.

But you don't need an object to specify the default values; you can also specify them inside the object literal, individually:

```
const providedData = {foo: 1};

const allData = {foo: 'a', bar: 'b', ...providedData};
assert.deepEqual(allData, {foo: 1, bar: 'b'});
```

28.3.3 Use case for spreading: non-destructively changing properties

So far, we have encountered one way of changing a property `.foo` of an object: We *set* it (line A) and mutate the object. That is, this way of changing a property is *destructive*.

```
const obj = {foo: 'a', bar: 'b'};
obj.foo = 1; // (A)
assert.deepEqual(obj, {foo: 1, bar: 'b'});
```

With spreading, we can change `.foo` *non-destructively* – we make a copy of `obj` where `.foo` has a different value:

```
const obj = {foo: 'a', bar: 'b'};
const updatedObj = {...obj, foo: 1};
assert.deepEqual(updatedObj, {foo: 1, bar: 'b'});
```

> **Exercise: Non-destructively updating a property via spreading (fixed key)**
> `exercises/single-objects/update_name_test.mjs`

28.4 Methods

28.4.1 Methods are properties whose values are functions

Let's revisit the example that was used to introduce methods:

```
const jane = {
  first: 'Jane',
  says(text) {
    return `${this.first} says "${text}"`;
  },
};
```

Somewhat surprisingly, methods are functions:

```
assert.equal(typeof jane.says, 'function');
```

Why is that? We learned in the chapter on callable values (p. 213), that ordinary functions play several roles. *Method* is one of those roles. Therefore, under the hood, jane roughly looks as follows.

```
const jane = {
  first: 'Jane',
  says: function (text) {
    return `${this.first} says "${text}"`;
```

},
};
```

## 28.4.2 `.call()`: specifying this via a parameter

Remember that each function `someFunc` is also an object and therefore has methods. One such method is `.call()` – it lets you call a function while specifying this via a parameter:

```
someFunc.call(thisValue, arg1, arg2, arg3);
```

28.4.2.1 Methods and `.call()`

If you make a method call, this is an implicit parameter that is filled in via the receiver of the call:

```
const obj = {
  method(x) {
    assert.equal(this, obj); // implicit parameter
    assert.equal(x, 'a');
  },
};

obj.method('a'); // receiver is `obj`
```

The method call in the last line sets up this as follows:

```
obj.method.call(obj, 'a');
```

As an aside, that means that there are actually two different dot operators:

1. One for accessing properties: `obj.prop`
2. One for making method calls: `obj.prop()`

They are different in that (2) is not just (1) followed by the function call operator (). Instead, (2) additionally specifies a value for this.

28.4.2.2 Functions and `.call()`

If you function-call an ordinary function, its implicit parameter this is also provided – it is implicitly set to undefined:

```
function func(x) {
  assert.equal(this, undefined); // implicit parameter
  assert.equal(x, 'a');
}

func('a');
```

The method call in the last line sets up this as follows:

```
func.call(undefined, 'a');
```

this being set to undefined during a function call, indicates that it is a feature that is only needed during a method call.
```

Next, we'll examine the pitfalls of using `this`. Before we can do that, we need one more tool: method `.bind()` of functions.

28.4.3 `.bind()`: pre-filling `this` and parameters of functions

`.bind()` is another method of function objects. This method is invoked as follows:

```
const boundFunc = someFunc.bind(thisValue, arg1, arg2);
```

`.bind()` returns a new function `boundFunc()`. Calling that function invokes `someFunc()` with `this` set to `thisValue` and these parameters: `arg1`, `arg2`, followed by the parameters of `boundFunc()`.

That is, the following two function calls are equivalent:

```
boundFunc('a', 'b')
someFunc.call(thisValue, arg1, arg2, 'a', 'b')
```

28.4.3.1 An alternative to `.bind()`

Another way of pre-filling `this` and parameters is via an arrow function:

```
const boundFunc2 = (...args) =>
  someFunc.call(thisValue, arg1, arg2, ...args);
```

28.4.3.2 An implementation of `.bind()`

Considering the previous section, `.bind()` can be implemented as a real function as follows:

```
function bind(func, thisValue, ...boundArgs) {
  return (...args) =>
    func.call(thisValue, ...boundArgs, ...args);
}
```

28.4.3.3 Example: binding a real function

Using `.bind()` for real functions is somewhat unintuitive because you have to provide a value for `this`. Given that it is `undefined` during function calls, it is usually set to `undefined` or `null`.

In the following example, we create `add8()`, a function that has one parameter, by binding the first parameter of `add()` to 8.

```
function add(x, y) {
  return x + y;
}

const add8 = add.bind(undefined, 8);
assert.equal(add8(1), 9);
```

28.4.3.4 Example: binding a method

In the following code, we turn method `.says()` into the stand-alone function `func()`:

```
const jane = {
  first: 'Jane',
  says(text) {
    return `${this.first} says "${text}"`; // (A)
  },
};

const func = jane.says.bind(jane, 'hello');
assert.equal(func(), 'Jane says "hello"');
```

Setting `this` to `jane` via `.bind()` is crucial here. Otherwise, `func()` wouldn't work properly because `this` is used in line A.

28.4.4 this pitfall: extracting methods

We now know quite a bit about functions and methods and are ready to take a look at the biggest pitfall involving methods and `this`: function-calling a method extracted from an object can fail if you are not careful.

In the following example, we fail when we extract method `jane.says()`, store it in the variable `func`, and function-call `func()`.

```
const jane = {
  first: 'Jane',
  says(text) {
    return `${this.first} says "${text}"`;
  },
};
const func = jane.says; // extract the method
assert.throws(
  () => func('hello'), // (A)
  {
    name: 'TypeError',
    message: "Cannot read property 'first' of undefined",
  });
```

The function call in line A is equivalent to:

```
assert.throws(
  () => jane.says.call(undefined, 'hello'), // `this` is undefined!
  {
    name: 'TypeError',
    message: "Cannot read property 'first' of undefined",
  });
```

So how do we fix this? We need to use `.bind()` to extract method `.says()`:

```
const func2 = jane.says.bind(jane);
assert.equal(func2('hello'), 'Jane says "hello"');
```

The .bind() ensures that this is always jane when we call func().

You can also use arrow functions to extract methods:

```
const func3 = text => jane.says(text);
assert.equal(func3('hello'), 'Jane says "hello"');
```

28.4.4.1 Example: extracting a method

The following is a simplified version of code that you may see in actual web development:

```
class ClickHandler {
  constructor(id, elem) {
    this.id = id;
    elem.addEventListener('click', this.handleClick); // (A)
  }
  handleClick(event) {
    alert('Clicked ' + this.id);
  }
}
```

In line A, we don't extract the method .handleClick() properly. Instead, we should do:

```
elem.addEventListener('click', this.handleClick.bind(this));
```

Exercise: Extracting a method
exercises/single-objects/method_extraction_exrc.mjs

28.4.5 this pitfall: accidentally shadowing this

Accidentally shadowing this is only an issue with ordinary functions

Arrow functions don't shadow this.

Consider the following problem: when you are inside an ordinary function, you can't access the this of the surrounding scope because the ordinary function has its own this. In other words, a variable in an inner scope hides a variable in an outer scope. That is called *shadowing* (p. 80). The following code is an example:

```
const prefixer = {
  prefix: '==> ',
  prefixStringArray(stringArray) {
    return stringArray.map(
      function (x) {
        return this.prefix + x; // (A)
      });
  },
};
```

28.4 Methods

```
assert.throws(
  () => prefixer.prefixStringArray(['a', 'b']),
  /^TypeError: Cannot read property 'prefix' of undefined$/);
```

In line A, we want to access the this of .prefixStringArray(). But we can't since the surrounding ordinary function has its own this that *shadows* (blocks access to) the this of the method. The value of the former this is undefined due to the callback being function-called. That explains the error message.

The simplest way to fix this problem is via an arrow function, which doesn't have its own this and therefore doesn't shadow anything:

```
const prefixer = {
  prefix: '==> ',
  prefixStringArray(stringArray) {
    return stringArray.map(
      (x) => {
        return this.prefix + x;
      });
  },
};
assert.deepEqual(
  prefixer.prefixStringArray(['a', 'b']),
  ['==> a', '==> b']);
```

We can also store this in a different variable (line A), so that it doesn't get shadowed:

```
prefixStringArray(stringArray) {
  const that = this; // (A)
  return stringArray.map(
    function (x) {
      return that.prefix + x;
    });
},
```

Another option is to specify a fixed this for the callback via .bind() (line A):

```
prefixStringArray(stringArray) {
  return stringArray.map(
    function (x) {
      return this.prefix + x;
    }.bind(this)); // (A)
},
```

Lastly, .map() lets us specify a value for this (line A) that it uses when invoking the callback:

```
prefixStringArray(stringArray) {
  return stringArray.map(
    function (x) {
      return this.prefix + x;
    },
```

```
  this); // (A)
},
```

28.4.6 Avoiding the pitfalls of `this`

We have seen two big `this`-related pitfalls:

1. Extracting methods (p. 271)
2. Accidentally shadowing `this` (p. 272)

One simple rule helps avoid the second pitfall:

> "Avoid the keyword `function`": Never use ordinary functions, only arrow functions (for real functions) and method definitions.

Following this rule has two benefits:

- It prevents the second pitfall because ordinary functions are never used as real functions.
- `this` becomes easier to understand because it will only appear inside methods (never inside ordinary functions). That makes it clear that `this` is an OOP feature.

However, even though I don't use (ordinary) function *expressions* anymore, I do like function *declarations* syntactically. You can use them safely if you don't refer to `this` inside them. The static checking tool ESLint can warn you during development when you do this wrong via a built-in rule[1].

Alas, there is no simple way around the first pitfall: whenever you extract a method, you have to be careful and do it properly – for example, by binding `this`.

28.4.7 The value of `this` in various contexts

What is the value of `this` in various contexts?

Inside a callable entity, the value of `this` depends on how the callable entity is invoked and what kind of callable entity it is:

- Function call:
    - Ordinary functions: `this === undefined` (in strict mode)
    - Arrow functions: `this` is same as in surrounding scope (lexical `this`)
- Method call: `this` is receiver of call
- `new`: `this` refers to newly created instance

You can also access `this` in all common top-level scopes:

- `<script>` element: `this === globalThis`
- ECMAScript modules: `this === undefined`
- CommonJS modules: `this === module.exports`

However, I like to pretend that you can't access `this` in top-level scopes because top-level `this` is confusing and rarely useful.

---

[1] https://eslint.org/docs/rules/no-invalid-this

28.5 Objects as dictionaries (advanced)

Objects work best as records. But before ES6, JavaScript did not have a data structure for dictionaries (ES6 brought Maps (p. 365)). Therefore, objects had to be used as dictionaries, which imposed a signficant constraint: keys had to be strings (symbols were also introduced with ES6).

We first look at features of objects that are related to dictionaries but also useful for objects-as-records. This section concludes with tips for actually using objects as dictionaries (spoiler: use Maps if you can).

28.5.1 Arbitrary fixed strings as property keys

So far, we have always used objects as records. Property keys were fixed tokens that had to be valid identifiers and internally became strings:

```
const obj = {
  mustBeAnIdentifier: 123,
};

// Get property
assert.equal(obj.mustBeAnIdentifier, 123);

// Set property
obj.mustBeAnIdentifier = 'abc';
assert.equal(obj.mustBeAnIdentifier, 'abc');
```

As a next step, we'll go beyond this limitation for property keys: In this section, we'll use arbitrary fixed strings as keys. In the next subsection, we'll dynamically compute keys.

Two techniques allow us to use arbitrary strings as property keys.

First, when creating property keys via object literals, we can quote property keys (with single or double quotes):

```
const obj = {
  'Can be any string!': 123,
};
```

Second, when getting or setting properties, we can use square brackets with strings inside them:

```
// Get property
assert.equal(obj['Can be any string!'], 123);

// Set property
obj['Can be any string!'] = 'abc';
assert.equal(obj['Can be any string!'], 'abc');
```

You can also use these techniques for methods:

```
const obj = {
  'A nice method'() {
```

```
    return 'Yes!';
  },
};

assert.equal(obj['A nice method'](), 'Yes!');
```

28.5.2 Computed property keys

So far, property keys were always fixed strings inside object literals. In this section we learn how to dynamically compute property keys. That enables us to use either arbitrary strings or symbols.

The syntax of dynamically computed property keys in object literals is inspired by dynamically accessing properties. That is, we can use square brackets to wrap expressions:

```
const obj = {
  ['Hello world!']: true,
  ['f'+'o'+'o']: 123,
  [Symbol.toStringTag]: 'Goodbye', // (A)
};

assert.equal(obj['Hello world!'], true);
assert.equal(obj.foo, 123);
assert.equal(obj[Symbol.toStringTag], 'Goodbye');
```

The main use case for computed keys is having symbols as property keys (line A).

Note that the square brackets operator for getting and setting properties works with arbitrary expressions:

```
assert.equal(obj['f'+'o'+'o'], 123);
assert.equal(obj['==> foo'.slice(-3)], 123);
```

Methods can have computed property keys, too:

```
const methodKey = Symbol();
const obj = {
  [methodKey]() {
    return 'Yes!';
  },
};

assert.equal(obj[methodKey](), 'Yes!');
```

For the remainder of this chapter, we'll mostly use fixed property keys again (because they are syntactically more convenient). But all features are also available for arbitrary strings and symbols.

> **Exercise: Non-destructively updating a property via spreading (computed key)**

28.5 Objects as dictionaries (advanced)

| exercises/single-objects/update_property_test.mjs

28.5.3 The `in` operator: is there a property with a given key?

The in operator checks if an object has a property with a given key:

```
const obj = {
  foo: 'abc',
  bar: false,
};

assert.equal('foo' in obj, true);
assert.equal('unknownKey' in obj, false);
```

28.5.3.1 Checking if a property exists via truthiness

You can also use a truthiness check to determine if a property exists:

```
assert.equal(
  obj.foo ? 'exists' : 'does not exist',
  'exists');
assert.equal(
  obj.unknownKey ? 'exists' : 'does not exist',
  'does not exist');
```

The previous checks work because `obj.foo` is truthy and because reading a missing property returns `undefined` (which is falsy).

There is, however, one important caveat: truthiness checks fail if the property exists, but has a falsy value (`undefined`, `null`, `false`, `0`, `""`, etc.):

```
assert.equal(
  obj.bar ? 'exists' : 'does not exist',
  'does not exist'); // should be: 'exists'
```

28.5.4 Deleting properties

You can delete properties via the `delete` operator:

```
const obj = {
  foo: 123,
};
assert.deepEqual(Object.keys(obj), ['foo']);

delete obj.foo;

assert.deepEqual(Object.keys(obj), []);
```

28.5.5 Listing property keys

Table 28.1: Standard library methods for listing *own* (non-inherited) property keys. All of them return Arrays with strings and/or symbols.

	enumerable	non-e.	string	symbol
`Object.keys()`	✓		✓	
`Object.getOwnPropertyNames()`	✓	✓	✓	
`Object.getOwnPropertySymbols()`	✓	✓		✓
`Reflect.ownKeys()`	✓	✓	✓	✓

Each of the methods in tbl. 28.1 returns an Array with the own property keys of the parameter. In the names of the methods, you can see that the following distinction is made:

- A *property key* can be either a string or a symbol.
- A *property name* is a property key whose value is a string.
- A *property symbol* is a property key whose value is a symbol.

The next section describes the term *enumerable* and demonstrates each of the methods.

28.5.5.1 Enumerability

Enumerability is an *attribute* (p. 284) of a property. Non-enumerable properties are ignored by some operations – for example, by `Object.keys()` (see tbl. 28.1) and by spread properties. By default, most properties are enumerable. The next example shows how to change that. It also demonstrates the various ways of listing property keys.

```
const enumerableSymbolKey = Symbol('enumerableSymbolKey');
const nonEnumSymbolKey = Symbol('nonEnumSymbolKey');

// We create enumerable properties via an object literal
const obj = {
  enumerableStringKey: 1,
  [enumerableSymbolKey]: 2,
}

// For non-enumerable properties, we need a more powerful tool
Object.defineProperties(obj, {
  nonEnumStringKey: {
    value: 3,
    enumerable: false,
  },
  [nonEnumSymbolKey]: {
    value: 4,
    enumerable: false,
  },
});

assert.deepEqual(
```

28.5 Objects as dictionaries (advanced)

```
  Object.keys(obj),
  [ 'enumerableStringKey' ]);
assert.deepEqual(
  Object.getOwnPropertyNames(obj),
  [ 'enumerableStringKey', 'nonEnumStringKey' ]);
assert.deepEqual(
  Object.getOwnPropertySymbols(obj),
  [ enumerableSymbolKey, nonEnumSymbolKey ]);
assert.deepEqual(
  Reflect.ownKeys(obj),
  [
    'enumerableStringKey', 'nonEnumStringKey',
    enumerableSymbolKey, nonEnumSymbolKey,
  ]);
```

`Object.defineProperties()` is explained later in this chapter (p. 284).

28.5.6 Listing property values via `Object.values()`

`Object.values()` lists the values of all enumerable properties of an object:

```
const obj = {foo: 1, bar: 2};
assert.deepEqual(
  Object.values(obj),
  [1, 2]);
```

28.5.7 Listing property entries via `Object.entries()`

`Object.entries()` lists key-value pairs of enumerable properties. Each pair is encoded as a two-element Array:

```
const obj = {foo: 1, bar: 2};
assert.deepEqual(
  Object.entries(obj),
  [
    ['foo', 1],
    ['bar', 2],
  ]);
```

> Exercise: `Object.entries()`
> exercises/single-objects/find_key_test.mjs

28.5.8 Properties are listed deterministically

Own (non-inherited) properties of objects are always listed in the following order:

1. Properties with string keys that contain integer indices (that includes Array indices (p. 326)):
   In ascending numeric order

2. Remaining properties with string keys:
   In the order in which they were added
3. Properties with symbol keys:
   In the order in which they were added

The following example demonstrates how property keys are sorted according to these rules:

```
> Object.keys({b:0,a:0, 10:0,2:0})
[ '2', '10', 'b', 'a' ]
```

> **The order of properties**
>
> The ECMAScript specification[a] describes in more detail how properties are ordered.
>
> ---
> [a]https://tc39.github.io/ecma262/#sec-ordinaryownpropertykeys

28.5.9 Assembling objects via `Object.fromEntries()`

Given an iterable over [key, value] pairs, `Object.fromEntries()` creates an object:

```
assert.deepEqual(
  Object.fromEntries([['foo',1], ['bar',2]]),
  {
    foo: 1,
    bar: 2,
  }
);
```

`Object.fromEntries()` does the opposite of `Object.entries()` (p. 279).

To demonstrate both, we'll use them to implement two tool functions from the library Underscore[2] in the next subsubsections.

28.5.9.1 Example: `pick(object, ...keys)`

`pick`[3] returns a copy of `object` that only has those properties whose keys are mentioned as arguments:

```
const address = {
  street: 'Evergreen Terrace',
  number: '742',
  city: 'Springfield',
  state: 'NT',
  zip: '49007',
};
assert.deepEqual(
  pick(address, 'street', 'number'),
  {
```

---
[2]https://underscorejs.org
[3]https://underscorejs.org/#pick

28.5 Objects as dictionaries (advanced)

```
    street: 'Evergreen Terrace',
    number: '742',
  }
);
```

We can implement `pick()` as follows:

```
function pick(object, ...keys) {
  const filteredEntries = Object.entries(object)
    .filter(([key, _value]) => keys.includes(key));
  return Object.fromEntries(filteredEntries);
}
```

28.5.9.2 Example: `invert(object)`

`invert`[4] returns a copy of `object` where the keys and values of all properties are swapped:

```
assert.deepEqual(
  invert({a: 1, b: 2, c: 3}),
  {1: 'a', 2: 'b', 3: 'c'}
);
```

We can implement `invert()` like this:

```
function invert(object) {
  const mappedEntries = Object.entries(object)
    .map(([key, value]) => [value, key]);
  return Object.fromEntries(mappedEntries);
}
```

28.5.9.3 A simple implementation of `Object.fromEntries()`

The following function is a simplified version of `Object.fromEntries()`:

```
function fromEntries(iterable) {
  const result = {};
  for (const [key, value] of iterable) {
    let coercedKey;
    if (typeof key === 'string' || typeof key === 'symbol') {
      coercedKey = key;
    } else {
      coercedKey = String(key);
    }
    result[coercedKey] = value;
  }
  return result;
}
```

---

[4] https://underscorejs.org/#invert

28.5.9.4 A polyfill for `Object.fromEntries()`

The npm package `object.fromentries`[5] is a *polyfill* (p. 258) for `Object.entries()`: it installs its own implementation if that method doesn't exist on the current platform.

> **Exercise: `Object.entries()` and `Object.fromEntries()`**
> `exercises/single-objects/omit_properties_test.mjs`

28.5.10 The pitfalls of using an object as a dictionary

If you use plain objects (created via object literals) as dictionaries, you have to look out for two pitfalls.

The first pitfall is that the `in` operator also finds inherited properties:

```
const dict = {};
assert.equal('toString' in dict, true);
```

We want `dict` to be treated as empty, but the `in` operator detects the properties it inherits from its prototype, `Object.prototype`.

The second pitfall is that you can't use the property key `__proto__` because it has special powers (it sets the prototype of the object):

```
const dict = {};

dict['__proto__'] = 123;
// No property was added to dict:
assert.deepEqual(Object.keys(dict), []);
```

So how do we avoid these pitfalls?

- Whenever you can, use Maps. They are the best solution for dictionaries.
- If you can't, use a library for objects-as-dictionaries that does everything safely.
- If you can't, use an object without a prototype.

The following code demonstrates using objects without prototypes as dictionaries:

```
const dict = Object.create(null); // no prototype

assert.equal('toString' in dict, false); // (A)

dict['__proto__'] = 123;
assert.deepEqual(Object.keys(dict), ['__proto__']);
```

We avoided both pitfalls: First, a property without a prototype does not inherit any properties (line A). Second, in modern JavaScript, `__proto__` is implemented via `Object.prototype`. That means that it is switched off if `Object.prototype` is not in the prototype chain.

---

[5] https://github.com/es-shims/Object.fromEntries

28.6 Standard methods (advanced)

> **Exercise: Using an object as a dictionary**
> exercises/single-objects/simple_dict_test.mjs

28.6 Standard methods (advanced)

Object.prototype defines several standard methods that can be overridden to configure how an object is treated by the language. Two important ones are:

- .toString()
- .valueOf()

28.6.1 .toString()

.toString() determines how objects are converted to strings:

```
> String({toString() { return 'Hello!' }})
'Hello!'
> String({})
'[object Object]'
```

28.6.2 .valueOf()

.valueOf() determines how objects are converted to numbers:

```
> Number({valueOf() { return 123 }})
123
> Number({})
NaN
```

28.7 Advanced topics

The following subsections give brief overviews of a few advanced topics.

28.7.1 Object.assign()

Object.assign() is a tool method:

```
Object.assign(target, source_1, source_2, ···)
```

This expression assigns all properties of source_1 to target, then all properties of source_2, etc. At the end, it returns target – for example:

```
const target = { foo: 1 };

const result = Object.assign(
  target,
  {bar: 2},
  {baz: 3, bar: 4});
```

```
assert.deepEqual(
  result, { foo: 1, bar: 4, baz: 3 });
// target was modified and returned:
assert.equal(result, target);
```

The use cases for `Object.assign()` are similar to those for spread properties. In a way, it spreads destructively.

28.7.2 Freezing objects

`Object.freeze(obj)` makes `obj` completely immutable: You can't change properties, add properties, or change its prototype – for example:

```
const frozen = Object.freeze({ x: 2, y: 5 });
assert.throws(
  () => { frozen.x = 7 },
  {
    name: 'TypeError',
    message: /^Cannot assign to read only property 'x'/,
  });
```

There is one caveat: `Object.freeze(obj)` freezes shallowly. That is, only the properties of `obj` are frozen but not objects stored in properties.

28.7.3 Property attributes and property descriptors

Just as objects are composed of properties, properties are composed of *attributes*. The value of a property is only one of several attributes. Others include:

- `writable`: Is it possible to change the value of the property?
- `enumerable`: Is the property considered by `Object.keys()`, spreading, etc.?

When you are using one of the operations for handling property attributes, attributes are specified via *property descriptors*: objects where each property represents one attribute. For example, this is how you read the attributes of a property `obj.foo`:

```
const obj = { foo: 123 };
assert.deepEqual(
  Object.getOwnPropertyDescriptor(obj, 'foo'),
  {
    value: 123,
    writable: true,
    enumerable: true,
    configurable: true,
  });
```

And this is how you set the attributes of a property `obj.bar`:

```
const obj = {
  foo: 1,
  bar: 2,
```

28.7 Advanced topics

```
  };

  assert.deepEqual(Object.keys(obj), ['foo', 'bar']);

  // Hide property `bar` from Object.keys()
  Object.defineProperty(obj, 'bar', {
    enumerable: false,
  });

  assert.deepEqual(Object.keys(obj), ['foo']);
```

Enumerability is covered in greater detail earlier in this chapter (p. 278). For more information on property attributes and property descriptors, consult *Speaking JavaScript*[6].

Quiz

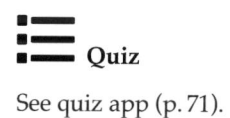

See quiz app (p. 71).

---

[6]http://speakingjs.com/es5/ch17.html#property_attributes

Chapter 29

Prototype chains and classes

Contents

29.1 Prototype chains	**288**
29.1.1 JavaScript's operations: all properties vs. own properties	289
29.1.2 Pitfall: only the first member of a prototype chain is mutated	289
29.1.3 Tips for working with prototypes (advanced)	290
29.1.4 Sharing data via prototypes	291
29.2 Classes	**293**
29.2.1 A class for persons	293
29.2.2 Classes under the hood	294
29.2.3 Class definitions: prototype properties	295
29.2.4 Class definitions: static properties	296
29.2.5 The `instanceof` operator	296
29.2.6 Why I recommend classes	296
29.3 Private data for classes	**297**
29.3.1 Private data: naming convention	297
29.3.2 Private data: WeakMaps	298
29.3.3 More techniques for private data	299
29.4 Subclassing	**299**
29.4.1 Subclasses under the hood (advanced)	300
29.4.2 `instanceof` in more detail (advanced)	301
29.4.3 Prototype chains of built-in objects (advanced)	301
29.4.4 Dispatched vs. direct method calls (advanced)	304
29.4.5 Mixin classes (advanced)	305
29.5 FAQ: objects	**307**
29.5.1 Why do objects preserve the insertion order of properties?	307

In this book, JavaScript's style of object-oriented programming (OOP) is introduced in four steps. This chapter covers steps 2–4, the previous chapter (p. 261) covers step 1. The steps are (fig. 29.1):

1. **Single objects (previous chapter):** How do *objects*, JavaScript's basic OOP building blocks, work in isolation?
2. **Prototype chains (this chapter):** Each object has a chain of zero or more *prototype objects*. Prototypes are JavaScript's core inheritance mechanism.
3. **Classes (this chapter):** JavaScript's *classes* are factories for objects. The relationship between a class and its instances is based on prototypal inheritance.
4. **Subclassing (this chapter):** The relationship between a *subclass* and its *superclass* is also based on prototypal inheritance.

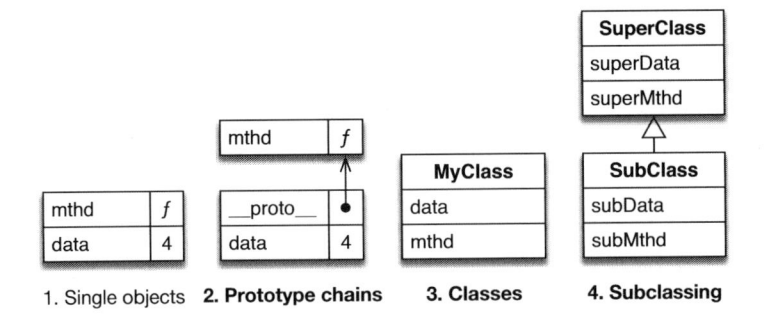

Figure 29.1: This book introduces object-oriented programming in JavaScript in four steps.

29.1 Prototype chains

Prototypes are JavaScript's only inheritance mechanism: each object has a prototype that is either `null` or an object. In the latter case, the object inherits all of the prototype's properties.

In an object literal, you can set the prototype via the special property `__proto__`:

```
const proto = {
  protoProp: 'a',
};
const obj = {
  __proto__: proto,
  objProp: 'b',
};

// obj inherits .protoProp:
assert.equal(obj.protoProp, 'a');
assert.equal('protoProp' in obj, true);
```

Given that a prototype object can have a prototype itself, we get a chain of objects – the so-called *prototype chain*. That means that inheritance gives us the impression that we are dealing with single objects, but we are actually dealing with chains of objects.

Fig. 29.2 shows what the prototype chain of `obj` looks like.

Non-inherited properties are called *own properties*. `obj` has one own property, `.objProp`.

29.1 Prototype chains

```
        proto
        ┌─__proto__─┬───┐ ──→ ...
        ├─protoProp─┼─'a'┤
        └───────────┴───┘
              ↑
        obj
        ┌─__proto__─┬───┐
        ├─objProp───┼─'b'┤
        └───────────┴───┘
```

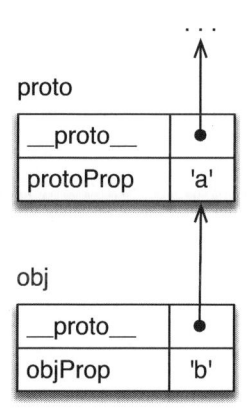

Figure 29.2: `obj` starts a chain of objects that continues with `proto` and other objects.

29.1.1 JavaScript's operations: all properties vs. own properties

Some operations consider all properties (own and inherited) – for example, getting properties:

```
> const obj = { foo: 1 };
> typeof obj.foo // own
'number'
> typeof obj.toString // inherited
'function'
```

Other operations only consider own properties – for example, `Object.keys()`:

```
> Object.keys(obj)
[ 'foo' ]
```

Read on for another operation that also only considers own properties: setting properties.

29.1.2 Pitfall: only the first member of a prototype chain is mutated

One aspect of prototype chains that may be counter-intuitive is that setting *any* property via an object – even an inherited one – only changes that very object – never one of the prototypes.

Consider the following object `obj`:

```
const proto = {
  protoProp: 'a',
};
const obj = {
  __proto__: proto,
  objProp: 'b',
};
```

In the next code snippet, we set the inherited property `obj.protoProp` (line A). That "changes" it by creating an own property: When reading `obj.protoProp`, the own property is found first and its value *overrides* the value of the inherited property.

```
// In the beginning, obj has one own property
assert.deepEqual(Object.keys(obj), ['objProp']);

obj.protoProp = 'x'; // (A)

// We created a new own property:
assert.deepEqual(Object.keys(obj), ['objProp', 'protoProp']);

// The inherited property itself is unchanged:
assert.equal(proto.protoProp, 'a');

// The own property overrides the inherited property:
assert.equal(obj.protoProp, 'x');
```

The prototype chain of `obj` is depicted in fig. 29.3.

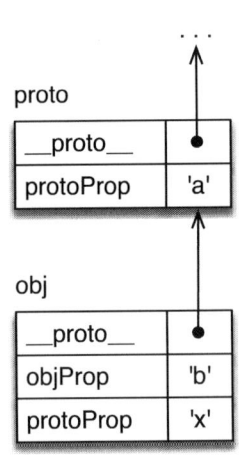

Figure 29.3: The own property `.protoProp` of `obj` overrides the property inherited from `proto`.

29.1.3 Tips for working with prototypes (advanced)

29.1.3.1 Best practice: avoid __proto__, except in object literals

I recommend to avoid the pseudo-property __proto__: As we will see later (p. 303), not all objects have it.

However, __proto__ in object literals is different. There, it is a built-in feature and always available.

The recommended ways of getting and setting prototypes are:

- The best way to get a prototype is via the following method:

29.1 Prototype chains

```
Object.getPrototypeOf(obj: Object) : Object
```

- The best way to set a prototype is when creating an object – via __proto__ in an object literal or via:

  ```
  Object.create(proto: Object) : Object
  ```

  If you have to, you can use `Object.setPrototypeOf()` to change the prototype of an existing object. But that may affect performance negatively.

This is how these features are used:

```
const proto1 = {};
const proto2 = {};

const obj = Object.create(proto1);
assert.equal(Object.getPrototypeOf(obj), proto1);

Object.setPrototypeOf(obj, proto2);
assert.equal(Object.getPrototypeOf(obj), proto2);
```

29.1.3.2 Check: is an object a prototype of another one?

So far, "p is a prototype of o" always meant "p is a *direct* prototype of o". But it can also be used more loosely and mean that p is in the prototype chain of o. That looser relationship can be checked via:

```
p.isPrototypeOf(o)
```

For example:

```
const a = {};
const b = {__proto__: a};
const c = {__proto__: b};

assert.equal(a.isPrototypeOf(b), true);
assert.equal(a.isPrototypeOf(c), true);

assert.equal(a.isPrototypeOf(a), false);
assert.equal(c.isPrototypeOf(a), false);
```

29.1.4 Sharing data via prototypes

Consider the following code:

```
const jane = {
  name: 'Jane',
  describe() {
    return 'Person named '+this.name;
  },
};
const tarzan = {
  name: 'Tarzan',
```

```
  describe() {
    return 'Person named '+this.name;
  },
};

assert.equal(jane.describe(), 'Person named Jane');
assert.equal(tarzan.describe(), 'Person named Tarzan');
```

We have two objects that are very similar. Both have two properties whose names are .name and .describe. Additionally, method .describe() is the same. How can we avoid duplicating that method?

We can move it to an object `PersonProto` and make that object a prototype of both jane and tarzan:

```
const PersonProto = {
  describe() {
    return 'Person named ' + this.name;
  },
};
const jane = {
  __proto__: PersonProto,
  name: 'Jane',
};
const tarzan = {
  __proto__: PersonProto,
  name: 'Tarzan',
};
```

The name of the prototype reflects that both jane and tarzan are persons.

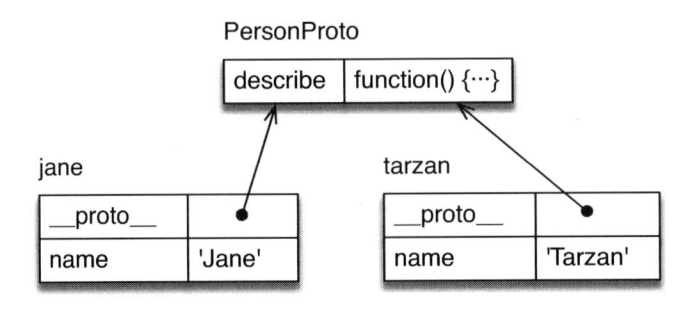

Figure 29.4: Objects jane and tarzan share method .describe(), via their common prototype PersonProto.

Fig. 29.4 illustrates how the three objects are connected: The objects at the bottom now contain the properties that are specific to jane and tarzan. The object at the top contains the properties that are shared between them.

When you make the method call jane.describe(), this points to the receiver of that method call, jane (in the bottom-left corner of the diagram). That's why the method still works. tarzan.describe() works similarly.

```
assert.equal(jane.describe(), 'Person named Jane');
assert.equal(tarzan.describe(), 'Person named Tarzan');
```

29.2 Classes

We are now ready to take on classes, which are basically a compact syntax for setting up prototype chains. Under the hood, JavaScript's classes are unconventional. But that is something you rarely see when working with them. They should normally feel familiar to people who have used other object-oriented programming languages.

29.2.1 A class for persons

We have previously worked with jane and tarzan, single objects representing persons. Let's use a *class declaration* to implement a factory for person objects:

```
class Person {
  constructor(name) {
    this.name = name;
  }
  describe() {
    return 'Person named '+this.name;
  }
}
```

jane and tarzan can now be created via new Person():

```
const jane = new Person('Jane');
assert.equal(jane.name, 'Jane');
assert.equal(jane.describe(), 'Person named Jane');

const tarzan = new Person('Tarzan');
assert.equal(tarzan.name, 'Tarzan');
assert.equal(tarzan.describe(), 'Person named Tarzan');
```

Class Person has two methods:

- The normal method .describe()
- The special method .constructor() which is called directly after a new instance has been created and initializes that instance. It receives the arguments that are passed to the new operator (after the class name). If you don't need any arguments to set up a new instance, you can omit the constructor.

29.2.1.1 Class expressions

There are two kinds of *class definitions* (ways of defining classes):

- *Class declarations*, which we have seen in the previous section.
- *Class expressions*, which we'll see next.

Class expressions can be anonymous and named:

```
// Anonymous class expression
const Person = class { ··· };

// Named class expression
const Person = class MyClass { ··· };
```

The name of a named class expression works similarly to the name of a named function expression (p. 213).

This was a first look at classes. We'll explore more features soon, but first we need to learn the internals of classes.

29.2.2 Classes under the hood

There is a lot going on under the hood of classes. Let's look at the diagram for jane (fig. 29.5).

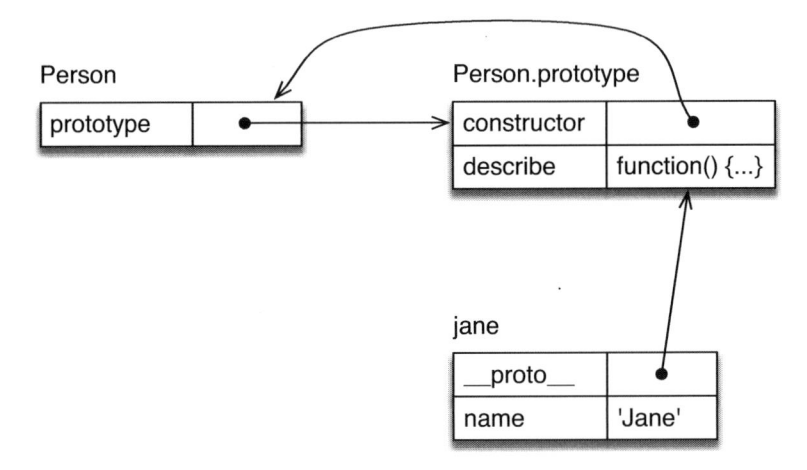

Figure 29.5: The class `Person` has the property `.prototype` that points to an object that is the prototype of all instances of `Person`. `jane` is one such instance.

The main purpose of class `Person` is to set up the prototype chain on the right (jane, followed by `Person.prototype`). It is interesting to note that both constructs inside class `Person` (`.constructor` and `.describe()`) created properties for `Person.prototype`, not for `Person`.

The reason for this slightly odd approach is backward compatibility: prior to classes, *constructor functions* (ordinary functions (p. 213), invoked via the new operator) were often used as factories for objects. Classes are mostly better syntax for constructor functions and therefore remain compatible with old code. That explains why classes are functions:

```
> typeof Person
'function'
```

In this book, I use the terms *constructor (function)* and *class* interchangeably.

It is easy to confuse `.__proto__` and `.prototype`. Hopefully, fig. 29.5 makes it clear how they differ:

29.2 Classes

- `.__proto__` is a pseudo-property for accessing the prototype of an object.
- `.prototype` is a normal property that is only special due to how the `new` operator uses it. The name is not ideal: `Person.prototype` does not point to the prototype of `Person`, it points to the prototype of all instances of `Person`.

29.2.2.1 `Person.prototype.constructor` (advanced)

There is one detail in fig. 29.5 that we haven't looked at, yet: `Person.prototype.constructor` points back to `Person`:

```
> Person.prototype.constructor === Person
true
```

This setup also exists due to backward compatibility. But it has two additional benefits.

First, each instance of a class inherits property `.constructor`. Therefore, given an instance, you can make "similar" objects using it:

```
const jane = new Person('Jane');

const cheeta = new jane.constructor('Cheeta');
// cheeta is also an instance of Person
// (the instanceof operator is explained later)
assert.equal(cheeta instanceof Person, true);
```

Second, you can get the name of the class that created a given instance:

```
const tarzan = new Person('Tarzan');

assert.equal(tarzan.constructor.name, 'Person');
```

29.2.3 Class definitions: prototype properties

All constructs in the body of the following class declaration create properties of `Foo.prototype`.

```
class Foo {
  constructor(prop) {
    this.prop = prop;
  }
  protoMethod() {
    return 'protoMethod';
  }
  get protoGetter() {
    return 'protoGetter';
  }
}
```

Let's examine them in order:

- `.constructor()` is called after creating a new instance of `Foo` to set up that instance.
- `.protoMethod()` is a normal method. It is stored in `Foo.prototype`.
- `.protoGetter` is a getter that is stored in `Foo.prototype`.

The following interaction uses class Foo:

```
> const foo = new Foo(123);
> foo.prop
123

> foo.protoMethod()
'protoMethod'
> foo.protoGetter
'protoGetter'
```

29.2.4 Class definitions: static properties

All constructs in the body of the following class declaration create so-called *static* properties – properties of Bar itself.

```
class Bar {
  static staticMethod() {
    return 'staticMethod';
  }
  static get staticGetter() {
    return 'staticGetter';
  }
}
```

The static method and the static getter are used as follows:

```
> Bar.staticMethod()
'staticMethod'
> Bar.staticGetter
'staticGetter'
```

29.2.5 The instanceof operator

The instanceof operator tells you if a value is an instance of a given class:

```
> new Person('Jane') instanceof Person
true
> ({}) instanceof Person
false
> ({}) instanceof Object
true
> [] instanceof Array
true
```

We'll explore the instanceof operator in more detail later (p. 301), after we have looked at subclassing.

29.2.6 Why I recommend classes

I recommend using classes for the following reasons:

- Classes are a common standard for object creation and inheritance that is now widely supported across frameworks (React, Angular, Ember, etc.). This is an improvement to how things were before, when almost every framework had its own inheritance library.
- They help tools such as IDEs and type checkers with their work and enable new features there.
- If you come from another language to JavaScript and are used to classes, then you can get started more quickly.
- JavaScript engines optimize them. That is, code that uses classes is almost always faster than code that uses a custom inheritance library.
- You can subclass built-in constructor functions such as `Error`.

That doesn't mean that classes are perfect:

- There is a risk of overdoing inheritance.
- There is a risk of putting too much functionality in classes (when some of it is often better put in functions).
- How they work superficially and under the hood is quite different. In other words, there is a disconnect between syntax and semantics. Two examples are:
    - A method definition inside a class `C` creates a method in the object `C.prototype`.
    - Classes are functions.

The motivation for the disconnect is backward compatibility. Thankfully, the disconnect causes few problems in practice; you are usually OK if you go along with what classes pretend to be.

Exercise: Writing a class

`exercises/proto-chains-classes/point_class_test.mjs`

29.3 Private data for classes

This section describes techniques for hiding some of the data of an object from the outside. We discuss them in the context of classes, but they also work for objects created directly, e.g., via object literals.

29.3.1 Private data: naming convention

The first technique makes a property private by prefixing its name with an underscore. This doesn't protect the property in any way; it merely signals to the outside: "You don't need to know about this property."

In the following code, the properties `._counter` and `._action` are private.

```
class Countdown {
  constructor(counter, action) {
    this._counter = counter;
    this._action = action;
  }
  dec() {
    this._counter--;
    if (this._counter === 0) {
      this._action();
    }
  }
}

// The two properties aren't really private:
assert.deepEqual(
  Object.keys(new Countdown()),
  ['_counter', '_action']);
```

With this technique, you don't get any protection and private names can clash. On the plus side, it is easy to use.

29.3.2 Private data: WeakMaps

Another technique is to use WeakMaps. How exactly that works is explained in the chapter on WeakMaps (p. 379). This is a preview:

```
const _counter = new WeakMap();
const _action = new WeakMap();

class Countdown {
  constructor(counter, action) {
    _counter.set(this, counter);
    _action.set(this, action);
  }
  dec() {
    let counter = _counter.get(this);
    counter--;
    _counter.set(this, counter);
    if (counter === 0) {
      _action.get(this)();
    }
  }
}

// The two pseudo-properties are truly private:
assert.deepEqual(
  Object.keys(new Countdown()),
  []);
```

This technique offers you considerable protection from outside access and there can't be

29.4 Subclassing

any name clashes. But it is also more complicated to use.

29.3.3 More techniques for private data

This book explains the most important techniques for private data in classes. There will also probably soon be built-in support for it. Consult the ECMAScript proposal "Class Public Instance Fields & Private Instance Fields"[1] for details.

A few additional techniques are explained in *Exploring ES6*[2].

29.4 Subclassing

Classes can also subclass ("extend") existing classes. As an example, the following class Employee subclasses Person:

```
class Person {
  constructor(name) {
    this.name = name;
  }
  describe() {
    return `Person named ${this.name}`;
  }
  static logNames(persons) {
    for (const person of persons) {
      console.log(person.name);
    }
  }
}

class Employee extends Person {
  constructor(name, title) {
    super(name);
    this.title = title;
  }
  describe() {
    return super.describe() +
      ` (${this.title})`;
  }
}

const jane = new Employee('Jane', 'CTO');
assert.equal(
  jane.describe(),
  'Person named Jane (CTO)');
```

Two comments:

---

[1] https://github.com/tc39/proposal-class-fields
[2] https://exploringjs.com/es6/ch_classes.html#sec_private-data-for-classes

- Inside a `.constructor()` method, you must call the super-constructor via `super()` before you can access `this`. That's because `this` doesn't exist before the super-constructor is called (this phenomenon is specific to classes).

- Static methods are also inherited. For example, `Employee` inherits the static method `.logNames()`:

  ```
  > 'logNames' in Employee
  true
  ```

> **Exercise: Subclassing**
> `exercises/proto-chains-classes/color_point_class_test.mjs`

29.4.1 Subclasses under the hood (advanced)

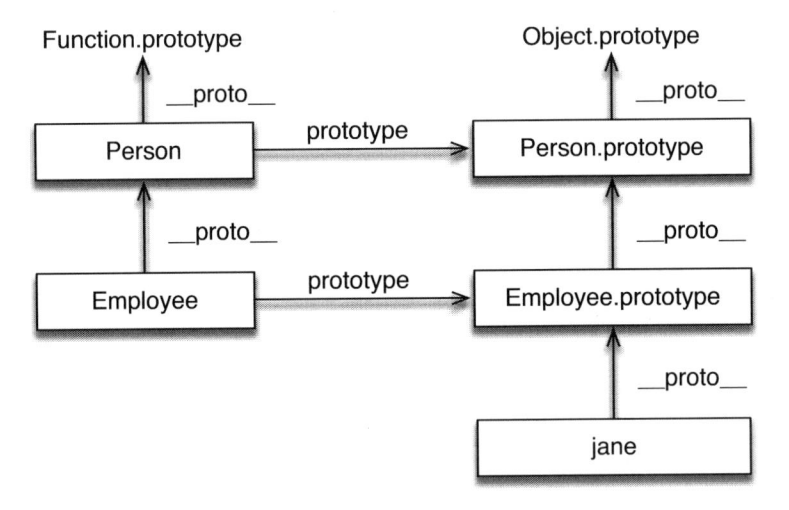

Figure 29.6: These are the objects that make up class `Person` and its subclass, `Employee`. The left column is about classes. The right column is about the `Employee` instance `jane` and its prototype chain.

The classes `Person` and `Employee` from the previous section are made up of several objects (fig. 29.6). One key insight for understanding how these objects are related is that there are two prototype chains:

- The instance prototype chain, on the right.
- The class prototype chain, on the left.

29.4.1.1 The instance prototype chain (right column)

The instance prototype chain starts with `jane` and continues with `Employee.prototype` and `Person.prototype`. In principle, the prototype chain ends at this point, but we get one more object: `Object.prototype`. This prototype provides services to virtually all objects, which is why it is included here, too:

```
> Object.getPrototypeOf(Person.prototype) === Object.prototype
true
```

29.4.1.2 The class prototype chain (left column)

In the class prototype chain, `Employee` comes first, `Person` next. Afterward, the chain continues with `Function.prototype`, which is only there because `Person` is a function and functions need the services of `Function.prototype`.

```
> Object.getPrototypeOf(Person) === Function.prototype
true
```

29.4.2 `instanceof` in more detail (advanced)

We have not yet seen how `instanceof` really works. Given the expression:

```
x instanceof C
```

How does `instanceof` determine if x is an instance of C (or a subclass of C)? It does so by checking if `C.prototype` is in the prototype chain of x. That is, the following expression is equivalent:

```
C.prototype.isPrototypeOf(x)
```

If we go back to fig. 29.6, we can confirm that the prototype chain does lead us to the following correct answers:

```
> jane instanceof Employee
true
> jane instanceof Person
true
> jane instanceof Object
true
```

29.4.3 Prototype chains of built-in objects (advanced)

Next, we'll use our knowledge of subclassing to understand the prototype chains of a few built-in objects. The following tool function `p()` helps us with our explorations.

```
const p = Object.getPrototypeOf.bind(Object);
```

We extracted method `.getPrototypeOf()` of `Object` and assigned it to p.

29.4.3.1 The prototype chain of {}

Let's start by examining plain objects:

```
> p({}) === Object.prototype
true
> p(p({})) === null
true
```

Fig. 29.7 shows a diagram for this prototype chain. We can see that {} really is an instance of `Object` – `Object.prototype` is in its prototype chain.

```
              null
               ↑
               | __proto__
        ┌──────────────────┐
        │ Object.prototype │
        └──────────────────┘
               ↑
               | __proto__
        ┌──────────────────┐
        │        {}        │
        └──────────────────┘
```

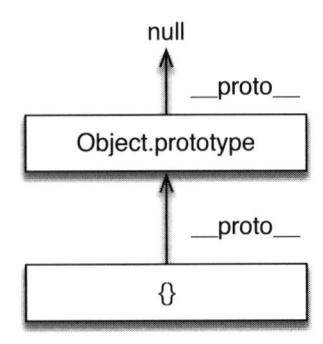

Figure 29.7: The prototype chain of an object created via an object literal starts with that object, continues with `Object.prototype`, and ends with `null`.

29.4.3.2 The prototype chain of []

What does the prototype chain of an Array look like?

```
> p([]) === Array.prototype
true
> p(p([])) === Object.prototype
true
> p(p(p([]))) === null
true
```

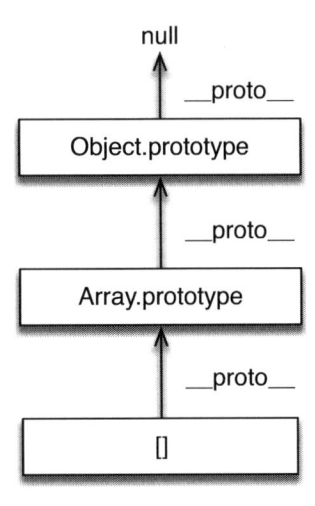

```
              null
               ↑
               | __proto__
        ┌──────────────────┐
        │ Object.prototype │
        └──────────────────┘
               ↑
               | __proto__
        ┌──────────────────┐
        │  Array.prototype │
        └──────────────────┘
               ↑
               | __proto__
        ┌──────────────────┐
        │        []        │
        └──────────────────┘
```

Figure 29.8: The prototype chain of an Array has these members: the Array instance, `Array.prototype`, `Object.prototype`, `null`.

This prototype chain (visualized in fig. 29.8) tells us that an Array object is an instance of `Array`, which is a subclass of `Object`.

29.4 Subclassing

29.4.3.3 The prototype chain of `function () {}`

Lastly, the prototype chain of an ordinary function tells us that all functions are objects:

```
> p(function () {}) === Function.prototype
true
> p(p(function () {})) === Object.prototype
true
```

29.4.3.4 Objects that aren't instances of `Object`

An object is only an instance of `Object` if `Object.prototype` is in its prototype chain. Most objects created via various literals are instances of `Object`:

```
> ({}) instanceof Object
true
> (() => {}) instanceof Object
true
> /abc/ug instanceof Object
true
```

Objects that don't have prototypes are not instances of `Object`:

```
> ({ __proto__: null }) instanceof Object
false
```

`Object.prototype` ends most prototype chains. Its prototype is `null`, which means it isn't an instance of `Object` either:

```
> Object.prototype instanceof Object
false
```

29.4.3.5 How exactly does the pseudo-property `.__proto__` work?

The pseudo-property `.__proto__` is implemented by class `Object` via a getter and a setter. It could be implemented like this:

```
class Object {
  get __proto__() {
    return Object.getPrototypeOf(this);
  }
  set __proto__(other) {
    Object.setPrototypeOf(this, other);
  }
  // ···
}
```

That means that you can switch `.__proto__` off by creating an object that doesn't have `Object.prototype` in its prototype chain (see the previous section):

```
> '__proto__' in {}
true
> '__proto__' in { __proto__: null }
false
```

29.4.4 Dispatched vs. direct method calls (advanced)

Let's examine how method calls work with classes. We are revisiting jane from earlier:

```
class Person {
  constructor(name) {
    this.name = name;
  }
  describe() {
    return 'Person named '+this.name;
  }
}
const jane = new Person('Jane');
```

Fig. 29.9 has a diagram with jane's prototype chain.

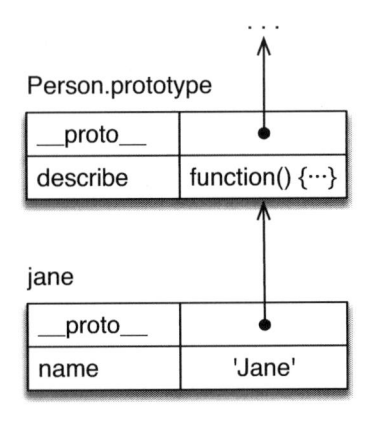

Figure 29.9: The prototype chain of jane starts with jane and continues with Person.prototype.

Normal method calls are *dispatched* – the method call jane.describe() happens in two steps:

- Dispatch: In the prototype chain of jane, find the first property whose key is 'describe' and retrieve its value.

    ```
    const func = jane.describe;
    ```

- Call: Call the value, while setting this to jane.

    ```
    func.call(jane);
    ```

This way of dynamically looking for a method and invoking it is called *dynamic dispatch*.

You can make the same method call *directly*, without dispatching:

```
Person.prototype.describe.call(jane)
```

This time, we directly point to the method via Person.prototype.describe and don't search for it in the prototype chain. We also specify this differently via .call().

29.4 Subclassing

Note that this always points to the beginning of a prototype chain. That enables .describe() to access .name.

29.4.4.1 Borrowing methods

Direct method calls become useful when you are working with methods of Object.prototype. For example, Object.prototype.hasOwnProperty(k) checks if this has a non-inherited property whose key is k:

```
> const obj = { foo: 123 };
> obj.hasOwnProperty('foo')
true
> obj.hasOwnProperty('bar')
false
```

However, in the prototype chain of an object, there may be another property with the key 'hasOwnProperty' that overrides the method in Object.prototype. Then a dispatched method call doesn't work:

```
> const obj = { hasOwnProperty: true };
> obj.hasOwnProperty('bar')
TypeError: obj.hasOwnProperty is not a function
```

The workaround is to use a direct method call:

```
> Object.prototype.hasOwnProperty.call(obj, 'bar')
false
> Object.prototype.hasOwnProperty.call(obj, 'hasOwnProperty')
true
```

This kind of direct method call is often abbreviated as follows:

```
> ({}).hasOwnProperty.call(obj, 'bar')
false
> ({}).hasOwnProperty.call(obj, 'hasOwnProperty')
true
```

This pattern may seem inefficient, but most engines optimize this pattern, so performance should not be an issue.

29.4.5 Mixin classes (advanced)

JavaScript's class system only supports *single inheritance*. That is, each class can have at most one superclass. One way around this limitation is via a technique called *mixin classes* (short: *mixins*).

The idea is as follows: Let's say we want a class C to inherit from two superclasses S1 and S2. That would be *multiple inheritance*, which JavaScript doesn't support.

Our workaround is to turn S1 and S2 into *mixins*, factories for subclasses:

```
const S1 = (Sup) => class extends Sup { /*···*/ };
const S2 = (Sup) => class extends Sup { /*···*/ };
```

Each of these two functions returns a class that extends a given superclass Sup. We create class C as follows:

```
class C extends S2(S1(Object)) {
  /*...*/
}
```

We now have a class C that extends a class S2 that extends a class S1 that extends Object (which most classes do implicitly).

29.4.5.1 Example: a mixin for brand management

We implement a mixin Branded that has helper methods for setting and getting the brand of an object:

```
const Branded = (Sup) => class extends Sup {
  setBrand(brand) {
    this._brand = brand;
    return this;
  }
  getBrand() {
    return this._brand;
  }
};
```

We use this mixin to implement brand management for a class Car:

```
class Car extends Branded(Object) {
  constructor(model) {
    super();
    this._model = model;
  }
  toString() {
    return `${this.getBrand()} ${this._model}`;
  }
}
```

The following code confirms that the mixin worked: Car has method .setBrand() of Branded.

```
const modelT = new Car('Model T').setBrand('Ford');
assert.equal(modelT.toString(), 'Ford Model T');
```

29.4.5.2 The benefits of mixins

Mixins free us from the constraints of single inheritance:

- The same class can extend a single superclass and zero or more mixins.
- The same mixin can be used by multiple classes.

29.5 FAQ: objects

29.5.1 Why do objects preserve the insertion order of properties?

In principle, objects are unordered. The main reason for ordering properties is so that operations that list entries, keys, or values are deterministic. That helps, e.g., with testing.

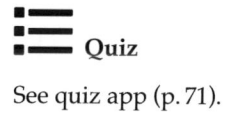

Quiz

See quiz app (p. 71).

Part VII

Collections

Chapter 30

Synchronous iteration

Contents

- 30.1 What is synchronous iteration about? ... 311
- 30.2 Core iteration constructs: iterables and iterators ... 312
- 30.3 Iterating manually ... 313
    - 30.3.1 Iterating over an iterable via `while` ... 313
- 30.4 Iteration in practice ... 314
    - 30.4.1 Iterating over Arrays ... 314
    - 30.4.2 Iterating over Sets ... 314
- 30.5 Quick reference: synchronous iteration ... 315
    - 30.5.1 Iterable data sources ... 315
    - 30.5.2 Iterating constructs ... 315

30.1 What is synchronous iteration about?

Synchronous iteration is a *protocol* (interfaces plus rules for using them) that connects two groups of entities in JavaScript:

- **Data sources:** On one hand, data comes in all shapes and sizes. In JavaScript's standard library, you have the linear data structure Array, the ordered collection Set (elements are ordered by time of addition), the ordered dictionary Map (entries are ordered by time of addition), and more. In libraries, you may find tree-shaped data structures and more.

- **Data consumers:** On the other hand, you have a whole class of constructs and algorithms that only need to access their input *sequentially*: one value at a time, until all values were visited. Examples include the `for-of` loop and spreading into function calls (via `...`).

The iteration protocol connects these two groups via the interface `Iterable`: data sources deliver their contents sequentially "through it"; data consumers get their input via it.

Data consumers   **Interface**   **Data sources**

for-of loop ─────────┐   Arrays
                     ├──► Iterable ◄────── Maps
spreading ───────────┘   Strings

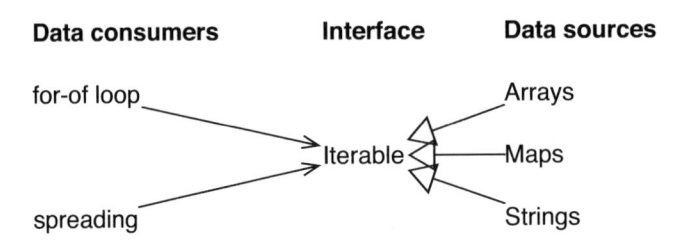

Figure 30.1: Data consumers such as the `for-of` loop use the interface `Iterable`. Data sources such as `Arrays` implement that interface.

Fig. 30.1 illustrates how iteration works: data consumers use the interface `Iterable`; data sources implement it.

> ⚙ **The JavaScript way of implementing interfaces**
>
> In JavaScript, an object *implements* an interface if it has all the methods that it describes. The interfaces mentioned in this chapter only exist in the ECMAScript specification.

Both sources and consumers of data profit from this arrangement:

- If you develop a new data structure, you only need to implement `Iterable` and a raft of tools can immediately be applied to it.
- If you write code that uses iteration, it automatically works with many sources of data.

30.2 Core iteration constructs: iterables and iterators

Two roles (described by interfaces) form the core of iteration (fig. 30.2):

- An *iterable* is an object whose contents can be traversed sequentially.
- An *iterator* is the pointer used for the traversal.

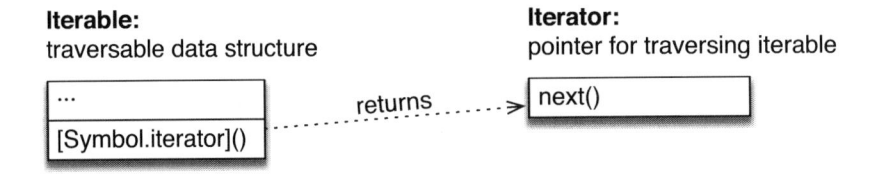

Iterable: **Iterator:**
traversable data structure   pointer for traversing iterable

| ... | returns | next() |
| [Symbol.iterator]() | ········►

Figure 30.2: Iteration has two main interfaces: `Iterable` and `Iterator`. The former has a method that returns the latter.

These are type definitions (in TypeScript's notation) for the interfaces of the iteration protocol:

```
interface Iterable<T> {
```

30.3 Iterating manually

```
  [Symbol.iterator]() : Iterator<T>;
}

interface Iterator<T> {
  next() : IteratorResult<T>;
}

interface IteratorResult<T> {
  value: T;
  done: boolean;
}
```

The interfaces are used as follows:

- You ask an Iterable for an iterator via the method whose key is Symbol.iterator.
- The Iterator returns the iterated values via its method .next().
- The values are not returned directly, but wrapped in objects with two properties:
    - .value is the iterated value.
    - .done indicates if the end of the iteration has been reached yet. It is true after the last iterated value and false beforehand.

30.3 Iterating manually

This is an example of using the iteration protocol:

```
const iterable = ['a', 'b'];

// The iterable is a factory for iterators:
const iterator = iterable[Symbol.iterator]();

// Call .next() until .done is true:
assert.deepEqual(
  iterator.next(), { value: 'a', done: false });
assert.deepEqual(
  iterator.next(), { value: 'b', done: false });
assert.deepEqual(
  iterator.next(), { value: undefined, done: true });
```

30.3.1 Iterating over an iterable via while

The following code demonstrates how to use a while loop to iterate over an iterable:

```
function logAll(iterable) {
  const iterator = iterable[Symbol.iterator]();
  while (true) {
    const {value, done} = iterator.next();
    if (done) break;
    console.log(value);
  }
}
```

```
}

logAll(['a', 'b']);
// Output:
// 'a'
// 'b'
```

> **Exercise: Using sync iteration manually**
> exercises/sync-iteration-use/sync_iteration_manually_exrc.mjs

30.4 Iteration in practice

We have seen how to use the iteration protocol manually, and it is relatively cumbersome. But the protocol is not meant to be used directly – it is meant to be used via higher-level language constructs built on top of it. This section shows what that looks like.

30.4.1 Iterating over Arrays

JavaScript's Arrays are iterable. That enables us to use the `for-of` loop:

```
const myArray = ['a', 'b', 'c'];

for (const x of myArray) {
  console.log(x);
}
// Output:
// 'a'
// 'b'
// 'c'
```

Destructuring via Array patterns (explained later) also uses iteration under the hood:

```
const [first, second] = myArray;
assert.equal(first, 'a');
assert.equal(second, 'b');
```

30.4.2 Iterating over Sets

JavaScript's Set data structure is iterable. That means `for-of` works:

```
const mySet = new Set().add('a').add('b').add('c');

for (const x of mySet) {
  console.log(x);
}
// Output:
// 'a'
```

```
// 'b'
// 'c'
```

As does Array-destructuring:

```
const [first, second] = mySet;
assert.equal(first, 'a');
assert.equal(second, 'b');
```

30.5 Quick reference: synchronous iteration

30.5.1 Iterable data sources

The following built-in data sources are iterable:

- Arrays
- Strings
- Maps
- Sets
- (Browsers: DOM data structures)

To iterate over the properties of objects, you need helpers such as `Object.keys()` and `Object.entries()`. That is necessary because properties exist at a different level that is independent of the level of data structures.

30.5.2 Iterating constructs

The following constructs are based on iteration:

- Destructuring via an Array pattern:

    ```
    const [x,y] = iterable;
    ```

- The for-of loop:

    ```
    for (const x of iterable) { /*···*/ }
    ```

- Array.from():

    ```
    const arr = Array.from(iterable);
    ```

- Spreading (via ...) into function calls and Array literals:

    ```
    func(...iterable);
    const arr = [...iterable];
    ```

- new Map() and new Set():

    ```
    const m = new Map(iterableOverKeyValuePairs);
    const s = new Set(iterableOverElements);
    ```

- Promise.all() and Promise.race():

    ```
    const promise1 = Promise.all(iterableOverPromises);
    const promise2 = Promise.race(iterableOverPromises);
    ```

- `yield*`:

  ```
  function* generatorFunction() {
    yield* iterable;
  }
  ```

Quiz

See quiz app (p. 71).

Chapter 31

Arrays (Array)

Contents

- 31.1 The two roles of Arrays in JavaScript 318
- 31.2 Basic Array operations 318
    - 31.2.1 Creating, reading, writing Arrays 318
    - 31.2.2 The .length of an Array 319
    - 31.2.3 Clearing an Array 319
    - 31.2.4 Spreading into Array literals 320
    - 31.2.5 Arrays: listing indices and entries 320
    - 31.2.6 Is a value an Array? 321
- 31.3 for-of and Arrays 321
    - 31.3.1 for-of: iterating over elements 321
    - 31.3.2 for-of: iterating over [index, element] pairs 322
- 31.4 Array-like objects 322
- 31.5 Converting iterable and Array-like values to Arrays 323
    - 31.5.1 Converting iterables to Arrays via spreading (...) 323
    - 31.5.2 Converting iterables and Array-like objects to Arrays via Array.from() (advanced) 323
- 31.6 Creating and filling Arrays with arbitrary lengths 324
    - 31.6.1 Do you need to create an empty Array that you'll fill completely later on? 324
    - 31.6.2 Do you need to create an Array filled with a primitive value? . . 324
    - 31.6.3 Do you need to create an Array filled with objects? 325
    - 31.6.4 Do you need to create a range of integers? 325
    - 31.6.5 Use a Typed Array if the elements are all integers or all floats . 325
- 31.7 Multidimensional Arrays 325
- 31.8 More Array features (advanced) 326
    - 31.8.1 Array indices are (slightly special) property keys 326
    - 31.8.2 Arrays are dictionaries and can have holes 327
- 31.9 Adding and removing elements (destructively and non-destructively) 329

        31.9.1 Prepending elements and Arrays 329
        31.9.2 Appending elements and Arrays 330
        31.9.3 Removing elements 330
    31.10 Methods: iteration and transformation (`.find()`, `.map()`, `.filter()`,
        etc.) 331
        31.10.1 Callbacks for iteration and transformation methods 331
        31.10.2 Searching elements: `.find()`, `.findIndex()` 332
        31.10.3 `.map()`: copy while giving elements new values 332
        31.10.4 `.flatMap()`: mapping to zero or more values 333
        31.10.5 `.filter()`: only keep some of the elements 335
        31.10.6 `.reduce()`: deriving a value from an Array (advanced) 336
    31.11 `.sort()`: sorting Arrays 338
        31.11.1 Customizing the sort order 339
        31.11.2 Sorting numbers 339
        31.11.3 Sorting objects 340
    31.12 Quick reference: `Array<T>` 340
        31.12.1 `new Array()` 340
        31.12.2 Static methods of `Array` 340
        31.12.3 Methods of `Array<T>.prototype` 341
        31.12.4 Sources 348

31.1 The two roles of Arrays in JavaScript

Arrays play two roles in JavaScript:

- Tuples: Arrays-as-tuples have a fixed number of indexed elements. Each of those elements can have a different type.
- Sequences: Arrays-as-sequences have a variable number of indexed elements. Each of those elements has the same type.

In practice, these two roles are often mixed.

Notably, Arrays-as-sequences are so flexible that you can use them as (traditional) arrays, stacks, and queues (see exercise later in this chapter).

31.2 Basic Array operations

31.2.1 Creating, reading, writing Arrays

The best way to create an Array is via an *Array literal*:

```
const arr = ['a', 'b', 'c'];
```

The Array literal starts and ends with square brackets []. It creates an Array with three *elements*: 'a', 'b', and 'c'.

To read an Array element, you put an index in square brackets (indices start at zero):

```
assert.equal(arr[0], 'a');
```

To change an Array element, you assign to an Array with an index:

```
arr[0] = 'x';
assert.deepEqual(arr, ['x', 'b', 'c']);
```

The range of Array indices is 32 bits (excluding the maximum length): [0, $2^{32}-1$)

31.2.2 The .length of an Array

Every Array has a property .length that can be used to both read and change(!) the number of elements in an Array.

The length of an Array is always the highest index plus one:

```
> const arr = ['a', 'b'];
> arr.length
2
```

If you write to the Array at the index of the length, you append an element:

```
> arr[arr.length] = 'c';
> arr
[ 'a', 'b', 'c' ]
> arr.length
3
```

Another way of (destructively) appending an element is via the Array method .push():

```
> arr.push('d');
> arr
[ 'a', 'b', 'c', 'd' ]
```

If you set .length, you are pruning the Array by removing elements:

```
> arr.length = 1;
> arr
[ 'a' ]
```

31.2.3 Clearing an Array

To clear (empty) an Array, you can either set its .length to zero:

```
const arr = ['a', 'b', 'c'];
arr.length = 0;
assert.deepEqual(arr, []);
```

or you can assign a new empty Array to the variable storing the Array:

```
let arr = ['a', 'b', 'c'];
arr = [];
assert.deepEqual(arr, []);
```

The latter approach has the advantage of not affecting other locations that point to the same Array. If, however, you do want to reset a shared Array for everyone, then you need the former approach.

> **Exercise: Removing empty lines via `.push()`**
> exercises/arrays/remove_empty_lines_push_test.mjs

31.2.4 Spreading into Array literals

Inside an Array literal, a *spread element* consists of three dots (...) followed by an expression. It results in the expression being evaluated and then iterated over. Each iterated value becomes an additional Array element – for example:

```
> const iterable = ['b', 'c'];
> ['a', ...iterable, 'd']
[ 'a', 'b', 'c', 'd' ]
```

That means that we can use spreading to create a copy of an Array:

```
const original = ['a', 'b', 'c'];
const copy = [...original];
```

Spreading is also convenient for concatenating Arrays (and other iterables) into Arrays:

```
const arr1 = ['a', 'b'];
const arr2 = ['c', 'd'];

const concatenated = [...arr1, ...arr2, 'e'];
assert.deepEqual(
  concatenated,
  ['a', 'b', 'c', 'd', 'e']);
```

Due to spreading using iteration, it only works if the value is iterable:

```
> [...'abc'] // strings are iterable
[ 'a', 'b', 'c' ]
> [...123]
TypeError: number 123 is not iterable
> [...undefined]
TypeError: undefined is not iterable
```

> ⚠️ **Spreading into Array literals is shallow**
>
> Similar to spreading into object literals (p. 266), spreading into Array literals creates *shallow* copies. That is, nested Arrays are not copied.

31.2.5 Arrays: listing indices and entries

Method `.keys()` lists the indices of an Array:

```
const arr = ['a', 'b'];
assert.deepEqual(
```

31.3 for-of and Arrays

```
  [...arr.keys()], // (A)
  [0, 1]);
```

`.keys()` returns an iterable. In line A, we spread to obtain an Array.

Listing Array indices is different from listing properties. The former produces numbers; the latter produces stringified numbers (in addition to non-index property keys):

```
const arr = ['a', 'b'];
arr.prop = true;

assert.deepEqual(
  Object.keys(arr),
  ['0', '1', 'prop']);
```

Method `.entries()` lists the contents of an Array as [index, element] pairs:

```
const arr = ['a', 'b'];
assert.deepEqual(
  [...arr.entries()],
  [[0, 'a'], [1, 'b']]);
```

31.2.6 Is a value an Array?

Following are two ways of checking if a value is an Array:

```
> [] instanceof Array
true
> Array.isArray([])
true
```

`instanceof` is usually fine. You need `Array.isArray()` if a value may come from another *realm*. Roughly, a realm is an instance of JavaScript's global scope. Some realms are isolated from each other (e.g., Web Workers (p. 421) in browsers), but there are also realms between which you can move data – for example, same-origin iframes in browsers. `x instanceof Array` checks the prototype chain of x and therefore returns `false` if x is an Array from another realm.

`typeof` categorizes Arrays as objects:

```
> typeof []
'object'
```

31.3 for-of and Arrays

We have already encountered the `for-of` loop. This section briefly recaps how to use it for Arrays.

31.3.1 for-of: iterating over elements

The following `for-of` loop iterates over the elements of an Array.

```
for (const element of ['a', 'b']) {
  console.log(element);
}
// Output:
// 'a'
// 'b'
```

31.3.2 `for-of`: iterating over [index, element] pairs

The following `for-of` loop iterates over [index, element] pairs. Destructuring (described later (p. 391)), gives us convenient syntax for setting up `index` and `element` in the head of `for-of`.

```
for (const [index, element] of ['a', 'b'].entries()) {
  console.log(index, element);
}
// Output:
// 0, 'a'
// 1, 'b'
```

31.4 Array-like objects

Some operations that work with Arrays require only the bare minimum: values must only be *Array-like*. An Array-like value is an object with the following properties:

- `.length`: holds the length of the Array-like object.
- `[0]`: holds the element at index 0 (etc.). Note that if you use numbers as property names, they are always coerced to strings. Therefore, `[0]` retrieves the value of the property whose key is `'0'`.

For example, `Array.from()` accepts Array-like objects and converts them to Arrays:

```
// If you omit .length, it is interpreted as 0
assert.deepEqual(
  Array.from({}),
  []);

assert.deepEqual(
  Array.from({length:2, 0:'a', 1:'b'}),
  [ 'a', 'b' ]);
```

The TypeScript interface for Array-like objects is:

```
interface ArrayLike<T> {
  length: number;
  [n: number]: T;
}
```

> Array-like objects are relatively rare in modern JavaScript

> Array-like objects used to be common before ES6; now you don't see them very often.

31.5 Converting iterable and Array-like values to Arrays

There are two common ways of converting iterable and Array-like values to Arrays: spreading and `Array.from()`.

31.5.1 Converting iterables to Arrays via spreading (...)

Inside an Array literal, spreading via ... converts any iterable object into a series of Array elements. For example:

```
// Get an Array-like collection from a web browser's DOM
const domCollection = document.querySelectorAll('a');

// Alas, the collection is missing many Array methods
assert.equal('map' in domCollection, false);

// Solution: convert it to an Array
const arr = [...domCollection];
assert.deepEqual(
  arr.map(x => x.href),
  ['https://2ality.com', 'https://exploringjs.com']);
```

The conversion works because the DOM collection is iterable.

31.5.2 Converting iterables and Array-like objects to Arrays via `Array.from()` (advanced)

`Array.from()` can be used in two modes.

31.5.2.1 Mode 1 of `Array.from()`: converting

The first mode has the following type signature:

```
.from<T>(iterable: Iterable<T> | ArrayLike<T>): T[]
```

Interface `Iterable` is shown in the chapter on synchronous iteration (p. 312). Interface `ArrayLike` appeared earlier in this chapter (p. 322).

With a single parameter, `Array.from()` converts anything iterable or Array-like to an Array:

```
> Array.from(new Set(['a', 'b']))
[ 'a', 'b' ]
> Array.from({length: 2, 0:'a', 1:'b'})
[ 'a', 'b' ]
```

31.5.2.2 Mode 2 of `Array.from()`: converting and mapping

The second mode of `Array.from()` involves two parameters:

```
.from<T, U>(
  iterable: Iterable<T> | ArrayLike<T>,
  mapFunc: (v: T, i: number) => U,
  thisArg?: any)
  : U[]
```

In this mode, `Array.from()` does several things:

- It iterates over `iterable`.
- It calls `mapFunc` with each iterated value. The optional parameter `thisArg` specifies a `this` for `mapFunc`.
- It applies `mapFunc` to each iterated value.
- It collects the results in a new Array and returns it.

In other words: we are going from an iterable with elements of type T to an Array with elements of type U.

This is an example:

```
> Array.from(new Set(['a', 'b']), x => x + x)
[ 'aa', 'bb' ]
```

31.6 Creating and filling Arrays with arbitrary lengths

The best way of creating an Array is via an Array literal. However, you can't always use one: The Array may be too large, you may not know its length during development, or you may want to keep its length flexible. Then I recommend the following techniques for creating, and possibly filling, Arrays.

31.6.1 Do you need to create an empty Array that you'll fill completely later on?

```
> new Array(3)
[ , , ,]
```

Note that the result has three *holes* (empty slots, p. 327) – the last comma in an Array literal is always ignored.

31.6.2 Do you need to create an Array filled with a primitive value?

```
> new Array(3).fill(0)
[0, 0, 0]
```

Caveat: If you use `.fill()` with an object, then each Array element will refer to this object (sharing it).

```
const arr = new Array(3).fill({});
arr[0].prop = true;
```

31.7 Multidimensional Arrays

```
assert.deepEqual(
  arr, [
    {prop: true},
    {prop: true},
    {prop: true},
  ]);
```

The next subsection explains how to fix this.

31.6.3 Do you need to create an Array filled with objects?

```
> Array.from({length: 3}, () => ({}))
[{}, {}, {}]
```

31.6.4 Do you need to create a range of integers?

```
function createRange(start, end) {
  return Array.from({length: end-start}, (_, i) => i+start);
}
assert.deepEqual(
  createRange(2, 5),
  [2, 3, 4]);
```

Here is an alternative, slightly hacky technique for creating integer ranges that start at zero:

```
/** Returns an iterable */
function createRange(end) {
  return new Array(end).keys();
}
assert.deepEqual(
  [...createRange(4)],
  [0, 1, 2, 3]);
```

This works because `.keys()` treats *holes* (p. 327) like undefined elements and lists their indices.

31.6.5 Use a Typed Array if the elements are all integers or all floats

If you are dealing with Arrays of integers or floats, consider *Typed Arrays* (p. 349), which were created for this purpose.

31.7 Multidimensional Arrays

JavaScript does not have real multidimensional Arrays; you need to resort to Arrays whose elements are Arrays:

```
function initMultiArray(...dimensions) {
  function initMultiArrayRec(dimIndex) {
    if (dimIndex >= dimensions.length) {
```

```
      return 0;
    } else {
      const dim = dimensions[dimIndex];
      const arr = [];
      for (let i=0; i<dim; i++) {
        arr.push(initMultiArrayRec(dimIndex+1));
      }
      return arr;
    }
  }
  return initMultiArrayRec(0);
}

const arr = initMultiArray(4, 3, 2);
arr[3][2][1] = 'X'; // last in each dimension
assert.deepEqual(arr, [
  [ [ 0, 0 ], [ 0, 0 ], [ 0, 0 ] ],
  [ [ 0, 0 ], [ 0, 0 ], [ 0, 0 ] ],
  [ [ 0, 0 ], [ 0, 0 ], [ 0, 0 ] ],
  [ [ 0, 0 ], [ 0, 0 ], [ 0, 'X' ] ],
]);
```

31.8 More Array features (advanced)

In this section, we look at phenomena you don't encounter often when working with Arrays.

31.8.1 Array indices are (slightly special) property keys

You'd think that Array elements are special because you are accessing them via numbers. But the square brackets operator [] for doing so is the same operator that is used for accessing properties. It coerces any value (that is not a symbol) to a string. Therefore, Array elements are (almost) normal properties (line A) and it doesn't matter if you use numbers or strings as indices (lines B and C):

```
const arr = ['a', 'b'];
arr.prop = 123;
assert.deepEqual(
  Object.keys(arr),
  ['0', '1', 'prop']); // (A)

assert.equal(arr[0], 'a');   // (B)
assert.equal(arr['0'], 'a'); // (C)
```

To make matters even more confusing, this is only how the language specification defines things (the theory of JavaScript, if you will). Most JavaScript engines optimize under the hood and do use actual integers to access Array elements (the practice of JavaScript, if you will).

31.8 More Array features (advanced)

Property keys (strings!) that are used for Array elements are called *indices*[1]. A string `str` is an index if converting it to a 32-bit unsigned integer and back results in the original value. Written as a formula:

```
ToString(ToUint32(str)) === str
```

31.8.1.1 Listing indices

When listing property keys, indices are treated specially (p. 279) – they always come first and are sorted like numbers (`'2'` comes before `'10'`):

```
const arr = [];
arr.prop = true;
arr[1] = 'b';
arr[0] = 'a';

assert.deepEqual(
  Object.keys(arr),
  ['0', '1', 'prop']);
```

Note that `.length`, `.entries()` and `.keys()` treat Array indices as numbers and ignore non-index properties:

```
assert.equal(arr.length, 2);
assert.deepEqual(
  [...arr.keys()], [0, 1]);
assert.deepEqual(
  [...arr.entries()], [[0, 'a'], [1, 'b']]);
```

We used a spread element (`...`) to convert the iterables returned by `.keys()` and `.entries()` to Arrays.

31.8.2 Arrays are dictionaries and can have holes

We distinguish two kinds of Arrays in JavaScript:

- An Array `arr` is *dense* if all indices `i`, with $0 \leq i <$ `arr.length`, exist. That is, the indices form a contiguous range.
- An Array is *sparse* if the range of indices has *holes* in it. That is, some indices are missing.

Arrays can be sparse in JavaScript because Arrays are actually dictionaries from indices to values.

> 💡 **Recommendation: avoid holes**
>
> So far, we have only seen dense Arrays and it's indeed recommended to avoid holes: They make your code more complicated and are not handled consistently by Array methods. Additionally, JavaScript engines optimize dense Arrays, making them faster.

---
[1]https://tc39.github.io/ecma262/#integer-index

31.8.2.1 Creating holes

You can create holes by skipping indices when assigning elements:

```
const arr = [];
arr[0] = 'a';
arr[2] = 'c';

assert.deepEqual(Object.keys(arr), ['0', '2']); // (A)

assert.equal(0 in arr, true); // element
assert.equal(1 in arr, false); // hole
```

In line A, we are using `Object.keys()` because `arr.keys()` treats holes as if they were undefined elements and does not reveal them.

Another way of creating holes is to skip elements in Array literals:

```
const arr = ['a', , 'c'];

assert.deepEqual(Object.keys(arr), ['0', '2']);
```

You can also delete Array elements:

```
const arr = ['a', 'b', 'c'];
assert.deepEqual(Object.keys(arr), ['0', '1', '2']);
delete arr[1];
assert.deepEqual(Object.keys(arr), ['0', '2']);
```

31.8.2.2 How do Array operations treat holes?

Alas, there are many different ways in which Array operations treat holes.

Some Array operations remove holes:

```
> ['a',,'b'].filter(x => true)
[ 'a', 'b' ]
```

Some Array operations ignore holes:

```
> ['a', ,'a'].every(x => x === 'a')
true
```

Some Array operations ignore but preserve holes:

```
> ['a',,'b'].map(x => 'c')
[ 'c', , 'c' ]
```

Some Array operations treat holes as `undefined` elements:

```
> Array.from(['a',,'b'], x => x)
[ 'a', undefined, 'b' ]
> [...['a',,'b'].entries()]
[[0, 'a'], [1, undefined], [2, 'b']]
```

Object.keys() works differently than .keys() (strings vs. numbers, holes don't have keys):

```
> [...['a',,'b'].keys()]
[ 0, 1, 2 ]
> Object.keys(['a',,'b'])
[ '0', '2' ]
```

There is no rule to remember here. If it ever matters how an Array operation treats holes, the best approach is to do a quick test in a console.

31.9 Adding and removing elements (destructively and non-destructively)

JavaScript's Array is quite flexible and more like a combination of array, stack, and queue. This section explores ways of adding and removing Array elements. Most operations can be performed both *destructively* (modifying the Array) and *non-destructively* (producing a modified copy).

31.9.1 Prepending elements and Arrays

In the following code, we destructively prepend single elements to arr1 and an Array to arr2:

```
const arr1 = ['a', 'b'];
arr1.unshift('x', 'y'); // prepend single elements
assert.deepEqual(arr1, ['x', 'y', 'a', 'b']);

const arr2 = ['a', 'b'];
arr2.unshift(...['x', 'y']); // prepend Array
assert.deepEqual(arr2, ['x', 'y', 'a', 'b']);
```

Spreading lets us unshift an Array into arr2.

Non-destructive prepending is done via spread elements:

```
const arr1 = ['a', 'b'];
assert.deepEqual(
  ['x', 'y', ...arr1], // prepend single elements
  ['x', 'y', 'a', 'b']);
assert.deepEqual(arr1, ['a', 'b']); // unchanged!

const arr2 = ['a', 'b'];
assert.deepEqual(
  [...['x', 'y'], ...arr2], // prepend Array
  ['x', 'y', 'a', 'b']);
assert.deepEqual(arr2, ['a', 'b']); // unchanged!
```

31.9.2 Appending elements and Arrays

In the following code, we destructively append single elements to `arr1` and an Array to `arr2`:

```
const arr1 = ['a', 'b'];
arr1.push('x', 'y'); // append single elements
assert.deepEqual(arr1, ['a', 'b', 'x', 'y']);

const arr2 = ['a', 'b'];
arr2.push(...['x', 'y']); // append Array
assert.deepEqual(arr2, ['a', 'b', 'x', 'y']);
```

Spreading lets us push an Array into `arr2`.

Non-destructive appending is done via spread elements:

```
const arr1 = ['a', 'b'];
assert.deepEqual(
  [...arr1, 'x', 'y'], // append single elements
  ['a', 'b', 'x', 'y']);
assert.deepEqual(arr1, ['a', 'b']); // unchanged!

const arr2 = ['a', 'b'];
assert.deepEqual(
  [...arr2, ...['x', 'y']], // append Array
  ['a', 'b', 'x', 'y']);
assert.deepEqual(arr2, ['a', 'b']); // unchanged!
```

31.9.3 Removing elements

These are three destructive ways of removing Array elements:

```
// Destructively remove first element:
const arr1 = ['a', 'b', 'c'];
assert.equal(arr1.shift(), 'a');
assert.deepEqual(arr1, ['b', 'c']);

// Destructively remove last element:
const arr2 = ['a', 'b', 'c'];
assert.equal(arr2.pop(), 'c');
assert.deepEqual(arr2, ['a', 'b']);

// Remove one or more elements anywhere:
const arr3 = ['a', 'b', 'c', 'd'];
assert.deepEqual(arr3.splice(1, 2), ['b', 'c']);
assert.deepEqual(arr3, ['a', 'd']);
```

`.splice()` is covered in more detail in the quick reference at the end of this chapter (p. 341).

Destructuring via a rest element lets you non-destructively remove elements from the beginning of an Array (destructuring is covered later (p. 391)).

```
const arr1 = ['a', 'b', 'c'];
// Ignore first element, extract remaining elements
const [, ...arr2] = arr1;

assert.deepEqual(arr2, ['b', 'c']);
assert.deepEqual(arr1, ['a', 'b', 'c']); // unchanged!
```

Alas, a rest element must come last in an Array. Therefore, you can only use it to extract suffixes.

Exercise: Implementing a queue via an Array

exercises/arrays/queue_via_array_test.mjs

31.10 Methods: iteration and transformation (.find(), .map(), .filter(), etc.)

In this section, we take a look at Array methods for iterating over Arrays and for transforming Arrays.

31.10.1 Callbacks for iteration and transformation methods

All iteration and transformation methods use callbacks. The former feed all iterated values to their callbacks; the latter ask their callbacks how to transform Arrays.

These callbacks have type signatures that look as follows:

```
callback: (value: T, index: number, array: Array<T>) => boolean
```

That is, the callback gets three parameters (it is free to ignore any of them):

- `value` is the most important one. This parameter holds the iterated value that is currently being processed.
- `index` can additionally tell the callback what the index of the iterated value is.
- `array` points to the current Array (the receiver of the method call). Some algorithms need to refer to the whole Array – e.g., to search it for answers. This parameter lets you write reusable callbacks for such algorithms.

What the callback is expected to return depends on the method it is passed to. Possibilities include:

- `.map()` fills its result with the values returned by its callback:
  ```
  > ['a', 'b', 'c'].map(x => x + x)
  [ 'aa', 'bb', 'cc' ]
  ```
- `.find()` returns the first Array element for which its callback returns `true`:

```
> ['a', 'bb', 'ccc'].find(str => str.length >= 2)
'bb'
```

Both of these methods are described in more detail later.

31.10.2 Searching elements: `.find()`, `.findIndex()`

`.find()` returns the first element for which its callback returns a truthy value (and undefined if it can't find anything):

```
> [6, -5, 8].find(x => x < 0)
-5
> [6, 5, 8].find(x => x < 0)
undefined
```

`.findIndex()` returns the index of the first element for which its callback returns a truthy value (and -1 if it can't find anything):

```
> [6, -5, 8].findIndex(x => x < 0)
1
> [6, 5, 8].findIndex(x => x < 0)
-1
```

`.findIndex()` can be implemented as follows:

```
function findIndex(arr, callback) {
  for (const [i, x] of arr.entries()) {
    if (callback(x, i, arr)) {
      return i;
    }
  }
  return -1;
}
```

31.10.3 `.map()`: copy while giving elements new values

`.map()` returns a modified copy of the receiver. The elements of the copy are the results of applying map's callback to the elements of the receiver.

All of this is easier to understand via examples:

```
> [1, 2, 3].map(x => x * 3)
[ 3, 6, 9 ]
> ['how', 'are', 'you'].map(str => str.toUpperCase())
[ 'HOW', 'ARE', 'YOU' ]
> [true, true, true].map((_x, index) => index)
[ 0, 1, 2 ]
```

`.map()` can be implemented as follows:

```
function map(arr, mapFunc) {
  const result = [];
  for (const [i, x] of arr.entries()) {
```

```
      result.push(mapFunc(x, i, arr));
    }
    return result;
}
```

> **Exercise: Numbering lines via `.map()`**
> `exercises/arrays/number_lines_test.mjs`

31.10.4 `.flatMap()`: mapping to zero or more values

The type signature of `Array<T>.prototype.flatMap()` is:

```
.flatMap<U>(
  callback: (value: T, index: number, array: T[]) => U|Array<U>,
  thisValue?: any
): U[]
```

Both `.map()` and `.flatMap()` take a function `callback` as a parameter that controls how an input Array is translated to an output Array:

- With `.map()`, each input Array element is translated to exactly one output element. That is, `callback` returns a single value.
- With `.flatMap()`, each input Array element is translated to zero or more output elements. That is, `callback` returns an Array of values (it can also return non-Array values, but that is rare).

This is `.flatMap()` in action:

```
> ['a', 'b', 'c'].flatMap(x => [x,x])
[ 'a', 'a', 'b', 'b', 'c', 'c' ]
> ['a', 'b', 'c'].flatMap(x => [x])
[ 'a', 'b', 'c' ]
> ['a', 'b', 'c'].flatMap(x => [])
[]
```

31.10.4.1 A simple implementation

You could implement `.flatMap()` as follows. Note: This implementation is simpler than the built-in version, which, for example, performs more checks.

```
function flatMap(arr, mapFunc) {
  const result = [];
  for (const [index, elem] of arr.entries()) {
    const x = mapFunc(elem, index, arr);
    // We allow mapFunc() to return non-Arrays
    if (Array.isArray(x)) {
      result.push(...x);
    } else {
      result.push(x);
    }
```

```
  }
  return result;
}
```

What is .flatMap() good for? Let's look at use cases!

31.10.4.2 Use case: filtering and mapping at the same time

The result of the Array method .map() always has the same length as the Array it is invoked on. That is, its callback can't skip Array elements it isn't interested in. The ability of .flatMap() to do so is useful in the next example.

We will use the following function processArray() to create an Array that we'll then filter and map via .flatMap():

```
function processArray(arr, callback) {
  return arr.map(x => {
    try {
      return { value: callback(x) };
    } catch (e) {
      return { error: e };
    }
  });
}
```

Next, we create an Array results via processArray():

```
const results = processArray([1, -5, 6], throwIfNegative);
assert.deepEqual(results, [
  { value: 1 },
  { error: new Error('Illegal value: -5') },
  { value: 6 },
]);

function throwIfNegative(value) {
  if (value < 0) {
    throw new Error('Illegal value: '+value);
  }
  return value;
}
```

We can now use .flatMap() to extract just the values or just the errors from results:

```
const values = results.flatMap(
  result => result.value ? [result.value] : []);
assert.deepEqual(values, [1, 6]);

const errors = results.flatMap(
  result => result.error ? [result.error] : []);
assert.deepEqual(errors, [new Error('Illegal value: -5')]);
```

31.10.4.3 Use case: mapping to multiple values

The Array method `.map()` maps each input Array element to one output element. But what if we want to map it to multiple output elements?

That becomes necessary in the following example:

```
> stringsToCodePoints(['many', 'a', 'moon'])
['m', 'a', 'n', 'y', 'a', 'm', 'o', 'o', 'n']
```

We want to convert an Array of strings to an Array of Unicode characters (code points). The following function achieves that via `.flatMap()`:

```
function stringsToCodePoints(strs) {
  return strs.flatMap(str => [...str]);
}
```

Exercises: `.flatMap()`

- exercises/arrays/convert_to_numbers_test.mjs
- exercises/arrays/replace_objects_test.mjs

31.10.5 `.filter()`: only keep some of the elements

The Array method `.filter()` returns an Array collecting all elements for which the callback returns a truthy value.

For example:

```
> [-1, 2, 5, -7, 6].filter(x => x >= 0)
[ 2, 5, 6 ]
> ['a', 'b', 'c', 'd'].filter((_x,i) => (i%2)===0)
[ 'a', 'c' ]
```

`.filter()` can be implemented as follows:

```
function filter(arr, filterFunc) {
  const result = [];
  for (const [i, x] of arr.entries()) {
    if (filterFunc(x, i, arr)) {
      result.push(x);
    }
  }
  return result;
}
```

Exercise: Removing empty lines via `.filter()`

exercises/arrays/remove_empty_lines_filter_test.mjs

31.10.6 .reduce(): deriving a value from an Array (advanced)

Method .reduce() is a powerful tool for computing a "summary" of an Array arr. A summary can be any kind of value:

- A number. For example, the sum of all elements of arr.
- An Array. For example, a copy of arr, where each element is twice the original element.
- Etc.

reduce is also known as foldl ("fold left") in functional programming and popular there. One caveat is that it can make code difficult to understand.

.reduce() has the following type signature (inside an Array<T>):

```
.reduce<U>(
  callback: (accumulator: U, element: T, index: number, array: T[]) => U,
  init?: U)
  : U
```

T is the type of the Array elements, U is the type of the summary. The two may or may not be different. accumulator is just another name for "summary".

To compute the summary of an Array arr, .reduce() feeds all Array elements to its callback one at a time:

```
const accumulator_0 = callback(init, arr[0]);
const accumulator_1 = callback(accumulator_0, arr[1]);
const accumulator_2 = callback(accumulator_1, arr[2]);
// Etc.
```

callback combines the previously computed summary (stored in its parameter accumulator) with the current Array element and returns the next accumulator. The result of .reduce() is the final accumulator – the last result of callback after it has visited all elements.

In other words: callback does most of the work; .reduce() just invokes it in a useful manner.

You could say that the callback folds Array elements into the accumulator. That's why this operation is called "fold" in functional programming.

31.10.6.1 A first example

Let's look at an example of .reduce() in action: function addAll() computes the sum of all numbers in an Array arr.

```
function addAll(arr) {
  const startSum = 0;
  const callback = (sum, element) => sum + element;
  return arr.reduce(callback, startSum);
}
assert.equal(addAll([1, 2, 3]), 6); // (A)
assert.equal(addAll([7, -4, 2]), 5);
```

31.10 Methods: iteration and transformation (`.find()`, `.map()`, `.filter()`, etc.)

In this case, the accumulator holds the sum of all Array elements that `callback` has already visited.

How was the result 6 derived from the Array in line A? Via the following invocations of `callback`:

```
callback(0, 1) --> 1
callback(1, 2) --> 3
callback(3, 3) --> 6
```

Notes:

- The first parameters are the current accumulators (starting with parameter `init` of `.reduce()`).
- The second parameters are the current Array elements.
- The results are the next accumulators.
- The last result of `callback` is also the result of `.reduce()`.

Alternatively, we could have implemented `addAll()` via a `for-of` loop:

```
function addAll(arr) {
  let sum = 0;
  for (const element of arr) {
    sum = sum + element;
  }
  return sum;
}
```

It's hard to say which of the two implementations is "better": the one based on `.reduce()` is a little more concise, while the one based on `for-of` may be a little easier to understand – especially if you are not familiar with functional programming.

31.10.6.2 Example: finding indices via `.reduce()`

The following function is an implementation of the Array method `.indexOf()`. It returns the first index at which the given `searchValue` appears inside the Array `arr`:

```
const NOT_FOUND = -1;
function indexOf(arr, searchValue) {
  return arr.reduce(
    (result, elem, index) => {
      if (result !== NOT_FOUND) {
        // We have already found something: don't change anything
        return result;
      } else if (elem === searchValue) {
        return index;
      } else {
        return NOT_FOUND;
      }
    },
    NOT_FOUND);
}
```

```
assert.equal(indexOf(['a', 'b', 'c'], 'b'), 1);
assert.equal(indexOf(['a', 'b', 'c'], 'x'), -1);
```

One limitation of `.reduce()` is that you can't finish early (in a `for-of` loop, you can `break`). Here, we always immediately return the result once we have found it.

31.10.6.3 Example: doubling Array elements

Function `double(arr)` returns a copy of `inArr` whose elements are all multiplied by 2:

```
function double(inArr) {
  return inArr.reduce(
    (outArr, element) => {
      outArr.push(element * 2);
      return outArr;
    },
    []);
}
assert.deepEqual(
  double([1, 2, 3]),
  [2, 4, 6]);
```

We modify the initial value `[]` by pushing into it. A non-destructive, more functional version of `double()` looks as follows:

```
function double(inArr) {
  return inArr.reduce(
    // Don't change `outArr`, return a fresh Array
    (outArr, element) => [...outArr, element * 2],
    []);
}
assert.deepEqual(
  double([1, 2, 3]),
  [2, 4, 6]);
```

This version is more elegant but also slower and uses more memory.

> **Exercises: `.reduce()`**
> - `map()` via `.reduce()`: `exercises/arrays/map_via_reduce_test.mjs`
> - `filter()` via `.reduce()`: `exercises/arrays/filter_via_reduce_test.mjs`
> - `countMatches()` via `.reduce()`: `exercises/arrays/count_matches_via_reduce_test.mjs`

31.11 `.sort()`: sorting Arrays

`.sort()` has the following type definition:

```
sort(compareFunc?: (a: T, b: T) => number): this
```

31.11 .sort(): sorting Arrays

By default, .sort() sorts string representations of the elements. These representations are compared via <. This operator compares *lexicographically* (the first characters are most significant). You can see that when sorting numbers:

```
> [200, 3, 10].sort()
[ 10, 200, 3 ]
```

When sorting human-language strings, you need to be aware that they are compared according to their code unit values (char codes):

```
> ['pie', 'cookie', 'éclair', 'Pie', 'Cookie', 'Éclair'].sort()
[ 'Cookie', 'Pie', 'cookie', 'pie', 'Éclair', 'éclair' ]
```

As you can see, all unaccented uppercase letters come before all unaccented lowercase letters, which come before all accented letters. Use Intl, the JavaScript internationalization API[2], if you want proper sorting for human languages.

Note that .sort() sorts *in place*; it changes and returns its receiver:

```
> const arr = ['a', 'c', 'b'];
> arr.sort() === arr
true
> arr
[ 'a', 'b', 'c' ]
```

31.11.1 Customizing the sort order

You can customize the sort order via the parameter compareFunc, which must return a number that is:

- negative if a < b
- zero if a === b
- positive if a > b

> 💡 **Tip for remembering these rules**
>
> A negative number is *less than* zero (etc.).

31.11.2 Sorting numbers

You can use this helper function to sort numbers:

```
function compareNumbers(a, b) {
  if (a < b) {
    return -1;
  } else if (a === b) {
    return 0;
  } else {
    return 1;
  }
}
```

---

[2]https://developer.mozilla.org/en-US/docs/Web/JavaScript/Reference/Global_Objects/Intl

```
}
assert.deepEqual(
  [200, 3, 10].sort(compareNumbers),
  [3, 10, 200]);
```

The following is a quick and dirty alternative.

```
> [200, 3, 10].sort((a,b) => a - b)
[ 3, 10, 200 ]
```

The downsides of this approach are:

- It is cryptic.
- There is a risk of numeric overflow or underflow, if a-b becomes a large positive or negative number.

31.11.3 Sorting objects

You also need to use a compare function if you want to sort objects. As an example, the following code shows how to sort objects by age.

```
const arr = [ {age: 200}, {age: 3}, {age: 10} ];
assert.deepEqual(
  arr.sort((obj1, obj2) => obj1.age - obj2.age),
  [{ age: 3 }, { age: 10 }, { age: 200 }] );
```

> **Exercise: Sorting objects by name**
> exercises/arrays/sort_objects_test.mjs

31.12 Quick reference: Array<T>

Legend:

- R: method does not change the Array (non-destructive).
- W: method changes the Array (destructive).

31.12.1 new Array()

new Array(n) creates an Array of length n that contains n holes:

```
// Trailing commas are always ignored.
// Therefore: number of commas = number of holes
assert.deepEqual(new Array(3), [,,,]);
```

new Array() creates an empty Array. However, I recommend to always use [] instead.

31.12.2 Static methods of Array

- Array.from<T>(iterable: Iterable<T> | ArrayLike<T>): T[] [ES6]

31.12 Quick reference: Array<T> 341

- Array.from<T,U>(iterable: Iterable<T> | ArrayLike<T>, mapFunc: (v: T, k: number) => U, thisArg?: any): U[] [ES6]

    Converts an iterable or an Array-like object (p. 322) to an Array. Optionally, the input values can be translated via mapFunc before they are added to the output Array.

    Examples:

    ```
    > Array.from(new Set(['a', 'b'])) // iterable
    [ 'a', 'b' ]
    > Array.from({length: 2, 0:'a', 1:'b'}) // Array-like object
    [ 'a', 'b' ]
    ```

- Array.of<T>(...items: T[]): T[] [ES6]

    This static method is mainly useful for subclasses of Array, where it serves as a custom Array literal:

    ```
    class MyArray extends Array {}

    assert.equal(
      MyArray.of('a', 'b') instanceof MyArray, true);
    ```

31.12.3 Methods of Array<T>.prototype

- .concat(...items: Array<T[] | T>): T[] [R, ES3]

    Returns a new Array that is the concatenation of the receiver and all items. Non-Array parameters (such as 'b' in the following example) are treated as if they were Arrays with single elements.

    ```
    > ['a'].concat('b', ['c', 'd'])
    [ 'a', 'b', 'c', 'd' ]
    ```

- .copyWithin(target: number, start: number, end=this.length): this [W, ES6]

    Copies the elements whose indices range from (including) start to (excluding) end to indices starting with target. Overlapping is handled correctly.

    ```
    > ['a', 'b', 'c', 'd'].copyWithin(0, 2, 4)
    [ 'c', 'd', 'c', 'd' ]
    ```

    If start or end is negative, then .length is added to it.

- .entries(): Iterable<[number, T]> [R, ES6]

    Returns an iterable over [index, element] pairs.

    ```
    > Array.from(['a', 'b'].entries())
    [ [ 0, 'a' ], [ 1, 'b' ] ]
    ```

- .every(callback: (value: T, index: number, array: Array<T>) => boolean, thisArg?: any): boolean [R, ES5]

Returns true if callback returns a truthy value for every element. Otherwise, it returns false. It stops as soon as it receives a falsy value. This method corresponds to universal quantification ("for all", ∀) in mathematics.

```
> [1, 2, 3].every(x => x > 0)
true
> [1, -2, 3].every(x => x > 0)
false
```

Related method: .some() ("exists").

- .fill(value: T, start=0, end=this.length): this [W, ES6]

Assigns value to every index between (including) start and (excluding) end.

```
> [0, 1, 2].fill('a')
[ 'a', 'a', 'a' ]
```

Caveat: Don't use this method to fill an Array with an object obj; then each element will refer to obj (sharing it). In this case, it's better to use Array.from() (p. 324).

- .filter(callback: (value: T, index: number, array: Array<T>) => any, thisArg?: any): T[] [R, ES5]

Returns an Array with only those elements for which callback returns a truthy value.

```
> [1, -2, 3].filter(x => x > 0)
[ 1, 3 ]
```

- .find(predicate: (value: T, index: number, obj: T[]) => boolean, thisArg?: any): T | undefined [R, ES6]

The result is the first element for which predicate returns a truthy value. If there is no such element, the result is undefined.

```
> [1, -2, 3].find(x => x < 0)
-2
> [1, 2, 3].find(x => x < 0)
undefined
```

- .findIndex(predicate: (value: T, index: number, obj: T[]) => boolean, thisArg?: any): number [R, ES6]

The result is the index of the first element for which predicate returns a truthy value. If there is no such element, the result is -1.

```
> [1, -2, 3].findIndex(x => x < 0)
1
> [1, 2, 3].findIndex(x => x < 0)
-1
```

- .flat(depth = 1): any[] [R, ES2019]

"Flattens" an Array: It descends into the Arrays that are nested inside the input Array and creates a copy where all values it finds at level depth or lower are moved to the top level.

```
> [ 1,2, [3,4], [[5,6]] ].flat(0) // no change
[ 1, 2, [3,4], [[5,6]] ]

> [ 1,2, [3,4], [[5,6]] ].flat(1)
[1, 2, 3, 4, [5,6]]

> [ 1,2, [3,4], [[5,6]] ].flat(2)
[1, 2, 3, 4, 5, 6]
```

- .flatMap<U>(callback: (value: T, index: number, array: T[]) => U|Array<U>, thisValue?: any): U[] [R, ES2019]

  The result is produced by invoking callback() for each element of the original Array and concatenating the Arrays it returns.

  ```
  > ['a', 'b', 'c'].flatMap(x => [x,x])
  [ 'a', 'a', 'b', 'b', 'c', 'c' ]
  > ['a', 'b', 'c'].flatMap(x => [x])
  [ 'a', 'b', 'c' ]
  > ['a', 'b', 'c'].flatMap(x => [])
  []
  ```

- .forEach(callback: (value: T, index: number, array: Array<T>) => void, thisArg?: any): void [R, ES5]

  Calls callback for each element.

  ```
  ['a', 'b'].forEach((x, i) => console.log(x, i))

  // Output:
  // 'a', 0
  // 'b', 1
  ```

  A for-of loop is usually a better choice: it's faster, supports break and can iterate over arbitrary iterables.

- .includes(searchElement: T, fromIndex=0): boolean [R, ES2016]

  Returns true if the receiver has an element whose value is searchElement and false, otherwise. Searching starts at index fromIndex.

  ```
  > [0, 1, 2].includes(1)
  true
  > [0, 1, 2].includes(5)
  false
  ```

- .indexOf(searchElement: T, fromIndex=0): number [R, ES5]

  Returns the index of the first element that is strictly equal to searchElement. Returns -1 if there is no such element. Starts searching at index fromIndex, visiting higher indices next.

```
> ['a', 'b', 'a'].indexOf('a')
0
> ['a', 'b', 'a'].indexOf('a', 1)
2
> ['a', 'b', 'a'].indexOf('c')
-1
```

- `.join(separator = ','): string` [R, ES1]

    Creates a string by concatenating string representations of all elements, separating them with `separator`.

    ```
    > ['a', 'b', 'c'].join('##')
    'a##b##c'
    > ['a', 'b', 'c'].join()
    'a,b,c'
    ```

- `.keys(): Iterable<number>` [R, ES6]

    Returns an iterable over the keys of the receiver.

    ```
    > [...['a', 'b'].keys()]
    [ 0, 1 ]
    ```

- `.lastIndexOf(searchElement: T, fromIndex=this.length-1): number` [R, ES5]

    Returns the index of the last element that is strictly equal to `searchElement`. Returns -1 if there is no such element. Starts searching at index `fromIndex`, visiting lower indices next.

    ```
    > ['a', 'b', 'a'].lastIndexOf('a')
    2
    > ['a', 'b', 'a'].lastIndexOf('a', 1)
    0
    > ['a', 'b', 'a'].lastIndexOf('c')
    -1
    ```

- `.map<U>(mapFunc: (value: T, index: number, array: Array<T>) => U, thisArg?: any): U[]` [R, ES5]

    Returns a new Array, in which every element is the result of `mapFunc` being applied to the corresponding element of the receiver.

    ```
    > [1, 2, 3].map(x => x * 2)
    [ 2, 4, 6 ]
    > ['a', 'b', 'c'].map((x, i) => i)
    [ 0, 1, 2 ]
    ```

- `.pop(): T | undefined` [W, ES3]

    Removes and returns the last element of the receiver. That is, it treats the end of the receiver as a stack. The opposite of `.push()`.

    ```
    > const arr = ['a', 'b', 'c'];
    > arr.pop()
    ```

```
'c'
> arr
[ 'a', 'b' ]
```

- .push(...items: T[]): number [W, ES3]

  Adds zero or more items to the end of the receiver. That is, it treats the end of the receiver as a stack. The return value is the length of the receiver after the change. The opposite of .pop().

  ```
  > const arr = ['a', 'b'];
  > arr.push('c', 'd')
  4
  > arr
  [ 'a', 'b', 'c', 'd' ]
  ```

- .reduce<U>(callback: (accumulator: U, element: T, index: number, array: T[]) => U, init?: U): U [R, ES5]

  This method produces a summary of the receiver: it feeds all Array elements to callback, which combines a current summary (in parameter accumulator) with the current Array element and returns the next accumulator:

  ```
  const accumulator_0 = callback(init, arr[0]);
  const accumulator_1 = callback(accumulator_0, arr[1]);
  const accumulator_2 = callback(accumulator_1, arr[2]);
  // Etc.
  ```

  The result of .reduce() is the last result of callback after it has visited all Array elements.

  ```
  > [1, 2, 3].reduce((accu, x) => accu + x, 0)
  6
  > [1, 2, 3].reduce((accu, x) => accu + String(x), '')
  '123'
  ```

  If no init is provided, the Array element at index 0 is used and the element at index 1 is visited first. Therefore, the Array must have at least length 1.

- .reduceRight<U>(callback: (accumulator: U, element: T, index: number, array: T[]) => U, init?: U): U [R, ES5]

  Works like .reduce(), but visits the Array elements backward, starting with the last element.

  ```
  > [1, 2, 3].reduceRight((accu, x) => accu + String(x), '')
  '321'
  ```

- .reverse(): this [W, ES1]

  Rearranges the elements of the receiver so that they are in reverse order and then returns the receiver.

  ```
  > const arr = ['a', 'b', 'c'];
  > arr.reverse()
  ```

```
[ 'c', 'b', 'a' ]
> arr
[ 'c', 'b', 'a' ]
```

- `.shift(): T | undefined` [W, ES3]

    Removes and returns the first element of the receiver. The opposite of `.unshift()`.

    ```
    > const arr = ['a', 'b', 'c'];
    > arr.shift()
    'a'
    > arr
    [ 'b', 'c' ]
    ```

- `.slice(start=0, end=this.length): T[]` [R, ES3]

    Returns a new Array containing the elements of the receiver whose indices are between (including) `start` and (excluding) `end`.

    ```
    > ['a', 'b', 'c', 'd'].slice(1, 3)
    [ 'b', 'c' ]
    > ['a', 'b'].slice() // shallow copy
    [ 'a', 'b' ]
    ```

    Negative indices are allowed and added to `.length`:

    ```
    > ['a', 'b', 'c'].slice(-2)
    [ 'b', 'c' ]
    ```

- `.some(callback: (value: T, index: number, array: Array<T>) => boolean, thisArg?: any): boolean` [R, ES5]

    Returns `true` if `callback` returns a truthy value for at least one element. Otherwise, it returns `false`. It stops as soon as it receives a truthy value. This method corresponds to existential quantification ("exists", ∃) in mathematics.

    ```
    > [1, 2, 3].some(x => x < 0)
    false
    > [1, -2, 3].some(x => x < 0)
    true
    ```

    Related method: `.every()` ("for all").

- `.sort(compareFunc?: (a: T, b: T) => number): this` [W, ES1]

    Sorts the receiver and returns it. By default, it sorts string representations of the elements. It does so lexicographically and according to the code unit values (char codes) of the characters:

    ```
    > ['pie', 'cookie', 'éclair', 'Pie', 'Cookie', 'Éclair'].sort()
    [ 'Cookie', 'Pie', 'cookie', 'pie', 'Éclair', 'éclair' ]
    > [200, 3, 10].sort()
    [ 10, 200, 3 ]
    ```

    You can customize the sort order via `compareFunc`, which returns a number that is:

31.12 Quick reference: Array<T>

- negative if a < b
- zero if a === b
- positive if a > b

Trick for sorting numbers (with a risk of numeric overflow or underflow):

```
> [200, 3, 10].sort((a, b) => a - b)
[ 3, 10, 200 ]
```

> **.sort() is stable**
>
> Since ECMAScript 2019, sorting is guaranteed to be stable: if elements are considered equal by sorting, then sorting does not change the order of those elements (relative to each other).

- .splice(start: number, deleteCount=this.length-start, ...items: T[]): T[] [W, ES3]

  At index start, it removes deleteCount elements and inserts the items. It returns the deleted elements.

  ```
  > const arr = ['a', 'b', 'c', 'd'];
  > arr.splice(1, 2, 'x', 'y')
  [ 'b', 'c' ]
  > arr
  [ 'a', 'x', 'y', 'd' ]
  ```

  start can be negative and is added to .length if it is:

  ```
  > ['a', 'b', 'c'].splice(-2, 2)
  [ 'b', 'c' ]
  ```

- .toString(): string [R, ES1]

  Converts all elements to strings via String(), concatenates them while separating them with commas, and returns the result.

  ```
  > [1, 2, 3].toString()
  '1,2,3'
  > ['1', '2', '3'].toString()
  '1,2,3'
  > [].toString()
  ''
  ```

- .unshift(...items: T[]): number [W, ES3]

  Inserts the items at the beginning of the receiver and returns its length after this modification.

  ```
  > const arr = ['c', 'd'];
  > arr.unshift('e', 'f')
  4
  ```

```
> arr
[ 'e', 'f', 'c', 'd' ]
```

- `.values(): Iterable<T>` [R, ES6]

    Returns an iterable over the values of the receiver.

    ```
    > [...['a', 'b'].values()]
    [ 'a', 'b' ]
    ```

31.12.4 Sources

- TypeScript's built-in typings[3]
- MDN web docs for JavaScript[4]
- ECMAScript language specification[5]

Quiz

See quiz app (p. 71).

---

[3]https://github.com/Microsoft/TypeScript/blob/master/lib/
[4]https://developer.mozilla.org/en-US/docs/Web/JavaScript
[5]https://tc39.github.io/ecma262/

Chapter 32

Typed Arrays: handling binary data (Advanced)

Contents

32.1 The basics of the API	350
32.1.1 Use cases for Typed Arrays	350
32.1.2 The core classes: `ArrayBuffer`, Typed Arrays, `DataView`	350
32.1.3 Using Typed Arrays	351
32.1.4 Using DataViews	352
32.2 Element types	352
32.2.1 Handling overflow and underflow	353
32.2.2 Endianness	354
32.3 More information on Typed Arrays	355
32.3.1 The static method «ElementType»`Array.from()`	355
32.3.2 Typed Arrays are iterable	356
32.3.3 Typed Arrays vs. normal Arrays	357
32.3.4 Converting Typed Arrays to and from normal Arrays	357
32.3.5 Concatenating Typed Arrays	358
32.4 Quick references: indices vs. offsets	358
32.5 Quick reference: ArrayBuffers	359
32.5.1 `new ArrayBuffer()`	359
32.5.2 Static methods of `ArrayBuffer`	359
32.5.3 Properties of `ArrayBuffer.prototype`	360
32.6 Quick reference: Typed Arrays	360
32.6.1 Static methods of `TypedArray<T>`	360
32.6.2 Properties of `TypedArray<T>.prototype`	361
32.6.3 `new «ElementType»Array()`	362
32.6.4 Static properties of «ElementType»`Array`	363
32.6.5 Properties of «ElementType»`Array.prototype`	363
32.7 Quick reference: DataViews	363

32.7.1   new DataView() 363
32.7.2   Properties of DataView.prototype 363

32.1 The basics of the API

Much data on the web is text: JSON files, HTML files, CSS files, JavaScript code, etc. JavaScript handles such data well via its built-in strings.

However, before 2011, it did not handle binary data well. The Typed Array Specification 1.0[1] was introduced on February 8, 2011 and provides tools for working with binary data. With ECMAScript 6, Typed Arrays were added to the core language and gained methods that were previously only available for normal Arrays (.map(), .filter(), etc.).

32.1.1 Use cases for Typed Arrays

The main uses cases for Typed Arrays, are:

- Processing binary data: managing image data, manipulating binary files, handling binary network protocols, etc.
- Interacting with native APIs: Native APIs often receive and return data in a binary format, which you could neither store nor manipulate well in pre-ES6 JavaScript. That meant that whenever you were communicating with such an API, data had to be converted from JavaScript to binary and back for every call. Typed Arrays eliminate this bottleneck. One example of communicating with native APIs is WebGL, for which Typed Arrays were initially created. Section "History of Typed Arrays"[2] of the article "Typed Arrays: Binary Data in the Browser"[3] (by Ilmari Heikkinen for HTML5 Rocks) has more information.

32.1.2 The core classes: `ArrayBuffer`, Typed Arrays, `DataView`

The Typed Array API stores binary data in instances of `ArrayBuffer`:

```
const buf = new ArrayBuffer(4); // length in bytes
// buf is initialized with zeros
```

An ArrayBuffer itself is a black box: if you want to access its data, you must wrap it in another object – a *view object*. Two kinds of view objects are available:

- Typed Arrays: let you access the data as an indexed sequence of elements that all have the same type. Examples include:
    - `Uint8Array`: Elements are unsigned 8-bit integers. *Unsigned* means that their ranges start at zero.
    - `Int16Array`: Elements are signed 16-bit integers. *Signed* means that they have a sign and can be negative, zero, or positive.
    - `Float32Array`: Elements are 32-bit floating point numbers.

---
[1] https://www.khronos.org/registry/typedarray/specs/1.0/
[2] http://www.html5rocks.com/en/tutorials/webgl/typed_arrays/#toc-history
[3] http://www.html5rocks.com/en/tutorials/webgl/typed_arrays/#toc-history

32.1 The basics of the API

- DataViews: let you interpret the data as various types (Uint8, Int16, Float32, etc.) that you can read and write at any byte offset.

Fig. 32.1 shows a class diagram of the API.

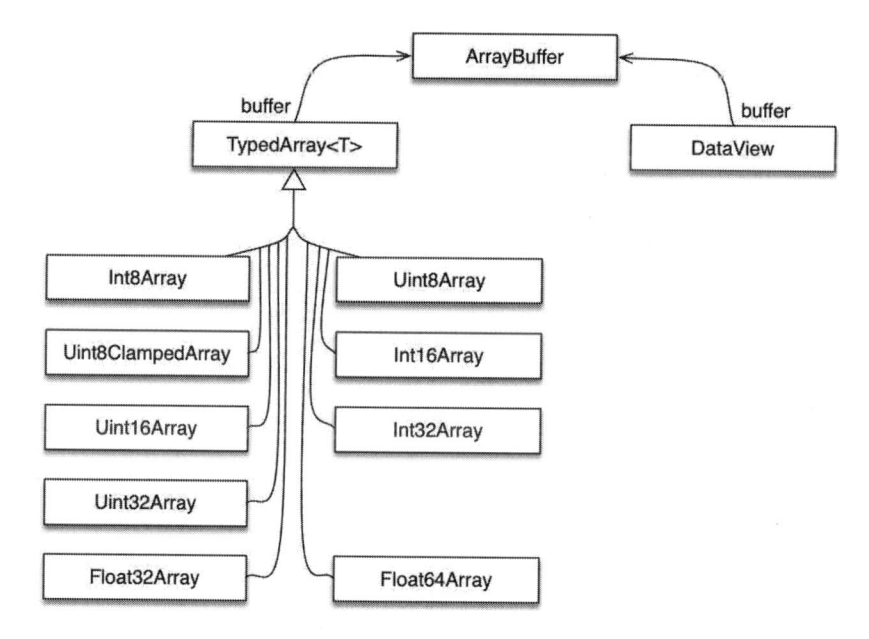

Figure 32.1: The classes of the Typed Array API.

32.1.3 Using Typed Arrays

Typed Arrays are used much like normal Arrays with a few notable differences:

- Typed Arrays store their data in ArrayBuffers.
- All elements are initialized with zeros.
- All elements have the same type. Writing values to a Typed Array coerces them to that type. Reading values produces normal numbers.
- The length of a Typed Array is immutable; it can't be changed.
- Typed Arrays can't have holes.

32.1.3.1 Creating Typed Arrays

The following code shows three different ways of creating the same Typed Array:

```
// Argument: Typed Array or Array-like object
const ta1 = new Uint8Array([0, 1, 2]);

const ta2 = Uint8Array.of(0, 1, 2);

const ta3 = new Uint8Array(3); // length of Typed Array
ta3[0] = 0;
ta3[1] = 1;
```

```
ta3[2] = 2;

assert.deepEqual(ta1, ta2);
assert.deepEqual(ta1, ta3);
```

32.1.3.2 The wrapped ArrayBuffer

```
const typedArray = new Int16Array(2); // 2 elements
assert.equal(typedArray.length, 2);

assert.deepEqual(
  typedArray.buffer, new ArrayBuffer(4)); // 4 bytes
```

32.1.3.3 Getting and setting elements

```
const typedArray = new Int16Array(2);

assert.equal(typedArray[1], 0); // initialized with 0
typedArray[1] = 72;
assert.equal(typedArray[1], 72);
```

32.1.4 Using DataViews

This is how DataViews are used:

```
const dataView = new DataView(new ArrayBuffer(4));
assert.equal(dataView.getInt16(0), 0);
assert.equal(dataView.getUint8(0), 0);
dataView.setUint8(0, 5);
```

32.2 Element types

Table 32.1: Element types supported by the Typed Array API.

Element	Typed Array	Bytes	Description	
Int8	Int8Array	1	8-bit signed integer	ES6
Uint8	Uint8Array	1	8-bit unsigned integer	ES6
Uint8C	Uint8ClampedArray	1	8-bit unsigned integer (clamped conversion)	ES6 ES6
Int16	Int16Array	2	16-bit signed integer	ES6
Uint16	Uint16Array	2	16-bit unsigned integer	ES6
Int32	Int32Array	4	32-bit signed integer	ES6
Uint32	Uint32Array	4	32-bit unsigned integer	ES6
Float32	Float32Array	4	32-bit floating point	ES6
Float64	Float64Array	8	64-bit floating point	ES6

32.2 Element types

Tbl. 32.1 lists the available element types. These types (e.g., Int32) show up in two locations:

- They are the types of the elements of Typed Arrays. For example, all elements of a Int32Array have the type Int32. The element type is the only aspect of Typed Arrays that differs.
- They are the lenses through which an ArrayBuffer accesses its DataView when you use methods such as .getInt32() and .setInt32().

The element type Uint8C is special: it is not supported by DataView and only exists to enable Uint8ClampedArray. This Typed Array is used by the canvas element (where it replaces CanvasPixelArray) and should otherwise be avoided. The only difference between Uint8C and Uint8 is how overflow and underflow are handled (as explained in the next subsection).

32.2.1 Handling overflow and underflow

Normally, when a value is out of the range of the element type, modulo arithmetic is used to convert it to a value within range. For signed and unsigned integers that means that:

- The highest value plus one is converted to the lowest value (0 for unsigned integers).
- The lowest value minus one is converted to the highest value.

The following function helps illustrate how conversion works:

```
function setAndGet(typedArray, value) {
  typedArray[0] = value;
  return typedArray[0];
}
```

Modulo conversion for unsigned 8-bit integers:

```
const uint8 = new Uint8Array(1);

// Highest value of range
assert.equal(setAndGet(uint8, 255), 255);
// Overflow
assert.equal(setAndGet(uint8, 256), 0);

// Lowest value of range
assert.equal(setAndGet(uint8, 0), 0);
// Underflow
assert.equal(setAndGet(uint8, -1), 255);
```

Modulo conversion for signed 8-bit integers:

```
const int8 = new Int8Array(1);

// Highest value of range
assert.equal(setAndGet(int8, 127), 127);
// Overflow
assert.equal(setAndGet(int8, 128), -128);
```

```
// Lowest value of range
assert.equal(setAndGet(int8, -128), -128);
// Underflow
assert.equal(setAndGet(int8, -129), 127);
```

Clamped conversion is different:

- All underflowing values are converted to the lowest value.
- All overflowing values are converted to the highest value.

```
const uint8c = new Uint8ClampedArray(1);

// Highest value of range
assert.equal(setAndGet(uint8c, 255), 255);
// Overflow
assert.equal(setAndGet(uint8c, 256), 255);

// Lowest value of range
assert.equal(setAndGet(uint8c, 0), 0);
// Underflow
assert.equal(setAndGet(uint8c, -1), 0);
```

32.2.2 Endianness

Whenever a type (such as `Uint16`) is stored as a sequence of multiple bytes, *endianness* matters:

- Big endian: the most significant byte comes first. For example, the `Uint16` value 0x4321 is stored as two bytes – first 0x43, then 0x21.
- Little endian: the least significant byte comes first. For example, the `Uint16` value 0x4321 is stored as two bytes – first 0x21, then 0x43.

Endianness tends to be fixed per CPU architecture and consistent across native APIs. Typed Arrays are used to communicate with those APIs, which is why their endianness follows the endianness of the platform and can't be changed.

On the other hand, the endianness of protocols and binary files varies, but is fixed per format, across platforms. Therefore, we must be able to access data with either endianness. DataViews serve this use case and let you specify endianness when you get or set a value.

Quoting Wikipedia on Endianness[4]:

- Big-endian representation is the most common convention in data networking; fields in the protocols of the Internet protocol suite, such as IPv4, IPv6, TCP, and UDP, are transmitted in big-endian order. For this reason, big-endian byte order is also referred to as network byte order.
- Little-endian storage is popular for microprocessors in part due to significant historical influence on microprocessor designs by Intel Corporation.

---

[4]https://en.wikipedia.org/wiki/Endianness

Other orderings are also possible. Those are generically called *middle-endian* or *mixed-endian*.

32.3 More information on Typed Arrays

In this section, «ElementType»Array stands for Int8Array, Uint8Array, etc. ElementType is Int8, Uint8, etc.

32.3.1 The static method «ElementType»Array.from()

This method has the type signature:

```
.from<S>(
  source: Iterable<S>|ArrayLike<S>,
  mapfn?: S => ElementType, thisArg?: any)
  : «ElementType»Array
```

.from() converts source into an instance of this (a Typed Array).

For example, normal Arrays are iterable and can be converted with this method:

```
assert.deepEqual(
  Uint16Array.from([0, 1, 2]),
  Uint16Array.of(0, 1, 2));
```

Typed Arrays are also iterable:

```
assert.deepEqual(
  Uint16Array.from(Uint8Array.of(0, 1, 2)),
  Uint16Array.of(0, 1, 2));
```

source can also be an *Array-like object* (p. 322):

```
assert.deepEqual(
  Uint16Array.from({0:0, 1:1, 2:2, length: 3}),
  Uint16Array.of(0, 1, 2));
```

The optional mapfn lets you transform the elements of source before they become elements of the result. Why perform the two steps *mapping* and *conversion* in one go? Compared to mapping separately via .map(), there are two advantages:

1. No intermediate Array or Typed Array is needed.
2. When converting between Typed Arrays with different precisions, less can go wrong.

Read on for an explanation of the second advantage.

32.3.1.1 Pitfall: mapping while converting between Typed Array types

The static method .from() can optionally both map and convert between Typed Array types. Less can go wrong if you use that method.

To see why that is, let us first convert a Typed Array to a Typed Array with a higher precision. If we use `.from()` to map, the result is automatically correct. Otherwise, you must first convert and then map.

```
const typedArray = Int8Array.of(127, 126, 125);
assert.deepEqual(
  Int16Array.from(typedArray, x => x * 2),
  Int16Array.of(254, 252, 250));

assert.deepEqual(
  Int16Array.from(typedArray).map(x => x * 2),
  Int16Array.of(254, 252, 250)); // OK
assert.deepEqual(
  Int16Array.from(typedArray.map(x => x * 2)),
  Int16Array.of(-2, -4, -6)); // wrong
```

If we go from a Typed Array to a Typed Array with a lower precision, mapping via `.from()` produces the correct result. Otherwise, we must first map and then convert.

```
assert.deepEqual(
  Int8Array.from(Int16Array.of(254, 252, 250), x => x / 2),
  Int8Array.of(127, 126, 125));

assert.deepEqual(
  Int8Array.from(Int16Array.of(254, 252, 250).map(x => x / 2)),
  Int8Array.of(127, 126, 125)); // OK
assert.deepEqual(
  Int8Array.from(Int16Array.of(254, 252, 250)).map(x => x / 2),
  Int8Array.of(-1, -2, -3)); // wrong
```

The problem is that if we map via `.map()`, then input type and output type are the same. In contrast, `.from()` goes from an arbitrary input type to an output type that you specify via its receiver.

32.3.2 Typed Arrays are iterable

Typed Arrays are iterable (p. 311). That means that you can use the `for-of` loop and other iteration-based mechanisms:

```
const ui8 = Uint8Array.of(0, 1, 2);
for (const byte of ui8) {
  console.log(byte);
}
// Output:
// 0
// 1
// 2
```

ArrayBuffers and DataViews are not iterable.

32.3.3 Typed Arrays vs. normal Arrays

Typed Arrays are much like normal Arrays: they have a .length, elements can be accessed via the bracket operator [], and they have most of the standard Array methods. They differ from normal Arrays in the following ways:

- Typed Arrays have buffers. The elements of a Typed Array ta are not stored in ta, they are stored in an associated ArrayBuffer that can be accessed via ta.buffer:

    ```
    const ta = new Uint16Array(2); // 2 elements
    assert.deepEqual(
      ta.buffer, new ArrayBuffer(4)); // 4 bytes
    ```

- Typed Arrays are initialized with zeros:
    - new Array(4) creates a normal Array without any elements. It only has four *holes* (indices less than the .length that have no associated elements).
    - new Uint8Array(4) creates a Typed Array whose four elements are all 0.

    ```
    assert.deepEqual(new Uint8Array(4), Uint8Array.of(0, 0, 0, 0));
    ```

- All of the elements of a Typed Array have the same type:
    - Setting elements converts values to that type.

        ```
        const ta = new Uint8Array(1);

        ta[0] = 257;
        assert.equal(ta[0], 1); // 257 % 256 (overflow)

        ta[0] = '2';
        assert.equal(ta[0], 2);
        ```

    - Getting elements returns numbers.

        ```
        const ta = new Uint8Array(1);
        assert.equal(ta[0], 0);
        assert.equal(typeof ta[0], 'number');
        ```

- The .length of a Typed Array is derived from its ArrayBuffer and never changes (unless you switch to a different ArrayBuffer).

- Normal Arrays can have holes; Typed Arrays can't.

32.3.4 Converting Typed Arrays to and from normal Arrays

To convert a normal Array to a Typed Array, you pass it to a Typed Array constructor (which accepts Array-like objects and Typed Arrays) or to «ElementType»Array.from() (which accepts iterables and Array-like objects). For example:

```
const ta1 = new Uint8Array([0, 1, 2]);
const ta2 = Uint8Array.from([0, 1, 2]);
assert.deepEqual(ta1, ta2);
```

To convert a Typed Array to a normal Array, you can use spreading or `Array.from()` (because Typed Arrays are iterable):

```
assert.deepEqual(
  [...Uint8Array.of(0, 1, 2)], [0, 1, 2] );
assert.deepEqual(
  Array.from(Uint8Array.of(0, 1, 2)), [0, 1, 2] );
```

32.3.5 Concatenating Typed Arrays

Typed Arrays don't have a method `.concat()`, like normal Arrays do. The workaround is to use their overloaded method `.set()`:

```
.set(typedArray: TypedArray, offset=0): void
.set(arrayLike: ArrayLike<number>, offset=0): void
```

It copies the existing `typedArray` or `arrayLike` into the receiver, at index `offset`. TypedArray is a fictitious abstract superclass of all concrete Typed Array classes.

The following function uses that method to copy zero or more Typed Arrays (or Array-like objects) into an instance of `resultConstructor`:

```
function concatenate(resultConstructor, ...arrays) {
  let totalLength = 0;
  for (const arr of arrays) {
    totalLength += arr.length;
  }
  const result = new resultConstructor(totalLength);
  let offset = 0;
  for (const arr of arrays) {
    result.set(arr, offset);
    offset += arr.length;
  }
  return result;
}
assert.deepEqual(
  concatenate(Uint8Array, Uint8Array.of(1, 2), [3, 4]),
  Uint8Array.of(1, 2, 3, 4));
```

32.4 Quick references: indices vs. offsets

In preparation for the quick references on ArrayBuffers, Typed Arrays, and DataViews, we need learn the differences between indices and offsets:

- Indices for the bracket operator [ ]: You can only use non-negative indices (starting at 0).

  In normal Arrays, writing to negative indices creates properties:

  ```
  const arr = [6, 7];
  arr[-1] = 5;
  ```

```
    assert.deepEqual(
      Object.keys(arr), ['0', '1', '-1']);
```

In Typed Arrays, writing to negative indices is ignored:

```
const tarr = Uint8Array.of(6, 7);
tarr[-1] = 5;
assert.deepEqual(
  Object.keys(tarr), ['0', '1']);
```

- Indices for methods of ArrayBuffers, Typed Arrays, and DataViews: Every index can be negative. If it is, it is added to the length of the entity to produce the actual index. Therefore, -1 refers to the last element, -2 to the second-last, etc. Methods of normal Arrays work the same way.

```
const ui8 = Uint8Array.of(0, 1, 2);
assert.deepEqual(ui8.slice(-1), Uint8Array.of(2));
```

- Offsets passed to methods of Typed Arrays and DataViews: must be non-negative – for example:

```
const dataView = new DataView(new ArrayBuffer(4));
assert.throws(
  () => dataView.getUint8(-1),
  {
    name: 'RangeError',
    message: 'Offset is outside the bounds of the DataView',
  });
```

Whether a parameter is an index or an offset can only be determined by looking at documentation; there is no simple rule.

32.5 Quick reference: ArrayBuffers

ArrayBuffers store binary data, which is meant to be accessed via Typed Arrays and DataViews.

32.5.1 new ArrayBuffer()

The type signature of the constructor is:

```
new ArrayBuffer(length: number)
```

Invoking this constructor via new creates an instance whose capacity is length bytes. Each of those bytes is initially 0.

You can't change the length of an ArrayBuffer; you can only create a new one with a different length.

32.5.2 Static methods of ArrayBuffer

- ArrayBuffer.isView(arg: any)

Returns true if arg is an object and a *view* for an ArrayBuffer (i.e., if it is a Typed Array or a DataView).

32.5.3 Properties of `ArrayBuffer.prototype`

- get .byteLength(): number

Returns the capacity of this ArrayBuffer in bytes.

- .slice(startIndex: number, endIndex=this.byteLength)

Creates a new ArrayBuffer that contains the bytes of this ArrayBuffer whose indices are greater than or equal to startIndex and less than endIndex. start and endIndex can be negative (see §32.4 "Quick references: indices vs. offsets" (p. 358)).

32.6 Quick reference: Typed Arrays

The properties of the various Typed Array objects are introduced in two steps:

1. TypedArray: First, we look at the abstract superclass of all Typed Array classes (which was shown in the class diagram at the beginning of this chapter). I'm calling that superclass TypedArray, but it is not directly accessible from JavaScript. TypedArray.prototype houses all methods of Typed Arrays.
2. «ElementType»Array: The concrete Typed Array classes are called Uint8Array, Int16Array, Float32Array, etc. These are the classes that you use via new, .of, and .from().

32.6.1 Static methods of `TypedArray<T>`

Both static TypedArray methods are inherited by its subclasses (Uint8Array, etc.). TypedArray is abstract. Therefore, you always use these methods via the subclasses, which are concrete and can have direct instances.

- .from<S>(source: Iterable<S>|ArrayLike<S>, mapfn?: S => T, thisArg?: any) : instanceof this

Converts an iterable (including Arrays and Typed Arrays) or an Array-like object (p. 322) to an instance of this (instanceof this is my invention to express that fact).

```
assert.deepEqual(
  Uint16Array.from([0, 1, 2]),
  Uint16Array.of(0, 1, 2));
```

The optional mapfn lets you transform the elements of source before they become elements of the result.

```
assert.deepEqual(
  Int16Array.from(Int8Array.of(127, 126, 125), x => x * 2),
  Int16Array.of(254, 252, 250));
```

- .of(...items: number[]): instanceof this

32.6 Quick reference: Typed Arrays

Creates a new instance of this whose elements are items (coerced to the element type).

```
assert.deepEqual(
  Int16Array.of(-1234, 5, 67),
  new Int16Array([-1234, 5, 67]) );
```

32.6.2 Properties of `TypedArray<T>.prototype`

Indices accepted by Typed Array methods can be negative (they work like traditional Array methods that way). Offsets must be non-negative. For details, see §32.4 "Quick references: indices vs. offsets" (p. 358).

32.6.2.1 Properties specific to Typed Arrays

The following properties are specific to Typed Arrays; normal Arrays don't have them:

- `get .buffer(): ArrayBuffer`

  Returns the buffer backing this Typed Array.

- `get .length(): number`

  Returns the length in elements of this Typed Array's buffer.

- `get .byteLength(): number`

  Returns the size in bytes of this Typed Array's buffer.

- `get .byteOffset(): number`

  Returns the offset where this Typed Array "starts" inside its ArrayBuffer.

- `.set(typedArray: TypedArray, offset=0): void`
- `.set(arrayLike: ArrayLike<number>, offset=0): void`

  Copies all elements of the first parameter to this Typed Array. The element at index 0 of the parameter is written to index offset of this Typed Array (etc.). For more information on Array-like objects, consult §31.4 "Array-like objects" (p. 322).

- `.subarray(startIndex=0, endIndex=this.length): TypedArray<T>`

  Returns a new Typed Array that has the same buffer as this Typed Array, but a (generally) smaller range. If startIndex is non-negative then the first element of the resulting Typed Array is this[startIndex], the second this[startIndex+1] (etc.). If startIndex in negative, it is converted appropriately.

32.6.2.2 Array methods

The following methods are basically the same as the methods of normal Arrays:

- `.copyWithin(target: number, start: number, end=this.length): this` [W, ES6]
- `.entries(): Iterable<[number, T]>` [R, ES6]
- `.every(callback: (value: T, index: number, array: TypedArray<T>) => boolean, thisArg?: any): boolean` [R, ES5]

- `.fill(value: T, start=0, end=this.length): this` [W, ES6]
- `.filter(callback: (value: T, index: number, array: TypedArray<T>) => any, thisArg?: any): T[]` [R, ES5]
- `.find(predicate: (value: T, index: number, obj: T[]) => boolean, thisArg?: any): T | undefined` [R, ES6]
- `.findIndex(predicate: (value: T, index: number, obj: T[]) => boolean, thisArg?: any): number` [R, ES6]
- `.forEach(callback: (value: T, index: number, array: TypedArray<T>) => void, thisArg?: any): void` [R, ES5]
- `.includes(searchElement: T, fromIndex=0): boolean` [R, ES2016]
- `.indexOf(searchElement: T, fromIndex=0): number` [R, ES5]
- `.join(separator = ','): string` [R, ES1]
- `.keys(): Iterable<number>` [R, ES6]
- `.lastIndexOf(searchElement: T, fromIndex=this.length-1): number` [R, ES5]
- `.map<U>(mapFunc: (value: T, index: number, array: TypedArray<T>) => U, thisArg?: any): U[]` [R, ES5]
- `.reduce<U>(callback: (accumulator: U, element: T, index: number, array: T[]) => U, init?: U): U` [R, ES5]
- `.reduceRight<U>(callback: (accumulator: U, element: T, index: number, array: T[]) => U, init?: U): U` [R, ES5]
- `.reverse(): this` [W, ES1]
- `.slice(start=0, end=this.length): T[]` [R, ES3]
- `.some(callback: (value: T, index: number, array: TypedArray<T>) => boolean, thisArg?: any): boolean` [R, ES5]
- `.sort(compareFunc?: (a: T, b: T) => number): this` [W, ES1]
- `.toString(): string` [R, ES1]
- `.values(): Iterable<number>` [R, ES6]

For details on how these methods work, please consult §31.12.3 "Methods of Array<T>.prototype" (p. 341).

32.6.3 new «ElementType»Array()

Each Typed Array constructor has a name that follows the pattern «ElementType»Array, where «ElementType» is one of the element types in the table at the beginning. That means that there are nine constructors for Typed Arrays:

- `Float32Array`, `Float64Array`
- `Int8Array`, `Int16Array`, `Int32Array`
- `Uint8Array`, `Uint8ClampedArray`, `Uint16Array`, `Uint32Array`

Each constructor has four *overloaded* versions – it behaves differently depending on how many arguments it receives and what their types are:

- new «ElementType»Array(buffer: ArrayBuffer, byteOffset=0, length=0)

    Creates a new «ElementType»Array whose buffer is buffer. It starts accessing the buffer at the given byteOffset and will have the given length. Note that length counts elements of the Typed Array (with 1–8 bytes each), not bytes.

- new «ElementType»Array(length=0)

Creates a new «ElementType»Array with the given length and the appropriate buffer. The buffer's size in bytes is:

```
length * «ElementType»Array.BYTES_PER_ELEMENT
```

- new «ElementType»Array(source: TypedArray)

    Creates a new instance of «ElementType»Array whose elements have the same values as the elements of source, but coerced to ElementType.

- new «ElementType»Array(source: ArrayLike<number>)

    Creates a new instance of «ElementType»Array whose elements have the same values as the elements of source, but coerced to ElementType. For more information on Array-like objects, consult §31.4 "Array-like objects" (p. 322).

32.6.4 Static properties of «ElementType»Array

- «ElementType»Array.BYTES_PER_ELEMENT: number

    Counts how many bytes are needed to store a single element:

    ```
    > Uint8Array.BYTES_PER_ELEMENT
    1
    > Int16Array.BYTES_PER_ELEMENT
    2
    > Float64Array.BYTES_PER_ELEMENT
    8
    ```

32.6.5 Properties of «ElementType»Array.prototype

- .BYTES_PER_ELEMENT: number

    The same as «ElementType»Array.BYTES_PER_ELEMENT.

32.7 Quick reference: DataViews

32.7.1 new DataView()

- newDataView(buffer:ArrayBuffer, byteOffset=0, byteLength=buffer.byteLength-byteOffset)

    Creates a new DataView whose data is stored in the ArrayBuffer buffer. By default, the new DataView can access all of buffer. The last two parameters allow you to change that.

32.7.2 Properties of DataView.prototype

In the remainder of this section, «ElementType» refers to either:

- Float32, Float64
- Int8, Int16, Int32
- Uint8, Uint16, Uint32

These are the properties of `DataView.prototype`:

- `get .buffer()`

  Returns the ArrayBuffer of this DataView.

- `get .byteLength()`

  Returns how many bytes can be accessed by this DataView.

- `get .byteOffset()`

  Returns at which offset this DataView starts accessing the bytes in its buffer.

- `.get«ElementType»(byteOffset: number, littleEndian=false)`

  Reads a value from the buffer of this DataView.

- `.set«ElementType»(byteOffset:number, value:number, littleEndian=false)`

  Writes `value` to the buffer of this DataView.

Chapter 33

Maps (`Map`)

Contents

- 33.1 Using Maps 366
  - 33.1.1 Creating Maps 366
  - 33.1.2 Copying Maps 366
  - 33.1.3 Working with single entries 366
  - 33.1.4 Determining the size of a Map and clearing it 367
  - 33.1.5 Getting the keys and values of a Map 367
  - 33.1.6 Getting the entries of a Map 367
  - 33.1.7 Listed in insertion order: entries, keys, values 368
  - 33.1.8 Converting between Maps and Objects 368
- 33.2 Example: Counting characters 369
- 33.3 A few more details about the keys of Maps (advanced) 369
  - 33.3.1 What keys are considered equal? 370
- 33.4 Missing Map operations 370
  - 33.4.1 Mapping and filtering Maps 370
  - 33.4.2 Combining Maps 371
- 33.5 Quick reference: `Map<K,V>` 372
  - 33.5.1 Constructor 372
  - 33.5.2 `Map<K,V>.prototype`: handling single entries 372
  - 33.5.3 `Map<K,V>.prototype`: handling all entries 373
  - 33.5.4 `Map<K,V>.prototype`: iterating and looping 373
  - 33.5.5 Sources of this section 374
- 33.6 FAQ: Maps 374
  - 33.6.1 When should I use a Map, and when should I use an object? . 374
  - 33.6.2 When would I use an object as a key in a Map? 375
  - 33.6.3 Why do Maps preserve the insertion order of entries? 375
  - 33.6.4 Why do Maps have a `.size`, while Arrays have a `.length`? .. 375

Before ES6, JavaScript didn't have a data structure for dictionaries and (ab)used objects as dictionaries from strings to arbitrary values. ES6 brought Maps, which are dictionaries from arbitrary values to arbitrary values.

33.1 Using Maps

An instance of Map maps keys to values. A single key-value mapping is called an *entry*.

33.1.1 Creating Maps

There are three common ways of creating Maps.

First, you can use the constructor without any parameters to create an empty Map:

```
const emptyMap = new Map();
assert.equal(emptyMap.size, 0);
```

Second, you can pass an iterable (e.g., an Array) over key-value "pairs" (Arrays with two elements) to the constructor:

```
const map = new Map([
  [1, 'one'],
  [2, 'two'],
  [3, 'three'], // trailing comma is ignored
]);
```

Third, the .set() method adds entries to a Map and is chainable:

```
const map = new Map()
  .set(1, 'one')
  .set(2, 'two')
  .set(3, 'three');
```

33.1.2 Copying Maps

As we'll see later, Maps are also iterables over key-value pairs. Therefore, you can use the constructor to create a copy of a Map. That copy is *shallow*: keys and values are the same; they are not duplicated.

```
const original = new Map()
  .set(false, 'no')
  .set(true, 'yes');

const copy = new Map(original);
assert.deepEqual(original, copy);
```

33.1.3 Working with single entries

.set() and .get() are for writing and reading values (given keys).

```
const map = new Map();

map.set('foo', 123);

assert.equal(map.get('foo'), 123);
// Unknown key:
```

33.1 Using Maps

```
assert.equal(map.get('bar'), undefined);
// Use the default value '' if an entry is missing:
assert.equal(map.get('bar') || '', '');
```

`.has()` checks if a Map has an entry with a given key. `.delete()` removes entries.

```
const map = new Map([['foo', 123]]);

assert.equal(map.has('foo'), true);
assert.equal(map.delete('foo'), true)
assert.equal(map.has('foo'), false)
```

33.1.4 Determining the size of a Map and clearing it

`.size` contains the number of entries in a Map. `.clear()` removes all entries of a Map.

```
const map = new Map()
  .set('foo', true)
  .set('bar', false)
;

assert.equal(map.size, 2)
map.clear();
assert.equal(map.size, 0)
```

33.1.5 Getting the keys and values of a Map

`.keys()` returns an iterable over the keys of a Map:

```
const map = new Map()
  .set(false, 'no')
  .set(true, 'yes')
;

for (const key of map.keys()) {
  console.log(key);
}
// Output:
// false
// true
```

We can use spreading (..., p. 320) to convert the iterable returned by `.keys()` to an Array:

```
assert.deepEqual(
  [...map.keys()],
  [false, true]);
```

`.values()` works like `.keys()`, but for values instead of keys.

33.1.6 Getting the entries of a Map

`.entries()` returns an iterable over the entries of a Map:

```
const map = new Map()
  .set(false, 'no')
  .set(true, 'yes')
;

for (const entry of map.entries()) {
  console.log(entry);
}
// Output:
// [false, 'no']
// [true, 'yes']
```

Spreading (..., p. 320) converts the iterable returned by .entries() to an Array:

```
assert.deepEqual(
  [...map.entries()],
  [[false, 'no'], [true, 'yes']]);
```

Map instances are also iterables over entries. In the following code, we use destructuring (p. 391) to access the keys and values of map:

```
for (const [key, value] of map) {
  console.log(key, value);
}
// Output:
// false, 'no'
// true, 'yes'
```

33.1.7 Listed in insertion order: entries, keys, values

Maps record in which order entries were created and honor that order when listing entries, keys, or values:

```
const map1 = new Map([
  ['a', 1],
  ['b', 2],
]);
assert.deepEqual(
  [...map1.keys()], ['a', 'b']);

const map2 = new Map([
  ['b', 2],
  ['a', 1],
]);
assert.deepEqual(
  [...map2.keys()], ['b', 'a']);
```

33.1.8 Converting between Maps and Objects

As long as a Map only uses strings and symbols as keys, you can convert it to an object (via Object.fromEntries() (p. 280)):

```
const map = new Map([
  ['a', 1],
  ['b', 2],
]);
const obj = Object.fromEntries(map);
assert.deepEqual(
  obj, {a: 1, b: 2});
```

You can also convert an object to a Map with string or symbol keys (via Object.entries() (p. 279)):

```
const obj = {
  a: 1,
  b: 2,
};
const map = new Map(Object.entries(obj));
assert.deepEqual(
  map, new Map([['a', 1], ['b', 2]]));
```

33.2 Example: Counting characters

countChars() returns a Map that maps characters to numbers of occurrences.

```
function countChars(chars) {
  const charCounts = new Map();
  for (let ch of chars) {
    ch = ch.toLowerCase();
    const prevCount = charCounts.get(ch) || 0;
    charCounts.set(ch, prevCount+1);
  }
  return charCounts;
}

const result = countChars('AaBccc');
assert.deepEqual(
  [...result],
  [
    ['a', 2],
    ['b', 1],
    ['c', 3],
  ]
);
```

33.3 A few more details about the keys of Maps (advanced)

Any value can be a key, even an object:

```
const map = new Map();
```

```
const KEY1 = {};
const KEY2 = {};

map.set(KEY1, 'hello');
map.set(KEY2, 'world');

assert.equal(map.get(KEY1), 'hello');
assert.equal(map.get(KEY2), 'world');
```

33.3.1 What keys are considered equal?

Most Map operations need to check whether a value is equal to one of the keys. They do so via the internal operation SameValueZero[1], which works like === but considers NaN to be equal to itself.

As a consequence, you can use NaN as a key in Maps, just like any other value:

```
> const map = new Map();

> map.set(NaN, 123);
> map.get(NaN)
123
```

Different objects are always considered to be different. That is something that can't be changed (yet – configuring key equality is on TC39's long-term roadmap).

```
> new Map().set({}, 1).set({}, 2).size
2
```

33.4 Missing Map operations

33.4.1 Mapping and filtering Maps

You can .map() and .filter() an Array, but there are no such operations for a Map. The solution is:

1. Convert the Map into an Array of [key, value] pairs.
2. Map or filter the Array.
3. Convert the result back to a Map.

I'll use the following Map to demonstrate how that works.

```
const originalMap = new Map()
.set(1, 'a')
.set(2, 'b')
.set(3, 'c');
```

Mapping originalMap:

```
const mappedMap = new Map( // step 3
  [...originalMap] // step 1
```

---

[1]http://www.ecma-international.org/ecma-262/6.0/#sec-samevaluezero

33.4 Missing Map operations

```
    .map(([k, v]) => [k * 2, '_' + v]) // step 2
);
assert.deepEqual([...mappedMap],
  [[2,'_a'], [4,'_b'], [6,'_c']]);
```

Filtering originalMap:

```
const filteredMap = new Map( // step 3
  [...originalMap] // step 1
    .filter(([k, v]) => k < 3) // step 2
);
assert.deepEqual([...filteredMap],
  [[1,'a'], [2,'b']]);
```

Step 1 is performed by spreading (...) in the Array literal.

33.4.2 Combining Maps

There are no methods for combining Maps, which is why we must use a workaround that is similar to the one from the previous section.

Let's combine the following two Maps:

```
const map1 = new Map()
  .set(1, '1a')
  .set(2, '1b')
  .set(3, '1c')
;

const map2 = new Map()
  .set(2, '2b')
  .set(3, '2c')
  .set(4, '2d')
;
```

To combine map1 and map2, we turn them into Arrays via spreading (...) and concatenate those Arrays. Afterward, we convert the result back to a Map. All of that is done in line A.

```
const combinedMap = new Map([...map1, ...map2]); // (A)
assert.deepEqual(
  [...combinedMap], // convert to Array for comparison
  [ [ 1, '1a' ],
    [ 2, '2b' ],
    [ 3, '2c' ],
    [ 4, '2d' ] ]
);
```

Exercise: Combining two Maps

exercises/maps/combine_maps_test.mjs

33.5 Quick reference: `Map<K,V>`

Note: For the sake of conciseness, I'm pretending that all keys have the same type `K` and that all values have the same type `V`.

33.5.1 Constructor

- `new Map<K, V>(entries?: Iterable<[K, V]>)` [ES6]

    If you don't provide the parameter `entries`, then an empty Map is created. If you do provide an iterable over [key, value] pairs, then those pairs are added as entries to the Map. For example:

    ```
    const map = new Map([
      [ 1, 'one' ],
      [ 2, 'two' ],
      [ 3, 'three' ], // trailing comma is ignored
    ]);
    ```

33.5.2 `Map<K,V>.prototype`: handling single entries

- `.get(key: K): V` [ES6]

    Returns the `value` that key is mapped to in this Map. If there is no key `key` in this Map, `undefined` is returned.

    ```
    const map = new Map([[1, 'one'], [2, 'two']]);
    assert.equal(map.get(1), 'one');
    assert.equal(map.get(5), undefined);
    ```

- `.set(key: K, value: V): this` [ES6]

    Maps the given key to the given value. If there is already an entry whose key is key, it is updated. Otherwise, a new entry is created. This method returns `this`, which means that you can chain it.

    ```
    const map = new Map([[1, 'one'], [2, 'two']]);
    map.set(1, 'ONE!')
       .set(3, 'THREE!');
    assert.deepEqual(
      [...map.entries()],
      [[1, 'ONE!'], [2, 'two'], [3, 'THREE!']]);
    ```

- `.has(key: K): boolean` [ES6]

    Returns whether the given key exists in this Map.

    ```
    const map = new Map([[1, 'one'], [2, 'two']]);
    assert.equal(map.has(1), true); // key exists
    assert.equal(map.has(5), false); // key does not exist
    ```

- `.delete(key: K): boolean` [ES6]

If there is an entry whose key is key, it is removed and true is returned. Otherwise, nothing happens and false is returned.

```
const map = new Map([[1, 'one'], [2, 'two']]);
assert.equal(map.delete(1), true);
assert.equal(map.delete(5), false); // nothing happens
assert.deepEqual(
  [...map.entries()],
  [[2, 'two']]);
```

33.5.3 Map<K,V>.prototype: handling all entries

- get .size: number [ES6]

Returns how many entries this Map has.

```
const map = new Map([[1, 'one'], [2, 'two']]);
assert.equal(map.size, 2);
```

- .clear(): void [ES6]

Removes all entries from this Map.

```
const map = new Map([[1, 'one'], [2, 'two']]);
assert.equal(map.size, 2);
map.clear();
assert.equal(map.size, 0);
```

33.5.4 Map<K,V>.prototype: iterating and looping

Both iterating and looping happen in the order in which entries were added to a Map.

- .entries(): Iterable<[K,V]> [ES6]

Returns an iterable with one [key, value] pair for each entry in this Map. The pairs are Arrays of length 2.

```
const map = new Map([[1, 'one'], [2, 'two']]);
for (const entry of map.entries()) {
  console.log(entry);
}
// Output:
// [1, 'one']
// [2, 'two']
```

- .forEach(callback: (value: V, key: K, theMap: Map<K,V>) => void, thisArg?: any): void [ES6]

The first parameter is a callback that is invoked once for each entry in this Map. If thisArg is provided, this is set to it for each invocation. Otherwise, this is set to undefined.

```
const map = new Map([[1, 'one'], [2, 'two']]);
map.forEach((value, key) => console.log(value, key));
```

```
// Output:
// 'one', 1
// 'two', 2
```

- `.keys(): Iterable<K>` [ES6]

    Returns an iterable over all keys in this Map.

    ```
    const map = new Map([[1, 'one'], [2, 'two']]);
    for (const key of map.keys()) {
      console.log(key);
    }
    // Output:
    // 1
    // 2
    ```

- `.values(): Iterable<V>` [ES6]

    Returns an iterable over all values in this Map.

    ```
    const map = new Map([[1, 'one'], [2, 'two']]);
    for (const value of map.values()) {
      console.log(value);
    }
    // Output:
    // 'one'
    // 'two'
    ```

- `[Symbol.iterator](): Iterable<[K,V]>` [ES6]

    The default way of iterating over Maps. Same as `.entries()`.

    ```
    const map = new Map([[1, 'one'], [2, 'two']]);
    for (const [key, value] of map) {
      console.log(key, value);
    }
    // Output:
    // 1, 'one'
    // 2, 'two'
    ```

33.5.5 Sources of this section

- TypeScript's built-in typings[2]

33.6 FAQ: Maps

33.6.1 When should I use a Map, and when should I use an object?

If you need a dictionary-like data structure with keys that are neither strings nor symbols, you have no choice: you must use a Map.

---
[2]https://github.com/Microsoft/TypeScript/blob/master/lib/

If, however, your keys are either strings or symbols, you must decide whether or not to use an object. A rough general guideline is:

- Is there a fixed set of keys (known at development time)?

    Then use an object `obj` and access the values via fixed keys:

    ```
    const value = obj.key;
    ```

- Can the set of keys change at runtime?

    Then use a Map `map` and access the values via keys stored in variables:

    ```
    const theKey = 123;
    map.get(theKey);
    ```

33.6.2 When would I use an object as a key in a Map?

You normally want Map keys to be compared by value (two keys are considered equal if they have the same content). That excludes objects. However, there is one use case for objects as keys: externally attaching data to objects. But that use case is served better by WeakMaps, where entries don't prevent keys from being garbage-collected (for details, consult the next chapter (p. 377)).

33.6.3 Why do Maps preserve the insertion order of entries?

In principle, Maps are unordered. The main reason for ordering entries is so that operations that list entries, keys, or values are deterministic. That helps, for example, with testing.

33.6.4 Why do Maps have a `.size`, while Arrays have a `.length`?

In JavaScript, indexable sequences (such as Arrays and strings) have a `.length`, while unindexed collections (such as Maps and Sets) have a `.size`:

- `.length` is based on indices; it is always the highest index plus one.
- `.size` counts the number of elements in a collection.

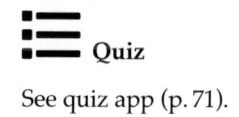

Quiz

See quiz app (p. 71).

Chapter 34

WeakMaps (`WeakMap`)

Contents

- 34.1 WeakMaps are black boxes 377
- 34.2 The keys of a WeakMap are *weakly held* 378
  - 34.2.1 All WeakMap keys must be objects 378
  - 34.2.2 Use case: attaching values to objects 378
- 34.3 Examples 379
  - 34.3.1 Caching computed results via WeakMaps 379
  - 34.3.2 Keeping private data in WeakMaps 379
- 34.4 WeakMap API 380

WeakMaps are similar to Maps, with the following differences:

- They are black boxes, where a value can only be accessed if you have both the WeakMap and the key.
- The keys of a WeakMap are *weakly held*: if an object is a key in a WeakMap, it can still be garbage-collected. That lets us use WeakMaps to attach data to objects.

The next two sections examine in more detail what that means.

34.1 WeakMaps are black boxes

It is impossible to inspect what's inside a WeakMap:

- For example, you can't iterate or loop over keys, values or entries. And you can't compute the size.
- Additionally, you can't clear a WeakMap either – you have to create a fresh instance.

These restrictions enable a security property. Quoting Mark Miller[1]:

---

[1] https://github.com/tc39/tc39-notes/blob/master/meetings/2014-11/nov-19.md#412-should-weakmapweakset-have-a-clear-method-markm

The mapping from weakmap/key pair value can only be observed or affected by someone who has both the weakmap and the key. With `clear()`, someone with only the WeakMap would've been able to affect the WeakMap-and-key-to-value mapping.

34.2 The keys of a WeakMap are *weakly held*

The keys of a WeakMap are said to be *weakly held*: Normally if one object refers to another one, then the latter object can't be garbage-collected as long as the former exists. With a WeakMap, that is different: If an object is a key and not referred to elsewhere, it can be garbage-collected while the WeakMap still exists. That also leads to the corresponding entry being removed (but there is no way to observe that).

34.2.1 All WeakMap keys must be objects

All WeakMap keys must be objects. You get an error if you use a primitive value:

```
> const wm = new WeakMap();
> wm.set(123, 'test')
TypeError: Invalid value used as weak map key
```

With primitive values as keys, WeakMaps wouldn't be black boxes anymore. But given that primitive values are never garbage-collected, you don't profit from weakly held keys anyway, and can just as well use a normal Map.

34.2.2 Use case: attaching values to objects

This is the main use case for WeakMaps: you can use them to externally attach values to objects – for example:

```
const wm = new WeakMap();
{
  const obj = {};
  wm.set(obj, 'attachedValue'); // (A)
}
// (B)
```

In line A, we attach a value to `obj`. In line B, `obj` can already be garbage-collected, even though `wm` still exists. This technique of attaching a value to an object is equivalent to a property of that object being stored externally. If `wm` were a property, the previous code would look as follows:

```
{
  const obj = {};
  obj.wm = 'attachedValue';
}
```

34.3 Examples

34.3.1 Caching computed results via WeakMaps

With WeakMaps, you can associate previously computed results with objects without having to worry about memory management. The following function countOwnKeys() is an example: it caches previous results in the WeakMap cache.

```
const cache = new WeakMap();
function countOwnKeys(obj) {
  if (cache.has(obj)) {
    return [cache.get(obj), 'cached'];
  } else {
    const count = Object.keys(obj).length;
    cache.set(obj, count);
    return [count, 'computed'];
  }
}
```

If we use this function with an object obj, you can see that the result is only computed for the first invocation, while a cached value is used for the second invocation:

```
> const obj = { foo: 1, bar: 2};
> countOwnKeys(obj)
[2, 'computed']
> countOwnKeys(obj)
[2, 'cached']
```

34.3.2 Keeping private data in WeakMaps

In the following code, the WeakMaps _counter and _action are used to store the values of virtual properties of instances of Countdown:

```
const _counter = new WeakMap();
const _action = new WeakMap();

class Countdown {
  constructor(counter, action) {
    _counter.set(this, counter);
    _action.set(this, action);
  }
  dec() {
    let counter = _counter.get(this);
    counter--;
    _counter.set(this, counter);
    if (counter === 0) {
      _action.get(this)();
    }
  }
}
```

```
// The two pseudo-properties are truly private:
assert.deepEqual(
  Object.keys(new Countdown()),
  []);
```

This is how `Countdown` is used:

```
let invoked = false;

const cd = new Countdown(3, () => invoked = true);

cd.dec(); assert.equal(invoked, false);
cd.dec(); assert.equal(invoked, false);
cd.dec(); assert.equal(invoked, true);
```

> **Exercise: WeakMaps for private data**
>
> `exercises/weakmaps/weakmaps_private_data_test.mjs`

34.4 WeakMap API

The constructor and the four methods of `WeakMap` work the same as their `Map` equivalents (p. 372):

- `new WeakMap<K, V>(entries?: Iterable<[K, V]>)` [ES6]
- `.delete(key: K) : boolean` [ES6]
- `.get(key: K) : V` [ES6]
- `.has(key: K) : boolean` [ES6]
- `.set(key: K, value: V) : this` [ES6]

> **Quiz**
>
> See quiz app (p. 71).

Chapter 35

Sets (Set)

Contents

- 35.1 Using Sets 382
  - 35.1.1 Creating Sets 382
  - 35.1.2 Adding, removing, checking membership 382
  - 35.1.3 Determining the size of a Set and clearing it ... 382
  - 35.1.4 Iterating over Sets 383
- 35.2 Examples of using Sets 383
  - 35.2.1 Removing duplicates from an Array 383
  - 35.2.2 Creating a set of Unicode characters (code points) ... 383
- 35.3 What Set elements are considered equal? 383
- 35.4 Missing Set operations 384
  - 35.4.1 Union (a ∪ b) 384
  - 35.4.2 Intersection (a ∩ b) 384
  - 35.4.3 Difference (a \ b) 385
  - 35.4.4 Mapping over Sets 385
  - 35.4.5 Filtering Sets 385
- 35.5 Quick reference: Set<T> 385
  - 35.5.1 Constructor 385
  - 35.5.2 Set<T>.prototype: single Set elements 385
  - 35.5.3 Set<T>.prototype: all Set elements 386
  - 35.5.4 Set<T>.prototype: iterating and looping 386
  - 35.5.5 Symmetry with Map 387
- 35.6 FAQ: Sets 387
  - 35.6.1 Why do Sets have a .size, while Arrays have a .length? ... 387

Before ES6, JavaScript didn't have a data structure for sets. Instead, two workarounds were used:

- The keys of an object were used as a set of strings.

- Arrays were used as sets of arbitrary values. The downside is that checking *membership* (if an Array contains a value) is slower.

Since ES6, JavaScript has the data structure `Set`, which can contain arbitrary values and performs membership checks quickly.

35.1 Using Sets

35.1.1 Creating Sets

There are three common ways of creating Sets.

First, you can use the constructor without any parameters to create an empty Set:

```
const emptySet = new Set();
assert.equal(emptySet.size, 0);
```

Second, you can pass an iterable (e.g., an Array) to the constructor. The iterated values become elements of the new Set:

```
const set = new Set(['red', 'green', 'blue']);
```

Third, the `.add()` method adds elements to a Set and is chainable:

```
const set = new Set()
.add('red')
.add('green')
.add('blue');
```

35.1.2 Adding, removing, checking membership

`.add()` adds an element to a Set.

```
const set = new Set();
set.add('red');
```

`.has()` checks if an element is a member of a Set.

```
assert.equal(set.has('red'), true);
```

`.delete()` removes an element from a Set.

```
assert.equal(set.delete('red'), true); // there was a deletion
assert.equal(set.has('red'), false);
```

35.1.3 Determining the size of a Set and clearing it

`.size` contains the number of elements in a Set.

```
const set = new Set()
  .add('foo')
  .add('bar');
assert.equal(set.size, 2)
```

`.clear()` removes all elements of a Set.

```
set.clear();
assert.equal(set.size, 0)
```

35.1.4 Iterating over Sets

Sets are iterable and the `for-of` loop works as you'd expect:

```
const set = new Set(['red', 'green', 'blue']);
for (const x of set) {
  console.log(x);
}
// Output:
// 'red'
// 'green'
// 'blue'
```

As you can see, Sets preserve *insertion order*. That is, elements are always iterated over in the order in which they were added.

Given that Sets are iterable, you can use spreading (..., p. 320) to convert them to Arrays:

```
const set = new Set(['red', 'green', 'blue']);
const arr = [...set]; // ['red', 'green', 'blue']
```

35.2 Examples of using Sets

35.2.1 Removing duplicates from an Array

Converting an Array to a Set and back, removes duplicates from the Array:

```
assert.deepEqual(
  [...new Set([1, 2, 1, 2, 3, 3, 3])],
  [1, 2, 3]);
```

35.2.2 Creating a set of Unicode characters (code points)

Strings are iterable and can therefore be used as parameters for new Set():

```
assert.deepEqual(
  new Set('abc'),
  new Set(['a', 'b', 'c']));
```

35.3 What Set elements are considered equal?

As with Map keys, Set elements are compared similarly to `===`, with the exception of NaN being equal to itself.

```
> const set = new Set([NaN, NaN, NaN]);
> set.size
1
```

```
> set.has(NaN)
true
```

As with ===, two different objects are never considered equal (and there is no way to change that at the moment):

```
> const set = new Set();

> set.add({});
> set.size
1

> set.add({});
> set.size
2
```

35.4 Missing Set operations

Sets are missing several common operations. Such an operation can usually be implemented by:

- Converting the input Sets to Arrays by spreading into Array literals (p. 320).
- Performing the operation on Arrays.
- Converting the result to a Set and returning it.

35.4.1 Union (a ∪ b)

Computing the union of two Sets a and b means creating a Set that contains the elements of both a and b.

```
const a = new Set([1,2,3]);
const b = new Set([4,3,2]);
// Use spreading to concatenate two iterables
const union = new Set([...a, ...b]);

assert.deepEqual([...union], [1, 2, 3, 4]);
```

35.4.2 Intersection (a ∩ b)

Computing the intersection of two Sets a and b means creating a Set that contains those elements of a that are also in b.

```
const a = new Set([1,2,3]);
const b = new Set([4,3,2]);
const intersection = new Set(
  [...a].filter(x => b.has(x)));

assert.deepEqual([...intersection], [2, 3]);
```

35.4.3 Difference (a \ b)

Computing the difference between two Sets a and b means creating a Set that contains those elements of a that are not in b. This operation is also sometimes called *minus* (−).

```
const a = new Set([1,2,3]);
const b = new Set([4,3,2]);
const difference = new Set(
  [...a].filter(x => !b.has(x)));

assert.deepEqual([...difference], [1]);
```

35.4.4 Mapping over Sets

Sets don't have a method .map(). But we can borrow the one that Arrays have:

```
const set = new Set([1, 2, 3]);
const mappedSet = new Set([...set].map(x => x * 2));

// Convert mappedSet to an Array to check what's inside it
assert.deepEqual([...mappedSet], [2, 4, 6]);
```

35.4.5 Filtering Sets

We can't directly .filter() Sets, so we need to use the corresponding Array method:

```
const set = new Set([1, 2, 3, 4, 5]);
const filteredSet = new Set([...set].filter(x => (x % 2) === 0));

assert.deepEqual([...filteredSet], [2, 4]);
```

35.5 Quick reference: Set<T>

35.5.1 Constructor

- new Set<T>(values?: Iterable<T>) [ES6]

    If you don't provide the parameter values, then an empty Set is created. If you do, then the iterated values are added as elements to the Set. For example:

    ```
    const set = new Set(['red', 'green', 'blue']);
    ```

35.5.2 Set<T>.prototype: single Set elements

- .add(value: T): this [ES6]

    Adds value to this Set. This method returns this, which means that it can be chained.

    ```
    const set = new Set(['red']);
    set.add('green').add('blue');
    assert.deepEqual([...set], ['red', 'green', 'blue']);
    ```

- .delete(value: T): boolean [ES6]

    Removes value from this Set. Returns true if something was deleted and false, otherwise.

    ```
    const set = new Set(['red', 'green', 'blue']);
    assert.equal(set.delete('red'), true); // there was a deletion
    assert.deepEqual([...set], ['green', 'blue']);
    ```

- .has(value: T): boolean [ES6]

    Checks whether value is in this Set.

    ```
    const set = new Set(['red', 'green']);
    assert.equal(set.has('red'), true);
    assert.equal(set.has('blue'), false);
    ```

35.5.3 Set<T>.prototype: all Set elements

- get .size: number [ES6]

    Returns how many elements there are in this Set.

    ```
    const set = new Set(['red', 'green', 'blue']);
    assert.equal(set.size, 3);
    ```

- .clear(): void [ES6]

    Removes all elements from this Set.

    ```
    const set = new Set(['red', 'green', 'blue']);
    assert.equal(set.size, 3);
    set.clear();
    assert.equal(set.size, 0);
    ```

35.5.4 Set<T>.prototype: iterating and looping

- .values(): Iterable<T> [ES6]

    Returns an iterable over all elements of this Set.

    ```
    const set = new Set(['red', 'green']);
    for (const x of set.values()) {
      console.log(x);
    }
    // Output:
    // 'red'
    // 'green'
    ```

- [Symbol.iterator](): Iterable<T> [ES6]

    Default way of iterating over Sets. Same as .values().

    ```
    const set = new Set(['red', 'green']);
    for (const x of set) {
      console.log(x);
    ```

```
        }
        // Output:
        // 'red'
        // 'green'
```

- .forEach(callback: (value: T, key: T, theSet: Set<T>) => void, thisArg?: any): void [ES6]

    Feeds each element of this Set to callback(). value and key both contain the current element. This redundancy was introduced so that this callback has the same type signature as the callback of Map.prototype.forEach().

    You can specify the this of callback via thisArg. If you omit it, this is undefined.

    ```
    const set = new Set(['red', 'green']);
    set.forEach(x => console.log(x));
    // Output:
    // 'red'
    // 'green'
    ```

35.5.5 Symmetry with Map

The following two methods mainly exist so that Sets and Maps have similar interfaces. Each Set element is handled as if it were a Map entry whose key and value are both the element.

- Set.prototype.entries(): Iterable<[T,T]> [ES6]
- Set.prototype.keys(): Iterable<T> [ES6]

.entries() enables you to convert a Set to a Map:

```
const set = new Set(['a', 'b', 'c']);
const map = new Map(set.entries());
assert.deepEqual(
  [...map.entries()],
  [['a','a'], ['b','b'], ['c','c']]);
```

35.6 FAQ: Sets

35.6.1 Why do Sets have a .size, while Arrays have a .length?

The answer to this question is given in §33.6.4 "Why do Maps have a .size, while Arrays have a .length?" (p. 375).

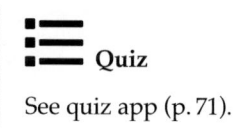

Quiz

See quiz app (p. 71).

Chapter 36

WeakSets (WeakSet)

Contents

    36.1 Example: Marking objects as safe to use with a method 389
    36.2 WeakSet API 390

WeakSets are similar to Sets, with the following differences:

- They can hold objects without preventing those objects from being garbage-collected.

- They are black boxes: we only get any data out of a WeakSet if we have both the WeakSet and a value. The only methods that are supported are .add(), .delete(), .has(). Consult the section on WeakMaps as black boxes (p. 377) for an explanation of why WeakSets don't allow iteration, looping, and clearing.

Given that we can't iterate over their elements, there are not that many use cases for WeakSets. They do enable us to mark objects.

36.1 Example: Marking objects as safe to use with a method

Domenic Denicola shows[1] how a class Foo can ensure that its methods are only applied to instances that were created by it:

```
const foos = new WeakSet();

class Foo {
  constructor() {
    foos.add(this);
  }
```

---

[1]https://mail.mozilla.org/pipermail/es-discuss/2015-June/043027.html

```
  method() {
    if (!foos.has(this)) {
      throw new TypeError('Incompatible object!');
    }
  }
}

const foo = new Foo();
foo.method(); // works

assert.throws(
  () => {
    const obj = {};
    Foo.prototype.method.call(obj); // throws an exception
  },
  TypeError
);
```

36.2 WeakSet API

The constructor and the three methods of WeakSet work the same as their Set equivalents (p. 385):

- `new WeakSet<T>(values?: Iterable<T>)` [ES6]
- `.add(value: T): this` [ES6]
- `.delete(value: T): boolean` [ES6]
- `.has(value: T): boolean` [ES6]

Chapter 37

Destructuring

Contents

- 37.1 A first taste of destructuring 392
- 37.2 Constructing vs. extracting 392
- 37.3 Where can we destructure? 393
- 37.4 Object-destructuring 394
  - 37.4.1 Property value shorthands 394
  - 37.4.2 Rest properties 395
  - 37.4.3 Syntax pitfall: assigning via object destructuring 395
- 37.5 Array-destructuring 395
  - 37.5.1 Array-destructuring works with any iterable 396
  - 37.5.2 Rest elements 396
- 37.6 Examples of destructuring 396
  - 37.6.1 Array-destructuring: swapping variable values 396
  - 37.6.2 Array-destructuring: operations that return Arrays 397
  - 37.6.3 Object-destructuring: multiple return values 397
- 37.7 What happens if a pattern part does not match anything? 398
  - 37.7.1 Object-destructuring and missing properties 398
  - 37.7.2 Array-destructuring and missing elements 398
- 37.8 What values can't be destructured? 398
  - 37.8.1 You can't object-destructure undefined and null 398
  - 37.8.2 You can't Array-destructure non-iterable values 399
- 37.9 (Advanced) 399
- 37.10 Default values 399
  - 37.10.1 Default values in Array-destructuring 400
  - 37.10.2 Default values in object-destructuring 400
- 37.11 Parameter definitions are similar to destructuring 400
- 37.12 Nested destructuring 401

37.1 A first taste of destructuring

With normal assignment, you extract one piece of data at a time – for example:

```
const arr = ['a', 'b', 'c'];
const x = arr[0]; // extract
const y = arr[1]; // extract
```

With destructuring, you can extract multiple pieces of data at the same time via patterns in locations that receive data. The left-hand side of = in the previous code is one such location. In the following code, the square brackets in line A are a destructuring pattern:

```
const arr = ['a', 'b', 'c'];
const [x, y] = arr; // (A)
assert.equal(x, 'a');
assert.equal(y, 'b');
```

This code does the same as the previous code.

Note that the pattern is "smaller" than the data: we are only extracting what we need.

37.2 Constructing vs. extracting

In order to understand what destructuring is, consider that JavaScript has two kinds of operations that are opposites:

- You can *construct* compound data, for example, by setting properties and via object literals.
- You can *extract* data out of compound data, for example, by getting properties.

Constructing data looks as follows:

```
// Constructing: one property at a time
const jane1 = {};
jane1.first = 'Jane';
jane1.last = 'Doe';

// Constructing: multiple properties
const jane2 = {
  first: 'Jane',
  last: 'Doe',
};

assert.deepEqual(jane1, jane2);
```

Extracting data looks as follows:

```
const jane = {
  first: 'Jane',
  last: 'Doe',
};
```

37.3 Where can we destructure?

```
// Extracting: one property at a time
const f1 = jane.first;
const l1 = jane.last;
assert.equal(f1, 'Jane');
assert.equal(l1, 'Doe');

// Extracting: multiple properties (NEW!)
const {first: f2, last: l2} = jane; // (A)
assert.equal(f2, 'Jane');
assert.equal(l2, 'Doe');
```

The operation in line A is new: we declare two variables f2 and l2 and initialize them via *destructuring* (multivalue extraction).

The following part of line A is a *destructuring pattern*:

```
{first: f2, last: l2}
```

Destructuring patterns are syntactically similar to the literals that are used for multivalue construction. But they appear where data is received (e.g., at the left-hand side of assignments), not where data is created (e.g., at the right-hand side of assignments).

37.3 Where can we destructure?

Destructuring patterns can be used at "data sink locations" such as:

- Variable declarations:
  ```
  const [a] = ['x'];
  assert.equal(a, 'x');

  let [b] = ['y'];
  assert.equal(b, 'y');
  ```
- Assignments:
  ```
  let b;
  [b] = ['z'];
  assert.equal(b, 'z');
  ```
- Parameter definitions:
  ```
  const f = ([x]) => x;
  assert.equal(f(['a']), 'a');
  ```

Note that variable declarations include const and let declarations in for-of loops:

```
const arr = ['a', 'b'];
for (const [index, element] of arr.entries()) {
    console.log(index, element);
}
// Output:
```

```
// 0, 'a'
// 1, 'b'
```

In the next two sections, we'll look deeper into the two kinds of destructuring: object-destructuring and Array-destructuring.

37.4 Object-destructuring

Object-destructuring lets you batch-extract values of properties via patterns that look like object literals:

```
const address = {
  street: 'Evergreen Terrace',
  number: '742',
  city: 'Springfield',
  state: 'NT',
  zip: '49007',
};

const { street: s, city: c } = address;
assert.equal(s, 'Evergreen Terrace');
assert.equal(c, 'Springfield');
```

You can think of the pattern as a transparent sheet that you place over the data: the pattern key `'street'` has a match in the data. Therefore, the data value `'Evergreen Terrace'` is assigned to the pattern variable s.

You can also object-destructure primitive values:

```
const {length: len} = 'abc';
assert.equal(len, 3);
```

And you can object-destructure Arrays:

```
const {0:x, 2:y} = ['a', 'b', 'c'];
assert.equal(x, 'a');
assert.equal(y, 'c');
```

Why does that work? Array indices are also properties (p. 326).

37.4.1 Property value shorthands

Object literals support property value shorthands and so do object patterns:

```
const { street, city } = address;
assert.equal(street, 'Evergreen Terrace');
assert.equal(city, 'Springfield');
```

> **Exercise: Object-destructuring**
>
> exercises/destructuring/object_destructuring_exrc.mjs

37.4.2 Rest properties

In object literals, you can have spread properties. In object patterns, you can have rest properties (which must come last):

```
const obj = { a: 1, b: 2, c: 3 };
const { a: propValue, ...remaining } = obj; // (A)

assert.equal(propValue, 1);
assert.deepEqual(remaining, {b:2, c:3});
```

A rest property variable, such as `remaining` (line A), is assigned an object with all data properties whose keys are not mentioned in the pattern.

`remaining` can also be viewed as the result of non-destructively removing property a from `obj`.

37.4.3 Syntax pitfall: assigning via object destructuring

If we object-destructure in an assignment, we are facing a pitfall caused by syntactic ambiguity (p. 51) – you can't start a statement with a curly brace because then JavaScript thinks you are starting a block:

```
let prop;
assert.throws(
  () => eval("{prop} = { prop: 'hello' };"),
  {
    name: 'SyntaxError',
    message: 'Unexpected token =',
  });
```

⚙ Why eval()?

`eval()` (p. 224) delays parsing (and therefore the `SyntaxError`) until the callback of `assert.throws()` is executed. If we didn't use it, we'd already get an error when this code is parsed and `assert.throws()` wouldn't even be executed.

The workaround is to put the whole assignment in parentheses:

```
let prop;
({prop} = { prop: 'hello' });
assert.equal(prop, 'hello');
```

37.5 Array-destructuring

Array-destructuring lets you batch-extract values of Array elements via patterns that look like Array literals:

```
const [x, y] = ['a', 'b'];
assert.equal(x, 'a');
```

```
assert.equal(y, 'b');
```

You can skip elements by mentioning holes inside Array patterns:

```
const [, x, y] = ['a', 'b', 'c']; // (A)
assert.equal(x, 'b');
assert.equal(y, 'c');
```

The first element of the Array pattern in line A is a hole, which is why the Array element at index 0 is ignored.

37.5.1 Array-destructuring works with any iterable

Array-destructuring can be applied to any value that is iterable, not just to Arrays:

```
// Sets are iterable
const mySet = new Set().add('a').add('b').add('c');
const [first, second] = mySet;
assert.equal(first, 'a');
assert.equal(second, 'b');

// Strings are iterable
const [a, b] = 'xyz';
assert.equal(a, 'x');
assert.equal(b, 'y');
```

37.5.2 Rest elements

In Array literals, you can have spread elements. In Array patterns, you can have rest elements (which must come last):

```
const [x, y, ...remaining] = ['a', 'b', 'c', 'd']; // (A)

assert.equal(x, 'a');
assert.equal(y, 'b');
assert.deepEqual(remaining, ['c', 'd']);
```

A rest element variable, such as `remaining` (line A), is assigned an Array with all elements of the destructured value that were not mentioned yet.

37.6 Examples of destructuring

37.6.1 Array-destructuring: swapping variable values

You can use Array-destructuring to swap the values of two variables without needing a temporary variable:

```
let x = 'a';
let y = 'b';

[x,y] = [y,x]; // swap
```

37.6 Examples of destructuring

```
assert.equal(x, 'b');
assert.equal(y, 'a');
```

37.6.2 Array-destructuring: operations that return Arrays

Array-destructuring is useful when operations return Arrays, as does, for example, the regular expression method `.exec()`:

```
// Skip the element at index 0 (the whole match):
const [, year, month, day] =
  /^([0-9]{4})-([0-9]{2})-([0-9]{2})$/
    .exec('2999-12-31');

assert.equal(year, '2999');
assert.equal(month, '12');
assert.equal(day, '31');
```

37.6.3 Object-destructuring: multiple return values

Destructuring is very useful if a function returns multiple values – either packaged as an Array or packaged as an object.

Consider a function `findElement()` that finds elements in an Array:

```
findElement(array, (value, index) => «boolean expression»)
```

Its second parameter is a function that receives the value and index of an element and returns a boolean indicating if this is the element the caller is looking for.

We are now faced with a dilemma: Should `findElement()` return the value of the element it found or the index? One solution would be to create two separate functions, but that would result in duplicated code because both functions would be very similar.

The following implementation avoids duplication by returning an object that contains both index and value of the element that is found:

```
function findElement(arr, predicate) {
  for (let index=0; index < arr.length; index++) {
    const value = arr[index];
    if (predicate(value)) {
      // We found something:
      return { value, index };
    }
  }
  // We didn't find anything:
  return { value: undefined, index: -1 };
}
```

Destructuring helps us with processing the result of `findElement()`:

```
const arr = [7, 8, 6];
```

```
const {value, index} = findElement(arr, x => x % 2 === 0);
assert.equal(value, 8);
assert.equal(index, 1);
```

As we are working with property keys, the order in which we mention `value` and `index` doesn't matter:

```
const {index, value} = findElement(arr, x => x % 2 === 0);
```

The kicker is that destructuring also serves us well if we are only interested in one of the two results:

```
const arr = [7, 8, 6];

const {value} = findElement(arr, x => x % 2 === 0);
assert.equal(value, 8);

const {index} = findElement(arr, x => x % 2 === 0);
assert.equal(index, 1);
```

All of these conveniences combined make this way of handling multiple return values quite versatile.

37.7 What happens if a pattern part does not match anything?

What happens if there is no match for part of a pattern? The same thing that happens if you use non-batch operators: you get `undefined`.

37.7.1 Object-destructuring and missing properties

If a property in an object pattern has no match on the right-hand side, you get undefined:

```
const {prop: p} = {};
assert.equal(p, undefined);
```

37.7.2 Array-destructuring and missing elements

If an element in an Array pattern has no match on the right-hand side, you get undefined:

```
const [x] = [];
assert.equal(x, undefined);
```

37.8 What values can't be destructured?

37.8.1 You can't object-destructure `undefined` and `null`

Object-destructuring only fails if the value to be destructured is either `undefined` or `null`. That is, it fails whenever accessing a property via the dot operator would fail too.

37.9 (Advanced)   399

```
assert.throws(
  () => { const {prop} = undefined; },
  {
    name: 'TypeError',
    message: "Cannot destructure property `prop` of " +
      "'undefined' or 'null'.",
  }
);
assert.throws(
  () => { const {prop} = null; },
  {
    name: 'TypeError',
    message: "Cannot destructure property `prop` of " +
      "'undefined' or 'null'.",
  }
);
```

37.8.2 You can't Array-destructure non-iterable values

Array-destructuring demands that the destructured value be iterable. Therefore, you can't Array-destructure `undefined` and `null`. But you can't Array-destructure non-iterable objects either:

```
assert.throws(
  () => { const [x] = {}; },
  {
    name: 'TypeError',
    message: '{} is not iterable',
  }
);
```

Quiz: basic

See quiz app (p. 71).

37.9 (Advanced)

All of the remaining sections are advanced.

37.10 Default values

Normally, if a pattern has no match, the corresponding variable is set to `undefined`:

```
const {prop: p} = {};
assert.equal(p, undefined);
```

If you want a different value to be used, you need to specify a *default value* (via =):

```
const {prop: p = 123} = {}; // (A)
assert.equal(p, 123);
```

In line A, we specify the default value for p to be 123. That default is used because the data that we are destructuring has no property named prop.

37.10.1 Default values in Array-destructuring

Here, we have two default values that are assigned to the variables x and y because the corresponding elements don't exist in the Array that is destructured.

```
const [x=1, y=2] = [];

assert.equal(x, 1);
assert.equal(y, 2);
```

The default value for the first element of the Array pattern is 1; the default value for the second element is 2.

37.10.2 Default values in object-destructuring

You can also specify default values for object-destructuring:

```
const {first: f='', last: l=''} = {};
assert.equal(f, '');
assert.equal(l, '');
```

Neither property key first nor property key last exist in the object that is destructured. Therefore, the default values are used.

With property value shorthands, this code becomes simpler:

```
const {first='', last=''} = {};
assert.equal(first, '');
assert.equal(last, '');
```

37.11 Parameter definitions are similar to destructuring

Considering what we have learned in this chapter, parameter definitions have much in common with an Array pattern (rest elements, default values, etc.). In fact, the following two function declarations are equivalent:

```
function f1(«pattern1», «pattern2») {
  // ···
}

function f2(...args) {
  const [«pattern1», «pattern2»] = args;
  // ···
}
```

37.12 Nested destructuring

Until now, we have only used variables as *assignment targets* (data sinks) inside destructuring patterns. But you can also use patterns as assignment targets, which enables you to nest patterns to arbitrary depths:

```
const arr = [
  { first: 'Jane', last: 'Bond' },
  { first: 'Lars', last: 'Croft' },
];
const [, {first}] = arr;
assert.equal(first, 'Lars');
```

Inside the Array pattern in line A, there is a nested object pattern at index 1.

Nested patterns can become difficult to understand, so they are best used in moderation.

Quiz: advanced

See quiz app (p. 71).

Chapter 38

Synchronous generators (advanced)

Contents

38.1 What are synchronous generators?	403
38.1.1 Generator functions return iterables and fill them via `yield`	404
38.1.2 `yield` pauses a generator function	404
38.1.3 Why does `yield` pause execution?	406
38.1.4 Example: Mapping over iterables	407
38.2 Calling generators from generators (advanced)	407
38.2.1 Calling generators via `yield*`	407
38.2.2 Example: Iterating over a tree	408
38.3 Background: external iteration vs. internal iteration	409
38.4 Use case for generators: reusing traversals	410
38.4.1 The traversal to reuse	410
38.4.2 Internal iteration (push)	410
38.4.3 External iteration (pull)	411
38.5 Advanced features of generators	411

38.1 What are synchronous generators?

Synchronous generators are special versions of function definitions and method definitions that always return synchronous iterables:

```
// Generator function declaration
function* genFunc1() { /*···*/ }

// Generator function expression
const genFunc2 = function* () { /*···*/ };
```

```
// Generator method definition in an object literal
const obj = {
  * generatorMethod() {
    // ···
  }
};

// Generator method definition in a class definition
// (class declaration or class expression)
class MyClass {
  * generatorMethod() {
    // ···
  }
}
```

Asterisks (*) mark functions and methods as generators:

- Functions: The pseudo-keyword function* is a combination of the keyword function and an asterisk.
- Methods: The * is a modifier (similar to static and get).

38.1.1 Generator functions return iterables and fill them via yield

If you call a generator function, it returns an iterable (actually, an iterator that is also iterable). The generator fills that iterable via the yield operator:

```
function* genFunc1() {
  yield 'a';
  yield 'b';
}

const iterable = genFunc1();
// Convert the iterable to an Array, to check what's inside:
assert.deepEqual([...iterable], ['a', 'b']);

// You can also use a for-of loop
for (const x of genFunc1()) {
  console.log(x);
}
// Output:
// 'a'
// 'b'
```

38.1.2 yield pauses a generator function

Using a generator function involves the following steps:

- Function-calling it returns an iterator iter (that is also an iterable).
- Iterating over iter repeatedly invokes iter.next(). Each time, we jump into the body of the generator function until there is a yield that returns a value.

38.1 What are synchronous generators?

Therefore, yield does more than just add values to iterables – it also pauses and exits the generator function:

- Like return, a yield exits the body of the function and returns a value (via .next()).
- Unlike return, if you repeat the invocation (of .next()), execution resumes directly after the yield.

Let's examine what that means via the following generator function.

```
let location = 0;
function* genFunc2() {
  location = 1; yield 'a';
  location = 2; yield 'b';
  location = 3;
}
```

In order to use genFunc2(), we must first create the iterator/iterable iter. genFunc2() is now paused "before" its body.

```
const iter = genFunc2();
// genFunc2() is now paused "before" its body:
assert.equal(location, 0);
```

iter implements the iteration protocol (p. 311). Therefore, we control the execution of genFunc2() via iter.next(). Calling that method resumes the paused genFunc2() and executes it until there is a yield. Then execution pauses and .next() returns the operand of the yield:

```
assert.deepEqual(
  iter.next(), {value: 'a', done: false});
// genFunc2() is now paused directly after the first `yield`:
assert.equal(location, 1);
```

Note that the yielded value 'a' is wrapped in an object, which is how iterators always deliver their values.

We call iter.next() again and execution continues where we previously paused. Once we encounter the second yield, genFunc2() is paused and .next() returns the yielded value 'b'.

```
assert.deepEqual(
  iter.next(), {value: 'b', done: false});
// genFunc2() is now paused directly after the second `yield`:
assert.equal(location, 2);
```

We call iter.next() one more time and execution continues until it leaves the body of genFunc2():

```
assert.deepEqual(
  iter.next(), {value: undefined, done: true});
// We have reached the end of genFunc2():
assert.equal(location, 3);
```

This time, property `.done` of the result of `.next()` is `true`, which means that the iterator is finished.

38.1.3 Why does `yield` pause execution?

What are the benefits of `yield` pausing execution? Why doesn't it simply work like the Array method `.push()` and fill the iterable with values without pausing?

Due to pausing, generators provide many of the features of *coroutines* (think processes that are multitasked cooperatively). For example, when you ask for the next value of an iterable, that value is computed *lazily* (on demand). The following two generator functions demonstrate what that means.

```
/**
 * Returns an iterable over lines
 */
function* genLines() {
  yield 'A line';
  yield 'Another line';
  yield 'Last line';
}

/**
 * Input: iterable over lines
 * Output: iterable over numbered lines
 */
function* numberLines(lineIterable) {
  let lineNumber = 1;
  for (const line of lineIterable) { // input
    yield lineNumber + ': ' + line; // output
    lineNumber++;
  }
}
```

Note that the `yield` in `numberLines()` appears inside a `for-of` loop. `yield` can be used inside loops, but not inside callbacks (more on that later).

Let's combine both generators to produce the iterable `numberedLines`:

```
const numberedLines = numberLines(genLines());
assert.deepEqual(
  numberedLines.next(), {value: '1: A line', done: false});
assert.deepEqual(
  numberedLines.next(), {value: '2: Another line', done: false});
```

The key benefit of using generators here is that everything works incrementally: via `numberedLines.next()`, we ask `numberLines()` for only a single numbered line. In turn, it asks `genLines()` for only a single unnumbered line.

This incrementalism continues to work if, for example, `genLines()` reads its lines from a large text file: If we ask `numberLines()` for a numbered line, we get one as soon as `genLines()` has read its first line from the text file.

Without generators, `genLines()` would first read all lines and return them. Then `numberLines()` would number all lines and return them. We therefore have to wait much longer until we get the first numbered line.

> **Exercise: Turning a normal function into a generator**
> exercises/sync-generators/fib_seq_test.mjs

38.1.4 Example: Mapping over iterables

The following function `mapIter()` is similar to the Array method `.map()`, but it returns an iterable, not an Array, and produces its results on demand.

```
function* mapIter(iterable, func) {
  let index = 0;
  for (const x of iterable) {
    yield func(x, index);
    index++;
  }
}

const iterable = mapIter(['a', 'b'], x => x + x);
assert.deepEqual([...iterable], ['aa', 'bb']);
```

> **Exercise: Filtering iterables**
> exercises/sync-generators/filter_iter_gen_test.mjs

38.2 Calling generators from generators (advanced)

38.2.1 Calling generators via `yield*`

`yield` only works directly inside generators – so far we haven't seen a way of delegating yielding to another function or method.

Let's first examine what does *not* work: in the following example, we'd like `foo()` to call `bar()`, so that the latter yields two values for the former. Alas, a naive approach fails:

```
function* bar() {
  yield 'a';
  yield 'b';
}
function* foo() {
  // Nothing happens if we call `bar()`:
  bar();
}
assert.deepEqual(
  [...foo()], []);
```

Why doesn't this work? The function call `bar()` returns an iterable, which we ignore.

What we want is for `foo()` to yield everything that is yielded by `bar()`. That's what the `yield*` operator does:

```
function* bar() {
  yield 'a';
  yield 'b';
}
function* foo() {
  yield* bar();
}
assert.deepEqual(
  [...foo()], ['a', 'b']);
```

In other words, the previous `foo()` is roughly equivalent to:

```
function* foo() {
  for (const x of bar()) {
    yield x;
  }
}
```

Note that `yield*` works with any iterable:

```
function* gen() {
  yield* [1, 2];
}
assert.deepEqual(
  [...gen()], [1, 2]);
```

38.2.2 Example: Iterating over a tree

`yield*` lets us make recursive calls in generators, which is useful when iterating over recursive data structures such as trees. Take, for example, the following data structure for binary trees.

```
class BinaryTree {
  constructor(value, left=null, right=null) {
    this.value = value;
    this.left = left;
    this.right = right;
  }

  /** Prefix iteration: parent before children */
  * [Symbol.iterator]() {
    yield this.value;
    if (this.left) {
      // Same as yield* this.left[Symbol.iterator]()
      yield* this.left;
    }
    if (this.right) {
```

```
      yield* this.right;
    }
  }
}
```

Method `[Symbol.iterator]()` adds support for the iteration protocol, which means that we can use a `for-of` loop to iterate over an instance of BinaryTree:

```
const tree = new BinaryTree('a',
  new BinaryTree('b',
    new BinaryTree('c'),
    new BinaryTree('d')),
  new BinaryTree('e'));

for (const x of tree) {
  console.log(x);
}
// Output:
// 'a'
// 'b'
// 'c'
// 'd'
// 'e'
```

> **Exercise: Iterating over a nested Array**
> `exercises/sync-generators/iter_nested_arrays_test.mjs`

38.3 Background: external iteration vs. internal iteration

In preparation for the next section, we need to learn about two different styles of iterating over the values "inside" an object:

- External iteration (pull): Your code asks the object for the values via an iteration protocol. For example, the `for-of` loop is based on JavaScript's iteration protocol:

  ```
  for (const x of ['a', 'b']) {
    console.log(x);
  }
  // Output:
  // 'a'
  // 'b'
  ```

- Internal iteration (push): You pass a callback function to a method of the object and the method feeds the values to the callback. For example, Arrays have the method `.forEach()`:

  ```
  ['a', 'b'].forEach((x) => {
    console.log(x);
  });
  ```

```
// Output:
// 'a'
// 'b'
```

The next section has examples for both styles of iteration.

38.4 Use case for generators: reusing traversals

One important use case for generators is extracting and reusing traversals.

38.4.1 The traversal to reuse

As an example, consider the following function that traverses a tree of files and logs their paths (it uses the Node.js API[1] for doing so):

```
function logPaths(dir) {
  for (const fileName of fs.readdirSync(dir)) {
    const filePath = path.resolve(dir, fileName);
    console.log(filePath);
    const stats = fs.statSync(filePath);
    if (stats.isDirectory()) {
      logPaths(filePath); // recursive call
    }
  }
}
```

Consider the following directory:

```
mydir/
    a.txt
    b.txt
    subdir/
        c.txt
```

Let's log the paths inside `mydir/`:

```
logPaths('mydir');

// Output:
// 'mydir/a.txt'
// 'mydir/b.txt'
// 'mydir/subdir'
// 'mydir/subdir/c.txt'
```

How can we reuse this traversal and do something other than logging the paths?

38.4.2 Internal iteration (push)

One way of reusing traversal code is via *internal iteration*: Each traversed value is passsed to a callback (line A).

---

[1] https://nodejs.org/en/docs/

```
function visitPaths(dir, callback) {
  for (const fileName of fs.readdirSync(dir)) {
    const filePath = path.resolve(dir, fileName);
    callback(filePath); // (A)
    const stats = fs.statSync(filePath);
    if (stats.isDirectory()) {
      visitPaths(filePath, callback);
    }
  }
}
const paths = [];
visitPaths('mydir', p => paths.push(p));
assert.deepEqual(
  paths,
  [
    'mydir/a.txt',
    'mydir/b.txt',
    'mydir/subdir',
    'mydir/subdir/c.txt',
  ]);
```

38.4.3 External iteration (pull)

Another way of reusing traversal code is via *external iteration*: We can write a generator that yields all traversed values (line A).

```
function* iterPaths(dir) {
  for (const fileName of fs.readdirSync(dir)) {
    const filePath = path.resolve(dir, fileName);
    yield filePath; // (A)
    const stats = fs.statSync(filePath);
    if (stats.isDirectory()) {
      yield* iterPaths(filePath);
    }
  }
}
const paths = [...iterPaths('mydir')];
```

38.5 Advanced features of generators

The chapter on generators[2] in *Exploring ES6* covers two features that are beyond the scope of this book:

- yield can also *receive* data, via an argument of .next().
- Generators can also return values (not just yield them). Such values do not become iteration values, but can be retrieved via yield*.

---
[2]https://exploringjs.com/es6/ch_generators.html

Part VIII

Asynchronicity

Chapter 39

Asynchronous programming in JavaScript

Contents

39.1 A roadmap for asynchronous programming in JavaScript 416
    39.1.1 Synchronous functions 416
    39.1.2 JavaScript executes tasks sequentially in a single process ... 416
    39.1.3 Callback-based asynchronous functions 416
    39.1.4 Promise-based asynchronous functions 417
    39.1.5 Async functions 417
    39.1.6 Next steps 418
39.2 The call stack 418
39.3 The event loop 419
39.4 How to avoid blocking the JavaScript process 420
    39.4.1 The user interface of the browser can be blocked 420
    39.4.2 How can we avoid blocking the browser? 421
    39.4.3 Taking breaks 421
    39.4.4 Run-to-completion semantics 422
39.5 Patterns for delivering asynchronous results 422
    39.5.1 Delivering asynchronous results via events 423
    39.5.2 Delivering asynchronous results via callbacks 425
39.6 Asynchronous code: the downsides 425
39.7 Resources 426

This chapter explains the foundations of asynchronous programming in JavaScript.

39.1 A roadmap for asynchronous programming in JavaScript

This section provides a roadmap for the content on asynchronous programming in JavaScript.

> 👁 **Don't worry about the details!**
>
> Don't worry if you don't understand everything yet. This is just a quick peek at what's coming up.

39.1.1 Synchronous functions

Normal functions are *synchronous*: the caller waits until the callee is finished with its computation. `divideSync()` in line A is a synchronous function call:

```
function main() {
  try {
    const result = divideSync(12, 3); // (A)
    assert.equal(result, 4);
  } catch (err) {
    assert.fail(err);
  }
}
```

39.1.2 JavaScript executes tasks sequentially in a single process

By default, JavaScript *tasks* are functions that are executed sequentially in a single process. That looks like this:

```
while (true) {
  const task = taskQueue.dequeue();
  task(); // run task
}
```

This loop is also called the *event loop* because events, such as clicking a mouse, add tasks to the queue.

Due to this style of cooperative multitasking, we don't want a task to block other tasks from being executed while, for example, it waits for results coming from a server. The next subsection explores how to handle this case.

39.1.3 Callback-based asynchronous functions

What if `divide()` needs a server to compute its result? Then the result should be delivered in a different manner: The caller shouldn't have to wait (synchronously) until the result is ready; it should be notified (asynchronously) when it is. One way of delivering the result asynchronously is by giving `divide()` a callback function that it uses to notify the caller.

39.1 A roadmap for asynchronous programming in JavaScript

```
function main() {
  divideCallback(12, 3,
    (err, result) => {
      if (err) {
        assert.fail(err);
      } else {
        assert.equal(result, 4);
      }
    });
}
```

When there is an asynchronous function call:

```
divideCallback(x, y, callback)
```

Then the following steps happen:

- `divideCallback()` sends a request to a server.
- Then the current task `main()` is finished and other tasks can be executed.
- When a response from the server arrives, it is either:
  - An error `err`: Then the following task is added to the queue.
    ```
    taskQueue.enqueue(() => callback(err));
    ```
  - A result r: Then the following task is added to the queue.
    ```
    taskQueue.enqueue(() => callback(null, r));
    ```

39.1.4 Promise-based asynchronous functions

Promises are two things:

- A standard pattern that makes working with callbacks easier.
- The mechanism on which *async functions* (the topic of the next subsection) are built.

Invoking a Promise-based function looks as follows.

```
function main() {
  dividePromise(12, 3)
    .then(result => assert.equal(result, 4))
    .catch(err => assert.fail(err));
}
```

39.1.5 Async functions

One way of looking at async functions is as better syntax for Promise-based code:

```
async function main() {
  try {
    const result = await dividePromise(12, 3); // (A)
    assert.equal(result, 4);
  } catch (err) {
    assert.fail(err);
  }
}
```

The `dividePromise()` we are calling in line A is the same Promise-based function as in the previous section. But we now have synchronous-looking syntax for handling the call. `await` can only be used inside a special kind of function, an *async function* (note the keyword `async` in front of the keyword `function`). `await` pauses the current async function and returns from it. Once the awaited result is ready, the execution of the function continues where it left off.

39.1.6 Next steps

- In this chapter, we'll see how synchronous function calls work. We'll also explore JavaScript's way of executing code in a single process, via its *event loop*.
- Asynchronicity via callbacks (p. 425) is also described in this chapter.
- The following chapters cover Promises (p. 427) and async functions (p. 447).
- This series of chapters on asynchronous programming concludes with the chapter on asynchronous iteration (p. 457), which is similar to synchronous iteration (p. 311), but iterated values are delivered asynchronously.

39.2 The call stack

Whenever a function calls another function, we need to remember where to return to after the latter function is finished. That is typically done via a stack – the *call stack*: the caller pushes onto it the location to return to, and the callee jumps to that location after it is done.

This is an example where several calls happen:

```
1  function h(z) {
2    const error = new Error();
3    console.log(error.stack);
4  }
5  function g(y) {
6    h(y + 1);
7  }
8  function f(x) {
9    g(x + 1);
10 }
11 f(3);
12 // done
```

Initially, before running this piece of code, the call stack is empty. After the function call `f(3)` in line 11, the stack has one entry:

- Line 12 (location in top-level scope)

After the function call `g(x + 1)` in line 9, the stack has two entries:

- Line 10 (location in `f()`)
- Line 12 (location in top-level scope)

After the function call `h(y + 1)` in line 6, the stack has three entries:

39.3 The event loop

- Line 7 (location in g())
- Line 10 (location in f())
- Line 12 (location in top-level scope)

Logging error in line 3, produces the following output:

```
Error:
    at h (demos/async-js/stack_trace.mjs:2:17)
    at g (demos/async-js/stack_trace.mjs:6:3)
    at f (demos/async-js/stack_trace.mjs:9:3)
    at demos/async-js/stack_trace.mjs:11:1
```

This is a so-called *stack trace* of where the Error object was created. Note that it records where calls were made, not return locations. Creating the exception in line 2 is yet another call. That's why the stack trace includes a location inside h().

After line 3, each of the functions terminates and each time, the top entry is removed from the call stack. After function f is done, we are back in top-level scope and the stack is empty. When the code fragment ends then that is like an implicit return. If we consider the code fragment to be a task that is executed, then returning with an empty call stack ends the task.

39.3 The event loop

By default, JavaScript runs in a single process – in both web browsers and Node.js. The so-called *event loop* sequentially executes *tasks* (pieces of code) inside that process. The event loop is depicted in fig. 39.1.

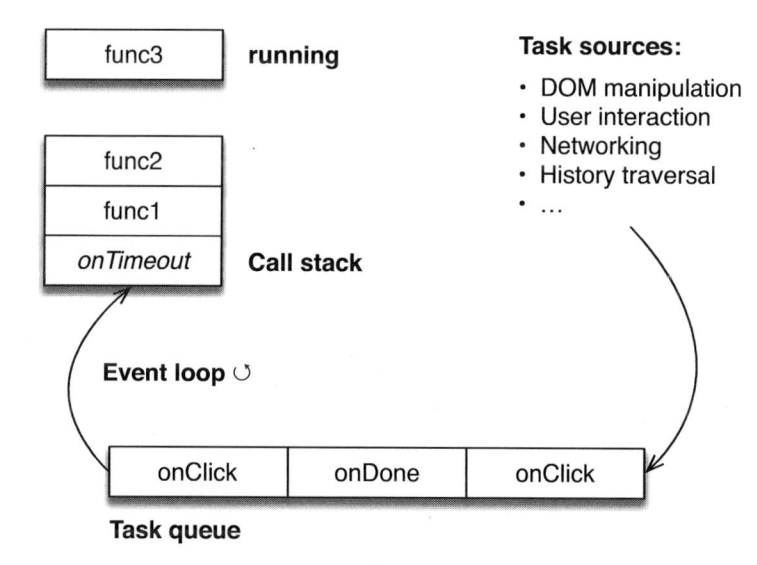

Figure 39.1: *Task sources* add code to run to the *task queue*, which is emptied by the *event loop*.

Two parties access the task queue:

- *Task sources* add tasks to the queue. Some of those sources run concurrently to the JavaScript process. For example, one task source takes care of user interface events: if a user clicks somewhere and a click listener was registered, then an invocation of that listener is added to the task queue.
- The *event loop* runs continuously inside the JavaScript process. During each loop iteration, it takes one task out of the queue (if the queue is empty, it waits until it isn't) and executes it. That task is finished when the call stack is empty and there is a return. Control goes back to the event loop, which then retrieves the next task from the queue and executes it. And so on.

The following JavaScript code is an approximation of the event loop:

```
while (true) {
  const task = taskQueue.dequeue();
  task(); // run task
}
```

39.4 How to avoid blocking the JavaScript process

39.4.1 The user interface of the browser can be blocked

Many of the user interface mechanisms of browsers also run in the JavaScript process (as tasks). Therefore, long-running JavaScript code can block the user interface. Let's look at a web page that demonstrates that. There are two ways in which you can try out that page:

- You can run it online[1].
- You can open the following file inside the repository with the exercises: `demos/async-js/blocking.html`

The following HTML is the page's user interface:

```
<a id="block" href="">Block</a>
<div id="statusMessage"></div>
<button>Click me!</button>
```

The idea is that you click "Block" and a long-running loop is executed via JavaScript. During that loop, you can't click the button because the browser/JavaScript process is blocked.

A simplified version of the JavaScript code looks like this:

```
document.getElementById('block')
  .addEventListener('click', doBlock); // (A)

function doBlock(event) {
  // ···
  displayStatus('Blocking...');
  // ···
  sleep(5000); // (B)
```

[1] http://rauschma.github.io/async-examples/blocking.html

39.4 How to avoid blocking the JavaScript process

```
    displayStatus('Done');
}

function sleep(milliseconds) {
  const start = Date.now();
  while ((Date.now() - start) < milliseconds);
}
function displayStatus(status) {
  document.getElementById('statusMessage')
    .textContent = status;
}
```

These are the key parts of the code:

- Line A: We tell the browser to call `doBlock()` whenever the HTML element is clicked whose ID is `block`.
- `doBlock()` displays status information and then calls `sleep()` to block the JavaScript process for 5000 milliseconds (line B).
- `sleep()` blocks the JavaScript process by looping until enough time has passed.
- `displayStatus()` displays status messages inside the `<div>` whose ID is `statusMessage`.

39.4.2 How can we avoid blocking the browser?

There are several ways in which you can prevent a long-running operation from blocking the browser:

- The operation can deliver its result *asynchronously*: Some operations, such as downloads, can be performed concurrently to the JavaScript process. The JavaScript code triggering such an operation registers a callback, which is invoked with the result once the operation is finished. The invocation is handled via the task queue. This style of delivering a result is called *asynchronous* because the caller doesn't wait until the results are ready. Normal function calls deliver their results synchronously.

- Perform long computations in separate processes: This can be done via so-called *Web Workers*. Web Workers are heavyweight processes that run concurrently to the main process. Each one of them has its own runtime environment (global variables, etc.). They are completely isolated and must be communicated with via message passing. Consult MDN web docs[2] for more information.

- Take breaks during long computations. The next subsection explains how.

39.4.3 Taking breaks

The following global function executes its parameter `callback` after a delay of `ms` milliseconds (the type signature is simplified – `setTimeout()` has more features):

```
function setTimeout(callback: () => void, ms: number): any
```

---
[2]https://developer.mozilla.org/en-US/docs/Web/API/Web_Workers_API

The function returns a *handle* (an ID) that can be used to *clear* the timeout (cancel the execution of the callback) via the following global function:

```
function clearTimeout(handle?: any): void
```

`setTimeout()` is available on both browsers and Node.js. The next subsection shows it in action.

> 💡 **setTimeout() lets tasks take breaks**
>
> Another way of looking at `setTimeout()` is that the current task takes a break and continues later via the callback.

39.4.4 Run-to-completion semantics

JavaScript makes a guarantee for tasks:

> Each task is always finished ("run to completion") before the next task is executed.

As a consequence, tasks don't have to worry about their data being changed while they are working on it (*concurrent modification*). That simplifies programming in JavaScript.

The following example demonstrates this guarantee:

```
console.log('start');
setTimeout(() => {
  console.log('callback');
}, 0);
console.log('end');

// Output:
// 'start'
// 'end'
// 'callback'
```

`setTimeout()` puts its parameter into the task queue. The parameter is therefore executed sometime after the current piece of code (task) is completely finished.

The parameter `ms` only specifies when the task is put into the queue, not when exactly it runs. It may even never run – for example, if there is a task before it in the queue that never terminates. That explains why the previous code logs `'end'` before `'callback'`, even though the parameter `ms` is `0`.

39.5 Patterns for delivering asynchronous results

In order to avoid blocking the main process while waiting for a long-running operation to finish, results are often delivered asynchronously in JavaScript. These are three popular patterns for doing so:

- Events

39.5 Patterns for delivering asynchronous results

- Callbacks
- Promises

The first two patterns are explained in the next two subsections. Promises are explained in the next chapter (p. 427).

39.5.1 Delivering asynchronous results via events

Events as a pattern work as follows:

- They are used to deliver values asynchronously.
- They do so zero or more times.
- There are three roles in this pattern:
    - The *event* (an object) carries the data to be delivered.
    - The *event listener* is a function that receives events via a parameter.
    - The *event source* sends events and lets you register event listeners.

Multiple variations of this pattern exist in the world of JavaScript. We'll look at three examples next.

39.5.1.1 Events: IndexedDB

IndexedDB is a database that is built into web browsers. This is an example of using it:

```
const openRequest = indexedDB.open('MyDatabase', 1); // (A)

openRequest.onsuccess = (event) => {
  const db = event.target.result;
  // ···
};

openRequest.onerror = (error) => {
  console.error(error);
};
```

indexedDB has an unusual way of invoking operations:

- Each operation has an associated method for creating *request objects*. For example, in line A, the operation is "open", the method is .open(), and the request object is openRequest.

- The parameters for the operation are provided via the request object, not via parameters of the method. For example, the event listeners (functions) are stored in the properties .onsuccess and .onerror.

- The invocation of the operation is added to the task queue via the method (in line A). That is, we configure the operation *after* its invocation has already been added to the queue. Only run-to-completion semantics saves us from race conditions here and ensures that the operation runs after the current code fragment is finished.

39.5.1.2 Events: `XMLHttpRequest`

The `XMLHttpRequest` API lets us make downloads from within a web browser. This is how we download the file `http://example.com/textfile.txt`:

```
const xhr = new XMLHttpRequest(); // (A)
xhr.open('GET', 'http://example.com/textfile.txt'); // (B)
xhr.onload = () => { // (C)
  if (xhr.status == 200) {
    processData(xhr.responseText);
  } else {
    assert.fail(new Error(xhr.statusText));
  }
};
xhr.onerror = () => { // (D)
  assert.fail(new Error('Network error'));
};
xhr.send(); // (E)

function processData(str) {
  assert.equal(str, 'Content of textfile.txt\n');
}
```

With this API, we first create a request object (line A), then configure it, then activate it (line E). The configuration consists of:

- Specifying which HTTP request method to use (line B): `GET`, `POST`, `PUT`, etc.
- Registering a listener (line C) that is notified if something could be downloaded. Inside the listener, we still need to determine if the download contains what we requested or informs us of an error. Note that some of the result data is delivered via the request object `xhr`. (I'm not a fan of this kind of mixing of input and output data.)
- Registering a listener (line D) that is notified if there was a network error.

39.5.1.3 Events: DOM

We have already seen DOM events in action in §39.4.1 "The user interface of the browser can be blocked" (p. 420). The following code also handles `click` events:

```
const element = document.getElementById('my-link'); // (A)
element.addEventListener('click', clickListener); // (B)

function clickListener(event) {
  event.preventDefault(); // (C)
  console.log(event.shiftKey); // (D)
}
```

We first ask the browser to retrieve the HTML element whose ID is `'my-link'` (line A). Then we add a listener for all `click` events (line B). In the listener, we first tell the browser not to perform its default action (line C) – going to the target of the link. Then we log to the console if the shift key is currently pressed (line D).

39.5.2 Delivering asynchronous results via callbacks

Callbacks are another pattern for handling asynchronous results. They are only used for one-off results and have the advantage of being less verbose than events.

As an example, consider a function readFile() that reads a text file and returns its contents asynchronously. This is how you call readFile() if it uses Node.js-style callbacks:

```
readFile('some-file.txt', {encoding: 'utf8'},
  (error, data) => {
    if (error) {
      assert.fail(error);
      return;
    }
    assert.equal(data, 'The content of some-file.txt\n');
  });
```

There is a single callback that handles both success and failure. If the first parameter is not null then an error happened. Otherwise, the result can be found in the second parameter.

> **Exercises: Callback-based code**
>
> The following exercises use tests for asynchronous code, which are different from tests for synchronous code. Consult §11.3.2 "Asynchronous tests in AVA" (p. 73) for more information.
>
> - From synchronous to callback-based code: `exercises/async-js/read_file_cb_exrc.mjs`
> - Implementing a callback-based version of .map(): `exercises/async-js/map_cb_test.mjs`

39.6 Asynchronous code: the downsides

In many situations, on either browsers or Node.js, you have no choice, you must use asynchronous code. In this chapter, we have seen several patterns that such code can use. All of them have two disadvantages:

- Asynchronous code is more verbose than synchronous code.
- If you call asynchronous code, your code must become asynchronous too. That's because you can't wait synchronously for an asynchronous result. Asynchronous code has an infectious quality.

The first disadvantage becomes less severe with Promises (covered in the next chapter (p. 427)) and mostly disappears with async functions (covered in the chapter after next (p. 447)).

Alas, the infectiousness of async code does not go away. But it is mitigated by the fact that switching between sync and async is easy with async functions.

39.7 Resources

- "Help, I'm stuck in an event-loop"[3] by Philip Roberts (video).
- "Event loops"[4], section in HTML5 spec.

---

[3] https://vimeo.com/96425312
[4] https://www.w3.org/TR/html5/webappapis.html#event-loops

Chapter 40

Promises for asynchronous programming

Contents

- 40.1 The basics of using Promises 428
  - 40.1.1 Using a Promise-based function 428
  - 40.1.2 What is a Promise? 428
  - 40.1.3 Implementing a Promise-based function 429
  - 40.1.4 States of Promises 429
  - 40.1.5 `Promise.resolve()`: create a Promise fulfilled with a given value 430
  - 40.1.6 `Promise.reject()`: create a Promise rejected with a given value 430
  - 40.1.7 Returning and throwing in `.then()` callbacks 430
  - 40.1.8 `.catch()` and its callback 432
  - 40.1.9 Chaining method calls 432
  - 40.1.10 Advantages of promises 433
- 40.2 Examples 433
  - 40.2.1 Node.js: Reading a file asynchronously 433
  - 40.2.2 Browsers: Promisifying `XMLHttpRequest` 435
  - 40.2.3 Node.js: `util.promisify()` 436
  - 40.2.4 Browsers: Fetch API 437
- 40.3 Error handling: don't mix rejections and exceptions 437
- 40.4 Promise-based functions start synchronously, settle asynchronously 439
- 40.5 `Promise.all()`: concurrency and Arrays of Promises 440
  - 40.5.1 Sequential execution vs. concurrent execution 440
  - 40.5.2 Concurrency tip: focus on when operations start 441
  - 40.5.3 `Promise.all()` is fork-join 441
  - 40.5.4 Asynchronous `.map()` via `Promise.all()` 442
- 40.6 Tips for chaining Promises 443
  - 40.6.1 Chaining mistake: losing the tail 443
  - 40.6.2 Chaining mistake: nesting 443

40.6.3	Chaining mistake: more nesting than necessary	444
40.6.4	Not all nesting is bad	444
40.6.5	Chaining mistake: creating Promises instead of chaining	445
40.7	**Advanced topics**	**445**

In this chapter, we explore Promises, yet another pattern for delivering asynchronous results.

> **Recommended reading**
>
> This chapter builds on the previous chapter (p. 415) with background on asynchronous programming in JavaScript.

40.1 The basics of using Promises

Promises are a pattern for delivering results asynchronously.

40.1.1 Using a Promise-based function

The following code is an example of using the Promise-based function `addAsync()` (whose implementation is shown soon):

```
addAsync(3, 4)
  .then(result => { // success
    assert.equal(result, 7);
  })
  .catch(error => { // failure
    assert.fail(error);
  });
```

Promises are similar to the event pattern (p. 423): There is an object (a *Promise*), where we register callbacks:

- Method `.then()` registers callbacks that handle results.
- Method `.catch()` registers callbacks that handle errors.

A Promise-based function returns a Promise and sends it a result or an error (if and when it is done). The Promise passes it on to the relevant callbacks.

In contrast to the event pattern, Promises are optimized for one-off results:

- A result (or an error) is cached so that it doesn't matter if we register a callback before or after the result (or error) was sent.
- We can chain the Promise methods `.then()` and `.catch()` because they both return Promises. That helps with sequentially invoking multiple asynchronous functions. More on that later.

40.1.2 What is a Promise?

What is a Promise? There are two ways of looking at it:

- On one hand, it is a placeholder or container for the final result that will eventually be delivered.
- On the other hand, it is an object with which we can register listeners.

40.1.3 Implementing a Promise-based function

This is an implementation of a Promise-based function that adds two numbers x and y:

```
function addAsync(x, y) {
  return new Promise(
    (resolve, reject) => { // (A)
      if (x === undefined || y === undefined) {
        reject(new Error('Must provide two parameters'));
      } else {
        resolve(x + y);
      }
    });
}
```

`addAsync()` immediately invokes the `Promise` constructor. The actual implementation of that function resides in the callback that is passed to that constructor (line A). That callback is provided with two functions:

- `resolve` is used for delivering a result (in case of success).
- `reject` is used for delivering an error (in case of failure).

40.1.4 States of Promises

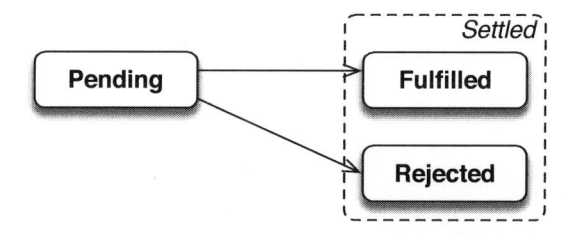

Figure 40.1: A Promise can be in either one of three states: pending, fulfilled, or rejected. If a Promise is in a final (non-pending) state, it is called *settled*.

Fig. 40.1 depicts the three states a Promise can be in. Promises specialize in one-off results and protect us against *race conditions* (registering too early or too late):

- If we register a `.then()` callback or a `.catch()` callback too early, it is notified once a Promise is settled.
- Once a Promise is settled, the settlement value (result or error) is cached. Thus, if `.then()` or `.catch()` are called after the settlement, they receive the cached value.

Additionally, once a Promise is settled, its state and settlement value can't change anymore. That helps make code predictable and enforces the one-off nature of Promises.

> **Some Promises are never settled**
>
> It is possible that a Promise is never settled. For example:
>
> ```
> new Promise(() => {})
> ```

40.1.5 `Promise.resolve()`: create a Promise fulfilled with a given value

`Promise.resolve(x)` creates a Promise that is fulfilled with the value x:

```
Promise.resolve(123)
  .then(x => {
    assert.equal(x, 123);
  });
```

If the parameter is already a Promise, it is returned unchanged:

```
const abcPromise = Promise.resolve('abc');
assert.equal(
  Promise.resolve(abcPromise),
  abcPromise);
```

Therefore, given an arbitrary value x, we can use `Promise.resolve(x)` to ensure we have a Promise.

Note that the name is `resolve`, not `fulfill`, because `.resolve()` returns a rejected Promise if its Parameter is a rejected Promise.

40.1.6 `Promise.reject()`: create a Promise rejected with a given value

`Promise.reject(err)` creates a Promise that is rejected with the value err:

```
const myError = new Error('My error!');
Promise.reject(myError)
  .catch(err => {
    assert.equal(err, myError);
  });
```

40.1.7 Returning and throwing in `.then()` callbacks

`.then()` handles Promise fulfillments. It also returns a fresh Promise. How that Promise is settled depends on what happens inside the callback. Let's look at three common cases.

40.1.7.1 Returning a non-Promise value

First, the callback can return a non-Promise value (line A). Consequently, the Promise returned by `.then()` is fulfilled with that value (as checked in line B):

```
Promise.resolve('abc')
  .then(str => {
    return str + str; // (A)
```

40.1 The basics of using Promises

```
  })
  .then(str2 => {
    assert.equal(str2, 'abcabc'); // (B)
  });
```

40.1.7.2 Returning a Promise

Second, the callback can return a Promise p (line A). Consequently, p "becomes" what .then() returns. In other words: the Promise that .then() has already returned is effectively replaced by p.

```
Promise.resolve('abc')
  .then(str => {
    return Promise.resolve(123); // (A)
  })
  .then(num => {
    assert.equal(num, 123);
  });
```

Why is that useful? We can return the result of a Promise-based operation and process its fulfillment value via a "flat" (non-nested) .then(). Compare:

```
// Flat
asyncFunc1()
  .then(result1 => {
    /*···*/
    return asyncFunc2();
  })
  .then(result2 => {
    /*···*/
  });

// Nested
asyncFunc1()
  .then(result1 => {
    /*···*/
    asyncFunc2()
    .then(result2 => {
      /*···*/
    });
  });
```

40.1.7.3 Throwing an exception

Third, the callback can throw an exception. Consequently, the Promise returned by .then() is rejected with that exception. That is, a synchronous error is converted into an asynchronous error.

```
const myError = new Error('My error!');
Promise.resolve('abc')
  .then(str => {
```

```
    throw myError;
  })
  .catch(err => {
    assert.equal(err, myError);
  });
```

40.1.8 .catch() and its callback

The only difference between .then() and .catch() is that the latter is triggered by rejections, not fulfillments. However, both methods turn the actions of their callbacks into Promises in the same manner. For example, in the following code, the value returned by the .catch() callback in line A becomes a fulfillment value:

```
const err = new Error();

Promise.reject(err)
  .catch(e => {
    assert.equal(e, err);
    // Something went wrong, use a default value
    return 'default value'; // (A)
  })
  .then(str => {
    assert.equal(str, 'default value');
  });
```

40.1.9 Chaining method calls

.then() and .catch() always return Promises. That enables us to create arbitrary long chains of method calls:

```
function myAsyncFunc() {
  return asyncFunc1() // (A)
    .then(result1 => {
      // ···
      return asyncFunc2(); // a Promise
    })
    .then(result2 => {
      // ···
      return result2 || '(Empty)'; // not a Promise
    })
    .then(result3 => {
      // ···
      return asyncFunc4(); // a Promise
    });
}
```

Due to chaining, the return in line A returns the result of the last .then().

In a way, .then() is the asynchronous version of the synchronous semicolon:

- .then() executes two asynchronous operations sequentially.

40.2 Examples

- The semicolon executes two synchronous operations sequentially.

We can also add `.catch()` into the mix and let it handle multiple error sources at the same time:

```
asyncFunc1()
  .then(result1 => {
    // ···
    return asyncFunction2();
  })
  .then(result2 => {
    // ···
  })
  .catch(error => {
    // Failure: handle errors of asyncFunc1(), asyncFunc2()
    // and any (sync) exceptions thrown in previous callbacks
  });
```

40.1.10 Advantages of promises

These are some of the advantages of Promises over plain callbacks when it comes to handling one-off results:

- The type signatures of Promise-based functions and methods are cleaner: if a function is callback-based, some parameters are about input, while the one or two callbacks at the end are about output. With Promises, everything output-related is handled via the returned value.

- Chaining asynchronous processing steps is more convenient.

- Promises handle both asynchronous errors (via rejections) and synchronous errors: Inside the callbacks for `new Promise()`, `.then()`, and `.catch()`, exceptions are converted to rejections. In contrast, if we use callbacks for asynchronicity, exceptions are normally not handled for us; we have to do it ourselves.

- Promises are a single standard that is slowly replacing several, mutually incompatible alternatives. For example, in Node.js, many functions are now available in Promise-based versions. And new asynchronous browser APIs are usually Promise-based.

One of the biggest advantages of Promises involves not working with them directly: they are the foundation of *async functions*, a synchronous-looking syntax for performing asynchronous computations. Asynchronous functions are covered in the next chapter (p. 447).

40.2 Examples

Seeing Promises in action helps with understanding them. Let's look at examples.

40.2.1 Node.js: Reading a file asynchronously

Consider the following text file `person.json` with JSON data (p. 497) in it:

```
{
  "first": "Jane",
  "last": "Doe"
}
```

Let's look at two versions of code that reads this file and parses it into an object. First, a callback-based version. Second, a Promise-based version.

40.2.1.1 The callback-based version

The following code reads the contents of this file and converts it to a JavaScript object. It is based on Node.js-style callbacks:

```
import * as fs from 'fs';
fs.readFile('person.json',
  (error, text) => {
    if (error) { // (A)
      // Failure
      assert.fail(error);
    } else {
      // Success
      try { // (B)
        const obj = JSON.parse(text); // (C)
        assert.deepEqual(obj, {
          first: 'Jane',
          last: 'Doe',
        });
      } catch (e) {
        // Invalid JSON
        assert.fail(e);
      }
    }
  });
```

fs is a built-in Node.js module for file system operations. We use the callback-based function fs.readFile() to read a file whose name is person.json. If we succeed, the content is delivered via the parameter text as a string. In line C, we convert that string from the text-based data format JSON into a JavaScript object. JSON is an object with methods for consuming and producing JSON. It is part of JavaScript's standard library and documented later in this book (p. 497).

Note that there are two error-handling mechanisms: the if in line A takes care of asynchronous errors reported by fs.readFile(), while the try in line B takes care of synchronous errors reported by JSON.parse().

40.2.1.2 The Promise-based version

The following code uses readFileAsync(), a Promise-based version of fs.readFile() (created via util.promisify(), which is explained later):

40.2 Examples

```
readFileAsync('person.json')
  .then(text => { // (A)
    // Success
    const obj = JSON.parse(text);
    assert.deepEqual(obj, {
      first: 'Jane',
      last: 'Doe',
    });
  })
  .catch(err => { // (B)
    // Failure: file I/O error or JSON syntax error
    assert.fail(err);
  });
```

Function `readFileAsync()` returns a Promise. In line A, we specify a success callback via method `.then()` of that Promise. The remaining code in then's callback is synchronous.

`.then()` returns a Promise, which enables the invocation of the Promise method `.catch()` in line B. We use it to specify a failure callback.

Note that `.catch()` lets us handle both the asynchronous errors of `readFileAsync()` and the synchronous errors of `JSON.parse()` because exceptions inside a `.then()` callback become rejections.

40.2.2 Browsers: Promisifying XMLHttpRequest

We have previously seen the event-based XMLHttpRequest API for downloading data in web browsers. The following function promisifies that API:

```
function httpGet(url) {
  return new Promise(
    (resolve, reject) => {
      const xhr = new XMLHttpRequest();
      xhr.onload = () => {
        if (xhr.status === 200) {
          resolve(xhr.responseText); // (A)
        } else {
          // Something went wrong (404, etc.)
          reject(new Error(xhr.statusText)); // (B)
        }
      }
      xhr.onerror = () => {
        reject(new Error('Network error')); // (C)
      };
      xhr.open('GET', url);
      xhr.send();
    });
}
```

Note how the results and errors of XMLHttpRequest are handled via `resolve()` and `reject()`:

- A successful outcome leads to the returned Promise being fullfilled with it (line A).
- An error leads to the Promise being rejected (lines B and C).

This is how to use `httpGet()`:

```
httpGet('http://example.com/textfile.txt')
  .then(content => {
    assert.equal(content, 'Content of textfile.txt\n');
  })
  .catch(error => {
    assert.fail(error);
  });
```

> **Exercise: Timing out a Promise**
> exercises/promises/promise_timeout_test.mjs

40.2.3 Node.js: `util.promisify()`

`util.promisify()` is a utility function that converts a callback-based function f into a Promise-based one. That is, we are going from this type signature:

```
f(arg_1, ···, arg_n, (err: Error, result: T) => void) : void
```

To this type signature:

```
f(arg_1, ···, arg_n) : Promise<T>
```

The following code promisifies the callback-based `fs.readFile()` (line A) and uses it:

```
import * as fs from 'fs';
import {promisify} from 'util';

const readFileAsync = promisify(fs.readFile); // (A)

readFileAsync('some-file.txt', {encoding: 'utf8'})
  .then(text => {
    assert.equal(text, 'The content of some-file.txt\n');
  })
  .catch(err => {
    assert.fail(err);
  });
```

> **Exercises: `util.promisify()`**
> - Using `util.promisify()`: exercises/promises/read_file_async_exrc.mjs
> - Implementing `util.promisify()` yourself: exercises/promises/my_promisify_test.mjs

40.2.4 Browsers: Fetch API

All modern browsers support Fetch, a new Promise-based API for downloading data. Think of it as a Promise-based version of `XMLHttpRequest`. The following is an excerpt of the API[1]:

```
interface Body {
  text() : Promise<string>;
  ...
}
interface Response extends Body {
  ...
}
declare function fetch(str) : Promise<Response>;
```

That means we can use `fetch()` as follows:

```
fetch('http://example.com/textfile.txt')
  .then(response => response.text())
  .then(text => {
    assert.equal(text, 'Content of textfile.txt\n');
  });
```

Exercise: Using the fetch API

`exercises/promises/fetch_json_test.mjs`

40.3 Error handling: don't mix rejections and exceptions

Rule for implementing functions and methods:

> Don't mix (asynchronous) rejections and (synchronous) exceptions.

This makes our synchronous and asynchronous code more predictable and simpler because we can always focus on a single error-handling mechanism.

For Promise-based functions and methods, the rule means that they should never throw exceptions. Alas, it is easy to accidentally get this wrong – for example:

```
// Don't do this
function asyncFunc() {
  doSomethingSync(); // (A)
  return doSomethingAsync()
    .then(result => {
      // ···
    });
}
```

The problem is that if an exception is thrown in line A, then `asyncFunc()` will throw an exception. Callers of that function only expect rejections and are not prepared for an

---

[1] https://fetch.spec.whatwg.org/#fetch-api

exception. There are three ways in which we can fix this issue.

We can wrap the whole body of the function in a `try-catch` statement and return a rejected Promise if an exception is thrown:

```
// Solution 1
function asyncFunc() {
  try {
    doSomethingSync();
    return doSomethingAsync()
      .then(result => {
        // ···
      });
  } catch (err) {
    return Promise.reject(err);
  }
}
```

Given that `.then()` converts exceptions to rejections, we can execute `doSomethingSync()` inside a `.then()` callback. To do so, we start a Promise chain via `Promise.resolve()`. We ignore the fulfillment value `undefined` of that initial Promise.

```
// Solution 2
function asyncFunc() {
  return Promise.resolve()
    .then(() => {
      doSomethingSync();
      return doSomethingAsync();
    })
    .then(result => {
      // ···
    });
}
```

Lastly, `new Promise()` also converts exceptions to rejections. Using this constructor is therefore similar to the previous solution:

```
// Solution 3
function asyncFunc() {
  return new Promise((resolve, reject) => {
      doSomethingSync();
      resolve(doSomethingAsync());
    })
    .then(result => {
      // ···
    });
}
```

40.4 Promise-based functions start synchronously, settle asynchronously

Most Promise-based functions are executed as follows:

- Their execution starts right away, synchronously (in the current task).
- But the Promise they return is guaranteed to be settled asynchronously (in a later task) – if ever.

The following code demonstrates that:

```
function asyncFunc() {
  console.log('asyncFunc');
  return new Promise(
    (resolve, _reject) => {
      console.log('new Promise()');
      resolve();
    });
}
console.log('START');
asyncFunc()
  .then(() => {
    console.log('.then()'); // (A)
  });
console.log('END');

// Output:
// 'START'
// 'asyncFunc'
// 'new Promise()'
// 'END'
// '.then()'
```

We can see that the callback of `new Promise()` is executed before the end of the code, while the result is delivered later (line A).

Benefits of this approach:

- Starting synchronously helps avoid race conditions because we can rely on the order in which Promise-based functions begin. There is an example in the next chapter (p. 455), where text is written to a file and race conditions are avoided.

- Chaining Promises won't starve other tasks of processing time because before a Promise is settled, there will always be a break, during which the event loop can run.

- Promise-based functions always return results asynchronously; we can be sure that there is never a synchronous return. This kind of predictability makes code easier to work with.

> **More information on this approach**
>
> "Designing APIs for Asynchrony"[a] by Isaac Z. Schlueter
>
> ---
> [a]http://blog.izs.me/post/59142742143/designing-apis-for-asynchrony

40.5 `Promise.all()`: concurrency and Arrays of Promises

40.5.1 Sequential execution vs. concurrent execution

Consider the following code:

```
const asyncFunc1 = () => Promise.resolve('one');
const asyncFunc2 = () => Promise.resolve('two');

asyncFunc1()
  .then(result1 => {
    assert.equal(result1, 'one');
    return asyncFunc2();
  })
  .then(result2 => {
    assert.equal(result2, 'two');
  });
```

Using `.then()` in this manner executes Promise-based functions *sequentially*: only after the result of `asyncFunc1()` is settled will `asyncFunc2()` be executed.

The static method `Promise.all()` helps execute Promise-based functions more concurrently:

```
Promise.all([asyncFunc1(), asyncFunc2()])
  .then(arr => {
    assert.deepEqual(arr, ['one', 'two']);
  });
```

Its type signature is:

```
Promise.all<T>(promises: Iterable<Promise<T>>): Promise<T[]>
```

The parameter `promises` is an iterable of Promises. The result is a single Promise that is settled as follows:

- If and when all input Promises are fulfilled, the output Promise is fulfilled with an Array of the fulfillment values.
- As soon as at least one input Promise is rejected, the output Promise is rejected with the rejection value of that input Promise.

In other words: We go from an iterable of Promises to a Promise for an Array.

40.5.2 Concurrency tip: focus on when operations start

Tip for determining how "concurrent" asynchronous code is: Focus on when asynchronous operations start, not on how their Promises are handled.

For example, each of the following functions executes `asyncFunc1()` and `asyncFunc2()` concurrently because they are started at nearly the same time.

```
function concurrentAll() {
  return Promise.all([asyncFunc1(), asyncFunc2()]);
}

function concurrentThen() {
  const p1 = asyncFunc1();
  const p2 = asyncFunc2();
  return p1.then(r1 => p2.then(r2 => [r1, r2]));
}
```

On the other hand, both of the following functions execute `asyncFunc1()` and `asyncFunc2()` sequentially: `asyncFunc2()` is only invoked after the Promise of `asyncFunc1()` is fulfilled.

```
function sequentialThen() {
  return asyncFunc1()
    .then(r1 => asyncFunc2()
      .then(r2 => [r1, r2]));
}

function sequentialAll() {
  const p1 = asyncFunc1();
  const p2 = p1.then(() => asyncFunc2());
  return Promise.all([p1, p2]);
}
```

40.5.3 `Promise.all()` is fork-join

`Promise.all()` is loosely related to the concurrency pattern "fork join" – for example:

```
Promise.all([
    // Fork async computations
    httpGet('http://example.com/file1.txt'),
    httpGet('http://example.com/file2.txt'),
  ])
  // Join async computations
  .then(([text1, text2]) => {
    assert.equal(text1, 'Content of file1.txt\n');
    assert.equal(text2, 'Content of file2.txt\n');
  });
```

`httpGet()` is the promisified version of `XMLHttpRequest` that we implemented earlier (p. 435).

40.5.4 Asynchronous `.map()` via `Promise.all()`

Array transformation methods such as `.map()`, `.filter()`, etc., are made for synchronous computations – for example:

```
function timesTwoSync(x) {
  return 2 * x;
}
const arr = [1, 2, 3];
const result = arr.map(timesTwoSync);
assert.deepEqual(result, [2, 4, 6]);
```

What happens if the callback of `.map()` is a Promise-based function (a function that maps normal values to Promises)? Then the result of `.map()` is an Array of Promises. Alas, that is not data that normal code can work with. Thankfully, we can fix that via `Promise.all()`: It converts an Array of Promises into a Promise that is fulfilled with an Array of normal values.

```
function timesTwoAsync(x) {
  return new Promise(resolve => resolve(x * 2));
}
const arr = [1, 2, 3];
const promiseArr = arr.map(timesTwoAsync);
Promise.all(promiseArr)
  .then(result => {
    assert.deepEqual(result, [2, 4, 6]);
  });
```

40.5.4.1 A more realistic example

The following code is a more realistic example: in the section on fork-join, there was an example where we downloaded two resources identified by two fixed URLs. Let's turn that code fragment into a function that accepts an Array of URLs and downloads the corresponding resources:

```
function downloadTexts(urls) {
  const promisedTexts = urls.map(httpGet);
  return Promise.all(promisedTexts);
}

downloadTexts([
    'http://example.com/file1.txt',
    'http://example.com/file2.txt',
  ])
  .then(texts => {
    assert.deepEqual(
      texts, [
        'Content of file1.txt\n',
        'Content of file2.txt\n',
      ]);
  });
```

40.6 Tips for chaining Promises

> Exercise: `Promise.all()` and listing files
> `exercises/promises/list_files_async_test.mjs`

40.6 Tips for chaining Promises

This section gives tips for chaining Promises.

40.6.1 Chaining mistake: losing the tail

Problem:

```
// Don't do this
function foo() {
  const promise = asyncFunc();
  promise.then(result => {
    // ···
  });

  return promise;
}
```

Computation starts with the Promise returned by `asyncFunc()`. But afterward, computation continues and another Promise is created via `.then()`. `foo()` returns the former Promise, but should return the latter. This is how to fix it:

```
function foo() {
  const promise = asyncFunc();
  return promise.then(result => {
    // ···
  });
}
```

40.6.2 Chaining mistake: nesting

Problem:

```
// Don't do this
asyncFunc1()
  .then(result1 => {
    return asyncFunc2()
    .then(result2 => { // (A)
      // ···
    });
  });
```

The `.then()` in line A is nested. A flat structure would be better:

```
asyncFunc1()
  .then(result1 => {
```

```
    return asyncFunc2();
  })
  .then(result2 => {
    // ···
  });
```

40.6.3 Chaining mistake: more nesting than necessary

This is another example of avoidable nesting:

```
// Don't do this
asyncFunc1()
  .then(result1 => {
    if (result1 < 0) {
      return asyncFuncA()
      .then(resultA => 'Result: ' + resultA);
    } else {
      return asyncFuncB()
      .then(resultB => 'Result: ' + resultB);
    }
  });
```

We can once again get a flat structure:

```
asyncFunc1()
  .then(result1 => {
    return result1 < 0 ? asyncFuncA() : asyncFuncB();
  })
  .then(resultAB => {
    return 'Result: ' + resultAB;
  });
```

40.6.4 Not all nesting is bad

In the following code, we actually benefit from nesting:

```
db.open()
  .then(connection => { // (A)
    return connection.select({ name: 'Jane' })
      .then(result => { // (B)
        // Process result
        // Use `connection` to make more queries
      })
      // ···
      .finally(() => {
        connection.close(); // (C)
      });
  })
```

We are receiving an asynchronous result in line A. In line B, we are nesting so that we have access to variable connection inside the callback and in line C.

40.6.5 Chaining mistake: creating Promises instead of chaining

Problem:

```
// Don't do this
class Model {
  insertInto(db) {
    return new Promise((resolve, reject) => { // (A)
      db.insert(this.fields)
        .then(resultCode => {
          this.notifyObservers({event: 'created', model: this});
          resolve(resultCode);
        }).catch(err => {
          reject(err);
        })
    });
  }
  // ···
}
```

In line A, we are creating a Promise to deliver the result of db.insert(). That is unnecessarily verbose and can be simplified:

```
class Model {
  insertInto(db) {
    return db.insert(this.fields)
      .then(resultCode => {
        this.notifyObservers({event: 'created', model: this});
        return resultCode;
      });
  }
  // ···
}
```

The key idea is that we don't need to create a Promise; we can return the result of the .then() call. An additional benefit is that we don't need to catch and re-reject the failure of db.insert(). We simply pass its rejection on to the caller of .insertInto().

40.7 Advanced topics

- In addition to Promise.all(), there is also Promise.race(), which is not used often and described in *Exploring ES6*[2].
- *Exploring ES6* has a section[3] that shows a very simple implementation of Promises. That may be helpful if you want a deeper understanding of how Promises work.

---

[2]https://exploringjs.com/es6/ch_promises.html#_timing-out-via-promiserace
[3]https://exploringjs.com/es6/ch_promises.html#sec_demo-promise

Chapter 41

Async functions

Contents

- 41.1 Async functions: the basics 447
  - 41.1.1 Async constructs 449
- 41.2 Returning from async functions 449
  - 41.2.1 Async functions always return Promises 449
  - 41.2.2 Returned Promises are not wrapped 450
  - 41.2.3 Executing async functions: synchronous start, asynchronous settlement (advanced) 450
- 41.3 `await`: working with Promises 451
  - 41.3.1 `await` and fulfilled Promises 452
  - 41.3.2 `await` and rejected Promises 452
  - 41.3.3 `await` is shallow (we can't use it in callbacks) ... 452
- 41.4 (Advanced) 453
- 41.5 Immediately invoked async arrow functions 453
- 41.6 Concurrency and `await` 454
  - 41.6.1 `await`: running asynchronous functions sequentially ... 454
  - 41.6.2 `await`: running asynchronous functions concurrently ... 454
- 41.7 Tips for using async functions 455
  - 41.7.1 We don't need `await` if we "fire and forget" 455
  - 41.7.2 It can make sense to `await` and ignore the result ... 456

Roughly, *async functions* provide better syntax for code that uses Promises. In order to use async functions, we should therefore understand Promises. They are explained in the previous chapter (p. 427).

41.1 Async functions: the basics

Consider the following async function:

```
async function fetchJsonAsync(url) {
  try {
    const request = await fetch(url); // async
    const text = await request.text(); // async
    return JSON.parse(text); // sync
  }
  catch (error) {
    assert.fail(error);
  }
}
```

The previous, rather synchronous-looking code is equivalent to the following code that uses Promises directly:

```
function fetchJsonViaPromises(url) {
  return fetch(url) // async
  .then(request => request.text()) // async
  .then(text => JSON.parse(text)) // sync
  .catch(error => {
    assert.fail(error);
  });
}
```

A few observations about the async function `fetchJsonAsync()`:

- Async functions are marked with the keyword `async`.

- Inside the body of an async function, we write Promise-based code as if it were synchronous. We only need to apply the `await` operator whenever a value is a Promise. That operator pauses the async function and resumes it once the Promise is settled:

    - If the Promise is fulfilled, `await` returns the fulfillment value.
    - If the Promise is rejected, `await` throws the rejection value.

- The result of an async function is always a Promise:

    - Any value that is returned (explicitly or implicitly) is used to fulfill the Promise.
    - Any exception that is thrown is used to reject the Promise.

Both `fetchJsonAsync()` and `fetchJsonViaPromises()` are called in exactly the same way, like this:

```
fetchJsonAsync('http://example.com/person.json')
.then(obj => {
  assert.deepEqual(obj, {
    first: 'Jane',
    last: 'Doe',
  });
});
```

41.2 Returning from async functions

> ⚙ **Async functions are as Promise-based as functions that use Promises directly**
>
> From the outside, it is virtually impossible to tell the difference between an async function and a function that returns a Promise.

41.1.1 Async constructs

JavaScript has the following async versions of synchronous callable entities. Their roles are always either real function or method.

```
// Async function declaration
async function func1() {}

// Async function expression
const func2 = async function () {};

// Async arrow function
const func3 = async () => {};

// Async method definition in an object literal
const obj = { async m() {} };

// Async method definition in a class definition
class MyClass { async m() {} }
```

> ⚙ **Asynchronous functions vs. async functions**
>
> The difference between the terms *asynchronous function* and *async function* is subtle, but important:
>
> - An *asynchronous function* is any function that delivers its result asynchronously – for example, a callback-based function or a Promise-based function.
> - An *async function* is defined via special syntax, involving the keywords `async` and `await`. It is also called async/await due to these two keywords. Async functions are based on Promises and therefore also asynchronous functions (which is somewhat confusing).

41.2 Returning from async functions

41.2.1 Async functions always return Promises

Each async function always returns a Promise.

Inside the async function, we fulfill the result Promise via `return` (line A):

```
async function asyncFunc() {
```

```
    return 123; // (A)
}

asyncFunc()
.then(result => {
  assert.equal(result, 123);
});
```

As usual, if we don't explicitly return anything, undefined is returned for us:

```
async function asyncFunc() {
}

asyncFunc()
.then(result => {
  assert.equal(result, undefined);
});
```

We reject the result Promise via throw (line A):

```
async function asyncFunc() {
  throw new Error('Problem!'); // (A)
}

asyncFunc()
.catch(err => {
  assert.deepEqual(err, new Error('Problem!'));
});
```

41.2.2 Returned Promises are not wrapped

If we return a Promise p from an async function, then p becomes the result of the function (or rather, the result "locks in" on p and behaves exactly like it). That is, the Promise is not wrapped in yet another Promise.

```
async function asyncFunc() {
  return Promise.resolve('abc');
}

asyncFunc()
.then(result => assert.equal(result, 'abc'));
```

Recall that any Promise q is treated similarly in the following situations:

- `resolve(q)` inside `new Promise((resolve, reject) => { ··· })`
- `return q` inside `.then(result => { ··· })`
- `return q` inside `.catch(err => { ··· })`

41.2.3 Executing async functions: synchronous start, asynchronous settlement (advanced)

Async functions are executed as follows:

- The Promise p for the result is created when the async function is started.
- Then the body is executed. There are two ways in which execution can leave the body:
  - Execution can leave **permanently** while settling p:
    * A `return` fulfills p.
    * A `throw` rejects p.
  - Execution can also leave **temporarily** when awaiting the settlement of another Promise q via `await`. The async function is paused and execution leaves it. It is resumed once q is settled.
- Promise p is returned after execution has left the body for the first time (permanently or temporarily).

Note that the notification of the settlement of the result p happens asynchronously, as is always the case with Promises.

The following code demonstrates that an async function is started synchronously (line A), then the current task finishes (line C), then the result Promise is settled – asynchronously (line B).

```
async function asyncFunc() {
  console.log('asyncFunc() starts'); // (A)
  return 'abc';
}
asyncFunc().
then(x => { // (B)
  console.log(`Resolved: ${x}`);
});
console.log('Task ends'); // (C)

// Output:
// 'asyncFunc() starts'
// 'Task ends'
// 'Resolved: abc'
```

41.3 `await`: working with Promises

The `await` operator can only be used inside async functions and async generators (which are explained in §42.2 "Asynchronous generators" (p. 460)). Its operand is usually a Promise and leads to the following steps being performed:

- The current async function is paused and returned from. This step is similar to how `yield` works in sync generators (p. 403).
- Eventually, the current task is finished and processing of the task queue continues.
- When and if the Promise is settled, the async function is resumed in a new task:
  - If the Promise is fulfilled, `await` returns the fulfillment value.
  - If the Promise is rejected, `await` throws the rejection value.

Read on to find out more about how `await` handles Promises in various states.

41.3.1 `await` and fulfilled Promises

If its operand ends up being a fulfilled Promise, `await` returns its fulfillment value:

```
assert.equal(await Promise.resolve('yes!'), 'yes!');
```

Non-Promise values are allowed, too, and simply passed on (synchronously, without pausing the async function):

```
assert.equal(await 'yes!', 'yes!');
```

41.3.2 `await` and rejected Promises

If its operand is a rejected Promise, then `await` throws the rejection value:

```
try {
  await Promise.reject(new Error());
  assert.fail(); // we never get here
} catch (e) {
  assert.equal(e instanceof Error, true);
}
```

Instances of `Error` (including instances of its subclasses) are treated specially and also thrown:

```
try {
  await new Error();
  assert.fail(); // we never get here
} catch (e) {
  assert.equal(e instanceof Error, true);
}
```

> **Exercise: Fetch API via async functions**
>
> `exercises/async-functions/fetch_json2_test.mjs`

41.3.3 `await` is shallow (we can't use it in callbacks)

If we are inside an async function and want to pause it via `await`, we must do so directly within that function; we can't use it inside a nested function, such as a callback. That is, pausing is *shallow*.

For example, the following code can't be executed:

```
async function downloadContent(urls) {
  return urls.map((url) => {
    return await httpGet(url); // SyntaxError!
  });
}
```

The reason is that normal arrow functions don't allow `await` inside their bodies.

OK, let's try an async arrow function then:

```
async function downloadContent(urls) {
  return urls.map(async (url) => {
    return await httpGet(url);
  });
}
```

Alas, this doesn't work either: Now .map() (and therefore downloadContent()) returns an Array with Promises, not an Array with (unwrapped) values.

One possible solution is to use Promise.all() to unwrap all Promises:

```
async function downloadContent(urls) {
  const promiseArray = urls.map(async (url) => {
    return await httpGet(url); // (A)
  });
  return await Promise.all(promiseArray);
}
```

Can this code be improved? Yes it can: in line A, we are unwrapping a Promise via await, only to re-wrap it immediately via return. If we omit await, we don't even need an async arrow function:

```
async function downloadContent(urls) {
  const promiseArray = urls.map(
    url => httpGet(url));
  return await Promise.all(promiseArray); // (B)
}
```

For the same reason, we can also omit await in line B.

> Exercise: Mapping and filtering asynchronously
> exercises/async-functions/map_async_test.mjs

41.4 (Advanced)

All remaining sections are advanced.

41.5 Immediately invoked async arrow functions

If we need an await outside an async function (e.g., at the top level of a module), then we can immediately invoke an async arrow function:

```
(async () => { // start
  const promise = Promise.resolve('abc');
  const value = await promise;
  assert.equal(value, 'abc');
})(); // end
```

The result of an immediately invoked async arrow function is a Promise:

```
const promise = (async () => 123)();
promise.then(x => assert.equal(x, 123));
```

41.6 Concurrency and await

In the next two subsections, we'll use the helper function paused():

```
/**
 * Resolves after `ms` milliseconds
 */
function delay(ms) {
  return new Promise((resolve, _reject) => {
    setTimeout(resolve, ms);
  });
}
async function paused(id) {
  console.log('START ' + id);
  await delay(10); // pause
  console.log('END ' + id);
  return id;
}
```

41.6.1 await: running asynchronous functions sequentially

If we prefix the invocations of multiple asynchronous functions with await, then those functions are executed sequentially:

```
async function sequentialAwait() {
  const result1 = await paused('first');
  assert.equal(result1, 'first');

  const result2 = await paused('second');
  assert.equal(result2, 'second');
}

// Output:
// 'START first'
// 'END first'
// 'START second'
// 'END second'
```

That is, paused('second') is only started after paused('first') is completely finished.

41.6.2 await: running asynchronous functions concurrently

If we want to run multiple functions concurrently, we can use the tool method Promise.all():

```
async function concurrentPromiseAll() {
  const result = await Promise.all([
```

```
    paused('first'), paused('second')
  ]);
  assert.deepEqual(result, ['first', 'second']);
}

// Output:
// 'START first'
// 'START second'
// 'END first'
// 'END second'
```

Here, both asynchronous functions are started at the same time. Once both are settled, await gives us either an Array of fulfillment values or – if at least one Promise is rejected – an exception.

Recall from §40.5.2 "Concurrency tip: focus on when operations start" (p. 441) that what counts is when we start a Promise-based computation; not how we process its result. Therefore, the following code is as "concurrent" as the previous one:

```
async function concurrentAwait() {
  const resultPromise1 = paused('first');
  const resultPromise2 = paused('second');

  assert.equal(await resultPromise1, 'first');
  assert.equal(await resultPromise2, 'second');
}
// Output:
// 'START first'
// 'START second'
// 'END first'
// 'END second'
```

41.7 Tips for using async functions

41.7.1 We don't need await if we "fire and forget"

await is not required when working with a Promise-based function; we only need it if we want to pause and wait until the returned Promise is settled. If we only want to start an asynchronous operation, then we don't need it:

```
async function asyncFunc() {
  const writer = openFile('someFile.txt');
  writer.write('hello'); // don't wait
  writer.write('world'); // don't wait
  await writer.close(); // wait for file to close
}
```

In this code, we don't await .write() because we don't care when it is finished. We do, however, want to wait until .close() is done.

Note: Each invocation of .write() starts synchronously. That prevents race conditions.

41.7.2 It can make sense to `await` and ignore the result

It can occasionally make sense to use `await`, even if we ignore its result – for example:

```
await longRunningAsyncOperation();
console.log('Done!');
```

Here, we are using `await` to join a long-running asynchronous operation. That ensures that the logging really happens *after* that operation is done.

Chapter 42

Asynchronous iteration

Contents

42.1 Basic asynchronous iteration	457
42.1.1 Protocol: async iteration	457
42.1.2 Using async iteration directly	458
42.1.3 Using async iteration via `for-await-of`	460
42.2 Asynchronous generators	460
42.2.1 Example: creating an async iterable via an async generator	461
42.2.2 Example: converting a sync iterable to an async iterable	462
42.2.3 Example: converting an async iterable to an Array	462
42.2.4 Example: transforming an async iterable	463
42.2.5 Example: mapping over asynchronous iterables	463
42.3 Async iteration over Node.js streams	464
42.3.1 Node.js streams: async via callbacks (push)	464
42.3.2 Node.js streams: async via async iteration (pull)	465
42.3.3 Example: from chunks to lines	465

> **Required knowledge**
>
> For this chapter, you should be familiar with:
>
> - Promises (p. 427)
> - Async functions (p. 447)

42.1 Basic asynchronous iteration

42.1.1 Protocol: async iteration

To understand how asynchronous iteration works, let's first revisit synchronous iteration (p. 311). It comprises the following interfaces:

```
interface Iterable<T> {
  [Symbol.iterator]() : Iterator<T>;
}
interface Iterator<T> {
  next() : IteratorResult<T>;
}
interface IteratorResult<T> {
  value: T;
  done: boolean;
}
```

- An Iterable is a data structure whose contents can be accessed via iteration. It is a factory for iterators.
- An Iterator is a factory for iteration results that we retrieve by calling the method .next().
- Each IterationResult contains the iterated .value and a boolean .done that is true after the last element and false before.

For the protocol for asynchronous iteration, we only want to change one thing: the values produced by .next() should be delivered asynchronously. There are two conceivable options:

- The .value could contain a Promise<T>.
- .next() could return Promise<IteratorResult<T>>.

In other words, the question is whether to wrap just values or whole iterator results in Promises.

It has to be the latter because when .next() returns a result, it starts an asynchronous computation. Whether or not that computation produces a value or signals the end of the iteration can only be determined after it is finished. Therefore, both .done and .value need to be wrapped in a Promise.

The interfaces for async iteration look as follows.

```
interface AsyncIterable<T> {
  [Symbol.asyncIterator]() : AsyncIterator<T>;
}
interface AsyncIterator<T> {
  next() : Promise<IteratorResult<T>>; // (A)
}
interface IteratorResult<T> {
  value: T;
  done: boolean;
}
```

The only difference to the synchronous interfaces is the return type of .next() (line A).

42.1.2 Using async iteration directly

The following code uses the asynchronous iteration protocol directly:

42.1 Basic asynchronous iteration

```
const asyncIterable = syncToAsyncIterable(['a', 'b']); // (A)
const asyncIterator = asyncIterable[Symbol.asyncIterator]();

// Call .next() until .done is true:
asyncIterator.next() // (B)
.then(iteratorResult => {
  assert.deepEqual(
    iteratorResult,
    { value: 'a', done: false });
  return asyncIterator.next(); // (C)
})
.then(iteratorResult => {
  assert.deepEqual(
    iteratorResult,
    { value: 'b', done: false });
  return asyncIterator.next(); // (D)
})
.then(iteratorResult => {
  assert.deepEqual(
    iteratorResult,
      { value: undefined, done: true });
})
;
```

In line A, we create an asynchronous iterable over the value 'a' and 'b'. We'll see an implementation of syncToAsyncIterable() later.

We call .next() in line B, line C and line D. Each time, we use .next() to unwrap the Promise and assert.deepEqual() to check the unwrapped value.

We can simplify this code if we use an async function. Now we unwrap Promises via await and the code looks almost like we are doing synchronous iteration:

```
async function f() {
  const asyncIterable = syncToAsyncIterable(['a', 'b']);
  const asyncIterator = asyncIterable[Symbol.asyncIterator]();

  // Call .next() until .done is true:
  assert.deepEqual(
    await asyncIterator.next(),
    { value: 'a', done: false });
  assert.deepEqual(
    await asyncIterator.next(),
    { value: 'b', done: false });
  assert.deepEqual(
    await asyncIterator.next(),
    { value: undefined, done: true });
}
```

42.1.3 Using async iteration via `for-await-of`

The asynchronous iteration protocol is not meant to be used directly. One of the language constructs that supports it is the `for-await-of` loop, which is an asynchronous version of the `for-of` loop. It can be used in async functions and *async generators* (which are introduced later in this chapter). This is an example of `for-await-of` in use:

```
for await (const x of syncToAsyncIterable(['a', 'b'])) {
  console.log(x);
}
// Output:
// 'a'
// 'b'
```

`for-await-of` is relatively flexible. In addition to asynchronous iterables, it also supports synchronous iterables:

```
for await (const x of ['a', 'b']) {
  console.log(x);
}
// Output:
// 'a'
// 'b'
```

And it supports synchronous iterables over values that are wrapped in Promises:

```
const arr = [Promise.resolve('a'), Promise.resolve('b')];
for await (const x of arr) {
  console.log(x);
}
// Output:
// 'a'
// 'b'
```

> **Exercise: Convert an async iterable to an Array**
>
> Warning: We'll soon see the solution for this exercise in this chapter.
>
> - `exercises/async-iteration/async_iterable_to_array_test.mjs`

42.2 Asynchronous generators

An asynchronous generator is two things at the same time:

- An async function (input): We can use `await` and `for-await-of` to retrieve data.
- A generator that returns an asynchronous iterable (output): We can use `yield` and `yield*` to produce data.

> **Asynchronous generators are very similar to synchronous generators**

42.2 Asynchronous generators

> Due to async generators and sync generators being so similar, I don't explain how exactly `yield` and `yield*` work. Please consult §38 "Synchronous generators" (p. 403) if you have doubts.

Therefore, an asynchronous generator has:

- Input that can be:
  - synchronous (single values, sync iterables) or
  - asynchronous (Promises, async iterables).
- Output that is an asynchronous iterable.

This looks as follows:

```
async function* asyncGen() {
  // Input: Promises, async iterables
  const x = await somePromise;
  for await (const y of someAsyncIterable) {
    // ···
  }

  // Output
  yield someValue;
  yield* otherAsyncGen();
}
```

42.2.1 Example: creating an async iterable via an async generator

Let's look at an example. The following code creates an async iterable with three numbers:

```
async function* yield123() {
  for (let i=1; i<=3; i++) {
    yield i;
  }
}
```

Does the result of `yield123()` conform to the async iteration protocol?

```
(async () => {
  const asyncIterable = yield123();
  const asyncIterator = asyncIterable[Symbol.asyncIterator]();
  assert.deepEqual(
    await asyncIterator.next(),
    { value: 1, done: false });
  assert.deepEqual(
    await asyncIterator.next(),
    { value: 2, done: false });
  assert.deepEqual(
    await asyncIterator.next(),
    { value: 3, done: false });
```

```
  assert.deepEqual(
    await asyncIterator.next(),
    { value: undefined, done: true });
})();
```

We wrapped the code in an immediately invoked async arrow function (p. 453).

42.2.2 Example: converting a sync iterable to an async iterable

The following asynchronous generator converts a synchronous iterable to an asynchronous iterable. It implements the function syncToAsyncIterable() that we have used previously.

```
async function* syncToAsyncIterable(syncIterable) {
  for (const elem of syncIterable) {
    yield elem;
  }
}
```

Note: The input is synchronous in this case (no await is needed).

42.2.3 Example: converting an async iterable to an Array

The following function is a solution to a previous exercise. It converts an async iterable to an Array (think spreading, but for async iterables instead of sync iterables).

```
async function asyncIterableToArray(asyncIterable) {
  const result = [];
  for await (const value of asyncIterable) {
    result.push(value);
  }
  return result;
}
```

Note that we can't use an async generator in this case: We get our input via for-await-of and return an Array wrapped in a Promise. The latter requirement rules out async generators.

This is a test for asyncIterableToArray():

```
async function* createAsyncIterable() {
  yield 'a';
  yield 'b';
}
const asyncIterable = createAsyncIterable();
assert.deepEqual(
  await asyncIterableToArray(asyncIterable), // (A)
  ['a', 'b']
);
```

Note the await in line A, which is needed to unwrap the Promise returned by asyncIterableToArray(). In order for await to work, this code fragment must be run inside an

42.2 Asynchronous generators

async function.

42.2.4 Example: transforming an async iterable

Let's implement an async generator that produces a new async iterable by transforming an existing async iterable.

```
async function* timesTwo(asyncNumbers) {
  for await (const x of asyncNumbers) {
    yield x * 2;
  }
}
```

To test this function, we use `asyncIterableToArray()` from the previous section.

```
async function* createAsyncIterable() {
  for (let i=1; i<=3; i++) {
    yield i;
  }
}
assert.deepEqual(
  await asyncIterableToArray(timesTwo(createAsyncIterable())),
  [2, 4, 6]
);
```

> **Exercise: Async generators**
>
> Warning: We'll soon see the solution for this exercise in this chapter.
>
> - exercises/async-iteration/number_lines_test.mjs

42.2.5 Example: mapping over asynchronous iterables

As a reminder, this is how to map over synchronous iterables:

```
function* mapSync(iterable, func) {
  let index = 0;
  for (const x of iterable) {
    yield func(x, index);
    index++;
  }
}
const syncIterable = mapSync(['a', 'b', 'c'], s => s.repeat(3));
assert.deepEqual(
  [...syncIterable],
  ['aaa', 'bbb', 'ccc']);
```

The asynchronous version looks as follows:

```
async function* mapAsync(asyncIterable, func) { // (A)
  let index = 0;
```

```
    for await (const x of asyncIterable) { // (B)
      yield func(x, index);
      index++;
    }
  }
```

Note how similar the sync implementation and the async implementation are. The only two differences are the async in line A and the await in line B. That is comparable to going from a synchronous function to an asynchronous function – we only need to add the keyword async and the occasional await.

To test mapAsync(), we use the helper function asyncIterableToArray() (shown earlier in this chapter, p. 462):

```
  async function* createAsyncIterable() {
    yield 'a';
    yield 'b';
  }
  const mapped = mapAsync(
    createAsyncIterable(), s => s.repeat(3));
  assert.deepEqual(
    await asyncIterableToArray(mapped), // (A)
    ['aaa', 'bbb']);
```

Once again, we await to unwrap a Promise (line A) and this code fragment must run inside an async function.

> **Exercise: filterAsyncIter()**
> exercises/async-iteration/filter_async_iter_test.mjs

42.3 Async iteration over Node.js streams

42.3.1 Node.js streams: async via callbacks (push)

Traditionally, reading asynchronously from Node.js streams is done via callbacks:

```
  function main(inputFilePath) {
    const readStream = fs.createReadStream(inputFilePath,
      { encoding: 'utf8', highWaterMark: 1024 });
    readStream.on('data', (chunk) => {
      console.log('>>> '+chunk);
    });
    readStream.on('end', () => {
      console.log('### DONE ###');
    });
  }
```

That is, the stream is in control and pushes data to the reader.

42.3.2 Node.js streams: async via async iteration (pull)

Starting with Node.js 10, we can also use asynchronous iteration to read from streams:

```
async function main(inputFilePath) {
  const readStream = fs.createReadStream(inputFilePath,
    { encoding: 'utf8', highWaterMark: 1024 });

  for await (const chunk of readStream) {
    console.log('>>> '+chunk);
  }
  console.log('### DONE ###');
}
```

This time, the reader is in control and pulls data from the stream.

42.3.3 Example: from chunks to lines

Node.js streams iterate over *chunks* (arbitrarily long pieces) of data. The following asynchronous generator converts an async iterable over chunks to an async iterable over lines:

```
/**
 * Parameter: async iterable of chunks (strings)
 * Result: async iterable of lines (incl. newlines)
 */
async function* chunksToLines(chunksAsync) {
  let previous = '';
  for await (const chunk of chunksAsync) { // input
    previous += chunk;
    let eolIndex;
    while ((eolIndex = previous.indexOf('\n')) >= 0) {
      // line includes the EOL (Windows '\r\n' or Unix '\n')
      const line = previous.slice(0, eolIndex+1);
      yield line; // output
      previous = previous.slice(eolIndex+1);
    }
  }
  if (previous.length > 0) {
    yield previous;
  }
}
```

Let's apply chunksToLines() to an async iterable over chunks (as produced by chunkIterable()):

```
async function* chunkIterable() {
  yield 'First\nSec';
  yield 'ond\nThird\nF';
  yield 'ourth';
}
const linesIterable = chunksToLines(chunkIterable());
```

```
  assert.deepEqual(
    await asyncIterableToArray(linesIterable),
    [
      'First\n',
      'Second\n',
      'Third\n',
      'Fourth',
    ]);
```

Now that we have an asynchronous iterable over lines, we can use the solution of a previous exercise, numberLines(), to number those lines:

```
async function* numberLines(linesAsync) {
  let lineNumber = 1;
  for await (const line of linesAsync) {
    yield lineNumber + ': ' + line;
    lineNumber++;
  }
}
const numberedLines = numberLines(chunksToLines(chunkIterable()));
assert.deepEqual(
  await asyncIterableToArray(numberedLines),
  [
    '1: First\n',
    '2: Second\n',
    '3: Third\n',
    '4: Fourth',
  ]);
```

Part IX

More standard library

Chapter 43

Regular expressions (RegExp)

Contents

- **43.1 Creating regular expressions** 470
  - 43.1.1 Literal vs. constructor 470
  - 43.1.2 Cloning and non-destructively modifying regular expressions 470
- **43.2 Syntax** 471
  - 43.2.1 Syntax characters 471
  - 43.2.2 Basic atoms 471
  - 43.2.3 Unicode property escapes [ES2018] 472
  - 43.2.4 Character classes 473
  - 43.2.5 Groups 474
  - 43.2.6 Quantifiers 474
  - 43.2.7 Assertions 474
  - 43.2.8 Disjunction (|) 475
- **43.3 Flags** 475
  - 43.3.1 Flag: Unicode mode via /u 477
- **43.4 Properties of regular expression objects** 479
  - 43.4.1 Flags as properties 479
  - 43.4.2 Other properties 479
- **43.5 Methods for working with regular expressions** 480
  - 43.5.1 In general, regular expressions match anywhere in a string 480
  - 43.5.2 `regExp.test(str)`: is there a match? [ES3] 480
  - 43.5.3 `str.search(regExp)`: at what index is the match? [ES3] 480
  - 43.5.4 `regExp.exec(str)`: capturing groups [ES3] 481
  - 43.5.5 `str.match(regExp)`: return all matching substrings [ES3] 482
  - 43.5.6 `str.replace(searchValue, replacementValue)` [ES3] 482
  - 43.5.7 Other methods for working with regular expressions 484
- **43.6 Flag /g and its pitfalls** 484
  - 43.6.1 Pitfall: You can't inline a regular expression with flag /g 485
  - 43.6.2 Pitfall: Removing /g can break code 485

43.6.3 Pitfall: Adding /g can break code 485
43.6.4 Pitfall: Code can break if `.lastIndex` isn't zero 486
43.6.5 Dealing with /g and `.lastIndex` 486
43.7 **Techniques for working with regular expressions** 487
43.7.1 Escaping arbitrary text for regular expressions 487
43.7.2 Matching everything or nothing 487

Availability of features

Unless stated otherwise, each regular expression feature has been available since ES3.

43.1 Creating regular expressions

43.1.1 Literal vs. constructor

The two main ways of creating regular expressions are:

- Literal: compiled statically (at load time).

    ```
    /abc/ui
    ```

- Constructor: compiled dynamically (at runtime).

    ```
    new RegExp('abc', 'ui')
    ```

Both regular expressions have the same two parts:

- The *body* abc – the actual regular expression.
- The *flags* u and i. Flags configure how the pattern is interpreted. For example, i enables case-insensitive matching. A list of available flags is given later in this chapter (p. 475).

43.1.2 Cloning and non-destructively modifying regular expressions

There are two variants of the constructor `RegExp()`:

- `new RegExp(pattern : string, flags = '')` [ES3]

    A new regular expression is created as specified via `pattern`. If `flags` is missing, the empty string `''` is used.

- `new RegExp(regExp : RegExp, flags = regExp.flags)` [ES6]

    `regExp` is cloned. If `flags` is provided, then it determines the flags of the clone.

The second variant is useful for cloning regular expressions, optionally while modifying them. Flags are immutable and this is the only way of changing them – for example:

```
function copyAndAddFlags(regExp, flagsToAdd='') {
  // The constructor doesn't allow duplicate flags;
  // make sure there aren't any:
```

```
    const newFlags = [...new Set(regExp.flags + flagsToAdd)].join('');
    return new RegExp(regExp, newFlags);
}
assert.equal(/abc/i.flags, 'i');
assert.equal(copyAndAddFlags(/abc/i, 'g').flags, 'gi');
```

43.2 Syntax

43.2.1 Syntax characters

At the top level of a regular expression, the following *syntax characters* are special. They are escaped by prefixing a backslash (\).

```
\ ^ $ . * + ? ( ) [ ] { } |
```

In regular expression literals, you must escape slashs:

```
> /\//.test('/')
true
```

In the argument of new RegExp(), you don't have to escape slashes:

```
> new RegExp('/').test('/')
true
```

43.2.2 Basic atoms

Atoms are the basic building blocks of regular expressions.

- *Pattern characters* are all characters *except* syntax characters (^, $, etc.). Pattern characters match themselves. Examples: A b %
- . matches any character. You can use the flag /s (dotall) to control if the dot matches line terminators or not (more below (p. 475)).
- *Character escapes* (each escape matches a single fixed character):
    - Control escapes (for a few control characters):
        * \f: form feed (FF)
        * \n: line feed (LF)
        * \r: carriage return (CR)
        * \t: character tabulation
        * \v: line tabulation
    - Arbitrary control characters: \cA (Ctrl-A), ..., \cZ (Ctrl-Z)
    - Unicode code units: \u00E4
    - Unicode code points (require flag /u): \u{1F44D}
- *Character class escapes* (each escape matches one out of a set of characters):
    - \d: digits (same as [0-9])
        * \D: non-digits
    - \w: "word" characters (same as [A-Za-z0-9_], related to identifiers in programming languages)
        * \W: non-word characters
    - \s: whitespace (space, tab, line terminators, etc.)
        * \S: non-whitespace

– *Unicode property escapes* [ES2018]: `\p{White_Space}`, `\P{White_Space}`, etc.
  * Require flag `/u`.
  * Described in the next subsection.

43.2.3 Unicode property escapes [ES2018]

43.2.3.1 Unicode character properties

In the Unicode standard, each character has *properties* – metadata describing it. Properties play an important role in defining the nature of a character. Quoting the Unicode Standard, Sect. 3.3, D3[1]:

> The semantics of a character are determined by its identity, normative properties, and behavior.

These are a few examples of properties:

- `Name`: a unique name, composed of uppercase letters, digits, hyphens, and spaces – for example:
  - A: `Name = LATIN CAPITAL LETTER A`
  - ☺: `Name = SLIGHTLY SMILING FACE`
- `General_Category`: categorizes characters – for example:
  - x: `General_Category = Lowercase_Letter`
  - $: `General_Category = Currency_Symbol`
- `White_Space`: used for marking invisible spacing characters, such as spaces, tabs and newlines – for example:
  - \t: `White_Space = True`
  - π: `White_Space = False`
- `Age`: version of the Unicode Standard in which a character was introduced – for example: The Euro sign € was added in version 2.1 of the Unicode standard.
  - €: `Age = 2.1`
- `Block`: a contiguous range of code points. Blocks don't overlap and their names are unique. For example:
  - S: `Block = Basic_Latin` (range U+0000..U+007F)
  - ☺: `Block = Emoticons` (range U+1F600..U+1F64F)
- `Script`: is a collection of characters used by one or more writing systems.
  - Some scripts support several writing systems. For example, the Latin script supports the writing systems English, French, German, Latin, etc.
  - Some languages can be written in multiple alternate writing systems that are supported by multiple scripts. For example, Turkish used the Arabic script before it transitioned to the Latin script in the early 20th century.
  - Examples:
    * α: `Script = Greek`
    * Д: `Script = Cyrillic`

43.2.3.2 Unicode property escapes

Unicode property escapes look like this:

---

[1] http://www.unicode.org/versions/Unicode9.0.0/ch03.pdf

43.2 Syntax

1. `\p{prop=value}`: matches all characters whose property `prop` has the value `value`.
2. `\P{prop=value}`: matches all characters that do not have a property `prop` whose value is `value`.
3. `\p{bin_prop}`: matches all characters whose binary property `bin_prop` is True.
4. `\P{bin_prop}`: matches all characters whose binary property `bin_prop` is False.

Comments:

- You can only use Unicode property escapes if the flag /u is set. Without /u, \p is the same as p.

- Forms (3) and (4) can be used as abbreviations if the property is General_Category. For example, the following two escapes are equivalent:

  ```
  \p{Lowercase_Letter}
  \p{General_Category=Lowercase_Letter}
  ```

Examples:

- Checking for whitespace:

  ```
  > /^\p{White_Space}+$/u.test('\t \n\r')
  true
  ```

- Checking for Greek letters:

  ```
  > /^\p{Script=Greek}+$/u.test('μετά')
  true
  ```

- Deleting any letters:

  ```
  > '1π2ü3é4'.replace(/\p{Letter}/ug, '')
  '1234'
  ```

- Deleting lowercase letters:

  ```
  > 'AbCdEf'.replace(/\p{Lowercase_Letter}/ug, '')
  'ACE'
  ```

Further reading:

- Lists of Unicode properties and their values: "Unicode Standard Annex #44: Unicode Character Database"[2] (Editors: Mark Davis, Laurențiu Iancu, Ken Whistler)

43.2.4 Character classes

A *character class* wraps *class ranges* in square brackets. The class ranges specify a set of characters:

- [«class ranges»] matches any character in the set.
- [^«class ranges»] matches any character not in the set.

Rules for class ranges:

- Non-syntax characters stand for themselves: [abc]

---
[2]https://unicode.org/reports/tr44/#Properties

- Only the following four characters are special and must be escaped via slashes:
  `^ \ - ]`
  - `^` only has to be escaped if it comes first.
  - `-` need not be escaped if it comes first or last.
- Character escapes (`\n`, `\u{1F44D}`, etc.) have the usual meaning.
  - Watch out: `\b` stands for backspace. Elsewhere in a regular expression, it matches word boundaries.
- Character class escapes (`\d`, `\p{White_Space}`, etc.) have the usual meaning.
- Ranges of characters are specified via dashes: `[a-z]`

43.2.5 Groups

- Positional capture group: `(#+)`
  - Backreference: `\1`, `\2`, etc.
- Named capture group [ES2018]: `(?<hashes>#+)`
  - Backreference: `\k<hashes>`
- Noncapturing group: `(?:#+)`

43.2.6 Quantifiers

By default, all of the following quantifiers are *greedy* (they match as many characters as possible):

- `?`: match never or once
- `*`: match zero or more times
- `+`: match one or more times
- `{n}`: match n times
- `{n,}`: match n or more times
- `{n,m}`: match at least n times, at most m times.

To make them *reluctant* (so that they match as few characters as possible), put question marks (?) after them:

```
> /".*"/.exec('"abc"def"')[0]   // greedy
'"abc"def"'
> /".*?"/.exec('"abc"def"')[0]  // reluctant
'"abc"'
```

43.2.7 Assertions

- `^` matches only at the beginning of the input
- `$` matches only at the end of the input
- `\b` matches only at a word boundary
  - `\B` matches only when not at a word boundary

43.2.7.1 Lookahead

Positive lookahead: (?=«pattern») matches if pattern matches what comes next.

Example: sequences of lowercase letters that are followed by an X.

```
> 'abcX def'.match(/[a-z]+(?=X)/g)
[ 'abc' ]
```

Note that the X itself is not part of the matched substring.

Negative lookahead: (?!«pattern») matches if pattern does not match what comes next.

Example: sequences of lowercase letters that are not followed by an X.

```
> 'abcX def'.match(/[a-z]+(?!X)/g)
[ 'ab', 'def' ]
```

43.2.7.2 Lookbehind [ES2018]

Positive lookbehind: (?<=«pattern») matches if pattern matches what came before.

Example: sequences of lowercase letters that are preceded by an X.

```
> 'Xabc def'.match(/(?<=X)[a-z]+/g)
[ 'abc' ]
```

Negative lookbehind: (?<!«pattern») matches if pattern does not match what came before.

Example: sequences of lowercase letters that are not preceded by an X.

```
> 'Xabc def'.match(/(?<!X)[a-z]+/g)
[ 'bc', 'def' ]
```

Example: replace ".js" with ".html", but not in "Node.js".

```
> 'Node.js: index.js and main.js'.replace(/(?<!Node)\.js/g, '.html')
'Node.js: index.html and main.html'
```

43.2.8 Disjunction (|)

Caveat: this operator has low precedence. Use groups if necessary:

- ^aa|zz$ matches all strings that start with aa and/or end with zz. Note that | has a lower precedence than ^ and $.
- ^(aa|zz)$ matches the two strings 'aa' and 'zz'.
- ^a(a|z)z$ matches the two strings 'aaz' and 'azz'.

43.3 Flags

Table 43.1: These are the regular expression flags supported by JavaScript.

Literal flag	Property name	ES	Description
g	global	ES3	Match multiple times
i	ignoreCase	ES3	Match case-insensitively
m	multiline	ES3	^ and $ match per line
s	dotall	ES2018	Dot matches line terminators
u	unicode	ES6	Unicode mode (recommended)
y	sticky	ES6	No characters between matches

The following regular expression flags are available in JavaScript (tbl. 43.1 provides a compact overview):

- /g (.global): fundamentally changes how the following methods work.
    - RegExp.prototype.test()
    - RegExp.prototype.exec()
    - String.prototype.match()

    How, is explained in §43.6 "Flag /g and its pitfalls" (p. 484). In a nutshell, without /g, the methods only consider the first match for a regular expression in an input string. With /g, they consider all matches.

- /i (.ignoreCase): switches on case-insensitive matching:

    ```
    > /a/.test('A')
    false
    > /a/i.test('A')
    true
    ```

- /m (.multiline): If this flag is on, ^ matches the beginning of each line and $ matches the end of each line. If it is off, ^ matches the beginning of the whole input string and $ matches the end of the whole input string.

    ```
    > 'a1\na2\na3'.match(/^a./gm)
    [ 'a1', 'a2', 'a3' ]
    > 'a1\na2\na3'.match(/^a./g)
    [ 'a1' ]
    ```

- /u (.unicode): This flag switches on the Unicode mode for a regular expression. That mode is explained in the next subsection.

- /y (.sticky): This flag mainly makes sense in conjunction with /g. When both are switched on, any match must directly follow the previous one (that is, it must start at index .lastIndex of the regular expression object). Therefore, the first match must be at index 0.

    ```
    > 'a1a2 a3'.match(/a./gy)
    [ 'a1', 'a2' ]
    > ' a1a2 a3'.match(/a./gy) // first match must be at index 0
    ```

43.3 Flags

```
null
> 'a1a2 a3'.match(/a./g)
[ 'a1', 'a2', 'a3' ]
> '_a1a2 a3'.match(/a./g)
[ 'a1', 'a2', 'a3' ]
```

The main use case for /y is tokenization (during parsing).

- /s (.dotall): By default, the dot does not match line terminators. With this flag, it does:

  ```
  > /./.test('\n')
  false
  > /./s.test('\n')
  true
  ```

  Workaround if /s isn't supported: Use [^] instead of a dot.

  ```
  > /[^]/.test('\n')
  true
  ```

43.3.1 Flag: Unicode mode via /u

The flag /u switches on a special Unicode mode for regular expressions. That mode enables several features:

- In patterns, you can use Unicode code point escapes such as \u{1F42A} to specify characters. Code unit escapes such as \u03B1 only have a range of four hexadecimal digits (which corresponds to the basic multilingual plane).

- In patterns, you can use Unicode property escapes such as \p{White_Space}.

- Many escapes are now forbidden. For example: \a \- \:

  Pattern characters always match themselves:

  ```
  > /pa-:/.test('pa-:')
  true
  ```

  Without /u, there are some pattern characters that still match themselves if you escape them with backslashes:

  ```
  > /\p\a\-\:/.test('pa-:')
  true
  ```

  With /u:

  - \p starts a Unicode property escape.
  - The remaining "self-matching" escapes are forbidden. As a consequence, they can now be used for new features in the future.

- The atomic units for matching are Unicode characters (code points), not JavaScript characters (code units).

The following subsections explain the last item in more detail. They use the following Unicode character to explain when the atomic units are Unicode characters and when they are JavaScript characters:

```
const codePoint = '☺';
const codeUnits = '\uD83D\uDE42'; // UTF-16

assert.equal(codePoint, codeUnits); // same string!
```

I'm only switching between ☺ and \uD83D\uDE42, to illustrate how JavaScript sees things. Both are equivalent and can be used interchangeably in strings and regular expressions.

43.3.1.1 Consequence: you can put Unicode characters in character classes

With /u, the two code units of ☺ are treated as a single character:

```
> /^[☺]$/u.test('☺')
true
```

Without /u, ☺ is treated as two characters:

```
> /^[\uD83D\uDE42]$/.test('\uD83D\uDE42')
false
> /^[\uD83D\uDE42]$/.test('\uDE42')
true
```

Note that ^ and $ demand that the input string have a single character. That's why the first result is false.

43.3.1.2 Consequence: the dot operator (.) matches Unicode characters, not JavaScript characters

With /u, the dot operator matches Unicode characters:

```
> '☺'.match(/./gu).length
1
```

.match() plus /g returns an Array with all the matches of a regular expression.

Without /u, the dot operator matches JavaScript characters:

```
> '\uD83D\uDE80'.match(/./g).length
2
```

43.3.1.3 Consequence: quantifiers apply to Unicode characters, not JavaScript characters

With /u, a quantifier applies to the whole preceding Unicode character:

```
> /^☺{3}$/u.test('☺☺☺')
true
```

Without /u, a quantifier only applies to the preceding JavaScript character:

```
> /^\uD83D\uDE80{3}$/.test('\uD83D\uDE80\uDE80\uDE80')
true
```

43.4 Properties of regular expression objects

Noteworthy:

- Strictly speaking, only .lastIndex is a real instance property. All other properties are implemented via getters.
- Accordingly, .lastIndex is the only mutable property. All other properties are read-only. If you want to change them, you need to copy the regular expression (consult §43.1.2 "Cloning and non-destructively modifying regular expressions" (p. 470) for details).

43.4.1 Flags as properties

Each regular expression flag exists as a property with a longer, more descriptive name:

```
> /a/i.ignoreCase
true
> /a/.ignoreCase
false
```

This is the complete list of flag properties:

- .dotall (/s)
- .global (/g)
- .ignoreCase (/i)
- .multiline (/m)
- .sticky (/y)
- .unicode (/u)

43.4.2 Other properties

Each regular expression also has the following properties:

- .source [ES3]: The regular expression pattern

    ```
    > /abc/ig.source
    'abc'
    ```

- .flags [ES6]: The flags of the regular expression

    ```
    > /abc/ig.flags
    'gi'
    ```

- .lastIndex [ES3]: Used when flag /g is switched on. Consult §43.6 "Flag /g and its pitfalls" (p. 484) for details.

43.5 Methods for working with regular expressions

43.5.1 In general, regular expressions match anywhere in a string

Note that, in general, regular expressions match anywhere in a string:

```
> /a/.test('__a__')
true
```

You can change that by using assertions such as ^ or by using the flag /y:

```
> /^a/.test('__a__')
false
> /^a/.test('a__')
true
```

43.5.2 regExp.test(str): is there a match? [ES3]

The regular expression method .test() returns true if regExp matches str:

```
> /bc/.test('ABCD')
false
> /bc/i.test('ABCD')
true
> /\.mjs$/.test('main.mjs')
true
```

With .test() you should normally avoid the /g flag. If you use it, you generally don't get the same result every time you call the method:

```
> const r = /a/g;
> r.test('aab')
true
> r.test('aab')
true
> r.test('aab')
false
```

The results are due to /a/ having two matches in the string. After all of those were found, .test() returns false.

43.5.3 str.search(regExp): at what index is the match? [ES3]

The string method .search() returns the first index of str at which there is a match for regExp:

```
> '_abc_'.search(/abc/)
1
> 'main.mjs'.search(/\.mjs$/)
4
```

43.5.4 regExp.exec(str): capturing groups [ES3]

43.5.4.1 Getting a match object for the first match

Without the flag /g, .exec() returns the captures of the first match for regExp in str:

```
assert.deepEqual(
  /(a+)b/.exec('ab aab'),
  {
    0: 'ab',
    1: 'a',
    index: 0,
    input: 'ab aab',
    groups: undefined,
  }
);
```

The result is a *match object* with the following properties:

- [0]: the complete substring matched by the regular expression
- [1]: capture of positional group 1 (etc.)
- .index: where did the match occur?
- .input: the string that was matched against
- .groups: captures of named groups

43.5.4.2 Named capture groups [ES2018]

The previous example contained a single positional group. The following example demonstrates named groups:

```
assert.deepEqual(
  /(?<as>a+)b/.exec('ab aab'),
  {
    0: 'ab',
    1: 'a',
    index: 0,
    input: 'ab aab',
    groups: { as: 'a' },
  }
);
```

In the result of .exec(), you can see that a named group is also a positional group – its capture exists twice:

- Once as a positional capture (property '1').
- Once as a named capture (property groups.as).

43.5.4.3 Looping over multiple matches

If you want to retrieve all matches of a regular expression (not just the first one), you need to switch on the flag /g. Then you can call .exec() multiple times and get one match each time. After the last match, .exec() returns null.

```
> const regExp = /(a+)b/g;
> regExp.exec('ab aab')
{ 0: 'ab', 1: 'a', index: 0, input: 'ab aab', groups: undefined }
> regExp.exec('ab aab')
{ 0: 'aab', 1: 'aa', index: 3, input: 'ab aab', groups: undefined }
> regExp.exec('ab aab')
null
```

Therefore, you can loop over all matches as follows:

```
const regExp = /(a+)b/g;
const str = 'ab aab';

let match;
// Check for null via truthiness
// Alternative: while ((match = regExp.exec(str)) !== null)
while (match = regExp.exec(str)) {
  console.log(match[1]);
}
// Output:
// 'a'
// 'aa'
```

Sharing regular expressions with /g has a few pitfalls, which are explained later (p. 484).

> **Exercise: Extract quoted text via .exec()**
> exercises/regexps/extract_quoted_test.mjs

43.5.5 str.match(regExp): return all matching substrings [ES3]

Without /g, .match() works like .exec() – it returns a single match object.

With /g, .match() returns all substrings of str that match regExp:

```
> 'ab aab'.match(/(a+)b/g)
[ 'ab', 'aab' ]
```

If there is no match, .match() returns null:

```
> 'xyz'.match(/(a+)b/g)
null
```

You can use the Or operator to protect yourself against null:

```
const numberOfMatches = (str.match(regExp) || []).length;
```

43.5.6 str.replace(searchValue, replacementValue) [ES3]

.replace() is overloaded – it works differently, depending on the types of its parameters:

- If searchValue is:

43.5 Methods for working with regular expressions

- Regular expression without /g: Replace first match of this regular expression.
- Regular expression with /g: Replace all matches of this regular expression.
- String: Replace first occurrence of this string (the string is interpreted verbatim, not as a regular expression). Alas, there is no way to replace every occurrence of a string. Later in this chapter (p. 487), we'll see a tool function that converts a string into a regular expression that matches this string (e.g., '*' becomes /*/).
- If replacementValue is:
    - String: Replace matches with this string. The character $ has special meaning and lets you insert captures of groups and more (read on for details).
    - Function: Compute strings that replace matches via this function.

The next two subsubsections assume that a regular expression with /g is being used.

43.5.6.1 replacementValue is a string

If the replacement value is a string, the dollar sign has special meaning – it inserts text matched by the regular expression:

Text	Result
$$	single $
$&	complete match
$`	text before match
$'	text after match
$n	capture of positional group n (n > 0)
$<name>	capture of named group name [ES2018]

Example: Inserting the text before, inside, and after the matched substring.

```
> 'a1 a2'.replace(/a/g, "($`|$&|$')")
'(|a|1 a2)1 (a1 |a|2)2'
```

Example: Inserting the captures of positional groups.

```
> const regExp = /^([A-Za-z]+): (.*)$/ug;
> 'first: Jane'.replace(regExp, 'KEY: $1, VALUE: $2')
'KEY: first, VALUE: Jane'
```

Example: Inserting the captures of named groups.

```
> const regExp = /^(?<key>[A-Za-z]+): (?<value>.*)$/ug;
> 'first: Jane'.replace(regExp, 'KEY: $<key>, VALUE: $<value>')
'KEY: first, VALUE: Jane'
```

43.5.6.2 replacementValue is a function

If the replacement value is a function, you can compute each replacement. In the following example, we multiply each non-negative integer that we find by two.

```
assert.equal(
  '3 cats and 4 dogs'.replace(/[0-9]+/g, (all) => 2 * Number(all)),
```

```
    '6 cats and 8 dogs'
);
```

The replacement function gets the following parameters. Note how similar they are to match objects. These parameters are all positional, but I've included how one might name them:

- `all`: complete match
- `g1`: capture of positional group 1
- Etc.
- `index`: where did the match occur?
- `input`: the string in which we are replacing
- `groups` [ES2018]: captures of named groups (an object)

> **Exercise: Change quotes via `.replace()` and a named group**
> `exercises/regexps/change_quotes_test.mjs`

43.5.7 Other methods for working with regular expressions

`String.prototype.split()` is described in the chapter on strings (p. 169). Its first parameter of `String.prototype.split()` is either a string or a regular expression. If it is the latter, then captures of groups appear in the result:

```
> 'a:b : c'.split(':')
[ 'a', 'b ', ' c' ]
> 'a:b : c'.split(/ *: */)
[ 'a', 'b', 'c' ]
> 'a:b : c'.split(/( *):( *)/)
[ 'a', '', '', 'b', ' ', ' ', 'c' ]
```

43.6 Flag /g and its pitfalls

The following two regular expression methods work differently if `/g` is switched on:

- `RegExp.prototype.exec()`
- `RegExp.prototype.test()`

Then they can be called repeatedly and deliver all matches inside a string. Property `.lastIndex` of the regular expression is used to track the current position inside the string – for example:

```
const r = /a/g;
assert.equal(r.lastIndex, 0);

assert.equal(r.test('aa'), true); // 1st match?
assert.equal(r.lastIndex, 1); // after 1st match

assert.equal(r.test('aa'), true); // 2nd match?
assert.equal(r.lastIndex, 2); // after 2nd match
```

43.6 Flag /g and its pitfalls

```
assert.equal(r.test('aa'), false); // 3rd match?
assert.equal(r.lastIndex, 0); // start over
```

The next subsections explain the pitfalls of using /g. They are followed by a subsection that explains how to work around those pitfalls.

43.6.1 Pitfall: You can't inline a regular expression with flag /g

A regular expression with /g can't be inlined. For example, in the following while loop, the regular expression is created fresh, every time the condition is checked. Therefore, its .lastIndex is always zero and the loop never terminates.

```
let count = 0;
// Infinite loop
while (/a/g.test('babaa')) {
  count++;
}
```

43.6.2 Pitfall: Removing /g can break code

If code expects a regular expression with /g and has a loop over the results of .exec() or .test(), then a regular expression without /g can cause an infinite loop:

```
function countMatches(regExp) {
  let count = 0;
  // Infinite loop
  while (regExp.exec('babaa')) {
    count++;
  }
  return count;
}
countMatches(/a/); // Missing: flag /g
```

Why? Because .exec() always returns the first result, a match object, and never null.

43.6.3 Pitfall: Adding /g can break code

With .test(), there is another caveat: if you want to check exactly once if a regular expression matches a string, then the regular expression must not have /g. Otherwise, you generally get a different result every time you call .test():

```
function isMatching(regExp) {
  return regExp.test('Xa');
}
const myRegExp = /^X/g;
assert.equal(isMatching(myRegExp), true);
assert.equal(isMatching(myRegExp), false);
```

Normally, you won't add /g if you intend to use .test() in this manner. But it can happen if, for example, you use the same regular expression for testing and for replacing.

43.6.4 Pitfall: Code can break if `.lastIndex` isn't zero

If you match a regular expression multiple times via `.exec()` or `.test()`, the current position inside the input string is stored in the regular expression property `.lastIndex`. Therefore, code that matches multiple times may break if `.lastIndex` is not zero:

```
function countMatches(regExp) {
  let count = 0;
  while (regExp.exec('babaa')) {
    count++;
  }
  return count;
}

const myRegExp = /a/g;
myRegExp.lastIndex = 4;
assert.equal(countMatches(myRegExp), 1); // should be 3
```

Note that `.lastIndex` is always zero in newly created regular expressions, but it may not be if the same regular expression is used multiple times.

43.6.5 Dealing with `/g` and `.lastIndex`

As an example of dealing with `/g` and `.lastIndex`, we will implement the following function:

```
countMatches(regExp, str)
```

It counts how often `regExp` has a match inside `str`. How do we prevent a wrong `regExp` from breaking our code? Let's look at three approaches.

First, we can throw an exception if `/g` isn't set or `.lastIndex` isn't zero:

```
function countMatches(regExp, str) {
  if (!regExp.global) {
    throw new Error('Flag /g of regExp must be set');
  }
  if (regExp.lastIndex !== 0) {
    throw new Error('regExp.lastIndex must be zero');
  }

  let count = 0;
  while (regExp.test(str)) {
    count++;
  }
  return count;
}
```

Second, we can clone the parameter. That has the added benefit that `regExp` won't be changed.

```
function countMatches(regExp, str) {
  const cloneFlags = regExp.flags + (regExp.global ? '' : 'g');
```

43.7 Techniques for working with regular expressions

```
  const clone = new RegExp(regExp, cloneFlags);

  let count = 0;
  while (clone.test(str)) {
    count++;
  }
  return count;
}
```

Third, we can use .match() to count occurrences, which doesn't change or depend on .lastIndex.

```
function countMatches(regExp, str) {
  if (!regExp.global) {
    throw new Error('Flag /g of regExp must be set');
  }
  return (str.match(regExp) || []).length;
}
```

43.7 Techniques for working with regular expressions

43.7.1 Escaping arbitrary text for regular expressions

The following function escapes an arbitrary text so that it is matched verbatim if you put it inside a regular expression:

```
function escapeForRegExp(str) {
  return str.replace(/[\\^$.*+?()[\]{}|]/g, '\\$&'); // (A)
}
assert.equal(escapeForRegExp('[yes?]'), String.raw`\[yes\?\]`);
assert.equal(escapeForRegExp('_g_'), String.raw`_g_`);
```

In line A, we escape all syntax characters. We have to be selective because the regular expression flag /u forbids many escapes – for example: \a \: \-

The regular expression method .replace() only lets you replace plain text once. With escapeForRegExp(), we can work around that limitation and replace plain text multiple times:

```
const plainText = ':-)';
const regExp = new RegExp(escapeForRegExp(plainText), 'ug');
assert.equal(
  ':-) :-) :-)'.replace(regExp, '☺'), '☺ ☺ ☺');
```

43.7.2 Matching everything or nothing

Sometimes, you may need a regular expression that matches everything or nothing – for example, as a default value.

- Match everything: /(?:)/

The empty group () matches everything. We make it non-capturing (via ?:), to avoid unnecessary work.

```
> /(?:)/.test('')
true
> /(?:)/.test('abc')
true
```

- Match nothing: `/.^/`

  ^ only matches at the beginning of a string. The dot moves matching beyond the first character and now ^ doesn't match anymore.

  ```
  > /.^/.test('')
  false
  > /.^/.test('abc')
  false
  ```

Chapter 44

Dates (Date)

Contents

    44.1 Best practice: avoid the built-in `Date` 489
        44.1.1 Things to look for in a date library 490
    44.2 Time standards 490
        44.2.1 Background: UTC vs. Z vs. GMT 490
        44.2.2 Dates do not support time zones 491
    44.3 Background: date time formats (ISO) 492
        44.3.1 Tip: append a Z to make date parsing deterministic 492
    44.4 Time values 493
        44.4.1 Creating time values 493
        44.4.2 Getting and setting time values 493
    44.5 Creating Dates 494
        44.5.1 Creating dates via numbers 494
        44.5.2 Parsing dates from strings 494
        44.5.3 Other ways of creating dates 494
    44.6 Getters and setters 495
        44.6.1 Time unit getters and setters 495
    44.7 Converting Dates to strings 495
        44.7.1 Strings with times 495
        44.7.2 Strings with dates 496
        44.7.3 Strings with dates and times 496
        44.7.4 Other methods 496

This chapter describes JavaScript's API for working with dates – the class `Date`.

44.1 Best practice: avoid the built-in `Date`

The JavaScript `Date` API is cumbersome to use. Hence, it's best to rely on a library for anything related to dates. Popular libraries include:

- Moment.js[1]
- Day.js[2]
- Luxon[3]
- js-joda[4]
- date-fns[5]

Consult the blog post "Why you shouldn't use Moment.js..."[6] for the pros and cons of these libraries.

Additionally, TC39 is working on a new date API for JavaScript: `temporal`[7].

44.1.1 Things to look for in a date library

Two things are important to keep in mind:

- *Tree-shaking* (p. 515) can considerably reduce the size of a library. It is a technique of only deploying those exports of a library to a web server that are imported somewhere. Functions are much more amenable to tree-shaking than classes.

- Support for time zones: As explained later (p. 491), `Date` does not support time zones, which introduces a number of pitfalls and is a key weakness. Make sure that your date library supports them.

44.2 Time standards

44.2.1 Background: UTC vs. Z vs. GMT

UTC, Z, and GMT are ways of specifying time that are similar, but subtly different:

- UTC (Coordinated Universal Time) is the time standard that all times zones are based on. They are specified relative to it. That is, no country or territory has UTC as its local time zone.

- Z (Zulu Time Zone) is a military time zone that is often used in aviation and the military as another name for UTC+0.

- GMT (Greenwich Mean Time) is a time zone used in some European and African countries. It is UTC plus zero hours and therefore has the same time as UTC.

Sources:

- "The Difference Between GMT and UTC"[8] at TimeAndDate.com
- "Z – Zulu Time Zone (Military Time)"[9] at TimeAndDate.com

---

[1] https://momentjs.com
[2] https://github.com/iamkun/dayjs
[3] https://moment.github.io/luxon/
[4] https://js-joda.github.io/js-joda/
[5] https://github.com/date-fns/date-fns
[6] https://inventi.studio/en/blog/why-you-shouldnt-use-moment-js
[7] https://github.com/maggiepint/proposal-temporal
[8] https://www.timeanddate.com/time/gmt-utc-time.html
[9] https://www.timeanddate.com/time/zones/z

44.2.2 Dates do not support time zones

Dates support the following time standards:

- The local time zone (which depends on the current location)
- UTC
- Time offsets (relative to UTC)

Depending on the operation, only some of those options are available. For example, when converting dates to strings or extracting time units such as the day of the month, you can only choose between the local time zone and UTC.

Internally, Dates are stored as UTC. When converting from or to the local time zone, the necessary offsets are determined via the date. In the following example, the local time zone is Europe/Paris:

```
// CEST (Central European Summer Time)
assert.equal(
  new Date('2122-06-29').getTimezoneOffset(), -120);

// CET (Central European Time)
assert.equal(
  new Date('2122-12-29').getTimezoneOffset(), -60);
```

Whenever you create or convert dates, you need to be mindful of the time standard being used – for example: new Date() uses the local time zone while .toISOString() uses UTC.

```
> new Date(2077, 0, 27).toISOString()
'2077-01-26T23:00:00.000Z'
```

Dates interpret 0 as January. The day of the month is 27 in the local time zone, but 26 in UTC.

> **Documenting the time standards supported by each operation**
>
> In the remainder of this chapter, the supported time standards are noted for each operation.

44.2.2.1 The downsides of not being able to specify time zones

Not being able to specify time zones has two downsides:

- It makes it impossible to support multiple time zones.

- It can lead to location-specific bugs. For example, the previous example produces different results depending on where it is executed. To be safe:
    - Use UTC-based operations whenever possible
    - Use Z or a time offset when parsing strings (see the next section for more information).

44.3 Background: date time formats (ISO)

Date time formats describe:

- The strings accepted by:
  - `Date.parse()`
  - `new Date()`
- The strings returned by (always longest format):
  - `Date.prototype.toISOString()`

The following is an example of a date time string returned by `.toISOString()`:

`'2033-05-28T15:59:59.123Z'`

Date time formats have the following structures:

- Date formats: Y=year; M=month; D=day

  ```
  YYYY-MM-DD
  YYYY-MM
  YYYY
  ```

- Time formats: T=separator (the string `'T'`); H=hour; m=minute; s=second and millisecond; Z=Zulu Time Zone (the string `'Z'`)

  ```
  THH:mm:ss.sss
  THH:mm:ss.sssZ

  THH:mm:ss
  THH:mm:ssZ

  THH:mm
  THH:mmZ
  ```

- Date time formats: are date formats followed by time formats.
  - For example (longest): `YYYY-MM-DDTHH:mm:ss.sssZ`

Instead of Z (which is UTC+0), we can also specify *time offsets* relative to UTC:

- `THH:mm+HH:mm` (etc.)
- `THH:mm-HH:mm` (etc.)

44.3.1 Tip: append a Z to make date parsing deterministic

If you add a Z to the end of a string, date parsing doesn't produce different results at different locations:

- Without Z: Input is January 27 (in the Europe/Paris time zone), output is January 26 (in UTC).

  ```
  > new Date('2077-01-27T00:00').toISOString()
  '2077-01-26T23:00:00.000Z'
  ```

- With Z: Input is January 27, output is January 27.

```
> new Date('2077-01-27T00:00Z').toISOString()
'2077-01-27T00:00:00.000Z'
```

44.4 Time values

A *time value* represents a date via the number of milliseconds since 1 January 1970 00:00:00 UTC.

Time values can be used to create Dates:

```
const timeValue = 0;
assert.equal(
  new Date(timeValue).toISOString(),
  '1970-01-01T00:00:00.000Z');
```

Coercing a Date to a number returns its time value:

```
> Number(new Date(123))
123
```

Ordering operators coerce their operands to numbers. Therefore, you can use these operators to compare Dates:

```
assert.equal(
  new Date('1972-05-03') < new Date('2001-12-23'), true);

// Internally:
assert.equal(73699200000 < 1009065600000, true);
```

44.4.1 Creating time values

The following methods create time values:

- `Date.now(): number` (UTC)

    Returns the current time as a time value.

- `Date.parse(dateTimeStr: string): number` (local time zone, UTC, time offset)

    Parses `dateTimeStr` and returns the corresponding time value.

- `Date.UTC(year,month,date?,hours?,minutes?,seconds?,milliseconds?): number` (UTC)

    Returns the time value for the specified UTC date time.

44.4.2 Getting and setting time values

- `Date.prototype.getTime(): number` (UTC)

    Returns the time value corresponding to the Date.

- `Date.prototype.setTime(timeValue)` (UTC)

    Sets this to the date encoded by `timeValue`.

44.5 Creating Dates

44.5.1 Creating dates via numbers

`new Date(year: number, month: number, date?: number, hours?: number, minutes?: number, seconds?: number, milliseconds?: number)` (local time zone)

Two of the parameters have pitfalls:

- For month, 0 is January, 1 is February, etc.
- If 0 ≤ year ≤ 99, then 1900 is added:

    ```
    > new Date(12, 1, 22, 19, 11).getFullYear()
    1912
    ```

    That's why, elsewhere in this chapter, we avoid the time unit `year` and always use `fullYear`. But in this case, we have no choice.

Example:

```
> new Date(2077,0,27, 21,49).toISOString() // CET (UTC+1)
'2077-01-27T20:49:00.000Z'
```

Note that the input hours (21) are different from the output hours (20). The former refer to the local time zone, the latter to UTC.

44.5.2 Parsing dates from strings

`new Date(dateTimeStr: string)` (local time zone, UTC, time offset)

If there is a Z at the end, UTC is used:

```
> new Date('2077-01-27T00:00Z').toISOString()
'2077-01-27T00:00:00.000Z'
```

If there is not Z or time offset at the end, the local time zone is used:

```
> new Date('2077-01-27T00:00').toISOString() // CET (UTC+1)
'2077-01-26T23:00:00.000Z'
```

If a string only contains a date, it is interpreted as UTC:

```
> new Date('2077-01-27').toISOString()
'2077-01-27T00:00:00.000Z'
```

44.5.3 Other ways of creating dates

- `new Date(timeValue: number)` (UTC)

    ```
    > new Date(0).toISOString()
    '1970-01-01T00:00:00.000Z'
    ```

- `new Date()` (UTC)

    The same as `new Date(Date.now())`.

44.6 Getters and setters

44.6.1 Time unit getters and setters

Dates have getters and setters for time units – for example:

- `Date.prototype.getFullYear()`
- `Date.prototype.setFullYear(num)`

These getters and setters conform to the following patterns:

- Local time zone:
    - `Date.prototype.get«Unit»()`
    - `Date.prototype.set«Unit»(num)`
- UTC:
    - `Date.prototype.getUTC«Unit»()`
    - `Date.prototype.setUTC«Unit»(num)`

These are the time units that are supported:

- Date
    - FullYear
    - Month: month (0–11). **Pitfall:** 0 is January, etc.
    - Date: day of the month (1–31)
    - Day (getter only): day of the week (0–6, 0 is Sunday)
- Time
    - Hours: hour (0–23)
    - Minutes: minutes (0–59)
    - Seconds: seconds (0–59)
    - Milliseconds: milliseconds (0–999)

There is one more getter that doesn't conform to the previously mentioned patterns:

- `Date.prototype.getTimezoneOffset()`

    Returns the time difference between local time zone and UTC in minutes. For example, for Europe/Paris, it returns -120 (CEST, Central European Summer Time) or -60 (CET, Central European Time):

    ```
    > new Date('2122-06-29').getTimezoneOffset()
    -120
    > new Date('2122-12-29').getTimezoneOffset()
    -60
    ```

44.7 Converting Dates to strings

Example Date:

```
const d = new Date(0);
```

44.7.1 Strings with times

- `Date.prototype.toTimeString()` (local time zone)

```
> d.toTimeString()
'01:00:00 GMT+0100 (Central European Standard Time)'
```

44.7.2 Strings with dates

- `Date.prototype.toDateString()` (local time zone)

  ```
  > d.toDateString()
  'Thu Jan 01 1970'
  ```

44.7.3 Strings with dates and times

- `Date.prototype.toString()` (local time zone)

  ```
  > d.toString()
  'Thu Jan 01 1970 01:00:00 GMT+0100 (Central European Standard Time)'
  ```

- `Date.prototype.toUTCString()` (UTC)

  ```
  > d.toUTCString()
  'Thu, 01 Jan 1970 00:00:00 GMT'
  ```

- `Date.prototype.toISOString()` (UTC)

  ```
  > d.toISOString()
  '1970-01-01T00:00:00.000Z'
  ```

44.7.4 Other methods

The following three methods are not really part of ECMAScript, but rather of the ECMAScript internationalization API[10]. That API has much functionality for formatting dates (including support for time zones), but not for parsing them.

- `Date.prototype.toLocaleTimeString()`
- `Date.prototype.toLocaleDateString()`
- `Date.prototype.toLocaleString()`

> **Exercise: Creating a date string**
>
> `exercises/dates/create_date_string_test.mjs`

---

[10]https://developer.mozilla.org/en-US/docs/Web/JavaScript/Reference/Global_Objects/Intl

Chapter 45

Creating and parsing JSON (JSON)

Contents

45.1 The discovery and standardization of JSON	498
45.1.1 JSON's grammar is frozen	498
45.2 JSON syntax	498
45.3 Using the JSON API	499
45.3.1 JSON.stringify(data, replacer?, space?)	499
45.3.2 JSON.parse(text, reviver?)	500
45.3.3 Example: converting to and from JSON	501
45.4 Customizing stringification and parsing (advanced)	501
45.4.1 .stringfy(): specifying which properties of objects to stringify	502
45.4.2 .stringify() and .parse(): value visitors	502
45.4.3 Example: visiting values	503
45.4.4 Example: stringifying unsupported values	503
45.4.5 Example: parsing unsupported values	504
45.5 FAQ	505
45.5.1 Why doesn't JSON support comments?	505

JSON ("JavaScript Object Notation") is a storage format that uses text to encode data. Its syntax is a subset of JavaScript expressions. As an example, consider the following text, stored in a file jane.json:

```
{
  "first": "Jane",
  "last": "Porter",
  "married": true,
  "born": 1890,
  "friends": [ "Tarzan", "Cheeta" ]
}
```

JavaScript has the global namespace object JSON that provides methods for creating and parsing JSON.

45.1 The discovery and standardization of JSON

A specification for JSON was published by Douglas Crockford in 2001, at json.org[1]. He explains:

> I discovered JSON. I do not claim to have invented JSON because it already existed in nature. What I did was I found it, I named it, I described how it was useful. I don't claim to be the first person to have discovered it; I know that there are other people who discovered it at least a year before I did. The earliest occurrence I've found was, there was someone at Netscape who was using JavaScript array literals for doing data communication as early as 1996, which was at least five years before I stumbled onto the idea.

Later, JSON was standardized as ECMA-404[2]:

- 1st edition: October 2013
- 2nd edition: December 2017

45.1.1 JSON's grammar is frozen

Quoting the ECMA-404 standard:

> Because it is so simple, it is not expected that the JSON grammar will ever change. This gives JSON, as a foundational notation, tremendous stability.

Therefore, JSON will never get improvements such as optional trailing commas, comments, or unquoted keys – independently of whether or not they are considered desirable. However, that still leaves room for creating supersets of JSON that compile to plain JSON.

45.2 JSON syntax

JSON consists of the following parts of JavaScript:

- Compound:
    - Object literals:
        * Property keys are double-quoted strings.
        * Property values are JSON values.
        * No trailing commas are allowed.
    - Array literals:
        * Elements are JSON values.
        * No holes or trailing commas are allowed.
- Atomic:
    - `null` (but not `undefined`)
    - Booleans
    - Numbers (excluding `NaN`, `+Infinity`, `-Infinity`)
    - Strings (must be double-quoted)

As a consequence, you can't (directly) represent cyclic structures in JSON.

---

[1] http://json.org/
[2] https://www.ecma-international.org/publications/standards/Ecma-404.htm

45.3 Using the JSON API

The global namespace object JSON contains methods for working with JSON data.

45.3.1 JSON.stringify(data, replacer?, space?)

.stringify() converts JavaScript data to a JSON string. In this section, we are ignoring the parameter replacer; it is explained in §45.4 "Customizing stringification and parsing" (p. 501).

45.3.1.1 Result: a single line of text

If you only provide the first argument, .stringify() returns a single line of text:

```
assert.equal(
  JSON.stringify({foo: ['a', 'b']}),
  '{"foo":["a","b"]}' );
```

45.3.1.2 Result: a tree of indented lines

If you provide a non-negative integer for space, then .stringify() returns one or more lines and indents by space spaces per level of nesting:

```
assert.equal(
JSON.stringify({foo: ['a', 'b']}, null, 2),
`{
  "foo": [
    "a",
    "b"
  ]
}`);
```

45.3.1.3 Details on how JavaScript data is stringified

Primitive values:

- Supported primitive values are stringified as expected:

    ```
    > JSON.stringify('abc')
    '"abc"'
    > JSON.stringify(123)
    '123'
    > JSON.stringify(null)
    'null'
    ```

- Unsupported numbers: 'null'

    ```
    > JSON.stringify(NaN)
    'null'
    > JSON.stringify(Infinity)
    'null'
    ```

- Other unsupported primitive values are not stringified; they produce the result undefined:

    ```
    > JSON.stringify(undefined)
    undefined
    > JSON.stringify(Symbol())
    undefined
    ```

Objects:

- If an object has a method .toJSON(), then the result of that method is stringified:

    ```
    > JSON.stringify({toJSON() {return true}})
    'true'
    ```

    Dates have a method .toJSON() that returns a string:

    ```
    > JSON.stringify(new Date(2999, 11, 31))
    '"2999-12-30T23:00:00.000Z"'
    ```

- Wrapped primitive values are unwrapped and stringified:

    ```
    > JSON.stringify(new Boolean(true))
    'true'
    > JSON.stringify(new Number(123))
    '123'
    ```

- Arrays are stringified as Array literals. Unsupported Array elements are stringified as if they were null:

    ```
    > JSON.stringify([undefined, 123, Symbol()])
    '[null,123,null]'
    ```

- All other objects – except for functions – are stringified as object literals. Properties with unsupported values are omitted:

    ```
    > JSON.stringify({a: Symbol(), b: true})
    '{"b":true}'
    ```

- Functions are not stringified:

    ```
    > JSON.stringify(() => {})
    undefined
    ```

45.3.2 JSON.parse(text, reviver?)

.parse() converts a JSON text to a JavaScript value. In this section, we are ignoring the parameter reviver; it is explained §45.4 "Customizing stringification and parsing" (p. 501).

This is an example of using .parse():

```
> JSON.parse('{"foo":["a","b"]}')
{ foo: [ 'a', 'b' ] }
```

45.3.3 Example: converting to and from JSON

The following class implements conversions from (line A) and to (line B) JSON.

```
class Point {
  static fromJson(jsonObj) { // (A)
    return new Point(jsonObj.x, jsonObj.y);
  }

  constructor(x, y) {
    this.x = x;
    this.y = y;
  }

  toJSON() { // (B)
    return {x: this.x, y: this.y};
  }
}
```

- Converting JSON to a point: We use the static method `Point.fromJson()` to parse JSON and create an instance of `Point`.

    ```
    assert.deepEqual(
      Point.fromJson(JSON.parse('{"x":3,"y":5}')),
      new Point(3, 5) );
    ```

- Converting a point to JSON: `JSON.stringify()` internally calls the previously mentioned method `.toJSON()` (p. 499).

    ```
    assert.equal(
      JSON.stringify(new Point(3, 5)),
      '{"x":3,"y":5}' );
    ```

> **Exercise: Converting an object to and from JSON**
> exercises/json/to_from_json_test.mjs

45.4 Customizing stringification and parsing (advanced)

Stringification and parsing can be customized as follows:

- `JSON.stringify(data, replacer?, space?)`

    The optional parameter `replacer` contains either:

    - An Array with names of properties. If a value in `data` is stringified as an object literal, then only the mentioned properties are considered. All other properties are ignored.
    - A *value visitor*, a function that can transform JavaScript data before it is stringified.

- `JSON.parse(text, reviver?)`

The optional parameter `reviver` contains a value visitor that can transform the parsed JSON data before it is returned.

45.4.1 `.stringfy()`: specifying which properties of objects to stringify

If the second parameter of `.stringify()` is an Array, then only object properties, whose names are mentioned there, are included in the result:

```
const obj = {
  a: 1,
  b: {
    c: 2,
    d: 3,
  }
};
assert.equal(
  JSON.stringify(obj, ['b', 'c']),
  '{"b":{"c":2}}');
```

45.4.2 `.stringify()` and `.parse()`: value visitors

What I call a *value visitor* is a function that transforms JavaScript data:

- `JSON.stringify()` lets the value visitor in its parameter `replacer` transform JavaScript data before it is stringified.
- `JSON.parse()` lets the value visitor in its parameter `reviver` transform parsed JavaScript data before it is returned.

In this section, JavaScript data is considered to be a tree of values. If the data is atomic, it is a tree that only has a root. All values in the tree are fed to the value visitor, one at a time. Depending on what the visitor returns, the current value is omitted, changed, or preserved.

A value visitor has the following type signature:

```
type ValueVisitor = (key: string, value: any) => any;
```

The parameters are:

- `value`: The current value.
- `this`: Parent of current value. The parent of the root value r is `{'': r}`.
  - Note: `this` is an implicit parameter and only available if the value visitor is an ordinary function.
- `key`: Key or index of the current value inside its parent. The key of the root value is `''`.

The value visitor can return:

- `value`: means there won't be any change.
- A different value x: leads to `value` being replaced with x in the output tree.
- `undefined`: leads to `value` being omitted in the output tree.

45.4 Customizing stringification and parsing (advanced)

45.4.3 Example: visiting values

The following code shows in which order a value visitor sees values:

```
const log = [];
function valueVisitor(key, value) {
  log.push({this: this, key, value});
  return value; // no change
}

const root = {
  a: 1,
  b: {
    c: 2,
    d: 3,
  }
};
JSON.stringify(root, valueVisitor);
assert.deepEqual(log, [
  { this: { '': root }, key: '',  value: root   },
  { this: root        , key: 'a', value: 1      },
  { this: root        , key: 'b', value: root.b },
  { this: root.b      , key: 'c', value: 2      },
  { this: root.b      , key: 'd', value: 3      },
]);
```

As we can see, the replacer of JSON.stringify() visits values top-down (root first, leaves last). The rationale for going in that direction is that we are converting JavaScript values to JSON values. And a single JavaScript object may be expanded into a tree of JSON-compatible values.

In contrast, the reviver of JSON.parse() visits values bottom-up (leaves first, root last). The rationale for going in that direction is that we are assembling JSON values into JavaScript values. Therefore, we need to convert the parts before we can convert the whole.

45.4.4 Example: stringifying unsupported values

JSON.stringify() has no special support for regular expression objects – it stringifies them as if they were plain objects:

```
const obj = {
  name: 'abc',
  regex: /abc/ui,
};
assert.equal(
  JSON.stringify(obj),
  '{"name":"abc","regex":{}}');
```

We can fix that via a replacer:

```
function replacer(key, value) {
  if (value instanceof RegExp) {
    return {
      __type__: 'RegExp',
      source: value.source,
      flags: value.flags,
    };
  } else {
    return value; // no change
  }
}
assert.equal(
JSON.stringify(obj, replacer, 2),
`{
  "name": "abc",
  "regex": {
    "__type__": "RegExp",
    "source": "abc",
    "flags": "iu"
  }
}`);
```

45.4.5 Example: parsing unsupported values

To `JSON.parse()` the result from the previous section, we need a reviver:

```
function reviver(key, value) {
  // Very simple check
  if (value && value.__type__ === 'RegExp') {
    return new RegExp(value.source, value.flags);
  } else {
    return value;
  }
}
const str = `{
  "name": "abc",
  "regex": {
    "__type__": "RegExp",
    "source": "abc",
    "flags": "iu"
  }
}`;
assert.deepEqual(
  JSON.parse(str, reviver),
  {
    name: 'abc',
    regex: /abc/ui,
  });
```

45.5 FAQ

45.5.1 Why doesn't JSON support comments?

Douglas Crockford explains why in a Google+ post from 1 May 2012[3]:

> I removed comments from JSON because I saw people were using them to hold parsing directives, a practice which would have destroyed interoperability. I know that the lack of comments makes some people sad, but it shouldn't.
>
> Suppose you are using JSON to keep configuration files, which you would like to annotate. Go ahead and insert all the comments you like. Then pipe it through JSMin [a minifier for JavaScript] before handing it to your JSON parser.

---

[3]https://web.archive.org/web/20190308024153/https://plus.google.com/+DouglasCrockfordEsq/posts/RK8qyGVaGSr

Part X

Miscellaneous topics

Chapter 46

Next steps: overview of web development (bonus)

Contents

46.1 Tips against feeling overwhelmed	509
46.2 Things worth learning for web development	510
46.2.1 Keep an eye on WebAssembly (Wasm)!	511
46.3 Example: tool-based JavaScript workflow	512
46.4 An overview of JavaScript tools	514
46.4.1 Building: getting from the JavaScript you write to the JavaScript you deploy	514
46.4.2 Static checking	515
46.4.3 Testing	516
46.4.4 Package managers	516
46.4.5 Libraries	516
46.5 Tools not related to JavaScript	517

You now know most of the JavaScript language. This chapter gives an overview of web development and describes next steps. It answers questions such as:

- What should I learn next for web development?
- What JavaScript-related tools should I know about?

46.1 Tips against feeling overwhelmed

Web development has become a vast field: Between JavaScript, web browsers, server-side JavaScript, JavaScript libraries, and JavaScript tools, there is a lot to know. Additionally, everything is always changing: some things go out of style, new things are invented, etc.

How can you avoid feeling overwhelmed when faced with this constantly changing vastness of knowledge?

- Focus on the web technologies that you work with most often and learn them well. If you do frontend development, that may be JavaScript, CSS, SVG, or something else.
- For JavaScript: Know the language, but also try out one tool in each of the following categories (which are covered in more detail later).
    - Compilers: compile future JavaScript or supersets of JavaScript to normal JavaScript.
    - Bundlers: combine all modules used by a web app into a single file (a script or a module). That makes loading faster and enables dead code elimination.
    - Static checkers. For example:
        * Linters: check for anti-patterns, style violations, and more.
        * Type checkers: type JavaScript statically and report errors.
    - Test libraries and tools
    - Version control (usually git)

> **Trust in your ability to learn on demand**
>
> It is commendable to learn something out of pure curiosity. But I'm wary of trying to learn everything and spreading yourself too thin. That also induces an anxiety of not knowing enough (because you never will). Instead, trust in your ability to learn things on demand!

46.2 Things worth learning for web development

These are a few things worth learning for web development:

- Browser APIs such as the *Document Object Model* (DOM), the browsers' representation of HTML in memory. They are the foundations of any kind of frontend development.

- JavaScript-adjacent technologies such as HTML and CSS.

- Frontend frameworks: When you get started with web development, it can be instructive to write user interfaces without any libraries. Once you feel more confident, frontend frameworks make many things easier, especially for larger apps. Popular frameworks include React, Angular, Vue, Ember, Svelte.

- Node.js is the most popular platform for server-side JavaScript. But it also lets you run JavaScript in the command line. Most JavaScript-related tools (even compilers!) are implemented in Node.js-based JavaScript and installed via npm. A good way to get started with Node.js, is to use it for shell scripting.

- JavaScript tooling: Modern web development involves many tools. Later in this chapter, there is an overview of the current tooling ecosystem.

- Progressive web apps: The driving idea behind *progressive web apps* is to give web apps features that, traditionally, only native apps had – for example: native installation on mobile and desktop operating systems; offline operation; showing notifications to users. Google has published a checklist[1] detailing what makes a web app *progressive*. The minimum requirements are:

- The app must be served over HTTPS (not the unsecure HTTP).
- The app must have a *Web App Manifest file*, specifying metadata such as app name and icon (often in multiple resolutions). The file(s) of the icon must also be present.
- The app must have a *service worker*: a base layer of the app that runs in the background, in a separate process (independently of web pages). One of its responsibilities is to keep the app functioning when there is no internet connection. Among others, two mechanisms help it do that: It is a local proxy that supervises all of the web resource requests of the app. And it has access to a browser's cache. Therefore, it can use the cache to fulfill requests when the app is offline – after initially caching all critical resources. Other capabilities of service workers include synchronizing data in the background; receiving server-sent push messages; and the aforementioned showing notifications to users.

One good resource for learning web development – including and beyond JavaScript – is MDN web docs[2].

46.2.1 Keep an eye on WebAssembly (Wasm)!

WebAssembly[3] is a universal virtual machine that is built into most JavaScript engines. You get the following distribution of work:

- JavaScript is for dynamic, higher-level code.
- WebAssembly is for static, lower-level code.

For static code, WebAssembly is quite fast: C/C++ code, compiled to WebAssembly, is about 50% as fast as the same code, compiled to native (source[4]). Use cases include support for new video formats, machine learning, gaming, etc.

WebAssembly works well as a compilation target for various languages. Does this mean JavaScript will be compiled to WebAssembly or replaced by another language?

46.2.1.1 Will JavaScript be compiled to WebAssembly?

JavaScript engines perform many optimizations for JavaScript's highly dynamic features. If you wanted to compile JavaScript to WebAssembly, you'd have to implement these optimizations on top of WebAssembly. The result would be slower than current engines and have a similar code base. Therefore, you wouldn't gain anything.

46.2.1.2 Will JavaScript be replaced by another language?

Does WebAssembly mean that JavaScript is about to be replaced by another language? WebAssembly does make it easier to support languages other than JavaScript in web browsers. But those languages face several challenges on that platform:

---
[1] https://developers.google.com/web/progressive-web-apps/checklist
[2] https://developer.mozilla.org/en-US/docs/Learn
[3] https://webassembly.org
[4] https://arxiv.org/abs/1901.09056

- All browser APIs are based on JavaScript.
- The runtimes (standard library, etc.) of other languages incur an additional memory overhead, whereas JavaScript's runtime is already built into web browsers.
- JavaScript is well-known, has many libraries and tools, etc.

Additionally, many parts of the WebAssembly ecosystem (e.g., debugging) are works in progress.

For dynamic code, JavaScript is comparatively fast. Therefore, for the foreseeable future, it will probably remain the most popular choice for high-level code. For low-level code, compiling more static languages (such as Rust) to WebAssembly is an intriguing option.

Given that it is just a virtual machine, there are not that many practically relevant things to learn about WebAssembly. But it is worth keeping an eye on its evolving role in web development. It is also becoming popular as a stand-alone virtual machine; e.g., supported by the WebAssembly System Interface[5].

46.3 Example: tool-based JavaScript workflow

```
<script src="code.js">
<script src="library.js">
```

index.html
  loads ↓   ↓ loads
code.js   library.js

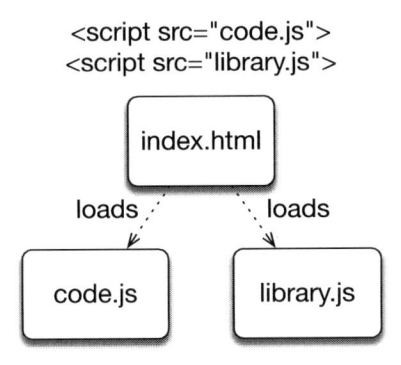

Figure 46.1: A classic, very simple web app: An HTML file refers to a JavaScript file `code.js`, which imbues the former with interactivity. `code.js` uses the library `library.js`, which must also be loaded by the HTML file.

Fig. 46.1 depicts a classic web app – when web development was less sophisticated (for better and for worse):

- `index.html` contains the HTML file that is opened in web browsers.
- `code.js` contains the JavaScript code loaded and used by `index.html`.
- That code depends on the library `library.js`, a file that was downloaded manually and put next to `code.js`. It is accessed via a global variable. Note that the HTML file needs to load the dependency `library.js` for `code.js`. `code.js` can't do that itself.

Since then, JavaScript workflows have become more complex. Fig. 46.2 shows such a workflow – one that is based on the JavaScript bundler *webpack*.

Let's examine the pieces (data, tools, technologies) involved in this workflow:

---

[5] https://github.com/WebAssembly/WASI

46.3 Example: tool-based JavaScript workflow

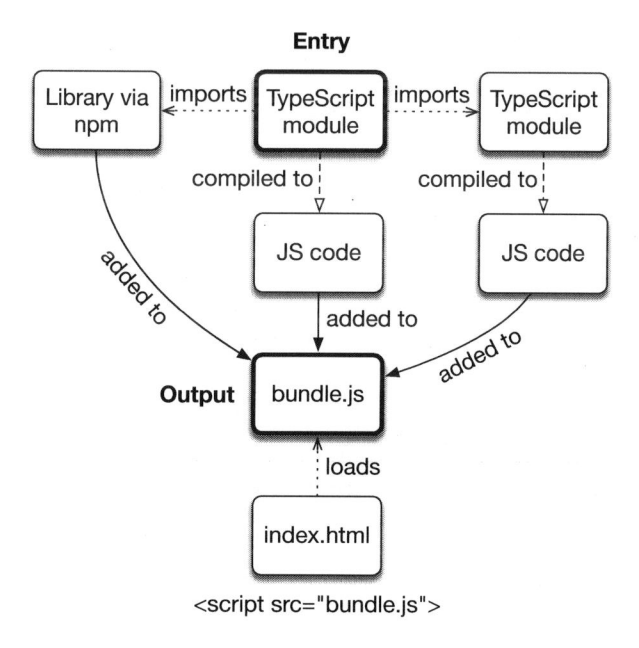

Figure 46.2: This is the workflow when developing a web app with the bundler *webpack*. Our web app consists of multiple modules. We tell webpack, in which one execution starts (the so-called *entry point*). It then analyzes the imports of the entry point, the imports of the imports, etc., to determine what code is needed to run the app. All of that code is put into a single script file.

- The app itself consists of multiple modules, written in *TypeScript* – a language that is a statically typed superset of JavaScript. Each file is an ECMAScript module, plus static type annotations.
- The library used by the app is now downloaded and installed via the npm package manager (p. 249). It also transparently handles *transitive dependencies* – if this package depends on other packages, etc.
- All TypeScript files are compiled to plain JS via a *loader*, a plugin for webpack.
- The tool *webpack* combines all plain JavaScript files into a single JavaScript script file. This process is called *bundling*. Bundling is done for two reasons:
  - Downloading a single file is usually faster in web browsers.
  - During bundling, you can perform various optimizations, such as leaving out code that isn't used.

The basic structure is still the same: the HTML file loads a JavaScript script file via a `<script>` element. However:

- The code is now modular without the HTML file having to know the modules.
- `bundle.js` only includes the code that is needed to run the app (vs. all of `library.js`).
- We used a package manager to install the libraries that our code depends on.
- The libraries aren't accessed via global variables but via ES module specifiers.

In modern browsers, you can also deliver the bundle as a module (vs. as a script file).

46.4 An overview of JavaScript tools

Now that we have seen one workflow, let's look at various categories of tools that are popular in the world of JavaScript. You'll see categories of tools and lots of names of specific tools. The former are much more important. The names change, as tools come into and out of style, but I wanted you to see at least some of them.

46.4.1 Building: getting from the JavaScript you write to the JavaScript you deploy

Building JavaScript means getting from the JavaScript you write to the JavaScript you deploy. The following tools are often involved in this process:

- Transpilers: A transpiler is a compiler that compiles source code to source code. Two transpilers that are popular in the JavaScript community are:
  - Babel compiles upcoming and modern JavaScript features to older versions of the language. That means you can use new features in your code and still run it on older browsers.
  - TypeScript is a superset of JavaScript. Roughly, it is the latest version of JavaScript plus static typing.
- Minifiers: A minifier compiles JavaScript to equivalent, smaller (as in fewer characters) JavaScript. It does so by renaming variables, removing comments, removing

46.4 An overview of JavaScript tools

whitespace, etc.

For example, given the following input:

```
let numberOfOccurrences = 5;
if (Math.random()) {
  // Math.random() is not zero
  numberOfOccurrences++
}
```

A minifier might produce:

```
let a=5;Math.random()&&a++;
```

- Popular minifiers include: UglifyJS[6], babel-minify[7], Terser[8], and Closure Compiler[9].

- Bundlers: compile and optimize the code of a JavaScript app. The input of a bundler is many files – all of the app's code plus the libraries it uses. A bundler combines these input files to produce fewer output files (which tends to improve performance[10]).

A bundler minimizes the size of its output via techniques such as *tree-shaking*. Tree-shaking is a form of dead code elimination: only those module exports are put in the output that are imported somewhere (across all code, while considering transitive imports).

It is also common to perform compilation steps such as transpiling and minification while bundling. In these cases, a bundler relies on the previously mentioned tools, packaged as libraries.

- Popular bundlers include webpack, browserify, Rollup, and Parcel.

All of these tools and build steps are usually coordinated via so-called *task runners* (think "make" in Unix). There are:

- Dedicated task runners: grunt, gulp, broccoli, etc.
- Tools that can be used as simple task runners: npm (via its "scripts") and webpack (via plugins).

46.4.2 Static checking

Static checking means analyzing source code *statically* (without running it). It can be used to detect a variety of problems. Tools include:

- Linters: check the source code for problematic patterns, unused variables, etc. Linters are especially useful if you are still learning the language because they point out if you are doing something wrong.
  - Popular linters include JSLint, JSHint, ESLint

---

[6] http://lisperator.net/uglifyjs/
[7] https://github.com/babel/minify
[8] https://github.com/terser-js/terser
[9] https://developers.google.com/closure/compiler/
[10] https://medium.com/@asyncmax/the-right-way-to-bundle-your-assets-for-faster-sites-over-http-2-437c37efe3ff

- Code style checkers: check if code is formatted properly. They consider indentation, spaces after brackets, spaces after commas, etc.
    - Example: JSCS (JavaScript Code Style checker)
- Code formatters: automatically format your code for you, according to rules that you can customize.
    - Example: Prettier
- Type checkers: add static type checking to JavaScript.
    - Popular type checkers: TypeScript (which is also a transpiler), Flow.

46.4.3 Testing

JavaScript has many testing frameworks – for example:

- Unit testing: Jasmine, Mocha, AVA, Jest, Karma, etc.
- Integration testing: Jenkins, Travis CI, etc.
- User interface testing: CasperJS, Protractor, Nightwatch.js, TestCafé, etc.

46.4.4 Package managers

The most popular package manager for JavaScript is npm. It started as a package manager for Node.js but has since also become dominant for client-side web development and tools of any kind.

There are alternatives to npm, but they are all based in one way or another on npm's software registry:

- Yarn[11] is a different take on npm; some of the features it pioneered are now also supported by npm.
- pnpm[12] focuses on saving space when installing packages locally.

46.4.5 Libraries

- Various helpers: lodash (which was originally based on the Underscore.js library) is one of the most popular general helper libraries for JavaScript.
- Data structures: The following libraries are two examples among many.
    - Immutable.js[13] provides immutable data structures for JavaScript.
    - Immer[14] is an interesting lightweight alternative to Immutable.js. It also doesn't mutate the data it operates on, but it works with normal objects and Arrays.
- Date libraries: JavaScript's built-in support for dates is limited and full of pitfalls. The chapter on dates lists libraries (p. 489) that you can use instead.
- Internationalization: In this area, ECMAScript's standard library is complemented by the ECMAScript Internationalization API (ECMA-402)[15]. It is accessed via the global variable `Intl` and available in most modern browsers.

---

[11] https://yarnpkg.com/en/
[12] https://github.com/pnpm/pnpm
[13] https://github.com/facebook/immutable-js/
[14] https://github.com/mweststrate/immer
[15] https://developer.mozilla.org/en-US/docs/Web/JavaScript/Reference/Global_Objects/Intl

- Implementing and accessing services: The following are two popular options that are supported by a variety of libraries and tools.
  - REST (Representative State Transfer) is one popular option for services and based on HTTP(S).
  - GraphQL[16] is more sophisticated (for example, it can combine multiple data sources) and supports a query language.

46.5 Tools not related to JavaScript

Given that JavaScript is just one of several kinds of artifacts involved in web development, more tools exist. These are but a few examples:

- CSS:
  - Minifiers: reduce the size of CSS by removing comments, etc.
  - Preprocessors: let you write compact CSS (sometimes augmented with control flow constructs, etc.) that is expanded into deployable, more verbose CSS.
  - Frameworks: provide help with layout, decent-looking user interface components, etc.
- Images: Automatically optimizing the size of bitmap images, etc.

---

[16]https://graphql.org/

Part XI

Appendices

Chapter 47

Index

!x, 121
++x, 126
x++, 126
+x, 126
, (comma operator), 107
--x, 126
x--, 126
-x, 126
x && y, 120
x + y, 102
x - y, 125
x / y, 125
x << y, 137
x === y, 105
x >>> y, 137
x >> y, 137
x & y, 136
x ** y, 125
x * y, 125
x ^ y, 136
x ¦ y, 136
x ¦¦ y, 120
x % y, 125
=, 103
c ? t : e, 119
__proto__, 288
~x, 137

accessor (object literal), 265
addition, 102
AMD module, 241

anonymous function expression, 212
argument, 219
argument vs. parameter, 219
Array, 317
Array hole, 327
Array index, 326
Array literal, 318
Array, dense, 327
Array, multidimensional, 325
Array, roles of an, 318
Array, sparse, 327
Array-destructuring, 395
Array-like object, 322
ArrayBuffer, 350
arrow function, 215
ASI (automatic semicolon insertion), 53
assert (module), 67
assertion, 65
assignment operator, 103
async, 449
async function, 447
async function*, 460
async-await, 447
asynchronous generator, 460
asynchronous iterable, 457
asynchronous iteration, 457
asynchronous iterator, 457
asynchronous programming, 415
attribute of a property, 284
automatic semicolon insertion (ASI), 53
await (async function), 451

await (asynchronous generator), 461

big endian, 354
binary integer literal, 124
binding (variable), 78
bitwise And, 136
bitwise Not, 137
bitwise Or, 136
bitwise Xor, 136
boolean, 115
Boolean(), 115
bound variable, 88
break, 194
bundler, 514
bundling, 514

call stack, 418
callback (asynchronous pattern), 425
callback function, 219
camel case, 47
catch, 207
class, 293
class, 293
class declaration, 293
class definition, 293
class expression, 293
class, mixin, 305
classes, private data for, 297
closure, 88
code point, 153
code unit, 153
coercion, 98
comma operator, 107
CommonJS module, 241
comparing by identity, 95
comparing by value, 94
computed property key, 276
concatenating strings, 161
conditional operator, 119
console, 59
console.error(), 62
console.log(), 61
const, 78
constant, 77
constructor function (role of an ordinary function), 213
continue, 195
Converting to [type], 115

Coordinated Universal Time (UTC), 490
copy object deeply, 267
copy object shallowly, 267
currying, 232

dash case, 47
DataView, 350
date, 489
date time format, 492
decimal floating point literal, 125
decimal integer literal, 124
decrementation operator (prefix), 126
decrementation operator (suffix), 126
deep copy of an object, 267
default export, 246
default value (destructuring), 399
default value (parameter), 220
delete, 277
deleting a property, 277
dense Array, 327
descriptor of a property, 284
destructive operation, 329
destructuring, 391
destructuring an Array, 395
destructuring an object, 394
dictionary (role of an object), 263
direct method call, 304
dispatched method call, 304
divided by operator, 125
division, 125
do-while, 200
dynamic this, 217
dynamic vs. static, 81

early activation, 86
Ecma, 32
ECMA-262, 32
ECMAScript, 32
ECMAScript module, 243
Eich, Brendan, 31
endianness (Typed Arrays), 354
enumerability, 278
enumerable (property attribute), 278
environment (variables), 227
equality operator, 105
ES module, 243
escaping HTML, 183

eval(), 224
evaluating an expression, 50
event (asynchronous pattern), 423
event loop, 419
exception, 205
exercises, getting started with, 71
exponentiation, 125
export, 243
export default, 246
export, default, 246
export, named, 243
expression, 50
extends, 299
external iteration, 409
extracting a method, 271

false, 115
falsiness, 116
falsy, 116
finally, 208
flags (regular expression), 470
Float32Array, 350
Float64Array, 350
floating point literal, 125
for, 200
for-await-of, 460
for-in, 203
for-of, 202
free variable, 88
freezing an object, 284
fulfilled (Promise state), 429
function declaration, 212
function expression, anonymous, 212
function expression, named, 212
function, arrow, 215
function, ordinary, 211
function, roles of an ordinary, 213
function, specialized, 211
function*, 403

garbage collection, 95
generator, asynchronous, 460
generator, synchronous, 403
getter (object literal), 265
global, 83
global object, 82
global scope, 82
global variable, 82

globalThis, 82
GMT (Greenwich Mean Time), 490
grapheme cluster, 156
Greenwich Mean Time (GMT), 490

heap, 95
hexadecimal integer literal, 124
hoisting, 88
hole in an Array, 327

identifier, 47
identity of an object, 94
if, 196
IIFE (immediately invoked function
   expression), 240
immediately invoked function
   expression (IIFE), 240
import, 244
import(), 254
import, named, 244
import, namespace, 245
in, 277
incrementation operator (prefix), 126
incrementation operator (suffix), 126
index of an Array, 326
Infinity, 130
inheritance, multiple, 305
inheritance, single, 305
instanceof, 95, 296
Int16Array, 350
Int32Array, 350
Int8Array, 350
integer, 133
integer, safe, 134
internal iteration, 409
iterable (asynchronous), 457
iterable (synchronous), 312
iteration, asynchronous, 457
iteration, external, 409
iteration, internal, 409
iteration, synchronous, 311
iterator (asynchronous), 457
iterator (synchronous), 312

JSON (data format), 497
JSON (namespace object), 497

kebab case, 47
keyword, 49

label, 195
left shift operator, 137
`let`, 78
lexical `this`, 217
listing properties, 277
little endian, 354
logical And, 120
logical Not, 121
logical Or, 120

Map, 365
`Map`, 365
Map vs. object, 374
`Math` (namespace object), 145
method, 268
method (object literal), 265
method (role of an ordinary function), 213
method call, direct, 304
method call, dispatched, 304
method, extracting a, 271
minification, 514
minifier, 514
minus operator (binary), 125
minus operator (unary), 126
mixin class, 305
module specifier, 252
module, AMD, 241
module, CommonJS, 241
multidimensional Array, 325
multiple inheritance, 305
multiple return values, 397
multiplication, 125

named export, 243
named function expression, 212
named import, 244
named parameter, 221
namespace import, 245
`NaN`, 128
`node_modules`, 250
npm, 249
npm package, 249
`null`, 111
number, 123
`Number()`, 127

object, 261
object literal, 263

object vs. Map, 374
object vs. primitive value, 93
`Object()`, 98
object, copy deeply, 267
object, copy shallowly, 267
object, freezing an, 284
object, identity of an, 94
object, roles of an, 263
object-destructuring, 394
`Object.is()`, 106
octal integer literal, 124
ordinary function, 211
ordinary function, roles of an, 213
override a property, 289

package, npm, 249
`package.json`, 249
parameter, 219
parameter default value, 220
parameter vs. argument, 219
partial application, 232
passing by identity, 94
passing by value, 93
pattern (regular expression), 470
pending (Promise state), 429
plus operator (binary), 102
plus operator (unary), 126
polyfill, 258
polyfill, speculative, 258
ponyfill, 258
primitive value, 93
primitive value vs. object, 93
private data for classes, 297
progressive web app, 510
prollyfill, 258
Promise, 427
Promise, states of a, 429
properties, listing, 277
property (object), 262
property attribute, 284
property descriptor, 284
property key, 277
property key, computed, 276
property key, quoted, 275
property name, 277
property symbol, 277
property value shorthand, 264
property, deleting a, 277

prototype, 288
prototype chain, 288
publicly known symbol, 188

quizzes, getting started with, 71
quoted property key, 275

real function (role of an ordinary function), 213
receiver, 265
record (role of an object), 263
RegExp, 469
regular expression, 469
regular expression literal, 470
rejected (Promise state), 429
remainder operator, 125
REPL, 60
replica, 258
RequireJS, 241
reserved word, 49
rest element (Array-destructuring), 396
rest parameter (function call), 220
rest property (object-destructuring), 395
return values, multiple, 397
revealing module pattern, 240
roles of an Array, 318
roles of an object, 263
roles of an ordinary function, 213
run-to-completion semantics, 422

safe integer, 134
scope of a variable, 79
script, 239
self, 83
sequence (role of an Array), 318
Set, 381
Set, 381
setter (object literal), 265
settled (Promise state), 429
shadowing, 81
shallow copy of an object, 267
shim, 258
signed right shift operator, 137
single inheritance, 305
sloppy mode, 55
snake case, 47
sparse Array, 327
specialized function, 211

specifier, module, 252
speculative polyfill, 258
spreading (...) into a function call, 222
spreading into an Array literal, 320
spreading into an object literal, 266
statement, 50
states of a Promise, 429
static, 296
static vs. dynamic, 81
strict mode, 55
string, 159
String(), 161
subclass, 299
subtraction, 125
switch, 197
symbol, 185
symbol, publicly known, 188
synchronous generator, 403
synchronous iterable, 312
synchronous iteration, 311
synchronous iterator, 312
syntax, 44

tagged template, 177
task queue, 419
task runner, 514
TC39, 33
TC39 process, 33
TDZ (temporal dead zone), 84
Technical Committee 39, 33
template literal, 176
temporal dead zone, 84
ternary operator, 119
this, 265
this, dynamic, 217
this, lexical, 217
this, pitfalls of, 274
this, values of, 274
throw, 206
time value, 493
times operator, 125
to the power of operator, 125
transpilation, 514
transpiler, 514
tree-shaking, 514
true, 115
truthiness, 116
truthy, 116

try, 207
tuple (role of an Array), 318
type, 91
type hierarchy, 92
type signature, 21
Typed Array, 349
typeof, 95
TypeScript, 514

Uint16Array, 350
Uint32Array, 350
Uint8Array, 350
Uint8ClampedArray, 350
undefined, 111
underscore case, 47
Unicode, 153
Unicode Transformation Format (UTF), 154
unit test, 72
unsigned right shift operator, 137
UTC (Coordinated Universal Time), 490
UTF (Unicode Transformation Format), 154
UTF-16, 155
UTF-32, 154
UTF-8, 155

variable, bound, 88
variable, free, 88
variable, scope of a, 79
void operator, 107

Wasm (WebAssembly), 511
WeakMap, 377
WeakMap, 377
WeakSet, 389
WeakSet, 389
Web Worker, 421
WebAssembly, 511
while, 199
window, 83
wrapper types (for primitive types), 98

yield (asynchronous generator), 461
yield (synchronous generator), 404
yield* (asynchronous generator), 461
yield* (synchronous generator), 407

Z (Zulu Time Zone), 490
Zulu Time Zone (Z), 490